Certificate Stage

Module D

Managerial Finance

Revision Series

9221/F99

British Library Cataloguing-in-Publication Data

A catalogue record for this book is available from the British Library.

Published by AT Foulks Lynch Ltd
Number 4
The Griffin Centre
Staines Road
Feltham
Middlesex
TW14 0HS

ISBN 07483 3922 1

© AT Foulks Lynch Ltd, 1999

Acknowledgements

The past ACCA examination questions are the copyright of the Association of Chartered Certified Accountants. The answers to the questions from June 1994 onwards are the answers produced by the examiners themselves and are the copyright of the Association of Chartered Certified Accountants. The answers to the questions prior to June 1994 have been produced by AT Foulks Lynch Ltd.

We are grateful to the Chartered Institute of Management Accountants and the Institute of Chartered Accountants in England and Wales for permission to reproduce past examination questions. The answers have been prepared by AT Foulks Lynch Ltd.

CONTENTS

PREFACE

The new edition of the ACCA Revision Series, published for the June and December 1999 examinations, contains a wealth of features to make your prospects of passing the exams even brighter.

Examiner Plus

This book contains all the new syllabus examinations from June 1994 up to and including December 1998 plus the examiner's official answers. All the exams are set out in chronological order at the back of the book.

We have cross referenced all these questions to their topic headings in the contents pages so you can see at a glance what questions have been set on each syllabus area to date, topic by topic.

The inclusion of these questions and answers really does give students an unparalleled view of the way the new syllabus examinations are set and, even more importantly, a tremendous insight into the mind of the Examiner. The Examiner's answers are in some cases fairly lengthy and whilst the Examiner would not necessarily expect you to include all the points that his answers include, they do nevertheless give you an excellent insight into the sorts of things that the Examiner is looking for and will help you produce answers in line with the Examiner's thinking.

Features

Step by Step Answer Plans and *'Did you answer the question?'* *checkpoints* will be fully explained on the following two pages.

Tutorial Notes

In some situations the examiner's official answers benefit from a little extra explanation when they are to be used as a learning aid. Where appropriate, we have incorporated extra workings or explanatory notes, so that you derive the maximum benefit from these answers in preparation for your own exam.

Topic Index

The topics covered in all the answers have been indexed. This means that you can easily access an answer relating to any topic which you want to consider by use of the index as well as by reference to the contents page at the front of the book.

The Revision Series also contains the following features:

- Practice questions and answers - a total bank of around 80 questions and answers

- An analysis of the new syllabus exams from June 1994 to December 1998

- Update notes to bring you up to date for new examinable documents and any changes to legislation as at 1st December 1998.

- The syllabus and format of the examination

- General Revision Guidance

- Examination Technique - an essential guide to ensure that you approach the examinations correctly

- Key Revision Topics

- Formulae and tables where appropriate

HOW TO USE THE ANSWER PLANS AND 'DID YOU ANSWER THE QUESTION?' CHECKPOINTS

STEP BY STEP ANSWER PLANS

A key feature in this year's Revision Series is the Step by Step Answer Plans, produced for all new syllabus exam questions from June 1995 to June 1998.

Students are always being told to plan their answers and this feature gives you positive assistance by showing you how you should plan your answer and the type of plan that you should produce before you attempt the question.

Of course, in the exam, your answer Plan can be less fully written than ours because you are writing it for yourself. We are producing an answer plan which communicates the details to you the student and therefore is of necessity much fuller. However, all the detail is there, written in a way which shows you the lines along which you should be thinking in order to produce the answer plan.

You will notice that the Answer Plans start and finish with the exhortation that you must make sure that you have read the question and that you are answering it correctly. Each time you write down the next step in the Answer Plan, you must ask yourself - 'Why am I including this step?' 'Is it relevant?' 'Is this what the Examiner has asked me to do and expected me to do?'

Help with the answer

In addition, if you really do get stuck with the question and cannot see how to approach it, you may find it helpful to turn to the answer page, **cover up the answer itself!,** and start to read the Answer Plan. This may trigger your memory such that you can then return to the question itself and gain all the benefit of doing the question properly without reference to the answer itself.

Practice makes perfect

Like all elements of examination technique the time to learn how to plan your answers is not in the examination itself. You have to practise them now - every time you produce an answer - so that when you come to the examination itself these answer plans will be second nature.

It is probably a good idea to sketch out your answer plans in the way we have produced them here (but remember they can be briefer) and then compare them swiftly to our Answer Plan at the back of the book (don't look at the answer itself at this stage!).

This may indicate that you have completely missed the point of the question or it might indicate one or two other areas that you might wish to explore.

Then, without having yet looked at the answer itself, start writing your answer proper and then compare that with the examiner's own answer.

'DID YOU ANSWER THE QUESTION?' CHECKPOINTS

This is another feature included in this year's edition of the Revision Series. They are included in the new syllabus exam answers from June 1995 to June 1998.

At various points of the answers, you will come across a box headed **'Did you answer the question',** followed by a brief note which shows you how the printed answer is answering the question and encourages you to make sure that your own answer has not wandered off the point or missed the point of the question completely.

This is an invaluable feature and it is a discipline you must develop as you practise answering questions. It is an area of examination technique that you must practise and practise again and again until it becomes second nature. How often do we read in an Examiner's report that candidates did not answer the question the Examiner had set but had simply answered the question that they wanted him to set or simply wandered off the point altogether? You must make sure that your answers do not fall into that particular trap and that they do rigorously follow the questions set.

A good way of practising this aspect of examination technique is to imagine an empty box headed up 'Did you answer the question?' at the end of the paragraph or paragraphs you are about to write on a particular topic. Try and imagine what you are going to write in that box; what are you going to say in that box which justifies the two or three paragraphs that you are about to write. If you can't imagine what you are going to put in that box, or when you imagine it you find that you are struggling to relate the next few paragraphs to the question, then think very hard before you start writing those paragraphs. Are they completely relevant? Why are you writing them? How are they relevant to the question?

You will find this 'imagining the box' a very useful way of focusing your mind on what you are writing and its relevance to the question.

SUMMARY

Use the two techniques together. They will help you to produce planned answers and they will help you make sure that your answers are focused very fully and carefully on the question the Examiner has actually set.

1 EXAMINATION FORMAT AND SYLLABUS

FORMAT OF THE EXAMINATION

	Number of marks
Section A: Compulsory mini case study	40
Section B: One question (out of two) on financial management	20
Section C: Two questions (out of three) on management accounting	40
	100

The management accounting content will account for approximately 40% of the marks and the financial management content for the remainder. Section A will be primarily financial management but may draw upon some management accounting concepts to a limited degree. Section B contains financial management questions only and section C contains only management accounting questions.

Time allowed: 3 hours

Introduction

Paper 8 examines two related subjects, Management Accounting (weighting of 40%) and Financial Management (weighting of 60%).

The paper builds on the overview of cost accounting from paper 3 and covers

- the application of the management accounting techniques used in planning, control and decision making and the interpretation of information available from their use

- the preparation, organisation, summarisation and presentation of management information/reports.

The paper introduces financial management areas, including

- the understanding of current practical methods used in making financial management decisions and the influence of the environment on such decisions

- the appreciation of the workings of the financial system, the evaluation of alternative sources of finance and the assessment of investment possibilities

- the communication of the consequences of financial management decisions to accountants and non-accountants.

Management Accounting

(1)   COST AND MANAGEMENT ACCOUNTING METHODS

      (a)   Determining and allocating/apportioning costs of activities and outputs through the use of appropriate concepts, methods and techniques

            (i)   absorption, marginal and opportunity cost approaches to the accumulation of costs for specific orders (job, batch, contract) or operations (process, service)

            (ii)   activity based costing; use of cost drivers and activities.

      (b)   Consideration and application of information required in relation to

            (i)   costing of products and services
            (ii)   preparing plans
            (iii)   monitoring/controlling performance
            (iv)   decision making.

(2)   INFORMATION FOR PLANNING AND CONTROL

      (a)   Budgeting and budgetary control

            (i)   identify objectives of budgetary planning and control systems (including an introduction to behavioural influences)

            (ii)   identify/evaluate budgetary systems such as fixed and flexible, zero based and incremental, periodic and continuous

            (iii)   developing/implementing budgeting systems: functional/subsidiary and master budgets (including cash budgeting)

            (iv)   monitoring and controlling performance; calculation of variances; determination of cause of variances

            (v)   quantitative aids in budgeting; least squares regression; scatter diagram with correlation; forecasting with regression; introduction to time series and seasonality to analyse time related data.

      (b)   Standard costing

            (i)   uses and limitations of standard costing

            (ii)   determination of standards

            (iii)   identification and calculation of variances; sales variances (including quantity and mix), cost variances (including mix and yield); absorption and marginal approaches

            (iv)   identify significance and inter-relationship of variances

            (v)   relevance to business performance measurement and control.

      (c)   Cost allocation/apportionment/absorption

            (i)   absorption and marginal costing; impact on profit reporting; relevance in planning and control

            (ii)   activity based costing; use in costing of products and services; use as a planning and control device.

(3)   THE COSTING/PRICING OF PRODUCTS AND SERVICES

    (a)   Consideration and application of information requirements in relation to

        (i)   job costs
        (ii)   process costs
        (iii)   service industries
        (iv)   internal services.

Financial management

(4)   FINANCIAL OBJECTIVES

    (a)   The nature, purpose and scope of financial management.

    (b)   The relationship between financial management, management accounting and financial accounting.

    (c)   The relationship of financial objectives to organisational strategy and ethos and to other organisational objectives. The constraints/conflicts which different objectives may put upon each other.

    (d)   The nature, scope and form (long term and short term) of financial objectives of different types of organisation, including not-for-profit organisations.

    (e)   The roles, responsibilities and relationships of key personnel involved in and with organisations (shareholders, lenders, managers, employees, customers, suppliers, government).

(5)   FINANCIAL MANAGEMENT FRAMEWORK

    (a)   The commercial and financial environment in which organisations operate (the nature and function of the money and capital markets including banks and other financial intermediaries, the Stock Exchange, the Unlisted Securities Market and Over the Counter markets).

    (b)   The economic environment in which organisations operate

        (i)   application of macro-economic theory as a basis for understanding the key economic variables affecting the business environment

        (ii)   fiscal policy, its nature, effectiveness of fiscal policy

        (iii)   money and interest rates, the role of money in the economy, the supply and demand for money

        (iv)   monetary policy, attitudes to monetary policy, problems of monetary policy

        (v)   supply-side policies, supply side problems, policies to improve supply side

        (vi)   policies towards monopolies and oligopolies, privatisation and deregulation

        (vii)   green policies; implications for management of the economy and the firm

        (viii) the significance of corporate securities (share capital, debt and preference shares) to commercial organisations and the markets in which they operate, and the influence of markets on organisations

        (ix)   the Efficient Markets Hypothesis and its relevance to decision making and to financial management practice.

(6)   MANAGEMENT OF WORKING CAPITAL

(a)   The nature and scope of working capital management.

(b)   The importance of effective working capital management to corporate survival.

(c)   Cash: selection of appropriate cash balances, managing cash surpluses and deficits. The nature and functions of the short term money market.

(d)   The management of debtors (including those overseas) involving credit evaluation, terms of credit, cash discounts, debt collection techniques, credit management monitoring and evaluation, factoring and invoice discounting.

(e)   Creditors: advantages and disadvantages of alternative methods of paying suppliers (including those overseas), the dangers of trading on credit.

(f)   Stock: alternative stock management systems and models including Total Quality Management (TQM), Just in Time (JIT), Economic Order Quantity (EOQ), etc.

(7)   SOURCES OF FINANCE

(a)   Sources and relative costs (including issue costs but not calculations of the cost of capital) of various types of finance and their suitability to different circumstances and organisations (both large and small companies, listed and unlisted) including

(i)   the nature and importance of internally generated funds

(ii)   capital markets (types of share capital, new issues, rights issues, loan capital, convertibles, warrants)

(iii)   the effect of dividend policy on financing needs

(iv)   bank finance (the various forms of short, medium and long term finance that are available, including leasing)

(v)   trade credit

(vi)   government sources: grants, regional and national aid schemes, tax incentives etc

(vii)   venture capital and financial sources particularly suited to the small company

(viii)   international money and capital markets, including an introduction to international banking, and the finance of foreign trade.

(b)   Determining requirements for finance (how much, for how long, for what purpose) in relation to a client's operational and strategic objectives. The importance of the choice of capital structure to an organisation.

(c)   Calculating financial gearing and other key financial ratios and analysing their significance to the organisation.

(d)   Determining appropriate sources of finance by identifying and evaluating appropriate sources, taking into account such factors as

(i)   cost of finance including its servicing
(ii)   timing of cash payments
(iii)   effect on gearing and other ratios
(iv)   effect on the company's existing investors.

(8)   CAPITAL EXPENDITURE AND INVESTMENT

(a)   Identifying potential investment opportunities.

(b)   Appraising capital investments (domestic) for commercial and non commercial organisations through the use of appropriate methods and techniques

     (i)   return on capital employed and payback

     (ii)   discounting based methods, including the importance of the cost of capital to investment appraisal (but not the calculation of cost of capital)

     (iii)   internal rate of return

     (iv)   net present value

     (v)   capital rationing (single and multi-period)

     (vi)   lease or buy decisions

including the effects of taxation and inflation on investment decisions, the handling of risk and uncertainty, eg through the use of probabilities, sensitivity analysis and simulations.

2 ANALYSIS OF PAST PAPERS

Topics	J94		D94		J95		D95		J96		D96		J97		D97		J98		D98	
Management accountant's role	2	●			2	●											4	○		
Process costing	2	●	4	○					2	●										
Absorption/marginal/activity based costing			3	○	4	○			3	●	4	○	4 5	●/○	4	○				
Service department costing									3	○	2	●	6	●						
Budgeting	2	●	1	□	2	●	1	□	2 4	●/○	1	□	5 6	●/○			5	○	5	○
Forecasting/statistical techniques					2	●	2	●	1	■			5	●						
Standard costing & variance analysis	3	○			2 3	●/○	3	○	2	●	3	○	4	○	5	○			6	○
Performance evaluation	4	○											6	●						
Decision making (including pricing)			2	●			4	○							6	○	6	○	4	○
Economic policies/macroeconomics	2	●			1 2	■/●	2	●	2	●	2 2	●/●					3	○		
Ratio analysis					6	○	1	□	5	●			1	□			2	●		
Management of working capital	5	○	2	●	2 5	●/●	2 1	●/□	5	○	5	○	1 3	■/●	1	□			3	○
Finance markets			2	●	6	●	2 1 5	●/■/○	2	●	2 2	●/●					1	■		
Sources of finance and gearing			5	○			6	○	1	□					2	●	1	□	2 3	○/●
Dividend policy															2	●				
Project financing	1	□			1	■	5	○	6	○	1 2	■/●	1	□						
Investment appraisal	6 1	○/■			5 1	○/□	2	●			6	○	2 3	○/○	3	○	2	○	1	□
Capital rationing			6	○																

Key

The number refers to the number of the question where this topic was examined in the exam.

Topics forming the whole or a substantial part of a question:

□ Compulsory   ○ Optional

Topics forming a non-substantial part of a question

■ Compulsory   ● Optional

3 GENERAL REVISION GUIDANCE

PLANNING YOUR REVISION

What is revision?

Revision is the process by which you remind yourself of the material you have studied during your course, clarify any problem areas and bring your knowledge to a state where you can retrieve it and present it in a way that will satisfy the Examiners.

Revision is not a substitute for hard work earlier in the course. The syllabus for this paper is too large to be hastily 'crammed' a week or so before the examination. You should think of your revision as the final stage in your study of any topic. It can only be effective if you have already completed earlier stages.

Ideally, you should begin your revision shortly after you begin an examination course. At the end of every week and at the end of every month, you should review the topics you have covered. If you constantly consolidate your work and integrate revision into your normal pattern of study, you should find that the final period of revision - and the examination itself - are much less daunting.

If you are reading this revision text while you are still working through your course, we strongly suggest that you begin now to review the earlier work you did for this paper. Remember, the more times you return to a topic, the more confident you will become with it.

The main purpose of this book, however, is to help you to make the best use of the last few weeks before the examination. In this section we offer some suggestions for effective planning of your final revision and discuss some revision techniques which you may find helpful.

Planning your time

Most candidates find themselves in the position where they have less time than they would like to revise, particularly if they are taking several papers at one diet. The majority of people must balance their study with conflicting demands from work, family or other commitments.

It is impossible to give hard and fast rules about the amount of revision you should do. You should aim to start your final revision at least four weeks before your examination. If you finish your course work earlier than this, you would be well advised to take full advantage of the extra time available to you. The number of hours you spend revising each week will depend on many factors, including the number of papers you are sitting. You should probably aim to do a minimum of about six to eight hours a week for each paper.

In order to make best use of the revision time that you have, it is worth spending a little of it at the planning stage. We suggest that you begin by asking yourself two questions:

- How much time do I have available for revision?
- What do I need to cover during my revision?

Once you have answered these questions, you should be able to draw up a detailed timetable. We will now consider these questions in more detail.

How much time do I have available for revision?

Many people find it helpful to work out a regular weekly pattern for their revision. We suggest you use the time planning chart provided to do this. Your aim should be to construct a timetable that is sustainable over a period of several weeks.

Time planning chart

	Monday	Tuesday	Wednesday	Thursday	Friday	Saturday	Sunday
00.00							
01.00							
02.00							
03.00							
04.00							
05.00							
06.00							
07.00							
08.00							
09.00							
10.00							
11.00							
12.00							
13.00							
14.00							
15.00							
16.00							
17.00							
18.00							
19.00							
20.00							
21.00							
22.00							
23.00							

1. First, block out all the time that is **definitely unavailable** for revision. This will include the hours when you normally sleep, the time you are at work and any other regular and clear commitments.

2. Think about **other people's claims on your time**. If you have a family, or friends whom you see regularly, you may want to discuss your plans with them. People are likely to be flexible in the demands they make on you in the run-up to your examinations, especially if they are aware that you have considered their needs as well as your own. If you consult the individuals who are affected by your plans, you may find that they are surprisingly supportive, instead of being resentful of the extra time you are spending studying.

3. Next, give some thought to the times of day when you **work most effectively**. This differs very much from individual to individual. Some people can concentrate first thing in the morning. Others work best in the early evening, or last thing at night. Some people find their day-to-day work so demanding that they are unable to do anything extra during the week, but must concentrate their study time at weekends. Mark the times when you feel you could do your best work on the

timetable. It is extremely important to acknowledge your personal preferences here. If you ignore them, you may devise a timetable that is completely unrealistic and which you will not be able to adhere to.

4   Consider your **other commitments**. Everybody has certain tasks, from doing the washing to walking the dog, that must be performed on a regular basis. These tasks may not have to be done at a particular time, but you should take them into consideration when planning your schedule. You may be able to find more convenient times to get these jobs done, or be able to persuade other people to help you with them.

5   Now mark some time for **relaxation**. If your timetable is to be sustainable, it must include some time for you to build up your reserves. If your normal week does not include any regular physical activity, make sure that you include some in your revision timetable. A couple of hours spent in a sports centre or swimming pool each week will probably enhance your ability to concentrate.

6   Your timetable should now be taking shape. You can probably see obvious study sessions emerging. It is not advisable to work for too long at any one session. Most people find that they can only really concentrate for one or two hours at a time. If your study sessions are longer than this, you should split them up.

What do I need to cover during my revision?

Most candidates are more confident about some parts of the syllabus than others. Before you begin your revision, it is important to have an overview of where your strengths and weaknesses lie.

One way to do this is to take a sheet of paper and divide it into three columns. Mark the columns:

OK   Marginal   Not OK

or use similar headings to indicate how confident you are with a topic. Then go through the syllabus (reprinted in Section 1) and list the topics under the appropriate headings. Alternatively, you could use the list of key topics in Section 5 of this book to compile your overview. You might also find it useful to skim through the introductions or summaries to the textbook or workbooks you have used in your course. These should remind you of parts of the course that you found particularly easy or difficult at the time. You could also use some of the exercises and questions in the workbooks or textbooks, or some of the questions in this book, as a diagnostic aid to discover the areas where you need to work hardest.

It is also important to be aware which areas of the syllabus are so central to the subject that they are likely to be examined in every diet, and which are more obscure, and not likely to come up so frequently. Your textbooks, workbooks and lecture notes will help you here, and section 2 of this book contains an analysis of past papers. Remember, the Examiner will be looking for broad coverage of the syllabus. There is no point in knowing one or two topics in exhaustive detail if you do so at the expense of the rest of the course.

Writing your revision timetable

You now have the information you need to write your timetable. You know how many weeks you have available, and the approximate amount of time that is available in each week.

You should stop all serious revision 48 hours before your examination. After this point, you may want to look back at your notes to refresh your memory, but you should not attempt to revise any new topics. A clear and rested brain is worth more than any extra facts you could memorise in this period.

Make one copy of this chart for each week you have available for revision.

Using your time planning chart, write in the times of your various study sessions during the week.

In the lower part of the chart, write in the topics that you will cover in each of these sessions.

Example of a revision timetable

Revision timetable Week beginning:	Monday	Tuesday	Wednesday	Thursday	Friday	Saturday	Sunday
Study sessions							
Topics							

Some revision techniques

There should be two elements in your revision. You must **look back** to the work you have covered in the course and **look forward** to the examination. The techniques you use should reflect these two aspects of revision.

Revision should not be boring. It is useful to try a variety of techniques. You probably already have some revision techniques of your own and you may also like to try some of the techniques suggested here, if they are new to you. However, don't waste time with methods of revision which are not effective for you.

- Go through your lecture notes, textbook or workbooks and use a highlighter pen to mark important points.

- Produce a new set of summarised notes. This can be a useful way of re-absorbing information, but you must be careful to keep your notes concise, or you may find that you are simply reproducing work you have done before. It is helpful to use a different format for your notes.

- Make a collection of key words which remind you of the essential concepts of a topic.

- Reduce your notes to a set of key facts and definitions which you must memorise. Write them on cards which you can keep with you all the time.

- When you come across areas which you were unsure about first time around, rework relevant questions in your course materials, then study the answers in great detail.

- If there are isolated topics which you feel are completely beyond you, identify exactly what it is that you cannot understand and find someone (such as a lecturer or recent graduate) who can explain these points to you.

- Practise as many exam standard questions as you can. The best way to do this is to work to time, under exam conditions. You should always resist looking at the answer until you have finished.

- If you have come to rely on a word processor in your day-to-day work, you may have got out of the habit of writing at speed. It is well worth reviving this skill before you sit down in the examination hall: it is something you will need.

- If you have a plentiful supply of relevant questions, you could use them to practise planning answers, and then compare your notes with the answers provided. This is not a substitute for writing full answers, but can be helpful additional practice.

- Go back to questions you have already worked on during the course. This time, complete them under exam conditions, paying special attention to the layout and organisation of your answers. Then compare them in detail with the suggested answers and think about the ways in which your answer differs. This is a useful way of 'fine tuning' your technique.

- During your revision period, do make a conscious effort to identify situations which illustrate concepts and ideas that may arise in the examination. These situations could come from your own work, or from reading the business pages of the quality press. This technique will give you a new perspective on your studies and could also provide material which you can use in the examination.

4 EXAMINATION TECHNIQUES

THE EXAMINATION

This section is divided into two parts. The first part considers the practicalities of sitting the examination. If you have taken other ACCA examinations recently, you may find that everything here is familiar to you. The second part discusses some examination techniques which you may find useful.

The practicalities

What to take with you

You should make sure that you have:

- your ACCA registration card
- your ACCA registration docket.

You may also take to your desk:

- pens and pencils
- a ruler and slide rule
- a calculator
- charting template and geometrical instruments
- eraser and correction fluid.

You are not allowed to take rough paper into the examination.

If you take any last-minute notes with you to the examination hall, make sure these are not on your person. You should keep notes or books in your bag or briefcase, which you will be asked to leave at the side of the examination hall.

Although most examination halls will have a clock, it is advisable to wear a watch, just in case your view is obscured.

If your calculator is solar-powered, make sure it works in artificial light. Some examination halls are not particularly well-lit. If you use a battery-powered calculator, take some spare batteries with you. For obvious reasons, you may not use a calculator which has a graphic/word display memory. Calculators with printout facilities are not allowed because they could disturb other candidates

Getting there

You should arrange to arrive at the examination hall at least half an hour before the examination is due to start. If the hall is a large one, the invigilator will start filling the hall half an hour before the starting time.

Make absolutely sure that you know how to get to the examination hall and how long it will take you. Check on parking or public transport. Leave yourself enough time so that you will not be anxious if the journey takes a little longer than you anticipated. Many people like to make a practice trip the day before their first examination.

At the examination hall

Examination halls differ greatly in size. Some only hold about ten candidates. Others can sit many hundreds of people. You may find that more than one examination is being taken at the hall at the same time, so don't panic if you hear people discussing a completely different subject from the one you have revised.

While you are waiting to go in, don't be put off by other people talking about how well, or badly, they have prepared for the examination.

You will be told when to come in to the examination hall. The desks are numbered. (Your number will be on your examination docket.) You will be asked to leave any bags at the side of the hall.

Inside the hall, the atmosphere will be extremely formal. The invigilator has certain things which he or she must tell candidates, often using a particular form of words. Listen carefully, in case there are any unexpected changes to the arrangements.

On your desk you will see a question paper and an answer booklet in which to write your answers. You will be told when to turn over the paper.

During the examination

You will have to leave your examination paper and answer booklet in the hall at the end of the examination. It is quite acceptable to write on your examination paper if it helps you to think about the questions. However, all workings should be in your answers. You may write any plans and notes in your answer booklet, as long as you cross them out afterwards.

If you require a new answer booklet, put your hand up and a supervisor will come and bring you one.

At various times during the examination, you will be told how much time you have left.

You should not need to leave the examination hall until the examination is finished. Put up your hand if you need to go to the toilet, and a supervisor will accompany you. If you feel unwell, put up your hand, and someone will come to your assistance. If you simply get up and walk out of the hall, you will not be allowed to reenter.

Before you finish, you must fill in the required information on the front of your answer booklet.

Examination techniques

Tackling Paper 8

The examination will consist of three sections. Section A, which is compulsory, will comprise a mini case study covering mainly financial management aspects. This will normally contain a mixture of four or five computational and discussion questions. This section is worth 40 marks, which will not be divided equally among the questions. The case study will be designed to test the depth of your understanding of the syllabus. You will be expected to provide your own assessment of the situation and to include your reasoned opinions. You should spend about an hour and 10 minutes on this case study.

In section B, you will have to answer one out of two problem-solving questions on financial management topics. In section C, you will have to answer two out of three questions on management accounting topics. These questions will be worth 20 marks each. All questions will include a mixture of computation and discussion. You should spend about 35 minutes on each question.

Your general strategy

You should spend the first ten minutes of the examination reading the paper and deciding which questions you will do. You must divide the time you spend on questions in proportion to the marks on offer. Don't be tempted to spend more time on a question you know a lot about, or one which you find particularly difficult. If a question has more than one part, you must try to complete each part.

On every question, the first marks are the easiest to gain. Even if things go wrong with your timing and you don't have time to complete a question properly, you will probably gain some marks by making a start.

Spend the last five minutes reading through your answers and making any additions or corrections.

You may answer written questions in any order you like. Some people start with their best question, to help them relax. Another strategy is to begin with your second best question, so that you are working even more effectively when you reach the question you are most confident about.

Once you have embarked on a question, you should try to stay with it, and not let your mind stray to other questions on the paper. You can only concentrate on one thing at once. However, if you get completely stuck with a question, leave space in your answer book and return to it later.

Answering the question

All Examiners say that the most frequent reason for failure in examinations, apart from basic lack of knowledge, is candidates' unwillingness to answer the question that the Examiner has asked. A great many people include every scrap of knowledge they have on a topic, just in case it is relevant. Stick to the question and tailor your answer to what you are asked. Pay particular attention to the verbs in the question.

You should be particularly wary if you come across a question which appears to be almost identical to one which you have practised during your revision. It probably isn't! Wishful thinking makes many people see the question they would like to see on the paper, not the one that is actually there. Read a question at least twice before you begin your answer. Underline key words on the question paper, if it helps focus your mind on what is required.

If you don't understand what a question is asking, state your assumptions. Even if you do not answer in precisely the way the Examiner hoped, you may be given some credit, if your assumptions are reasonable.

Presentation

You should do everything you can to make things easy for the marker. Although you will not be marked on your handwriting, the marker will find it easier to identify the points you have made if your answers are legible. The same applies to spelling and grammar. Use blue or black ink. The marker will be using red or green.

Use the margin to clearly identify which question, or part of a question, you are answering.

Start each answer on a new page. The order in which you answer the questions does not matter, but if a question has several parts, these parts should appear in the correct order in your answer book.

If there is the slightest doubt when an answer continues on another page, indicate to the marker that he or she must turn over. It is irritating for a marker to think he or she has reached the end of an answer, only to turn the page and find that the answer continues.

Use columnar layouts for computations. This will help you to avoid mistakes, and is easier to follow.

Use headings and numbered sentences if they help to show the structure of your answer. However, don't write your answers in one-word note form.

If your answers include diagrams, don't waste time making them great works of art. Keep them clear, neat and simple. Use your rule and any templates or geometric instruments you have with you. Remember to label the axes of graphs properly. Make reference to any diagrams in the body of your text so that they form an integral part of your answer.

It is a good idea to make a rough plan of an answer before you begin to write. Do this in your answer booklet, but make sure you cross it out neatly afterwards. The marker needs to be clear whether he or she is looking at your rough notes, or the answer itself.

Computations

Before you begin a computation, you may find it helpful to jot down the stages you will go through.

It is essential to include all your workings and to indicate where they fit in to your answer. It is important that the marker can see where you got the figures in your answer from. Even if you make mistakes in your computations, you will be given credit for using a principle correctly, if it is clear from your workings and the structure of your answer.

If you spot an arithmetical error which has implications for figures later in your answer, it almost certainly is not worth spending a lot of time reworking your computation.

If you are asked to comment or make recommendations on a computation, you must do so. There are important marks to be gained here. Even if your computation contains mistakes, you may still gain marks if your reasoning is correct.

Use the layouts which you see in the answers given in this booklet and in model answers. A clear layout will help you avoid errors and will impress the marker.

Essay questions

In this paper you could be asked to write a short essay of up to about 12 marks.

You must plan an essay before you start writing. One technique is to quickly jot down any ideas which you think are relevant. Re-read the question and cross out any points in your notes which are not relevant. Then number your points. Remember to cross out your plan afterwards.

Your essay should have a clear structure. It should contain a brief introduction, a main section and a conclusion. Don't waste time by restating the question at the start of your essay.

Break your essay up into paragraphs. Use sub-headings and numbered sentences if they help show the structure of your answer.

Be concise. It is better to write a little about a lot of different points than a great deal about one or two points.

The Examiner will be looking for evidence that you have understood the syllabus and can apply your knowledge in new situations. You will also be expected to give opinions and make judgements. These should be based on reasoned and logical arguments.

Case studies

The case study asks you to apply your knowledge in a particular situation. Expect to spend up to a quarter of the time available for the question on reading and analysing the information and planning your answer.

Start by reading the questions based on the case study. Then read the case study, trying to grasp the main points. Read the case study through again and make notes of the key points. Then analyse the case and identify the relevant issues and concepts. Before you start your answer, read the questions again along with relevant parts of the case study.

If alternative answers present themselves, mention them. You may sometimes find it helpful to consider short and long term recommendations separately.

Reports, memos and other documents

Some questions ask you to present your answer in the form of a report or a memo or other document. It is important that you use the correct format - there are easy marks to be gained here. Adopt the format used in sample questions, or use the format you are familiar with in your day-to-day work, as long as it contains all the essential elements.

You should also consider the audience for any document you are writing. How much do they know about the subject? What kind of information and recommendations are required? The Examiner will be looking for evidence that you can present your ideas in an appropriate form.

5 KEY REVISION TOPICS

The aim of this section is to provide you with a checklist of key information relating to this Paper. You should use it as a reminder of topics to be revised rather than as a summary of all you need to know. Aim to revise as many topics as possible because many of the questions in the exam draw on material from more than one section of the syllabus. You will get more out of this section if you read through Section 3, General Revision Guidance first.

MANAGEMENT ACCOUNTING

1, 2 COST ACCUMULATION AND PRODUCT COSTING

You should be

- able to compare and contrast the nature, format and purpose of *financial/management/ cost accounting, and management accounting/financial management*

- familiar with basic *costing terminology* - investment/profit/cost centres; cost units; cost classifications

- wholly conversant with the techniques involved in *overhead cost allocation and apportionment*, including reapportionment of service department costs and *activity based costing (ABC)*

- prepared to critically compare the traditional and ABC absorption methods

Refer to chapters 1 and 2 of the Lynchpin, and attempt all the questions shown under this heading on the contents page of this book

3 - 5 JOB, CONTRACT, PROCESS AND SERVICE COSTING

You need to have a good working knowledge of

- the types of work or production for which each of the *job*, *batch* and *contract* costing methods would be used

- how the techniques of overhead absorption and mark-ups can be used within the costing approaches

- how *attributable profit* may be calculated on a long term contract, and circumstances under which it may be recognised in the accounts

- the type of production for which *process costing* would be used, and the basic computation of cost per unit

- the treatment of *normal* and *abnormal* losses

- the concept of *equivalent units* and their use in valuing *work in process* (FIFO and weighted average)

- the bookkeeping entries to process and loss accounts

- the difference between *joint* and *by-products*, in nature and costing treatment

- the ways in which *joint costs* may be allocated between joint products

- the types of *cost units* that may be used for various service operations/businesses

- compute appropriate *costs per cost uni*t and other *performance measures* within a given service industry context and comment upon them

Refer to chapters 3 to 5 of the Lynchpin, and attempt all the questions shown under the heading "job, contract and process costing" on the contents page of this book - also question 15 in the budgeting section, which considers a service business.

6   MARGINAL AND ABSORPTION COSTING

You need to be able to

- explain and illustrate the effect of *marginal* and *absorption* costing on stock valuation and profit reporting

- comparatively discuss the two methods

Refer to chapter 6 of the Lynchpin, and attempt all the questions shown under this heading on the contents page of this book

7 - 11   BUDGETING AND CONTROL

The main areas with which you must be familiar are:

- the role the budget plays in corporate planning, its administration and general steps in preparation

- the preparation of *functional*, *cash* and *master* budgets

- the behavioural aspects

- the uses and limitations of quantitative aids in budgeting and forecasting - *regression, correlation, time series analysis*

- alternative budgeting systems - *zero based budgeting (versus incremental), programme planning budgeting systems*

Refer to chapters 7 to 11 of the Lynchpin, and attempt all the questions shown under this heading on the contents page of this book

12,13   STANDARD COSTING AND VARIANCE ANALYSIS

You need to be able to

- outline the uses, features and limitations of standard costing systems, and explain how standards are determined

- compute and interpret *variances* relating to:
    - materials (including mix and yield)
    - labour variances
    - overhead variances (including expenditure, capacity and efficiency)
    - sales (including quantity and mix)

- prepare reconciliations between budget and actual profits using *operating statements*

- discuss possible *causes* and *inter-relationship*s between variances

Refer to chapters 12 to 14 of the Lynchpin, and attempt all the questions shown under this heading on the contents page of this book

14   DECISION MAKING

You may be required to

- identify relevant information for planning, monitoring and decision making - incorporating the principles of *opportunity costing*

- employ contribution analysis (cost volume profit) measures and techniques such as break-even, contribution-sales ratio, profit targeting

- apply marginal costing principles to problems involving *limiting factors, make or buy* decisions and general proposal evaluation

Refer to chapter 15 of the Lynchpin, and attempt all the questions shown under this heading on the contents page of this book. Also look at Q 50, the case study from June 1996's paper, which includes break-even aspects in a financial management context

FINANCIAL MANAGEMENT

16 - 19 THE ECONOMIC ENVIRONMENT

You need to have an appreciation of

- the principal objectives of UK *macroeconomic policy* , and how the UK has performed in recent years

- the role and problems of *monetary policy*, and how the money supply may be measured

- the meaning and role of *fiscal policy*, and how it relates to monetary policy

- the definition, causes and measurement of *inflation,* and its consequences for the economy in general and companies in particular

- how inflation may distort the evaluation of business performance

- how Government may intervene in the economy, by operating a *competition policy,* incorporating *deregulation* or *privatisation*, and the implementation of *supply side policies.*

Refer to chapters 16 to 19 of the Lynchpin. These areas used to be principally examined by way of short-form questions - you should look at question 2 of each of the past papers up to December 1996. They are now likely to be short parts of questions in any section of the paper.

20   THE NATURE AND SCOPE OF FINANCIAL MANAGEMENT

You should be prepared to

- discuss the various possible *objectives* (financial, non-financial and social) of different types of organisations, including private and public sector businesses, and not-for-profit organisations

- identify and compute *ratios* and other suitable measures for the performance evaluation of a company, highlighting *profitability*, *liquidity* and *finance (gearing)* aspects

Refer to chapter 20 of the Lynchpin, and attempt all the questions shown under this heading on the contents page of this book. You should also look at the case study from June 1997 (Q 62)

21 THE FINANCIAL MANAGEMENT FRAMEWORK

You should have a general awareness of:

- the nature and role of *financial intermediaries*, *commercial banks* and *financial markets* in the provision of finance to companies

- the *creation of credit* by the banking system

- The main types of financial markets (capital and money), including international

- The operations of the *Stock Exchange* (including the Alternative Investment Market)

- the *Efficient Market Hypothesis*, and its implications for financial management

- the general factors determining *money market interest rates* and other rates of return, including the *risk-return trade off*

Refer to chapter 21 of the Lynchpin, and attempt all the questions shown under this heading on the contents page of this book

22 MANAGEMENT OF WORKING CAPITAL

You need to be prepared to discuss:

- the meaning of necessity for and general aims of working capital management

- the methods by which *debtors* can be monitored and controlled, including customer vetting, credit rating and collection procedures

- the roles of *factoring*, *invoice discounting* and *settlement discounts* in the administration and financing of debtors

- the benefits and potential costs associated with taking extended credit from *suppliers*

- the problems associated with *overseas trading*, including export credit risk and foreign exchange risk

- the particular factors (costs and benefits) to be taken into account when determining an optimum *stock* holding/ordering policy

- the relevance of *stock ratios*, the *economic order quantity* (EOQ) and *re-order level* in stock control, and to carry out appropriate calculations (the latter two under certain and uncertain demand conditions)

- the different types of stock system that may operate in practice, including *just in time*

- the formal models of *cash management* (EOQ, Miller-Orr, probability based), their application in determining optimal cash balances and their limitations

- the function and benefits of centralised *treasury management*

- the conditions under which the various *cash transmission* methods are available, and their role in cash flow management

Refer to chapters 22 and 23 of the Lynchpin, and attempt all the questions shown under this heading on the contents page of this book. You should also look at the case study questions from December 1995 (Q 44) and December 1996 (Q56)

24-26 LONG TERM FINANCE

You should be familiar with

- the methods by which *equity finance* may be obtained (internally and externally) including the various methods of *issuing shares*

- the principles and assumptions of the dividend valuation model, with and without growth

- the various types of *debt finance* that may be used, and its relative merits/demerits in comparison with equity, including taxation aspects

- the features and potential benefits of *convertible securities* and *warrants*

- the potential effects on EPS of conversion and option rights

- the various ways in which *financial gearing* may be measured (and how it compares with *operational gearing)*

- the possible *effects of financial gearing* on investors' required rates of return, share values and risks faced by the company and its investors

Refer to chapter 24 - 26 of the Lynchpin, and attempt all the questions shown under this heading on the contents page of this book; the case studies will also generally include aspects of this topic, in particular those from papers set in June 1994 (Q26) June 1996 (Q50), December 1996 (Q56) and June 1997 (Q62)

27-28 CAPITAL EXPENDITURE AND INVESTMENT - PRINCIPLES AND METHODS

You should be able to

- appreciate the difference between the meaning and treatment of *capital* and *revenue* expenditure

- discuss the ways in which firms identify potential investment opportunities - *strategic analysis*

- explain the *payback period* and *return on capital employed (ROCE)* (also known as *accounting rate of return (ARR))* methods, carry out related computations and examine their potential benefits and limitations

- explain the importance of the *time value of money* in investment appraisal, and the extent to which *discounted cash flow (DCF)* techniques take this into account

- explain this and other advantages of DCF methods over others

- calculate present values to derive the *net present value (NPV)* and *internal rate of return (IRR)* measures of investment worth.

- assess the relative merits of the IRR and NPV methods, including in the circumstances of *mutually exclusive* investments and investments with *multiple yields*.

- apply the DCF principles to *replacement decisions*

- explain the effect of *inflation* on investment appraisal, distinguishing between *real* and *money* terms, and evaluate projects on either basis

- allow for the effect of *taxation* on both cash flows and cost of capital within a project evaluation

Refer to chapters 27 - 29 of the Lynchpin, and attempt all the questions shown under this heading on the contents page of this book. Also look at the case study question from December 1996's paper (Q56)

30-32   CAPITAL EXPENDITURE AND INVESTMENT - SPECIAL SITUATIONS

You should be prepared to apply the DCF methods where:

- there is risk and/or uncertainty involved - using expected values, decision tree analysis, sensitivity analysis and simulation as appropriate

- there is an element of *capital rationing*, both single period (using *profitability indices)* and multi-period (formulating the *linear programme*)

- you are considering *leasing* as a method of project finance. As well as appreciating the effect of different types of finance (HP, finance leases and operating leases) on cash flows, you should be able to evaluate the *lease or borrow-and-buy* decision, both with and without tax.

Refer to chapters 30 to 32 of the Lynchpin, and attempt all the questions shown under this heading on the contents page of this book. Also look at the case study question from June 1995's paper (Q38)

6 UPDATES

INTRODUCTION

Examinable documents

Every six months ACCA publish a list of 'examinable documents' as at 1 June and 1 December which form the basis of the legislation and accounting regulations that will be examinable at the following diet.

The ACCA Official Textbooks published in June 1998 were fully up-to-date for these examinable documents published as at 1 June 1998. There are no examinable documents as such for Paper 8.

NEW EXAMINER

A new examiner was appointed for the Financial Management section of the paper with effect from the June 1998 examination. She issued some comments on her approach to the paper, which are set out below:

'Candidates and tutors should be aware that the financial management section of the paper builds on the economics already covered in paper 4, and also serves to introduce finance topics which will be examined in greater depth in paper 14.

I intend to set questions which may incorporate aspects of both economics and corporate financial management. As an example, the impact of inflation on pricing decisions and profit management requires understanding of how basic economic concepts or measures can impinge on businesses.

The case study question may be broad ranging in its syllabus coverage. I do not wish to set a 40 mark question which focuses on a single syllabus area - the question will contain both computational and discursive elements.

I am concerned that the finance questions should cover the full spectrum of business types and company sizes. Issues of funding for small firms, and the problems of financing growth in a business are, therefore, given equal importance to the type of difficulties facing larger concerns by the cost of raising debenture finance.

I also consider it important for students to recognise that the financial management skills required in the exam are introductory in level, and so appropriate to the Certificate Stage level of the examination. More advanced skills such as the computation of, and comment upon, a weighted average cost of capital are not examinable, as they form part of the paper 14 syllabus. The syllabus breakdown and exam notes should be used as the reference point for what is to be examined.

I do not, at this stage, propose any changes to the reading list and students will find that articles relevant to paper 8 will be published regularly in the *Students' Newsletter*. Such articles are essential reading.'

7 PRACTICE QUESTIONS

1	A POLYTECHNIC

A polytechnic offers a range of degree courses. The polytechnic organisation structure consist of three faculties each with a number of teaching departments. In addition, there is a polytechnic administrative/management function and a central services function.

The following cost information is available for the year ended 30 June 19X7:

(1) **Occupancy costs**

Total £1,500,000. Such costs are apportioned on the basis of area used which is:

	Square feet
Faculties	7,500
Teaching departments	20,000
Administration/management	7,000
Central services	3,000

(2) **Administration/management costs**

Direct costs: £1,775,000

Indirect costs: an apportionment of occupancy costs.

Direct and indirect costs are charged to degree courses on a percentage basis.

(3) **Faculty costs**

Direct costs: £700,000.

Indirect costs: an apportionment of occupancy costs and central service costs.

Direct and indirect costs are charged to teaching departments.

(4) **Teaching departments**

Direct costs: £5,525,000.

Indirect costs: an apportionment of occupancy costs and central service costs plus all faculty costs.

Direct and indirect costs are charged to degree courses on a percentage basis.

(5) **Central services**

Direct costs: £1,000,000.

Indirect costs: an apportionment of occupancy costs.

Direct and indirect costs of central services have in previous years been charged to users on a percentage basis. A study has now been completed which has estimated what user areas would have paid external suppliers for the same services on an individual basis. For the year ended 30 June 19X7, the apportionment of the central services cost is to be recalculated in a manner which recognises the cost savings achieved by using the central services facilities instead of using external service companies. This is to be done by apportioning the overall savings to user areas in proportion to their share of the estimated external costs.

The estimated external costs of service provision are as follows:

	£'000
Faculties	240
Teaching departments	800
Degree courses:	
Business studies	32
Mechanical engineering	48
Catering studies	32
All other degrees	448
	1,600

(6) Additional data relating to the degree courses is as follows:

	Degree course		
	Business Studies	*Mechanical Engineering*	*Catering Studies*
Number of graduates	80	50	120
Apportioned costs (as % of totals)			
Teaching departments	3%	2.5%	7%
Administration/management	2.5%	5%	4%

Central services are to be apportioned as detailed in (v) above.

The total number of graduates from the polytechnic in the year to 30 June 19X7 was 2,500.

You are required:

(a) to prepare a flow diagram which shows the apportionment of costs to user areas. No values need be shown; **(3 marks)**

(b) to calculate the average cost per graduate, for the year ended 30 June 19X7, for the polytechnic and for each of the degrees in business studies, mechanical engineering and catering studies, showing all relevant cost analysis; **(13 marks)**

(c) to suggest reasons for any differences in the average cost per graduate from one degree to another, and discuss briefly the relevance of such information to the polytechnic management. **(4 marks)**

(Total: 20 marks)
(ACCA June 88)

2 A LTD

Product X, one of the products manufactured by A Ltd is sold exclusively to B Ltd. The annual quantity is 250,000 units. A change in the final packing of the product is to be introduced in order to save costs.

Currently the product is packed into boxes, each containing four units of the product. These boxes are then packed in larger boxes (eight small boxes per large box). The new packaging operation will eliminate the packing into small boxes. The product is to be packed into a single box containing twenty units. The new box is available immediately. Savings will result in packaging materials and also in labour and overheads incurred in the packaging operation.

Details of the costs of manufacturing the product currently are as follows:

> Raw materials total £0.452 per unit. Packaging materials (excluding the cost of boxes) total £0.103 per unit. Inner and outer boxes cost £114.00 and £547.20 per thousand boxes respectively. There is 5% wastage on usage of both small and large boxes.

The product is manufactured in batches of 2,000 units, which pass through two stages - fabrication and packaging. 40 units of the product are fabricated per hour of direct labour; units are packaged at a rate of 120 units per direct labour hour. The hourly rates for direct labour in fabrication and packaging are £4.80 and £3.60 respectively.

A direct labour hour rate is established in both the fabrication and packaging departments in order to absorb overheads into the cost of products manufactured. Overheads currently incurred per period are as follows:

	Fabrication £'000	Packaging £'000	General services £'000
Variable	88.0	24.0	-
Fixed	359.4	53.6	253.0

General services overheads are apportioned to fabrication and packaging in the ratio 9:2. Direct labour hours per period in fabrication and packaging are currently 40,000 and 10,000 respectively.

Supplies of the two boxes, currently used for packaging the product, are in stock. These stocks are sufficient to produce 50,000 units. They have no alternative use.

The new box to be used for packaging the product will cost £475.00 per thousand boxes. 5% wastage will occur on usage. Units will be packed at a rate of 400 per direct labour hour. The selling price charged by A Ltd to B Ltd will be reduced from £1.55 to £1.53 per unit when the packaging change is introduced.

You are required:

(a) to calculate the current total manufacturing cost per unit of the product to A Ltd; **(13 marks)**

(b) to write a letter to the general manager of A Ltd:

(i) showing the savings that will result from the packaging change;

(ii) advising him when, from A Ltd's point of view, the packaging change should be introduced. (Explain and demonstrate fully the basis for your advice.) **(12 marks)**
(Total: 25 marks)
(ACCA Dec 89)

---

3 AMAZON PLC

Amazon plc manufactures two types of industrial sealant by passing materials through two consecutive processes. The results of operating the two processes during the previous month are shown below:

Process 1

Costs incurred (£):	
Materials 7,000 kg @ £0.50 per kg	3,500
Labour and overheads	4,340

Output (kg):
Transferred to Process 2	6,430
Defective production	570

Process 2

Costs incurred (£):
Labour and overheads	12,129

Output (kg):
Type E sealant	2,000
Type F sealant	4,000
By-product	430

It is considered normal for 10% of the total output from process 1 to be defective and all defective output is sold as scrap at £0.40 kg. Losses are not expected in process 2.

There was no work in process at the beginning or end of the month and no opening stocks of sealants.

Sales of the month's output from Process 2 were:

Type E sealant	1,100 kg
Type F sealant	3,200 kg
By-product	430 kg

The remainder of the output from Process 2 was in stock at the end of the month.

The selling prices of the products are: Type E sealant £7 per kg and Type F sealant £2.50 per kg. No additional costs are incurred on either of the two main products after the second process. The by-product is sold for £1.80 per kg after being sterilised, at a cost of £0.30 per kg, in a subsequent process. The operating costs of process 2 are reduced by the net income receivable from sales of the by-product.

You are required

(a)   to calculate, for the previous month, the cost of the output transferred from process 1 into process 2 and the net cost or saving arising from any abnormal losses or gains in process 1.   **(6 marks)**

(b)   to calculate the value of the closing stock of each sealant and the profit earned by each sealant during the previous month using the following method of apportioning costs to joint products:

(i)   according to weight of output,
(ii)   according to market value of output.   **(10 marks)**

(c)   to consider whether apportioning process costs to joint products is useful. Briefly illustrate with examples from your answer to (b) above.   **(4 marks)**
    (Total: 20 marks)

4   MANUFACTURING PRODUCT X

A new subsidiary of a group of companies was established for the manufacture and sale of Product X. During the first year of operations 90,000 units were sold at £20 per unit. At the end of the year, the closing stocks were 8,000 units in finished goods store and 4,000 units in work-in-progress which were complete as regards material content but only half complete in respect of labour and overheads. You are to assume that there were no opening stocks.

The work-in-progress account had been debited during the year with the following costs:

	£
Direct materials	714,000
Direct labour	400,000
Variable overhead	100,000
Fixed overhead	350,000

Selling and administration costs for the year were:

	Variable cost per unit sold £	Fixed cost £
Selling	1.50	200,000
Administration	0.10	50,000

The accountant of the subsidiary company had prepared a profit statement on the absorption costing principle which showed a profit of £11,000.

The financial controller of the group, however, had prepared a profit statement on a marginal costing basis which showed a loss. Faced with these two profit statements, the director responsible for this particular subsidiary company is confused.

You are required:

(a)   to prepare a statement showing the equivalent units produced and the production cost of one unit of Product X by element of cost and in total;   **(5 marks)**

(b)   to prepare a profit statement on the absorption costing principle which agrees with the company accountant's statement;   **(9 marks)**

(c)   to prepare a profit statement on the marginal costing basis;   **(6 marks)**

(d)   to explain the differences between the two statements given for (b) and (c) above to the director in such a way as to eliminate his confusion and state why both statements may be acceptable.
    (5 marks)
    (Total: 25 marks)

---

5   MIOZIP CO

The Miozip Co operates an absorption costing system which incorporates a factory-wide overhead absorption rate per direct labour hour. For 19X0 and 19X1 this rate was £2.10 per hour. The fixed factory overhead for 19X1 was £600,000 and this would have been fully absorbed if the company had operated at full capacity, which is estimated at 400,000 direct labour hours. Unfortunately, only 200,000 hours were worked in that year so that the overhead was seriously under-absorbed. Fixed factory overheads are expected to be unchanged in 19X2 and 19X3.

The outcome for 19X1 was a loss of £70,000 and the management believed that a major cause of this loss was the low overhead absorption rate which had led the company to quote selling prices which were uneconomic.

For 19X2 the overhead absorption rate was increased to £3.60 per direct labour hour and selling prices were raised in line with the established pricing procedures which involve adding a profit mark-up of 50% onto the full factory cost of the company's products. The new selling prices were also charged on the stock of finished goods held at the beginning of 19X2. In December 19X2 the company's accountant prepared an estimated profit and loss account for 19X2 and a budgeted profit and loss account for 19X3. Although sales were considered to be depressed in 19X1, they were even lower in 19X2 but, nevertheless, it seems that the company will make a profit for that year. A worrying feature of the estimated accounts is the high level of finished goods stock held and the 19X3 budget provides for a reduction in the stock level at 31 December 19X3 to the (physical) level which obtained at 1 January 19X1. Budgeted sales for 19X3 are set at the 19X2 sales level.

The summarised profit statements for the three years to 31 December 19X3 are as follows:

Summarised profit and loss accounts

	Actual 19X1 £	Actual 19X1 £	Estimated 19X2 £	Estimated 19X2 £	Budgeted 19X3 £	Budgeted 19X3 £
Sales revenue		1,350,000		1,316,250		1,316,250
Opening stock of finished goods	100,000		200,000		357,500	
Factory cost of production	1,000,000		975,000		650,000	
	1,100,000		1,175,000		1,007,500	
Less: Closing stock of finished goods	200,000		357,500		130,000	
Factory cost of goods sold		900,000		817,500		877,500
		450,000		498,750		438,750
Less: Factory overhead under-absorbed		300,000		150,000		300,000
		150,000		348,750		138,750
Administrative and financial costs		220,000		220,000		220,000
Profit/(loss)		(70,000)		128,750		(81,250)

You are required:

(a)   to write a short report to the board of Miozip explaining why the budgeted income for 19X3 is so different from that of 19X2 when the sales revenue is the same for both years;   **(5 marks)**

(b)   to restate the profit and loss account for 19X1, the estimated profit and loss account for 19X2 and the budgeted profit and loss account for 19X3 using marginal factory cost for stock valuation purposes;   **(7 marks)**

(c)   to comment on the problems which may follow from a decision to increase the overhead absorption rate in conditions when cost plus pricing is used and overhead is currently under-absorbed;   **(3 marks)**

(d)   to explain why the majority of businesses use full costing systems whilst most management accounting theorists favour marginal costing.   **(5 marks)**

Note: assume in your answers to this question that the value of the £ and the efficiency of the company have been constant over the period under review.

(Total: 20 marks)
(ACCA Dec 82)

6   LIMITATION PLC

Limitation plc commenced the manufacture and sale of a new product in the fourth quarter of 19X1. In order to facilitate the budgeting process for Quarters 1 and 2 of 19X2, the following information has been collected:

(1)   Forecast product/sales (batches of product):

Quarter 4, 19X1	30 batches
Quarter 1,19X2	45 batches
Quarter 2, 19X2	45 batches

(2)   It is estimated that direct labour is subject to a learning curve effect of 90%. The labour cost of batch 1 of Quarter 4, 19X1 was £600 (at £5 per hour). The labour output rates from the commencement of production of the product, after adjusting for learning effects, are as follows:

Total batches produced (batches)	Overall average time per batch (hours)
15	79.51
30	71.56
45	67.28
60	64.40
75	62.25
90	60.55
105	50.15
120	57.96

Labour hours worked and paid for will be adjusted to eliminate spare capacity during each quarter. All time will be paid for at £5 per hour.

(3)   Direct material is used at the rate of 200 units per batch of product for the first 20 batches of Quarter 4, 19X1. Units of material used per batch will fall by 2% of the original level for each 20 batches thereafter as the learning curve effect improves the efficiency with which the material is used. All material will be bought at £1.80 per unit during 19X2. Delivery of the total material requirement for a quarter will be made on day one of the quarter. Stock will be held in storage capacity hired at a cost of 30p per quarter per unit held in stock. Material will be used at an even rate throughout each quarter.

(4)   Variable overhead is estimated at 150% of direct labour cost during 19X2.

(5)   All units produced will be sold in the quarter of production at £1,200 per batch.

Required:

(a)   Calculate the labour hours requirement for the second batch and the sum of the labour hours for the third and fourth batches produced in Quarter 4, 19X1.   **(3 marks)**

(b)   Prepare a budget for each of Quarters 1 and 2, 19X2 showing the contribution earned from the product. Show all relevant workings.   **(14 marks)**

(c)   The supplier of the raw material has offered to deliver on a 'just-in-time' basis in return for a price increase to £1.90 per unit in Quarter 1, 19X2 and £2 per unit thereafter.

     (i)   Use information for Quarters 1 and 2 19X2 to determine whether the offer should be accepted on financial grounds.

(ii)   Comment on other factors which should be considered before a final decision is reached.

(8 marks)

(Total: 25 marks)

(ACCA December 1991 Paper 2.4 Management Accounting Adapted)

---

7   A AND B

A company has two machines - A and B - each of which may be used to produce Products X and Y. The products are fabric, made in a number of widths by passing untreated fabric across one of the machines and then adding a colour dye.

Budget/forecast data for 19X8 are as follows:

(1)   Stocks at 1 January 19X8:

Product X	30,000 metres at 120 cm width
Product Y	5,000 metres at 200 cm width
Untreated fabric:	25,000 sq metres
Fabric dye	25 kilos

(2)   The closing stock of untreated fabric is budgeted at 10% of the required input to production during 19X8. No closing stocks of X or Y are budgeted.

(3)   Fabric yield is budgeted at 90% of input for Machine A and 80% of input for Machine B, due to processing losses.

(4)   Fabric dye is used at the rate of 1 kilo per 500 square metres of **output** for both Products X and Y. The maximum quantity available from suppliers during 19X8 is 520 kilos. If there is insufficient dye to meet production requirements, the output of the narrowest product would be reduced as required.

(5)   The budgeted rates of good output for Machines A and B are the same and vary with the width of products according to the following table:

Product width (cm)	Good output per machine hour (metres)
100	120
120	100
140	90
160	80
180	70
200	50
240	40

(6)   The maximum output width of product from each machine is Machine A: 140 cm, Machine B: 240 cm. It is company policy not to use Machine B for product widths less than 125 cm.

(7)   Each machine is manned for 35 hours per week for 46 weeks in the year. Part of this is budgeted to be lost as idle time as follows, Machine A: 20% of manned hours; Machine B; 30% of manned hours. This idle time does not include any idle time caused by a shortage of fabric dye.

(8)   The sales forecast for 19X8 is as follows:

Product X	90,000 metres at 120 cm width
	70,000 metres at 160 cm width
Product Y	30,000 metres at 200 cm width
	100,000 metres at 100 cm width

(9)   If production capacity is not sufficient to allow the sales forecast to be achieved, the budgets for production on each machine will be set by limiting the quantity of the narrowest product on that machine.

You are required:

(a)   to prepare budgets for 19X8 analysed by product type and width for (i) production quantities and (ii) sales quantities. The budgets should make maximum use of the available resources; **(8 marks)**

(b)   to prepare a purchases budget for untreated fabric. Express the budget in terms of square metres purchased;   **(6 marks)**

(c)   to suggest ways in which the company might attempt to overcome any inability to meet the sales forecast. Comment on any problems likely to arise in the implementation of each of these ways.
(6 marks)
(Total: 20 marks)
(Pilot Paper)

---

8   MATERIAL VARIANCES

A company makes a product using two materials, X and Y, in the production process. A system of standard costing and variance analysis is in operation. The standard material requirement per tonne of mixed output is 60% material X at £30 per tonne and 40% material Y at £45 per tonne, with a standard yield of 90%.

The following information has been gathered for the three months January to March:

	January	February	March
Output achieved (tonnes)	810	765	900
Actual material input:			
X (tonnes)	540	480	700
Y (tonnes)	360	360	360
Actual material cost (X plus Y) (£)	32,400	31,560	38,600

The actual price per tonne of material Y throughout the January to March period was £45.

You are required:

(a)   to prepare material variance summaries for each of January, February and March which include yield and mix variances in total plus usage and price variances for each material and in total;
(15 marks)

(b)   to prepare comments for management on each variance including variance trend.   **(9 marks)**

(c)   to discuss the relevance of the variances calculated above in the light of the following additional information:

The company has an agreement to purchase 360 tonnes of material Y each month and the perishable nature of the material means that it must be used in the month of purchase and additional supplies in excess of 360 tonnes per month are not available.   **(6 marks)**
(Total: 30 marks)
(ACCA June 91)

9   AB LTD

AB Ltd manufactures a range of products. One of the products, Product M, requires the use of Materials X and Y. Standard material costs for the manufacture of an item of Product M in Period 1 included:

Material X: 9 kilos at £1.20 per kilo.

Total purchases of Material X in Period 1, for use in all products, were 142,000 kilos costing £171,820. 16,270 kilos were used in the period in the manufacture of 1,790 units of Product M.

In Period 2 the standard price of Material X was increased by 6%, whilst the standard usage of the material in Product M was left unchanged. 147,400 kilos of Material X were purchased in Period 2 at a favourable price variance of £1,031.80. A favourable usage variance of 0.5% of standard occurred on Material X in the manufacture of Product M in the period.

Required

(a)   Calculate:

  (i)   the total price variance on purchases of Material X in Period 1;   **(2 marks)**

  (ii)   the Material X usage variance arising from the manufacture of Product M in Period 1;
                                                                                              (2 marks)

  (iii)   the actual cost inflation on Material X from Period 1 to Period 2. Calculate as a percentage increase to one decimal place.   **(4 marks)**

  (iv)   the percentage change in actual usage of Material X per unit of Product M from Period 1 to Period 2. Calculate to one decimal place.   **(4 marks)**

(b)   Describe, and contrast, the different types of standards that may be set for raw material usage and labour efficiency.   **(8 marks)**
                                                                                        (Total: 20 marks)
                                                                                          (ACCA June 92)

10   MATERIAL A

A company manufacturers two components in one of its factories. Material A is one of several materials used in the manufacture of both components.

The standard direct labour hours per unit of production, and budgeted production quantities, for a 13 week period were:

	Standard direct labour hours	Budgeted production quantities
Component X	0.40 hours	36,000 units
Component Y	0.56 hours	22,000 units

The standard wage rate for all direct workers was £5.00 per hour. Throughout the 13 week period 53 direct workers were employed, working a standard 40 hour week.

The following actual information for the 13 week period is available:

Production:
   Component X, 35,000 units
   Component Y, 25,000 units
Direct wages paid, £138,500
Material A purchases, 47,000 kilos costing £85,110
Material A price variance, £430 F
Material A usage (component X), 33,426 kilos
Material A usage variance (component X), £320.32A

Required

(a)   Calculate the direct labour variances for the period.   **(5 marks)**

(b)   Calculate the standard purchase price for Material A for the period and the standard usage of
       Material A per unit of production for Component X.   **(8 marks)**

(c)   Describe the steps, and information, required to establish the material purchase quantity budget for
       Material A for a period.   **(7 marks)**
                                                                                                        (Total: 20 marks)
                                                                                                         (ACCA Dec 92)

---

11   STOBO PLC

Stobo plc must decide whether to produce and sell either Product X or Product Y in the coming period.

The estimated demand probabilities for the period and the selling prices which have been set are as follows:

	Product X		*Product Y*	
Selling price per unit	£75		£150	
Sales (units)	5,600	1,400	3,200	1,600
Probability	0.6	0.4	0.3	0.7

The average direct material cost per product unit is expected to vary according to quantity purchased as
follows:

Product X		*Product Y*	
Units purchased up to -	*Average material cost per unit £*	*Units purchased up to -*	*Average material cost per unit £*
1,000	6.50	1,000	33
2,000	6.00	2,000	30
3,000	5.50	3,000	28
4,000	5.00	4,000	26
5,000	4.75		
6,000	4.50		

Each product would pass through two departments - making and finishing - where the maximum available
labour hours are sufficient for all possible quantities. It may be assumed that labour hours which are paid
for are balanced by natural wastage, so that labour hours which are surplus to actual production
requirements do not need to be paid for.

The labour operations are subject to a learning curve effect of 80% for Product X and 90% for Product Y
which would apply in both the making and finishing departments.

Initial batch sizes will be 700 units for Product X and 800 units for Product Y. For these sizes, the hours required per product unit are as follows:

	Product X Hours per unit	Product Y Hours per unit
Making department	4	5
Finishing department	3	4

Wages are paid at £4 per hour in the making department and £3.75 per hour in the finishing department.

Variable overheads would be incurred at 200% on productive wage costs for the making department and 250% on productive wage costs for the finishing department.

Company fixed overheads are normally apportioned to products as a percentage of sales revenue. During the coming period, when total sales revenue of Stobo plc is estimated at £12,000,000, the overheads have been budgeted at 17.5% of sales revenue. The fixed overheads which would be avoidable if Products X or Y were not produced are as follows:

Product X	£36,000
Product Y	£5,000

Production would be adjusted to equate with sales in the period and the purchase of raw material would be matched with production requirements.

You are required:

(a)   showing all relevant calculations, to explain which product Stobo plc should produce and sell;

(14 marks)

(b)   showing all relevant calculations, to explain how the choice of product might be affected if the maximum available labour hours must be retained and paid for in the making and finishing departments but all other conditions are as above. **(6 marks)**

(Total: 20 marks)

(Pilot Paper)

12   A LTD

Budgeted information for A Ltd for the following period, analysed by product, is shown below:

	Product I	Product II	Product III
Sales units (000s)	225	376	190
Selling price (£ per unit)	11.00	10.50	8.00
Variable costs (£ per unit)	5.80	6.00	5.20
Attributable fixed costs (£000s)	275	337	296

General fixed costs, which are apportioned to products as a percentage of sales, are budgeted at £1,668,000.

Required

(a)   Calculate the budgeted profit of A Ltd, and of each of its products. **(5 marks)**

(b)   Recalculate the budgeted profit of A Ltd on the assumption that Product III is discontinued, with no effect on sales of the other two products. State and justify other assumptions made.

(5 marks)

(c)   Additional advertising, to that included in the budget for Product I, is being considered.

Calculate the minimum extra sales required of Product I to cover additional advertising expenditure of £80,000. Assume that all other existing fixed costs would remain unchanged.

(5 marks)

(d)   Calculate the increase in sales volume of Product II that is necessary in order to compensate the effect of profit of a 10% reduction in the selling price of the product. State clearly any assumptions made.   **(5 marks)**

(Total: 20 marks)

(ACCA June 92)

---

13   BORROWS PLC

Borrows plc has decided to embark upon a new investment strategy. Traditionally a mining company operating coal, silver, gold and other mines throughout the world, it has now decided to use its expertise and move into international oil exploration with a view to setting up joint ventures to exploit any oilfields it discovers. The company feels that it requires another £200 million finance to support new operations for the next 8 years and it has identified three possible sources:

(a)   an issue of ordinary shares. The company proposes to make a rights issue at a 10% discount to the current market price.

(b)   an issue of a ten year 7% $300 million Eurodollar bond

(c)   a sale of 8% convertible unsecured loan stock of £100 each. Each of these can be converted by holders at any time into 40 ordinary shares. Any outstanding stocks will be redeemed at par in five years time.

The balance sheet for Borrows at 31 March 1994 is as follows:

	£m	£m
Fixed assets		1,400
Current assets	600	
Less: Current liabilities*	(200)	
Net current assets	——	400
		1,800
Less: Long term liabilities:		
10% Debentures		(300)
Net assets		1,500
Capital and Reserves		
Issued ordinary shares (50p par)		500
Reserves		1,000
		1,500

* Current liabilities include £80 million overdraft

The current market price per share is 210p, and price per debenture £90 per cent.

The current exchange rate of £1=$1.50 is expected to be maintained in the medium term.

The profit and loss account (year end 31 March 1994) for the company is:

	£m
Operating profit*	208
- interest	40
Earnings before tax	168
- tax (33%)	55
Earnings attributable to ordinary shareholders	113

* The new finance is expected to increase operating profit by 20% per annum of the amount of the finance, but this may take 4 or 5 years to materialise.

You are required:

(a)   to explain why a rights issue generally results in a fall in the market price of shares. Calculate the theoretical ex-rights price of the share if the issue is undertaken. Under what circumstances would you expect the share price to actually go to this price? Ignore issue costs in this question.

(10 marks)

(b)   to discuss the financial implications of all three options by calculating appropriate accounting ratios.

(12 marks)

(c)   to briefly consider the main risks connected with the investment project itself, and how Borrows might attempt to allow for these.

(8 marks)

(d)   to advise Borrows on the choice of finance, using the data calculated in the above sections as well as any other information that you perceive to be relevant. What other information would be useful to the company in making this decision?

(10 marks)

(Total: 40 marks)

---

14   MANRAY PLC

Manray plc manufactures and distributes automatic security lighting systems, which are purchased primarily by households, but also by business customers. When formed, some dozen years ago, Manray issued four million 25p ordinary shares, and one million £1 nominal 8% cumulative preference shares. Although Manray still relies on a single product, this has been modified numerous times in order to remain abreast of competitors. It is now contemplating investment in computer-controlled manufacturing technology which will further improve the product. It will also significantly alter the cost structure by raising fixed costs by £400,000 but lowering variable cost by £10 per unit, as a result of increased automation.

The improvement in the quality of the product is also expected to raise annual sales by 10,000 units, with no price change. Despite the volume increase, there is expected to be no increase in working capital requirements due to the introduction of a JIT system of stock control. In the trading period ended 31 March 19X3, Manray sold 80,000 units largely to edge-of-town DIY outlets, at a price of £35 per unit.

The new production facility will be financed by borrowing £3m from its present bankers, who currently provide overdraft facilities. The interest rate will be variable, but is initially set at 10% pa. £1m of the loan will be used to repay the existing overdraft. The loan itself will be repaid in three equal instalments, every two years over the anticipated lifetime of the equipment. If the equipment is purchased in the very near future, the company can begin to claim capital allowances against taxation liability. (Tax is paid a year in arrears.) At present, these operate on a **straight-line basis** over four years. The equipment is not expected to have any resale value.

Exhibit 1 shows Manray's profit and loss account for the year ended 31 March 19X3.

Exhibit 1

		£'000
Sales		2,800
Less: Variable expenses	1,600	
Fixed expenses	250	
		1,850
Operating profit		950
Less: Interest payable		150
Taxable profit		800
Less: Corporation tax*: at 33%		264
Profit after tax		536
Less: Preference dividend		80
Profit available for ordinary shareholders		456
Less: Dividend		228
Retained profit		228

* *Note:* a full tax charge was payable, there being no depreciation allowances available for the year in question.

You are required:

(a)   Using a 15% discount rate, to determine whether the project is worthwhile, taking account of corporation tax and the depreciation allowance;   **(12 marks)**

(b)   to calculate the change in earnings per share if Manray introduces the new production facility at once;   **(6 marks)**

(c)   to explain the term 'operating gearing', and illustrate your answer using data relating to Manray;
                                                                                                                                                            (7 marks)

(d)   to determine the break-even volumes for Manray, both before and after the introduction of the new facility;   **(5 marks)**

(e)   One of Manray's directors argues that the proposed method of finance over-exposes Manray to increases in interest rates.

What macro-economic factors might be expected to cause increases in interest rates?   What difficulties might such an increase cause?   **(10 marks)**
                                                                                                                                        (Total 40 marks)
                                                                                                                                            (Pilot Paper)

15   COMPANY OBJECTIVES

Justify and criticise the usual assumption made in financial management literature that the objective of a company is to maximise the wealth of the shareholders. (Do not consider how this wealth is to be measured).

Outline other goals that companies claim to follow, and explain why these might be adopted in preference to the maximisation of shareholder wealth.

(20 marks)

16   EFFICIENT MARKET HYPOTHESIS

You are presented with the following different views of stock market behaviour.

(1)   If a company publishes an earnings figure that is better than the market expects, the shares of that company will usually experience an abnormally high return both on the day of the earnings announcement and over the two or three days following the date of the announcement.

(2)   The return on professionally managed portfolios of equities is likely to be no better than that which could be achieved by a naive investor who holds the market portfolio.

(3)   Share prices usually seem to rise sharply in the first few days of a new fiscal year. However, this can be explained by the fact that many investors sell losing stocks just before the fiscal year end in order to establish a tax loss for Capital Gains Tax purposes. This causes abnormal downward pressure which is released when the new fiscal year begins.

You are required:

(a)   to describe the three forms of the Efficient Market Hypothesis;   **(10 marks)**

(b)   to discuss what each of the above three statements would tell you about the efficiency of the stock market. Where appropriate relate your comments to one or more forms of the Efficient Market Hypothesis.
(10 marks)
(Total 20 marks)

17   FLOW OF FUNDS

(a)   Describe and explain the pattern of the flow of funds that occurs between the major sectors of an economy, and identify the sectors that are normally in surplus and those that are normally in deficit.
(7 marks)

(b)   Many borrowers wish to borrow large sums of money for long periods of time. Many savers wish to invest small sums of money for short periods of time.

Explain how financial intermediaries can help to satisfy the needs of both borrowers and lenders and describe the nature and functions of four major types of financial intermediary.   **(13 marks)**
(Total: 20 marks)
(ACCA June 86)

18   HEXICON PLC

(a)   Give reasons, with a brief explanation, why the net present value (NPV) method of investment appraisal is thought to be superior to other approaches.

(5 marks)

(b)   Hexicon plc manufactures and markets automatic washing machines. Among the many hundreds of components which it purchases each year from external suppliers for assembling into the finished article are drive belts, of which it uses 40,000 units pa. It is considering converting its purchasing, delivery and stock control of this item to a just-in-time system. This will raise the number of orders placed but lower the administrative and other costs of placing and receiving orders. If successful, this will provide the model for switching most of its inwards supplies on to this system. Details of actual and expected ordering and carrying costs are given in the table below.

			Actual	*Proposed*
O	=	Ordering cost per order	£100	£25
P	=	Purchase cost per item	£2.5	£2.5
I	=	Inventory holding cost (as a percentage of the purchase cost)	20%	20%

To implement the new arrangements will require 'one-off' reorganisation costs estimated at £4,000 which will be treated as a revenue item for tax purposes. The rate of corporation tax is 33% and Hexicon can obtain finance at 12%. The effective life span of the new system can be assumed to be eight years.

You are required:

(i)   to determine the effect of the new system on the economic order quantity (EOQ);

(ii)   to determine whether the new system is worthwhile in financial terms;

Note: EOQ is given by $Q = \sqrt{\dfrac{2 \times D \times O}{I \times P}}$ where D = demand, or usage.   **(10 marks)**

(c)   **You are required:** to briefly explain the nature and objectives of JIT purchasing agreements concluded between components users and suppliers.   **(5 marks)**

(Total: 20 marks)
(Pilot paper)

19   HN LTD

The directors of HN Ltd, a small manufacturing company, are worried about the company's cash flows during the next three months when sales receipts are at their lowest for the year. Cash budgets have been produced for the next three months under different economic assumptions. The Government's Budget is due in two weeks and there are concerns that there will be changes in corporate tax rates and credit controls. Cash flows in months two and three depend upon previous months' cash flows.

Net cash flow estimates (£000)

Month 1 Probable cash flow		Month 2 Probable cash flow		Month 3 Probable cash flow	
				.50	25
		.20	20	.50	15
				.50	5
.20	(55)	.50	10	.50	(5)
				.50	(5)
		.30	5	.50	(10)
				.50	5
		.20	10	.50	0
				.50	0
.50	(65)	.50	(5)	.50	(5)
				.50	(10)
		.30	(10)	.50	(15)
				.50	0
		.20	0	.50	(10)
				.50	(10)
.30	(72)	.50	(10)	.50	(20)
				.50	(20)
		.30	(15)	.50	(30)

The company currently has a cash flow of £20,000 which it keeps for 'transactions' and 'precautionary' purposes, and an overdraft facility of £80,000. The current overdraft is £12,000.

Required:

(a)   If the company wishes to maintain a month-end cash float of £20,000 at all times, what is the probability that the overdraft facility will be large enough to maintain this cash balance in each of months one, two and three? Interest on the overdraft can be ignored.   **(11 marks)**

(b)   What is the probability that the company will totally run out of cash (including using the overdraft) in each of months one, two and three?   **(4 marks)**

(c)   If, in better economic times, the company consistently generated a cash surplus and had no plans to increase dividends or to undertake further capital investment, discuss possible alternative uses for this cash flow surplus.   **(5 marks)**
   (Total: 20 marks)
   (ACCA 3.2 Financial Management June 93)

Tutorial note:

For parts (a) and (b) it is necessary to calculate the effects of each month's possible cash flows on the company's overdraft and cash float. The probabilities and joint probabilities of each cash flow profile will be used in the answer.

Part (c) requires a discussion of the reasons for holding cash and alternative uses for it.

20   COMFYLOT PLC

Comfylot plc produces garden seats which are sold on both domestic and export markets. Sales during the next year are forecast to be £16 million, 70% to the UK domestic market and 30% to the export market, and are expected to occur steadily throughout the year. 80% of UK sales are on credit terms, with payment due in 30 days. On average UK domestic customers take 57 days to make payment. An initial deposit of 15% of the sales price is paid by all export customers.

All export sales are on 60 days credit with an average collection period for credit sales of 75 days. Bad debts are currently 0.75% of UK credit sales, and 1.25% of export sales (net of the deposit).

Comfylot wishes to investigate the effects of each of three possible operational changes:

(1)   Domestic credit management could be undertaken by a non-recourse factoring company. The factor would charge a service fee of 1.5% and would provide finance on 80% of the debts factored at a cost of base rate +2.5%. The finance element must be taken as part of the agreement with the factor. Using a factor would save an initial £85,000 per year in administration costs, but would lead to immediate redundancy payments of £15,000.

(2)   As an alternative to using the factor a cash discount of 1.5% for payment in seven days could be offered on UK domestic sales. It is expected that 40% of domestic credit customers would use the cash discount. The discount would cost an additional £25,000 per year to administer, and would reduce bad debts to 0.50% of UK credit sales.

(3)   Extra advertising could be undertaken to stimulate export sales. Comfylot has been approached by a European satellite TV company which believes that £300,000 of advertising could increase export sales in the coming year by up to 30%. There is a 0.2 chance of a 20% increase in export sales, a 0.5 chance of a 25% increase and a 0.3 chance of a 30% increase. Direct costs of production are 65% of the sales price. Administration costs would increase by £30,000, £40,000 and £50,000 for the 20%, 25% and 30% increases in export sales respectively. Increased export sales are likely to result in the average collection period of the credit element of all exports lengthening by five days, and bad debts will increase to 1.5% of all export credit sales.

Bank base rate is currently 13% per year, and Comfylot can borrow overdraft finance at 15% per year. These rates are not expected to change in the near future.

Taxation may be ignored.

Required:

Discuss whether any of the three suggested changes should be adopted by Comfylot plc. All relevant calculations must be shown.   **(20 marks)**

(ACCA 3.2 Financial Management June 92)

*(**Tutorial note:** This question requires an analysis of three possible strategies to improve cash flow. The first two strategies involve working capital management changes. Calculate the extra costs and the extra benefits of each strategy in turn. Remember that holding debtors has an opportunity cost.*

For the third alternative, the company is projecting an increase in sales from extra advertising. Rather than calculate an expected value, the company will find it more useful to know the cost/saving implications of all three possible increases in sales.)

21   ENGOT PLC

Three senior managers of Engot plc are discussing the company's financial gearing. Mr R believes that the financial gearing is 55%, Mr Y believes that it is 89% and Mr Z 134%.

Summarised consolidated profit and loss account for the year ended 31 December 19X1

	£'000
Turnover	56,300
Less: Cost of sales	45,100
Gross profit	11,200
Less: Administrative and other expenses	6,450
Operating profit	4,750
Less: Interest payable	1,154
Profit before taxation	3,596
Less: Taxation	1,259
Profit for the financial year	2,337
Less: Dividends paid and proposed	970
Retained profit for the year	1,367

Summarised consolidated balance sheet as at 31 December 19X1

	£'000
Fixed assets	16,700
Current assets	
Stocks	7,040
Debtors	4,800
Cash at the bank and in hand	2,700
	14,540
Creditors: amounts falling due within one year	
8% loan stock 19X2	1,000
Bank loans and overdrafts	2,800
Trade creditors	7,200
Corporation tax	1,140
Proposed dividends	510
Accruals and deferred income	2,860
	15,510
Net current liabilities	970

Total assets less current liabilities	15,730
Creditors: amounts falling due after more than one year	
Bank loans	(5,600)
12% debentures repayable in 14 years' time	(1,800)
Net assets	8,330
Capital and reserves	£'000
Called-up share capital (10p par value)	2,200
Share premium account	1,940
Profit and loss account	4,190
	8,330

Current market data for Engot plc   Ordinary share price 94p
8% loan stock price £98
12% debentures price £108

You are required:

(a) to explain how each manager has estimated the financial gearing and suggest how each manager might argue that his is the most appropriate measure of financial gearing. State with reasons which measure of gearing you prefer;   **(7 marks)**

(b) to explain why financial gearing might be important to a company;   **(3 marks)**

(c) to discuss what factors might limit the amount of debt finance that a company uses;   **(5 marks)**

(d) to explain what mezzanine financing is and to describe the situations where it may be used to advantage.   **(5 marks)**
     (Total: 20 marks)

---

22   ARMADA LEISURE

(a) Discuss the main factors which a company should consider when determining the appropriate mix of long-term and short-term debt in its capital structure.   **(6 marks)**

(b) Armada Leisure Industries plc is already highly geared by industry standards, but wishes to raise external capital to finance the development of a new bowling alley in Plymouth. The stock market has recently reached a record level but economic forecasters are expressing doubts about the future prospects for the UK economy.

     You are required to assess the arguments for and against a rights issue by Armada;   **(8 marks)**

(c) **You are required** to examine the relative merits of leasing versus hire-purchase as means of acquiring capital assets.   **(6 marks)**
     (Total: 20 marks)
     (Pilot Paper)

---

23   AMBLE PLC

Amble plc is evaluating the manufacture of a new consumer product. The product can be introduced quickly, and has an expected life of four years before it is replaced by a more efficient model. Costs associated with the product are expected to be as follows.

Direct costs (per unit)

Labour

3.5 skilled labour hours at £5 per hour.   *17·50*
4 unskilled labour hours at £3 per hour.   *12*

Materials

6 kg of material Z at £1.46 per kg.
Three units of component P at £4.80 per unit
One unit of component Q at £6.40
Other variable costs: £2.10 per unit

Indirect costs

Apportionment of management salaries, £105,000 per year
Tax-allowable depreciation of machinery, £213,000 per year
Selling expenses (not including any salaries), £166,000 per year
Apportionment of head office costs, £50,000 per year
Rental of buildings, £100,000 per year
Interest charges, £104,000 per year
Other overheads, £70,000 per year (including apportionment of building rates £20,000. **Note**: rates are a local tax on property).

If the new product is introduced it will be manufactured in an existing factory, and will have no effect on rates payable. The factory could be rented for £120,000 per year (not including rates) to another company if the product is not introduced.

New machinery costing £864,000 will be required. The machinery is to be depreciated on a straight-line basis over four years, and has an expected salvage value of £12,000 after four years. The machinery will be financed by a four year fixed rate bank loan, at an interest rate of 12% per year. Additional working capital requirements may be ignored.

The product will require two additional managers to be recruited at an annual gross cost of £25,000 each, and one manager currently costing £20,000 will be moved from another factory where he will be replaced by a deputy manager at a cost of £17,000 per year. 70,000 kg of material Z are already in stock and are not required for other production. The realisable value of this material is £99,000.

The price per unit of the product in the first year will be £110, and demand is projected at 12,000, 17,500, 18,000 and 18,500 units in years 1 to 4 respectively. The inflation rate is expected to be approximately 5% per year, and prices will be increased in line with inflation. Wage and salary costs are expected to increase by 7% per year, and all other costs (including rent) by 5% per year. No price or cost increases are expected in the first year of production.

Corporation tax is at the rate of 35% payable in the year the profit occurs. Assume that all sales and costs are on a cash basis and occur at the end of the year, except for the initial purchase of machinery which would take place immediately. No stocks will be held at the end of any year.

Required:

(a)   Calculate the expected internal rate of return (IRR) associated with the manufacture of the new product.   **(15 marks)**

(b)   Amble is worried that the government might increase corporate tax rates.

Show by how much the tax rate would have to change before the project is not financially viable. A discount rate of 17% per year may be assumed for part (b).   **(10 marks)**

(Total: 25 marks)

(ACCA 3.2 Financial Management June 89)

Tutorial notes:

(1)   In order to calculate a project's IRR, it is necessary to identify the relevant cash flows. You will remember from your studies that the relevant cash flows for investment appraisal are those that are:

-     future not past (sunk)
-     incremental to the project not allocated to it
-     opportunity costs not original costs
-     operating costs to the project not financing costs (these are included in the discount rate).

(2)   This is an example of sensitivity analysis.

24   ZEDLAND

The general manager of the nationalised postal service of a small country, Zedland, wishes to introduce a new service. This service would offer same-day delivery of letters and parcels posted before 10 am within a distance of 150 kilometres. The service would require 100 new vans costing $8,000 each and 20 trucks costing $18,000 each. 180 new workers would be employed at an average annual wage of $13,000 and five managers at average annual salaries of $20,000 would be moved from their existing duties, where they would not be replaced.

Two postal rates are proposed. In the first year of operation letters will cost $0.525 and parcels $5.25. Market research undertaken at a cost of $50,000 forecasts that demand will average 15,000 letters per working day and 500 parcels per working day during the first year, and 20,000 letters per day and 750 parcels per day thereafter. There is a five-day working week. Annual running and maintenance costs on similar new vans and trucks are currently estimated in the first year of operation to be $2,000 per van and $4,000 per truck. These costs will increase by 20% per year (excluding the effects of inflation). Vehicles are depreciated over a five-year period on a straight-line basis. Depreciation is tax allowable and the vehicles will have negligible scrap value at the end of five years. Advertising in year one will cost $500,000 and in year two $250,000. There will be no advertising after year two. Existing premises will be used for the new service but additional costs of $150,000 per year will be incurred.

All the above cost data are current estimates and exclude any inflation effects. Wage and salary costs and all other costs are expected to rise because of inflation by approximately 5% per year during the five-year planning horizon of the postal service. The government of Zedland will not permit annual price increases within nationalised industries to exceed the level of inflation.

Nationalised industries are normally required by the government to earn at least an annual after-tax return of 5% on average investment and to achieve, on average, at least zero net present value on their investments.

The new service would be financed half with internally generated funds and half by borrowing on the capital market at an interest rate of 12% per year. The opportunity cost of capital for the postal service is estimated to be 14% per year. Corporate taxes in Zedland, to which the postal service is subject, are at the rate of 30% for annual profits of up to $500,000 and 40% for the balance in excess of $500,000. Tax is payable one year in arrears. All transactions may be assumed to be on a cash basis and to occur at the end of the year, with the exception of the initial investment which would be required almost immediately.

Required:

Acting as an independent consultant prepare a report advising as to whether the new postal service should be introduced. Include in your report a discussion of other factors that might need to be taken into account before a final decision can be made with respect to the introduction of the new postal service.

State clearly any assumptions that you make.   **(20 marks)**

(ACCA 3.2 Financial Management Dec 89)

Tutorial notes:

(1)   This project must be appraised by the two criteria mentioned in the question, return on investment based upon accounting profit, and NPV based upon cash flows. Assume a 40% tax rate for your answer. Since the required rate is assumed to be a nominal rate (i.e. it includes inflation), then the cash flows to be discounted must include inflation too. Note that the question gives the income expected in year 1, but that all expenses are in current value terms and must therefore have inflation added to find the expected year 1 outflow.

(2)   This is a straightforward question on one method of dealing with uncertainty of cash flows in investment appraisal.

---

25   BANDEN LTD

Banden Ltd is a highly geared company that wishes to expand its operations. Six possible capital investments have been identified, but the company only has access to a total of £620,000. The projects are not divisible and may not be postponed until a future period. After the projects end it is unlikely that similar investment opportunities will occur.

Expected net cash inflows (including salvage value)

Project	Year 1 £	2 £	3 £	4 £	5 £	Initial outlay £
A	70,000	70,000	70,000	70,000	70,000	246,000
B	75,000	87,000	64,000			180,000
C	48,000	48,000	63,000	73,000		175,000
D	62,000	62,000	62,000	62,000		180,000
E	40,000	50,000	60,000	70,000	40,000	180,000
F	35,000	82,000	82,000			150,000

Projects A and E are mutually exclusive. All projects are believed to be of similar risk to the company's existing capital investments.

Any surplus funds may be invested in the money market to earn a return of 9% per year. The money market may be assumed to be an efficient market.

Banden's cost of capital is 12% per year.

Required:

(a)   Calculate:

   (i)   The expected net present value;

   (ii)   The expected profitability index associated with each of the six projects, and rank the projects according to both of these investment appraisal methods.

   Explain briefly why these rankings differ;   **(8 marks)**

(b)   Give reasoned advice to Banden Ltd recommending which projects should be selected;   **(7 marks)**

(c)   A director of the company has suggested that using the company's normal cost of capital might not be appropriate in a capital rationing situation. Explain whether you agree with the director;

(5 marks)
(Total: 20 marks)
(ACCA June 88)

ANSWERS TO PRACTICE QUESTIONS

1   A POLYTECHNIC

(Tutorial notes: the flow diagram is not difficult, but the time allowance for 3 marks does present problems. However, time spent on ensuring that a correct picture of the cost apportionments is depicted will not only gain these marks but help a great deal in answering part (b).

Part (b) is basically an arithmetic exercise. Good use of the flow diagram will help in breaking this down into a series of apportionments. The model answer uses a 'step' approach. Students should adopt this approach; any attempt to apportion all the costs in a single table is likely to fail.

There is no one answer for part (c). Use your common sense and make brief general statements.)

(a)   **Flow diagram**

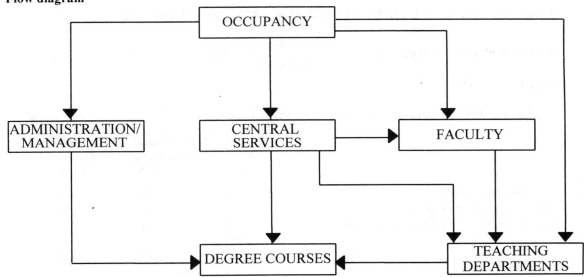

(b)   **Average cost per graduate**

Step 1

Apportion occupancy costs: $\left(\dfrac{£1,500,000}{37,500 \text{ sq ft}} = £40 \text{ per sq ft} \right)$

	£'000
Administration/Management	280
Central Services	120
Faculty	300
Teaching Departments	800
	1,500

Step 2

Apportion central services costs:

$$\left(\frac{£1,000,000+£120,000}{\text{External Costs }£1,600,000}\right) = 70\text{p per £ of external cost}$$

	£'000
Faculty	168
Teaching Departments	560
Degree Courses	392
	1,120

Step 3

Apportion teaching department costs (includes 100% of Faculty costs) and Administration/Management costs, to degree courses.

Teaching department: £800,000 + £560,000 + (£300,000 + £168,000 + £700,000) + £5,525,000 = £8,053,000

Administration/management: £280,000 + £1,775,000 = £2,055,000.

Total degree courses costs: £8,053,000 + £2,055,000 + £392,000 = £10,500,000.

$$\text{Average polytechnic cost per student} = \frac{£10,500,000}{2,500 \text{ students}} = £4,200$$

Step 4

Analyse £10,500,000 by degree course (in round £'000s).

	Business Studies £'000	Mechanical Engineering £'000	Catering Studies £'000
Teaching department	242	201	564
Administration/management	51	103	82
Central services (based on external costs)	22	34	22
	315	338	668
Average cost per graduate	£3,938	£6,760	£5,567

(c)   **Discussion**

The average cost per graduate will differ from one degree course to another for several reasons, the most obvious of which is the very different nature of the courses.

The engineering and catering courses will require much greater use of expensive machinery and equipment, which in turn will need more room. In addition these courses will probably require much greater lecturer input than on the business studies courses. The much lower staff/student ratio will push up the teaching costs per student.

Another factor to be considered is the variability in the student numbers. This variable is unlikely to have an impact on many of the polytechnic costs, which are mainly fixed in nature. For example, if in the following year intake is up to sixty on the mechanical engineering degree, with a similar level of costs, the average cost per student would fall to nearly that being reported for a catering studies student.

These average cost figures must be interpreted with great care by the management. They give a 'rough' guide to the relative cost of degree courses but the arbitrary apportionments render them very nearly useless for decision-making. For decision-making, incremental costs are required.

---

2   A LTD

(Tutorial notes:

(1)   The main advice here is to take one piece of information at a time and gradually build up what is a rather unusual cost per unit figure. It is necessary to use overhead incurred for the absorption rates which would appear to be consistent with budgeted figures.

(2)   It is necessary to identify which costs are affected by changing the packaging method - the obvious changes are in cost of boxes and packaging labour; the less obvious effect is the saving in variance overhead ie, as less hours are worked in packaging, less overhead will be incurred.)

(a)   **Calculation of current total manufacturing cost per unit**

	£
Direct material	0.45200
Packaging materials	0.10300

Packing boxes:

Small boxes 4 units per box $\dfrac{£114}{1,000} \times \tfrac{1}{4} \times \tfrac{105}{100}$ 0.02990

Larger boxes $4 \times 8 = 32$ units per box $\dfrac{£547.20}{1,000} \times \tfrac{1}{32} \times \tfrac{105}{100}$ 0.01796

Labour:

Fabrication £4.80 × $\tfrac{1}{40}$	0.12000
Packaging £3.60 × $\tfrac{1}{120}$	0.03000

Overhead (see working):

Fabrication £16.36 × $\tfrac{1}{40}$	0.40900
Packaging £12.36 × $\tfrac{1}{120}$	0.10300
	1.26486

Working - Overhead recovery rates

	Fabrication £	Packaging £	General £
Variable	88.0	24.0	
Fixed	359.4	53.6	253
General (9:2)	207.0	46.0	
	654.4	123.6	

Recovery rate:		
$\dfrac{\text{Overhead}}{\text{Direct labour hours}}$	$\dfrac{654.4}{40}$	$\dfrac{123.6}{10}$
	= £16.36 per hour	= £12.36 per hour

(b)   Address

Date   XX-X-19XX

General manager, A Ltd

Dear Sir,

Change in packaging of Product X

I am writing to advise you on the effect on costs of changing the method of packaging Product X.

(i)   The overall saving possible is shown below, calculated on a per unit basis:

	£	£
Revised cost of boxes: $\frac{475}{1,000} \times \frac{1}{20} \times \frac{105}{100}$		0.02494
Labour for packaging: $£3.60 \times \frac{1}{400}$		0.00900
		0.03394
Existing costs:		
Boxes £(0.02990 + 0.01796)	0.04786	
Labour for packaging	0.03000	
		0.07786
Saving in cost of boxes and labour		0.04392
Add: Saving in labour related variable overhead:		
$\left(\dfrac{\text{Variable overhead}}{\text{rate for packaging}} = \frac{24}{10} = £2.40 \text{ per hour} \right)$		
$\therefore$ Saving $= £2.40 \times \left(\frac{1}{120} - \frac{1}{400} \right)$		0.01400
Total saving per unit		0.05792

(ii)   This is the saving that can be achieved in the long run. It is in excess of the proposed reduction in selling price of (1.55 - 1.53) = £0.02. The bulk of this saving is not possible until existing stocks of the current boxes have been utilised ie, the figure of £0.05792 assumes the cost per unit of current boxes of £0.04786 can be avoided ie, the saving would initially only be (0.05792 - 0.04786) = £0.01 and therefore not cover the 2p reduction in selling price.

It is assumed:

(1)   that packaging and labour costs can be saved ie, that this labour is a variable cost.
(2)   the costs of packaging materials are not affected;
(3)   fixed overheads are unaffected by the change; and
(4)   that the change will be acceptable to B Ltd.

On the basis of the figures calculated the recommendation is for the packaging change to be introduced once existing box stocks have been exhausted.

Should you require any further information, please contact me again.

Yours faithfully

Cost accountant

3   AMAZON PLC

(a)   Cost per kg $= \dfrac{\text{Total cost} - \text{Scrap value of normal loss}}{\text{Expected output}} = \dfrac{3,500 + 4,340 - (700 \times 0.40)}{7,000 - (10\% \times 7,000)} = £1.20/\text{kg}$

Transfer to process 2 $= 6,430 \text{ kg} \times 1.20 = £7,716$

Expected output	$= 7,000 - (10\% \times 7,000) =$	6,300 kg
Actual output		6,430 kg
Abnormal gain		130 kg

Net gain $= 130 \text{ kg} \times (1.20 - 0.40) = £104$

(b)   *Costs of process 2*

		£
Transfer from process 1	$6,430 \times 1.20$	7,716
Labour and overhead		12,129
		19,845
Less net income of by-product $(1.80 - 0.30) \times 430$		645
		£19,200

(i)

	Weight of output kg		Share of joint costs £
E	2,000	$\dfrac{2,000}{6,000} \times 19,200$	6,400
F	4,000	$\dfrac{4,000}{6,000} \times 19,200$	12,800
	6,000 kg		£19,200

Cost/kg

Type E	$£6,400/2,000\text{kg} = £3.20/\text{kg}$
Type F	$£12,800/4,000\text{kg} = £3.20/\text{kg}$

Profits/(losses)

Type E	$1,100\text{kg} \times (7 - 3.20) = £4,180$
Type F	$3,200\text{kg} \times (2.50 - 3.20) = (£2,240)$

Stock values

Type E	$(2,000 \text{ kg} - 1,100\text{kg}) \times 3.20 = £2,880$
Type F	$(4,000\text{kg} - 3,200\text{kg}) \times 3.20 = £2,560$

(ii)

	Market value of output £			Share of joint costs £
Type E	$2,000\text{kg} \times £7 =$	14,000	$14/24 \times 19,200$	11,200
Type F	$4,000\text{kg} \times £2.50 =$	10,000	$10/24 \times 19,200$	8,000
		£24,000		£19,200

Cost/kg	Type E	£11,200/2,000kg	=	£5.60/kg
	Type F	£8,000/4,000kg	=	£2/kg
Profits	Type E	$(7 - 5.60) \times 1,100$kg	=	£1,540
	Type F	$(2.50 - 2) \times 3,200$kg	=	£1,600
Stock values	Type E	$(2,000$kg $- 1,100$kg$) \times 5.60$	=	£5,040
	Type F	$(4,000$kg $- 3,200$kg$) \times 2$	=	£1,600

(c)   The main purpose of apportioning joint costs is for financial reporting. We apportion the joint costs in order to calculate the stock value and the cost of sales. The main problem is that the choice of apportionment method is subjective and can have a profound effect on stock values and profits. For instance in part (b) above:

(1)   Type E was valued at £3.20/kg or £5.60/kg and gave a profit of £4,180 or £1,540.

(2)   Type F was valued at £3.20/kg or £2/kg and gave a loss of £2,240 or a profit of £1,600.

4   MANUFACTURING PRODUCT X

(a)

Input units	Output units		Elements of cost – equivalent units			
			Direct material	Direct labour	Variable overhead	Fixed overhead
102,000	90,000	Sold	90,000	90,000	90,000	90,000
	8,000	Finished goods	8,000	8,000	8,000	8,000
	4,000	Work-in-progress (W1)	4,000	2,000	2,000	2,000
Equivalent units			102,000	100,000	100,000	100,000
Total cost			£714,000	£400,000	£100,000	£350,000
per unit (W2)			£7	£4	£1	£3.5

Total cost per unit of X $= £(7 + 4 + 1 + 3.50) = £15.50$

(b)   **Profit statement based on absorption costing**

	£	£
Sales 90,000 units at £20		1,800,000
Production costs:		
Direct materials	714,000	
Direct labour	400,000	
Variable overhead	100,000	
	1,214,000	
Fixed overhead	350,000	
	1,564,000	

Less:	Closing stock				£000		
	8,000 units	×	£15.50	=	124		
	4,000 units	×	£7.00	=	28		
	2,000 units	×	£4.00	=	8		
	2,000 units	×	£1.00	=	2		
	2,000 units	×	£3.50	=	7		
					169		
						169,000	1,395,000
Gross profit							405,000

Less:	Selling costs:	Variable	90,000 × £1.50 =	135,000	
		Fixed		200,000	
	Administration:	Variable	90,000 × £0.10 =	9,000	
		Fixed		50,000	
					394,000

Net profit £11,000

This agrees with the accountant's profit of £11,000.

(c)

Profit statement based on marginal costing

	£	£	£
Sales 90,000 units at £20 each			1,800,000
Production costs:			
Direct materials		714,000	
Direct labour		400,000	
Variable overhead		100,000	
Variable cost		1,214,000	
Less: Closing stock			
8,000 units at £12 each	96,000		
4,000 units at £ 7 each	28,000		
2,000 units at £ 4 each	8,000		
2,000 units at £ 1 each	2,000		
		134,000	
			1,080,000
Gross contribution			720,000
Less: Variable selling costs		135,000	
Variable administration cost		9,000	
			144,000
Net contribution			576,000
Less: Fixed manufacturing overheads		350,000	
Fixed selling costs		200,000	
Fixed administration costs		50,000	
			600,000
Net loss			£(24,000)

(d) **Reconciliation**

	£
Profit under absorption costing	11,000
Loss under marginal costing	(24,000)
Difference	£35,000

The difference arises due to the different treatment of fixed overheads. Using absorption costing , fixed overheads are absorbed into the costs of production during the period. Using marginal costing, all fixed overheads are charged against the profits of the period. When sales and production volumes differ, this will result in different profit figures being stated.

The closing stocks using absorption costing included fixed costs ie:

			£
Finished goods	8,000 at £3.50 =		28,000
Work in progress	2,000 at £3.50 =		7,000
Total difference			£35,000

Both statements are acceptable for internal accounting purpose, most accountants preferring marginal costing for decision-making purposes. The absorption costing approach is necessary for external reporting, to comply with the requirements of *SSAP 9*.

WORKINGS

(W1)   4,000 units × degree of completion.
(W2)   Total cost/number of equivalent units.

---

5   MIOZIP CO

(Tutorial notes:

(1)   An average standard question but, having no 'units' with which to work, does present problems.

(2)   Part (a) is the standard question about absorption costing with changing stock levels resulting in different profits.

(3)   Part (b) is not difficult, but with no variable costs per unit with which to work, it is necessary to use total amounts after deducting the fixed factory overhead.

(4)   Part (c) is reasonably straightforward. Remember the problem of using pre-determined absorption rates in periods of changing activity levels.

(5)   Concentrate on the usefulness of marginal costs in decision-making but full cost systems ensure that no costs are ignored.)

(a)   **Report**

To:	The board of directors, Miozip Co
From:	The company accountant
Date:	XX-XX-19XX
Subject:	**Profitability**

From the summarised profit and loss accounts (estimated 19X2, budgeted 19X3), it is apparent that two periods with equal sales revenue are reporting profits/losses which differ by £210,000. The difference can be entirely attributed to the valuation of opening/closing stock.

The factory cost of goods sold for 19X2 is £60,000 lower than that expected for the level of sales achieved because of the lower overhead absorption rate used in 19X1. Some of the goods produced in this period, being attributed with a lower cost, were sold in 19X2. All units budgeted to be sold in 19X3 carry the full £3.60 overhead.

In addition, the level of activity budgeted in 19X3 (100,000 direct labour hours) is only two-thirds of that achieved in 19X2. This will result in an increased under-absorption of overhead charge of £150,000. This, together with the £60,000 above, accounts for the £210,000 differential.

(b) **Marginal costing statement**

WORKINGS

	£	%
19X1:		
Factory cost of production	1,000,000	100.00
Fixed factory overhead absorbed		
(£600,000 - £300,000)	300,000	30.00
∴ Other variable factory costs	700,000	70.00
19X2 (similar percentage for 19X3):		
Factory cost of production	975,000	100.00
Fixed factory overhead absorbed		
(£600,000 - £150,000)	450,000	46.15
∴ Other variable factory costs	525,000	53.85

Based on marginal costs:

	Actual 19X1		*Estimated 19X2*		*Budgeted 19X3*	
	£	£	£	£	£	£
Sales		1,350,000		1,316,250		1,316,250
Opening stock	70,000		140,000		192,500	
Variable factory cost of production	700,000		525,000		350,000	
	770,000		665,000		542,500	
Closing stock	(140,000)		(192,500)		(70,000)	
Variable cost of goods sold		630,000		472,500		472,500
Contribution		720,000		843,750		843,750
Fixed costs:						
Factory overheads		(600,000)		(600,000)		(600,000)
Administrative and financial costs		(220,000)		(220,000)		(220,000)
Net profit/(loss)		(100,000)		23,750		23,750

(c) **Potential problems**

The decision to increase the selling price by using the cost-plus formula without considering the effect upon demand from customers, could result in an increase in the under-absorbed overhead. The higher price might result in a fall in demand and a fall in the number of direct labour hours worked. Thus, the absorption of overheads would fall with the reduction in direct labour hours and a larger proportion of the overheads incurred would not be absorbed.

(d) **Use of absorption and marginal costing**

Management accounting theorists favour marginal costing because it will tend to give the most relevant costs to assist a decision-maker. Marginal costs are usually differential, incremental costs and are important in most decisions, including pricing special orders, production scheduling with limiting factors, and make or buy decisions. By contrast, full costing systems, by including fixed costs in product costs, can often lead to sub-optimal decisions being taken if the effect of 'fixed costs per unit' is not fully understood.

However, full costing systems appear to be used extensively in practice. This could be for the following reasons:

(i)   automatically ensures compliance with SSAP 9;

(ii)   provides more realistic matching of total costs with revenues;

(iii) a large part of the costs of most companies are now fixed; using marginal costing may result in these substantial costs being overlooked eg, under-pricing using a marginal cost-plus formula resulting in losses;

(iv)   analysis of under/over-absorbed overhead is useful to identify inefficient utilisation of production resources.

6   LIMITATION PLC

Your answer should look something like that which follows:

(a)   **Use of learning curves**

Hours for the first batch of Quarter 4, 19X1 = £600/£5 = 120 hours

Given a 90% learning curve, the average time per batch for all batches is 90% of that for the preceding level each time the number of batches is doubled. We have therefore:

Number of batches	Average time per batch (hours)	Total time (hours)
1	120	120
2	108 (120 × 0.9)	216
4	97.2 (108 × 0.9)	388.8

Hours for batch 2 = 216 - 120 = 96 hours
Hours for batch 3 + batch 4 = 388.8 - 216 = 172.8 hours

(b)   **Budget for quarters 1 and 2**

Workings:

Calculation of labour cost:

Time for first 30 batches = 30 × 71.56	=	2,146.8 hrs
Time for first 75 batches = 75 × 62.25	=	4,668.75 hrs
Hence time for Quarter 1 19X2 (45 batches)		2,521.95 hrs
Labour cost for Quarter 1 = 2,521.95 × £5	=	£12,610 approx
Time for first 75 batches = 75 × 62.25	=	4,668.75 hrs
Time for first 120 batches = 120 × 57.96	=	6,955.20 hrs
Hence time for Quarter 2 19X2 (45 batches)	=	2,286.45 hrs
Labour cost for quarter 2 = 2,286.45 × £5	=	£11,432 approx

Calculation of material cost:

Quarter 1 19X2	Units per batch	Total units
First 10 batches 200 × 0.98	196	1,960
Next 20 batches 200 × 0.96	192	3,840
Final 15 batches 200 × 0.94	188	2,820
Total Quarter 1 19X2		8,620

Material cost Quarter 1 19X2 = 8,620 × £1.80 = £15,516

Quarter 2 19X2	Units per batch	Total units
First 5 batches 200 × 0.04	188	940
Next 20 batches 200 × 0.92	184	3,680
Final 20 batches 200 × 0.90	180	3,600
Total Quarter 2 19X2		8,220

Material cost Quarter 2 19X2 = 8,220 × £1.80 = £14,796

Stock holding costs:

Quarter 1, 19X2 (8,620/2) × 30p	=	£1,293
Quarter 2, 19X2 (8,220/2) × 30p	=	£1,233

Limitation plc
Budget Quarters 1 and 2 19X2

	Quarter 1		Quarter 2	
	£	£	£	£
Sales revenue (45 × £1,200)		54,000		54,000
Less: Variable costs:				
Direct material	15,516		14,796	
Holding costs	1,293		1,233	
Direct labour	12,610		11,432	
Variable overhead	18,915	48,334	17,148	44,609
(150% of direct labour)				
Contribution		5,666		9,391

(c) **Effect of JIT supplies**

(i)

	Quarter 1		Quarter 2
	£		£
Increased cost (8,620 × £0.1)	862	(8,220 × £0.2)	1,644
Holding costs avoided	1,293		1,233
Net (increase)/decrease in cost	431		(411)

Hence on financial grounds using the information available just-in-time delivery offer would be acceptable in Quarter 1 but should be rejected thereafter.

(ii)   It is unlikely that Limitation plc will accept the offer based on the quarter 1 figures alone, even though they indicate a decrease in cost. Management should consider other factors, however, before rejecting the offer. There may be other costs associated with the present storage method such as transport costs from store due to deterioration and the cost of capital tied up in stock. The just-in-time delivery may cause additional costs if there is no buffer stock to allow for late delivery, changes in demand pattern and changes in level of process losses. Such factors would have an opportunity cost of idle capacity until material was available.

7   A AND B

(a)   **Budgets for 19X8**

(*Tutorial note:* There are two production constraints:

- dye
- machine time.

Realistically there is an element of luck as to which is dealt with first. Logic will eventually dictate that machine time be considered first since this will reduce the amount of two types of cloth made which, in turn, will reduce the need for dye.)

(i)   **Production budget**

		Machine A (≤ 140 cm) 35 × 46 = 1,610 hrs 80% = 1,288 hrs		Machine B (≥ 125 cm) 35 × 46 = 1,610 hrs 70% = 1,127 hrs	
Machine hours:	manned	35 × 46 = 1,610 hrs		35 × 46 = 1,610 hrs	
	used	80% = 1,288 hrs		70% = 1,127 hrs	
Product		X	Y	X	Y
Width		120cm	100cm	160cm	200cm
		m	m	m	m
Maximum demand		90,000	100,000	70,000	30,000
Opening stocks		(30,000)	-	-	(5,000)
Required production		60,000m	100,000m	70,000m	25,000m
		hrs	hrs	hrs	hrs
Production time/m		1/100	1/120	1/80	1/50
Total time required		600	833	875	500
Shortfall - on narrower		-	(145)	(248)	-
Total time available		600 hrs	688 hrs	627 hrs	500 hrs
Possible machine output		60,000m	82,560m	50,160m	25,000m
		kg	kg	kg	kg
Dye required/'000m (1 kg/500m^2)					
1,000 × 1.20 ÷ 500		2.40			
1,000 × 1.00 ÷ 500			2.00		
1,000 × 1.60 ÷ 500				3.20	
1,000 × 2.00 ÷ 500					4.00
Total dye required		144	165.120	160.512	100
Shortfall - on narrowest		-	(24.632)	-	-
Available/used (25 + 520)		144	140.488	160.512	100
Final production levels		60,000m	70,244m	50,160m	25,000m

(ii)   **Sales budget**

	Width	120cm	100cm	160cm	200cm
		m	m	m	m
	Production (i)	60,000	70,244	50,160	25,000
	Opening	30,000	-	-	5,000
	Closing stock	-	-	-	-
	Sales (metres)	90,000	70,244	50,160	30,000

(b)   **Purchases budget (m²)**

(*Tutorial note:* The amount of material used depends on the width of material, amount of production **and** the machine used. Therefore, separate calculations for machines A and B are needed).

		A m²	B m²	C m²
Output:	X 60,000m × 1.2m	72,000	-	72,000
	50,160m × 1.6m	-	80,256	80,256
	Y 70,244m × 1.0m	70,244	-	70,244
	25,000m × 2.0m	-	50,000	50,000
		142,244	130,256	272,500
Losses:	A $\frac{1}{9}$	15,805	-	15,805
	B $\frac{1}{4}$	-	32,564	32,564
		158,049	162,820	320,869
Closing stocks (10%)				32,087
Opening stocks				(25,000)
Purchases				327,956 m²

(c)   **Improving output, etc**

There are two binding constraints, dye and type B machine time; there is a surplus of type A machine time.

The dye constraint may be overcome by using different suppliers or negotiating a greater supply for a higher price. The problems with this approach are:

(i)   that the dye supplied may be of lesser quality than that currently used; and

(ii)   any higher prices will reduce profits on the existing production.

The machine time constraint can be overcome by:

(i)   sub contracting some of the production which uses type B machines - this may be costly and a quality control system is needed for the sub-contract work.

(ii)   installing additional type B machines, this is costly and time consuming - management must be satisfied that there is a long-term need for machine B time,

(iii)   modify type A machines so that they can be used to manufacture the 160cm width and thereby utilise the spare type A machine capacity. The modifications, if possible, may be costly and may reduce the efficiency of the machines which may lead to an overall reduction of profit despite the greater output being achieved.

WORKING

If output is 90% of input, the loss is 10% of input. The adjustment is thus $\frac{10\%}{90\%}$ or $\frac{1}{9}$ of output.

Similarly an 80% yield requires an adjustment of $\frac{2}{8}$ (or $\frac{1}{4}$) of output.

---

8   MATERIAL VARIANCES

(*Tutorial note:* part (a) is a very basic mix/yield question although it is designed to 'unnerve' students by including variances of zero in January.

In part (b) the zero variances should be mentioned.)

(a)   **Standard cost**

Material X	60% @ £30		18
Material Y	40% @ £45		18
	100%		36
Standard loss	10%		
Standard yield	90%	= $\dfrac{£36}{90\%}$ =	£40 per tonne

Price variance

	January £	February £	March £
Material Y	Nil	Nil	Nil
Material X:			
Total material cost	32,400	31,560	38,600
Less: Cost of Y 360 × £45	16,200	16,200	16,200
Actual cost of material X	16,200	15,360	22,400
Standard price @ Actual quantity:			
540 × £30	16,200		
480 × £30		14,400	
700 × £30			21,000
Price variance	Nil	960 A	1,400 A

Material variance summaries

	January Product X	January Product Y	January Total	February Product X	February Product Y	February Total	March Product X	March Product Y	March Total
Mix variance									
Actual quantity @ Actual mix	540	360	900	480	360	840	700	360	1,060
Actual quantity @ Standard mix	540	360	900	504	336	800	636	424	1,060
Mix variance			Nil	24 @ £30 = £720 F	24 @ £45 = £1,080 A	360 A	64 @ £30 = £1,920 A	64 @ £45 = £2,880 F	£960 F
Yield variance									
Actual quantity @ Standard mix	540	360	900	504	336	800	636	424	1,060
Standard quantity for actual production @ Standard mix	540	360	$810 \times \frac{100}{90}$ = 900	510	340	$765 \times \frac{100}{90}$ = 850	600	400	$900 \times \frac{100}{90}$ = 1,000
Yield variance			Nil	6 @ £30 = £180 F	4 @ £45 = £180 F	£360 F	36 @ £30 = £1,080 A	24 @ £45 = £1,080 A	£2,160 A
Usage variance									
Actual quantity @ Actual mix	540	360		480	360		700	360	
Standard quantity for actual production @ Standard mix	540	360		510	340		600	400	
Usage variance			£Nil	30 @ £30 = £900 F	20 @ £45 = £900 A	Nil	100 @ £30 = £3,000 A	40 @ £45 = £1,800 F	£1,200 A

(b)   Production in January is exactly according to standard. The price of Y has remained at standard for the whole period. The price of X is £2 $\left(\dfrac{960}{480} \text{ and } \dfrac{1,400}{700} \right)$ in excess of standard in February and March. If this continues the standard price of X will need to be increased. The proportion of X in the mix changed to $\dfrac{4,400}{840} = 57\%$ and $\dfrac{700}{1,060} = 66\%$ in February and March respectively. The cost increase in February, shown as an adverse mix variance of £360, is caused by dearer Y being used instead of cheaper X. There is an improvement in yield in February. The increased yield could be viewed as an abnormal gain of 9 tons (840 × 90% = (756 - 765) × £40 = £360). There is also a reduction in volume produced in February.

In March the significant increase in the proportion of X (which is cheaper) used has caused a favourable mix variance and may have contributed to the large adverse yield variance. Production in March is considerably higher than for January and February - this may be a reason for the adverse yield variance.

Overall there appears to be a link between mix and yield. If the proportion of Y is increased, causing adverse mix variance as Y is more expensive, the yield is improved - as occurred in February; the opposite took place in March.

There could also be a link between yield and the volume of production - in February production is low and yield is high, whereas in March production is high and yield is low.

(c)   This information helps to explain the increased proportion of Y used in February - if not used Y would be wasted, which could involve disposal costs. It could therefore be argued that the adverse mix variance on Y of £1,080 in February is a sunk cost ie, using a greater proportion of Y has not increased the purchase quantity. Using more of Y has improved yield.

In March the restriction on Y has resulted in adverse yield arising from the increased proportion of X needed to increase production volume - this has resulted in an overall adverse usage variance of £1,200. This excess cost should be included in the evaluation of decisions to try to obtain more of Y by, for example, paying a premium price.

It would be necessary to ascertain whether and how quality of the final product is affected by changes in mix and whether the quality is then acceptable to customers.

9   AB LTD

(a)   (i)   Actual cost: 142,000 kils at £1.21/kilo = £171,820
Standard cost: 142,000 kilos at £1.20/kilo = £170,400
Price variance = £1,420 A

(ii)   Actual usage (at standard price): 16,270 kilos at £1.20/kilo = £19,524
Standard usage: 1,790 units × £9 × £1.80/unit = £19,332
Usage variance = £192 A

(iii) Cost inflation:
Standard price = £1.272 (1.20 × 1.06) × 147,400 kilos = £187,492.80
less price variance £1,031.80
= actual cost £186,461 ÷ 147,400 = £1.265 per kil
∴ Cost inflation = $(\dfrac{1.265}{1.21} - 1) \times 100\% = 4.5\%$

(iv)   Actual usage of Material X:

Period 1: 16,270 kilos ÷ 1,790 units = 9.0894 kilos per unit
Period 2: 9 kilos per unit × 0.995 = 8.955 kilos per unit
∴ Change in usage = $(\dfrac{9.0894 - 8.955}{9.0894}) \times 100\% = 1.5\%$ improvement.

(b) There are four types of standards that may be set for raw material usage and labour efficiency:

(i) *Basic standards*: these are standards which are set out with a view to their remaining unchanged in the longer term, so as to provide a basis for identifying trends over time. They are not frequently used as they do not provide a measure of efficiency, and because actual usage and efficiency can be used instead to establish trends.

(ii) *Current standards*: in stark contrast to basic standards, current standards change frequently (eg, monthly) in order to reflect current operating conditions. If set correctly they can provide motivation to achieve. The danger is that they are frequently reset to what is being achieved rather than what may be reasonably achievable.

(iii) *Normal standards*: these are standards which are expected achievable performance over a longer period eg, one year. Such standards are most frequently encountered, being an integral part of the normal annual budgeting process. Normal standards should provide a tough but attainable target in order to provide motivation to improve efficiency. Allowances are made for a certain level of wastage, downtime etc, where these are an inevitable aspect of production operations.

(iv) *Ideal standards*: these are standards which can only be achieved under perfect operating conditions. Such standards provide a measure of the additional costs incurred by imperfect operating conditions and thus a target for cost reduction. They can, however, have a negative effect on motivation. They would be changed only when basic operating methods change ie, infrequently.

---

10 MATERIAL A

(a) Standard direct labour cost per unit of production:

Component X, 0.40 hours × £5.00/hour = £2.00/unit
Component Y, 0.56 hours × £5.00/hour = £2.80/unit

Actual hours per period = 53 × 40 × 13 = 27,560 hours

Variances		£
Actual wages		138,500
− Actual hours at standard rate		137,800
		700A

	£	£
Efficiency variance:		
Actual hours at standard rate		137,800
− Standard wages		
(Component X:		
35,000 units × £2.00/unit	70,000	
Component Y:		
25,000 units × £2.80/unit)	70,000	
		140,000
		2,200 F

(b) Standard purchase price of Material A:

	£
Actual cost of purchases	85,110
Plus: favourable price variance	430
	85,540
	÷ 47,000 kilos
	= £1.82 per kilo

Standard usage of material A per unit of production of Component X:

	£
Actual usage at standard price (33,426 kilos × £1.82/kilo)	60,835.32
Less: unfavourable usage variance	320.32
Standard usage	60,515.00
	÷ £1.82 per kilo
	= 33,250 kilos
	÷ 35,000 units
	= 0.95 kilos per unit of Component X

(c)   The first requirement is to establish the sales budget for components X and Y and to consider whether there is likely to be any factor of production which will prevent demand from being satisfied (limiting factor).

The existence of a limiting factor would influence, in conjunction with expected demand, the determination of the production budget for components X and Y.

In the absence of any limiting factor of production, the production budget will be determined by the sales budget with adjustment as necessary for budgeted changes in the level of finished stock of the components. A planned increase in finished component stock would require a production budget in excess of sales and vice versa.

Once the production budget for the two components has been established, the production quantity of each component multiplied by the expected usage of Material A per unit of component output determines the required quantity of material for production. Expected usage may be different to standard usage depending upon the type of standards that are set.

The budgeted purchase quantity of Material A must be sufficient to meet budgeted production usage requirements, with an adjustment to take account of any planned change in the level of raw material stock. A required increase in stock will lead to purchases in excess of usage and vice versa.

11   STOBO PLC

(a)   Product costs/unit:

	Product X		Product Y	
Volume	5,600	1,400	3,200	1,600
	£	£	£	£
Material cost	4.50	6.00	26.00	30.00
Wages cost (W3):				
Making	8.19	12.80	16.20	18.00
Finishing	5.76	9.00	12.15	13.50
Variable overheads:				
Making (200%)	16.38	25.60	32.40	36.00
Finishing (250%)	14.40	22.50	30.38	33.75
Variable costs/unit	49.23	75.90	117.13	131.25
Selling price	75.00	75.00	150.00	150.00
Contribution/unit	£25.77	£(0.90)	£32.87	£18.75
Total gross contribution (W4)	£144,312	(£1,260)	£105,184	£30,000

Demand probability	0.6	0.4	0.3	0.7
Expected gross contribution	£86,587	(£504)	£31,555	£21,000
Expected product gross contribution	£86,083		£52,555	
Relevant avoidable fixed costs	£36,000		£5,000	
Expected relevant profit	£50,083		£47,555	

Product X is preferred because it has the higher expected relevant profit.

(b)   If the maximum labour hours must be paid for then it is a fixed cost and the contribution/unit must be adjusted:

	Product X		Product Y	
Volume	5,600	1,400	3,200	1,600
	£	£	£	£
Contribution/unit (a)	25.77	(0.90)	32.87	18.75
Add: Wages cost:				
Making	8.19	12.80	16.20	18.00
Finishing	5.76	9.00	12.15	13.50
Revised contribution/unit	£39.72	£20.90	£61.22	£50.25
Total gross contribution (W4)	£222,432	£29,260	£195,904	£80,400
Demand probability	0.6	0.4	0.3	0.7
Expected gross contribution	£133,459	£11,704	£58,771	£56,280
Expected product gross contribution	£145,163		£115,051	
Relevant avoidable fixed costs	£36,000		£5,000	
Expected relevant profit	£109,163		£110,051	

Product Y now has the higher expected profit value and may be preferred.

WORKINGS

(W1)   Average unit times - Product X:

700 units	=	7 hours	
1,400 units	=	80% of 7 hours	= 5.6 hours
2,800 units	=	80% of 5.6 hours	= 4.48 hours
5,600 units	=	80% of 4.48 hours	= 3.584 hours

(W2)   Average unit times - Product Y:

800 units	=	9 hours	
1,600 units	=	90% of 9 hours	= 8.1 hours
3,200 units	=	90% of 8.1 hours	= 7.29 hours

(W3)   Making: X 5,600 = $\frac{4}{7}$ × £4 × 3.584 hours = £8.19
   X 1,400 = $\frac{4}{7}$ × £4 × 5.6 hours = £12.80
   Y 3,200 = $\frac{5}{9}$ × £4 × 7.29 hours = £16.20
   Y 1,600 = $\frac{5}{9}$ × £4 × 8.1 hours = £18.00

Finishing: X 5,600 = ³⁄₇ × £3.75 × 3.584 hours = £5.76
$\quad$ X 1,400 = ³⁄₇ × £3.75 × 5.6 hours = £9.00
$\quad$ Y 3,200 = ⁴⁄₉ × £3.75 × 7.29 hours = £12.15
$\quad$ Y 1,600 = ⁴⁄₉ × £3.75 × 8.1 hours = £13.50

(W4) Contribution/unit × volume

---

12   A LTD

(a)

	Product I £'000	Product II £'000	Product III £'000	Total £'000
Sales	2,475	3,948	1,520	7,943
Contribution	1,170	1,692	532	3,394
Attributable fixed costs	(275)	(337)	(296)	(908)
General fixed costs	(520)	(829)	(319)	(1,668)
	(795)	(1,166)	(615)	(2,576)
Profit	375	526	(83)	(818)
	= £1.60/unit	= £1.40/unit	= (£0.04/unit)	

(b)   If Product III is discontinued it may be assumed that, as well as variable costs, the fixed costs attributable to the product would be saved. The term 'attributable' fixed costs refers to costs which, although not variable with activity in the short-term, are directly incurred by a particular product and thus should be avoidable in the event of the activity ceasing altogether. However, an important question is whether the cost quoted is the true opportunity cost.

It is reasonable to assume that the level of general fixed costs would be unaffected by Product III's discontinuation as they are not specific to the product. Over time, however, it could be expected that they would be affected to some extent by large changes in activity.

The analysis would be as follows:

	£'000
Contribution of Products I and II	2,862
Attributable fixed costs of Products I and II	(612)
General fixed costs	(1,668)
	(2,280)
Profit	582

Thus profit would be reduced by £236,000, the net contribution (variable contribution minus attributable fixed costs) budgeted for Product III (ie, £532,000 − £296,000).

(c)   On the assumption that all existing fixed costs would be unaffected by any change in activity the extra sales units required would be:

$$\frac{£80,000 \text{ expenditure}}{£5.20 \text{ contribution per unit}} = 15,385$$

(d)   As with (iii) above it is reasonable to assume that fixed costs would be unaffected by the change in activity. Product contribution per unit would become:

	£
Selling price	9.45
Variable cost	6.00
Contribution	£3.45

Required sales would be:

$$\frac{£1,692,000}{£3.45} \quad \frac{\text{existing total contribution}}{\text{new contribution per unit}}$$

= 490,435 units, an increase of 30.4% over the budgeted sales of 376,000 units

13   BORROWS PLC

(a) **Effects of rights issues on share price**

Rights issues tend to reduce the market price of shares because they are sold at a discount to the market price. This is a necessary (but not a sufficient) requirement of a successful rights issue (potential investors still need to be convinced that taking up the rights represents a good investment on their part).

The theoretical ex-rights price is:

New finance required	£200m
Issue price (210p less 10%)	189p
Number of new shares	105.82m
(i.e. £200m ÷ £1.89)	
Existing number of shares	1,000.00m
New number of shares	1,105.82m
Existing market value	
(1,000m × £2.10)	£2,100m
Value of new issue	£200m
New market value	£2,300m
New share price	
(£2,300/1,105.82)	£2.08

The actual market price will be greater than the theoretical ex-rights price if the new money is invested in positive NPV projects, i.e. the money will earn a greater return than the required return for that investment. Thus the market price of the share will only equal the theoretical ex-rights price if the new money earns just the required return for the investment (i.e. the NPV of the investment is zero).

(b) **Financial implications of three options**

Gearing:

The current market value of debt is:

Long-term debt	£270m
Overdraft	£80m
	£350m

Gearing using market value is currently £350m/£2,100m = 16.7% (use market value in preference to book value to give a more meaningful figure). This is relatively low reflecting the risky nature of current operations.

With a new share issue, gearing will fall to £350m/£2,300m = 15.2%. With more debt, it will rise to £550m/£2,100m = 26.2%

Interest cover and EPS:

The projected P&L account is (£m)

	Ordinary	Eurodollar	CULS
Operating profit	249.6	249.6	249.6
Interest	40.0	54.0*	56.0
Earnings before tax	209.6	195.6	193.6
Tax	69.2	64.5	63.9
Earnings after tax	140.4	131.1	129.7
Number of shares	1,106	1,000	1,000
EPS	12.7p	13.1p	13.0p

*The existing £40 + ($300m × 7% ÷ 1.50) = £54m

The current EPS is 11.3p.

The higher EPS for debt may compensate for the higher financial risk borne by the ordinary shareholders.

Interest cover is currently 5.2, i.e. 208/40, and changes to:

	Ordinary	Eurodollar	CULS
	6.2	4.6	4.5

All look relatively comfortable.

(c)   **Risks of the investment**

The main areas of risk may include:

(i)   Exchange rate risks. Sterling will fluctuate (often significantly) against other currencies. Dealing in 'soft' currencies may also provide problems of convertibility if funds are repatriated. There are various hedging techniques available to insure against these risks, e.g. the forward markets, options etc.

(i)   The risk of finding any oil. This is business risk - the company will rely on survey reports.

(iii)   The risk of fluctuations in the oil price. This is affected by world supply and demand. Fixing long-term contracts, or selling oil forward (thereby confirming the price) may alleviate this problem.

(iv)   The period of time of the investment depends on the success and scale of any oil finds. This will also affect future cash flow profiles.

(d)   **Advice to Borrows plc**

This is a risky project. Even though this is a mining company, it is in a different location. Future cash flow requirements are extremely difficult to predict with no guarantee of a return, or when one might occur. This would suggest equity finance so that the company does not commit itself to higher interest charges than necessary. Equity finance is also permanent; the debt will have to be repaid.

Other information that would be useful in this decision includes:

(i)   financial and accounting information relating to other companies in this sector

(ii)   knowledge of the countries where exploration is to take place, with their economic and political profile.

14	MANRAY PLC

(a)   **NPV of project**

In order to determine whether or not the project is worthwhile it is necessary to compare the present value of the inflows and outflows of the project after tax adjustments. In this scenario the discount rate (cost of capital) is set at 15%. The actual interest rate of the borrowing being used is therefore irrelevant as this is deemed to be inherent in the discount rate.

The project outflow is £2m (£3m borrowed less £1m used to repay the overdraft).

The project will be eligible for capital allowances of 25% per annum over 4 years. This amounts to £500,000 per annum, assumed to be available from year 1 (when the equipment is brought into use) until year 4 inclusive. After tax this allowance amounts to £500,000 × 33% = £165,000 per annum. The present value of this tax saving is found using the 4-year annuity factor for years 2-5 inclusive (because tax is paid one year in arrears).

15% annuity factor years 1 - 5	=	3.352
15% annuity factor year 1	=	(0.870)
15% annuity factor years 2 - 5	=	2.482

The present value of the capital allowance is thus: £165,000 × 2.482 = £409,530

The change in costs and revenues arising from the project is as follows:

		£
Revenue: Additional 10,000 units @ £35 =		350,000
Variable costs:	New cost = 90,000 × £10 (W1)	
	Old cost = 80,000 × £20 (W1)	
	Saving = (80,000 × £20) - (90,000 × £10) =	700,000
		1,050,000
Fixed costs:	Increase by	(400,000)
Net pre-tax operating inflow		650,000

Since the loan is to be repaid 'in three equal instalments, every two years over the anticipated lifetime of the equipment' the project has a life of 6 years.

The present value of the net pre tax operating inflow is thus found using the 15% annuity factor for years 1–6:

$$£650,000 × 3.784 = £2,459,600$$

The tax charge resulting from the increase in pre-tax operating inflow is £650,000 × 33% = £214,500 which will arise in years 2–7 inclusive (because tax is paid 1 year in arrears. The 15% annuity factor for years 2 - 7 inclusive is:

15% annuity factor years 1–7	=	4.160
15% annuity factor year 1	=	(0.870)
15% annuity factor years 2–7		3.290

The present value of the tax charge is thus: £214,500 × 3.290 = £705,705

Present value summary:

	£
Investment outflow	(2,000,000)
Capital allowance inflow	409,530
Operating inflow	2,459,600
Operating tax outflow	(705,705)
Net present value	£163,425

Since the project has a positive net present value it is clearly worthwhile.

(b)   **Earnings per share (EPS)**

$$\text{Earnings per share} = \frac{\text{Profit available for ordinary shareholders}}{\text{Number of ordinary shares}}$$

$$= \frac{£456,000}{4m} = 11.4 \text{ pence per share}$$

If the new project is introduced the revised profit and loss account is:

	£'000	£'000
Sales		3,150
Less: Variable expenses	900	
Fixed costs	650	(1,550)
Operating profit		1,600
Less: Interest payable (£3m × 10%) (W2)		(300)
Profit before tax		1,300
Taxation (33% × £800,000 (W3))		(264)
		1,036
Less: Preference dividend		(80)
Profit available for ordinary shareholders		956

The new earnings for share is thus: $\dfrac{£956,000}{4m} = 23.9$ pence per share

This represents an increase of 12.5 pence per share or 110%.

(*Tutorial note:* Although this is the answer that was published by the ACCA as part of the Pilot Paper, there is clearly an inconsistency over the treatment of fixed costs. In (a) the additional £400,000 has been taken as extra **cash** fixed costs. However, on purchasing a new asset, additional **depreciation** of £2m ÷ 6 = £$^1/_3$m will be charged in the profit and loss and **should** appear in (b).)

(c)   **Operating gearing**

Operating gearing is the relationship between the level of fixed and variable costs incurred by a business. In relative terms the higher the level of fixed costs the greater is the proportion of revenue required to cover those costs. As a consequence the greater the level of relative fixed costs, the greater the risk of making losses (due to the impact of sales volume changes). In contrast, once the fixed costs have been covered the greater the proportionate fixed costs, the greater is the growth in profits.

Operating gearing can be measured by:

$$\frac{\text{Fixed costs}}{\text{Total costs}} \quad \text{or} \quad \frac{\text{Fixed costs}}{\text{Sales}}$$

In the case of Manray these calculations before and after the introduction of the project are:

Before: $\dfrac{£250,000}{£1,850,000} = 13.5\%$ $\qquad$ $\dfrac{£250,000}{£2,800,000} = 8.9\%$

After: $\dfrac{£650,000}{£1,550,000} = 41.9\%$ $\qquad$ $\dfrac{£650,000}{£3,150,000} = 20.6\%$

(*Tutorial note:* The most common definition is percentage change in profit ÷ percentage change in sales or contribution ÷ profit. Using this formula, operating gearing has increased from 126% to 178%.)

(d) **Break-even analysis**

The breakeven point equals:

$$\frac{\text{Fixed costs}}{\text{Contribution / unit}}$$

In the case of Manray this can be calculated before and after the project is introduced:

Before: $\dfrac{£250,000}{(£35-£20)} = 16,667 \text{ units}$

After: $\dfrac{£650,000}{(£35-£10)} = 26,000 \text{ units}$

Both of these calculations ignore interest, which if included has the following effect:

Before: $\dfrac{(£250,000+£150,000)}{(£35-£20)} = 26,667 \text{ units}$

After: $\dfrac{(£650,000+£300,000)}{(£35-£10)} = 38,000 \text{ units}$

(*Note:* the preference dividend is ignored because although it is fixed rate capital it is an appropriation of profit and not a cost).

(e) **Cause of interest rate rises and problems**

There are a number of economic reasons why interest rates change. Possible reasons for an increase in interest rates include:

(i) increased borrowing by the government; interest rates rise so as to increase the funds available for gilt purchase by taking funds away from other investments;

(ii) an increase in the funds demanded by the private sector; again interest rates rise to encourage such investors;

(iii) a rise in actual price inflation; causing notional interest rates to rise so that real interest rates remain constant;

(iv) a rise in the expected rate of inflation; so that investors, especially in respect of fixed rate investments, raise their interest rate demands so as to maintain a constant level of real income;

(v) government legislation to reduce the funds available for lending (eg, by banks); so that interest rates rise to reduce the demand for funds;

(vi) government action to strengthen the value of currency on the world currency markets.

When measuring difficulties in this way it is necessary to identify how such a difficulty would be measured. In the following it is assumed that the director is concerned about the company's ability to earn profits and make appropriate dividend payments to shareholders. Manray's level of interest cover after the introduction of the new project is:

$$\frac{\text{Operating profit}}{\text{Interest payable}} = \frac{£1,600,000}{£300,000} = 5.33\,\text{times}$$

This means that the interest payable can increase more than five-fold before the operating profit is eliminated, however this would then result in no dividends to either preference or ordinary shareholders. The ordinary shareholders, as the risk-takers, would expect their return to increase in line with interest rate changes in the longer term. Thus it can be stated that any significant increase of the interest cost in isolation has an important implication if it becomes the norm in the longer-term. However, when considering the added effects of reductions in operating income together with increases in interest rates the problem becomes more acute.

WORKINGS

(W1)   Present variable costs are £1,600,000/80,000 = £20/unit

The saving of £10/unit reduces the variable cost to £10/unit.

(W2)   The interest charge assumes that the present overdraft is refinanced - this would appear worthwhile as the present interest rate on the overdraft is 15% (£150,000/£1m) and the new loan rate is only 10%.

(W3)   Taxable profit = £1,300 - £500 (capital allowances).

---

15   COMPANY OBJECTIVES

Financial management is concerned with making decisions about the provisions and use of a firm's finances. A rational approach to decision-making necessitates a fairly clear idea of what the objectives of the decision maker are or, more importantly, of what are the objectives of those on behalf of whom the decisions are being made.

There is little agreement in the literature as to what objectives of firms are or even what they ought to be. However, most financial management textbooks make the assumption that the objective of a limited company is to maximise the wealth of its shareholders. This assumption is normally justified in terms of classical economic theory. In a market economy firms that achieve the highest returns for their investors will be the firms that are providing customers with what they require. In turn these companies, because they provide high returns to investors, will also find it easiest to raise new finance. Hence the so called 'invisible hand' theory will ensure optimal resource allocation and this should automatically maximise the overall economic welfare of the nation.

This argument can be criticised on several grounds. Firstly it ignores market imperfections. For example it might not be in the public interest to allow monopolies to maximise profits. Secondly it ignores social needs like health, police, defence etc.

From a more practical point of view directors have a legal duty to run the company on behalf of their shareholders. This however begs the question as to what do shareholders actually require from firms.

Another justification from the individual firm's point of view is to argue that it is in competition with other firms for further capital and it therefore needs to provide returns at least as good as the competition. If it does not it will lose the support of existing shareholders and will find it difficult to raise funds in the future, as well as being vulnerable to potential take-over bids.

Against the traditional and 'legal' view that the firm is run in order to maximise the wealth of ordinary shareholders, there is an alternative view that the firm is a coalition of different groups: equity shareholders, preference shareholders and lenders, employees, customers and suppliers. Each of these groups must be paid a minimum 'return' to encourage them to participate in the firm. Any excess wealth created by the firm should be and is the subject of bargaining between these groups.

At first sight this seems an easy way out of the 'objectives' problem. The directors of a company could say 'Let's just make the profits first, then we'll argue about who gets them at a later stage'. In other words, maximising profits leads to the largest pool of benefits to be distributed among the participants in the bargaining process. However, it does imply that all such participants must value profits in the same way and that they are all willing to take the same risks.

In fact the real risk position and the attitude to risk of ordinary shareholders, loan creditors and employees are likely to be very different. For instance, a shareholder who has a diversified portfolio is likely not to be so worried by the bankruptcy of one of his companies as will an employee of that company, or a supplier whose main customer is that company. The problem of risk is one major reason why there cannot be a single simple objective which is common to all companies.

Separate from the problem of which goal a company ought to pursue are the questions of which goals companies claim to pursue and which goals they actually pursue.

Many objectives are quoted by large companies and sometimes are included in their annual accounts. Examples are:

(a)   to produce an adequate return for shareholders;
(b)   to grow and survive autonomously;
(c)   to improve productivity;
(d)   to give the highest quality service to customers;
(e)   to maintain a contented workforce;
(f)   to be technical leaders in their field;
(g)   to be market leaders;
(h)   to acknowledge their social responsibilities.

Some of these stated objectives are probably a form of public relations exercise. At any rate, it is possible to classify most of them into four categories which are related to profitability:

(a)   Pure profitability goals eg, adequate return for shareholders.
(b)   'Surrogate' goals of profitability eg, improving productivity, happy workforce.
(c)   Constraints on profitability eg, acknowledging social responsibilities, no pollution, etc.
(d)   'Dysfunctional' goals.

The last category are goals which should not be followed because they do not benefit in the long run. Examples here include the pursuit of market leadership at any cost, even profitability. This may arise because management assumes that high sales equal high profits which is not necessarily so.

In practice the goals which a company actually pursues are affected to a large extent by the management. As a last resort, the directors may always be removed by the shareholders or the shareholders could vote for a take-over bid, but in large companies individual shareholders lack voting power and information. These companies can, therefore, be dominated by the management.

There are two levels of argument here. Firstly, if the management do attempt to maximise profits, then they are in a much more powerful position to decide how the profits are 'carved up' than are the shareholders.

Secondly, the management may actually be seeking 'prestige' goals rather than profit maximisation. Such goals might include growth for its own sake, including empire building or maximising turnover for its own sake, or becoming leaders in the technical field for no reason other than general prestige. Such goals are usually 'dysfunctional'.

The dominance of management depends on individual shareholders having no real voting power, and in this respect institutions have usually preferred to sell their shares rather than interfere with the management of companies. There is some evidence, however, that they are now taking a more active role in major company decisions.

From all that has been said above, it appears that each company should have its own unique decision model. For example, it is possible to construct models where the objective is to maximise profit subject to first fulfilling the target levels of other goals. However, it is not possible to develop the general theory of financial management very far without making an initial simplifying assumption about objectives. The objective of maximising the wealth of equity shareholders seems the least objectionable.

16   EFFICIENT MARKET HYPOTHESIS

Answer Plan

Weak form: past price movements only.

Semi-strong form: all current publicly available information.

Strong form: all information, public and non-public.

(a)   The **weak form** of the efficient market hypothesis states that the current share price reflects all information contained in the past price movements of that share. This implies that a study of the trends in share prices over a prior period will not help in predicting the way in which the value or price of those shares will move in the future. In other words there is no place for chartism or technical analysis. Statistical evidence suggests that the efficient market hypothesis does hold in its weak form.

The **semi-strong form** of the efficient market hypothesis encompasses the weak form and adds that share prices also reflect all current publicly available information, for instance information contained in recently published accounts. If the semi-strong form holds, then a detailed analysis of published will not assist in a prediction of future share price movements, since the share price already contains all relevant information shown in those accounts or made public since the issue of those accounts. As such it would only be possible to predict share price movements if unpublished information were known, in other words through insider information. Statistical evidence suggests that the semi-strong form of the efficient market hypothesis is valid.

The **strong form** of the efficient market hypothesis proposes that the current share price reflects all information relevant to the company, whether or not that information has been made public. If this is the case then it will never be possible to predict share price movements. The implication of this statement is that there would be no scope for gains to be made on share trading through the obtaining of inside (unpublished) information. Clearly this appears not to hold in practice, since legislation has been set to prevent insider dealing.

(b)   **Share price rises after announcement of high earnings**

The market will have assessed the likely level of the company's earnings from information which has been available to the public and the share price will be based on that assessment. If subsequent information suggests that the estimate of earnings was inaccurate the share price should adjust immediately under the semi-strong form of the efficient market hypothesis. In the situation described there was an immediate share price movement, but this continued over the following two or three days. This would suggest that the market is not absolutely efficient in the semi-strong form, because if it were the entire adjustment should have occurred immediately on announcement of the earnings figure.

It is also true that the market is not efficient in the strong form, otherwise the high earnings figure would have been known before it was published and as such reflected in the share price. Since the share price moved on announcement of the earnings, the strong form cannot hold.

Return on professionally managed portfolios

The suggestion that the return on professionally managed portfolios is likely to be no better than that which could be achieved by any investor would be supported by the strong form of the efficient market hypothesis. Assuming portfolio managers are not party to inside, unpublished information, this view would also be held by the semi-strong form of the efficient market hypothesis. However, if this proposition were to be unduly accepted there would be no demand for professionally managed portfolios. Since this is not the case, investors must perceive some benefit of placing their funds in the hands of portfolio managers. This would therefore suggest that the market is not efficient in either the semi-strong or strong form.

Share price movements around the fiscal year end

The downward movement on share prices just before the year end followed up a subsequent upward movement is due more to supply and demand effects than the efficient market hypothesis. There is no information specific to a particular security which causes the managers of portfolios or other investors to sell and then re-buy: it is simply the result of tax effects which apply universally to all shares across the market.

17   FLOW OF FUNDS

(a)   For flow of funds purposes the economy may be conveniently divided into four sectors: the personal, business, government and overseas sectors. Direct two-way flows of funds (of differing magnitudes) exist between each of these sectors through wages, payments for goods, taxation and other means. In addition, substantial flows are channelled between and within the four sectors via financial intermediaries which facilitate the flow of funds from those with a surplus of funds to those requiring funds, and also improve the consumption and investment opportunities available to individuals, organisations and the government.

The personal sector is always in surplus whilst the government sector is usually in deficit. In most countries the business sector is normally a net borrower but the overseas sector is more variable and may be either a net provider or a net borrower of funds.

(b)   Most personal sector savers invest relatively small sums of money, wish to maintain a reasonable level of liquidity and do not wish to take substantial risks. Many borrowers, especially in the corporate sector, require large amounts of finance for periods of several years to invest in projects which often involve considerable risk. Financial intermediaries satisfy the requirements of these and other borrowers and lenders by:

(i)   Collecting together small savings and 'parcelling' them into larger units which may be borrowed by companies and other organisations.

(ii)   Performing a 'transformational function' by being prepared to borrow funds for a relatively short period of time, and to lend those funds for a longer period of time. Building societies are the extreme example of this transformation, where very short-term deposits are often loaned out for 20 or more years. The financial intermediary relies upon only a proportion of deposits being withdrawn at any time, and keeps sufficient liquid funds to meet such withdrawals.

(iii)   Spreading risks. The small saver is given the opportunity to obtain a well diversified portfolio with only a small investment eg, via a unit trust or investment trust.

(iv)   Reducing transactions costs to both borrowers and lenders.

(v)   Providing financial advice and other services (eg, insurance).

Four types of financial intermediary (using the United Kingdom as an example) might include:

(1)   **Deposit institutions**

(a)   **Clearing banks**

Clearing banks are the dominant force in retail banking in the United Kingdom, and are also very active in wholesale and international banking. They are responsible for most of the country's cash distribution and money transmission facilities. Clearing banks, especially the 'big four', maintain large branch networks and offer a variety of accounts to the saver, from non-interest earning accounts to accounts yielding money market rates. These banks offer loan facilities, mostly of a short and medium term nature, to industry, commerce and the personal sector.

In recent years the clearing banks, mainly through subsidiaries, have expanded their operations into merchant banking, hire purchase leasing and other financial activities and are moving towards offering 'universal banking' facilities.

(b)   **Merchant and other banks**

Merchant banks concentrate upon the wholesale market and provide specialist services eg, analysis of investment projects, assistance with mergers and take-overs, underwriting facilities, syndicated credits and portfolio management. They do not maintain large branch networks and rely primarily upon money market funds for their deposit base.

Overseas banks, of which there are approximately four hundred represented in the United Kingdom, are also very active in wholesale banking and provide approximately 30% of bank lending to manufacturing industry. Some of the larger overseas banks are also establishing retail banking branch networks.

(c)   **Savings banks**

The National Savings Bank is operated by the Post Office and collects deposits from small savers which are used to help finance government borrowing requirements. (Other 'national savings' schemes include National Savings Certificates, Premium Bonds, and Income Bonds.)

(d)   **Finance houses**

Finance houses offer credit facilities (hire purchase especially) and leasing at the point of sale of goods and via branch networks. Their funds are derived partially through deposits, but mainly by borrowing from banks and other sources. Most of the major finance houses are owned by, or controlled by, the clearing banks.

(e)   **Building societies**

Building societies have recently experienced very rapid growth. They rely almost entirely upon personal sector deposits for their funds and exist primarily to provide mortgage finance to the personal sector, although they are now providing some of the retail banking facilities of the clearing banks.

(2)   **Insurance and provident institutions**

(a)   **Insurance companies**

Insurance companies operate both long-term business (life assurance and long-term sickness insurance) and general business (especially motor, property and personal accident insurance). Long-term business generates through the payment of premiums (either on a regular or lump sum basis) funds which are invested often for long periods, mainly in government securities, company securities, land and property. The maturities of investments are approximately matched with the anticipated needs to meet the requirements of policy holders.

(b)   **Pension funds**

Occupational pension funds collect contributions on a regular basis from employees and employers in order to make provision for pensions for employees upon retirement or upon early death. The asset portfolio of pension funds is similar to that of long-term insurance business and some pension funds are managed by insurance companies.

(3)   **Portfolio institutions**

(a)   **Unit trusts.** Unit trusts collect funds from investors and invest these funds primarily in equities. They allow relatively small investors to obtain the benefits of diversified portfolios (although many unit trusts offer portfolios specialising in particular industrial sectors or countries).

(b)   **Investment trusts**

Investment trusts are not 'trusts' but limited liability companies that can issue both equity and debt (unlike unit trusts). They also offer the benefits of diversification to their investors and invest primarily in corporate shares and government securities.

(4)   **Other financial intermediaries**

These include 3i plc (including the ICFC division and Ventures division), Equity Capital for Industry and the British Technology Group (incorporating the National Enterprise Board and the National Research Development Corporation).

18	HEXICON PLC

(a)   The following reasons may be cited for using the net present value (NPV) method of investment appraisal:

   (i)   Compared to accounting rate of return (ARR), it discounts real cashflows as opposed to accounting profits which are affected by non-cash items.

   (ii)   Compared to measuring internal rate of return (IRR), the NPV method only gives one solution. In some circumstances, (when there are a number of outflows occurring at different times), multiple IRR solutions are possible.

   (iii)   Compared to the payback method, NPV considers all of the cashflows of a project.

   (iv)   By using a discount rate it measures the opportunity cost of the money invested by a person in a project.

   (v)   The interest rate used can be increased/decreased depending upon the level of perceived risk in the investment.

   (vi)   The NPV of a project can be shown to be equal to the increase in the value of shareholder's equity in the company. Thus the method is consistent with the objective of shareholder wealth maximisation.

(b)   (i)   The present EOQ is $\sqrt{\dfrac{2 \times £100 \times 40,000}{20\% \times £2.50}}$ = 4,000 units/order

           The revised EOQ = $\sqrt{\dfrac{2 \times £25 \times 40,000}{20\% \times £2.50}}$ = 2,000 units/order

           From this it can be seen that the EOQ is halved.

   (ii)   The number of orders has increased from (40,000/4,000) 10 orders to (40,000/2,000) 20 orders; however, ordering costs are reduced by:

               (10 × £100) - (20 × £25) = £500 per annum

           Average stocks have also reduced from $\dfrac{4,000}{2}$ (2,000 units) to $\dfrac{2,000}{2}$ (1,000 units). Consequently carrying costs have reduced by 20% × £2.50 × 1,000 = £500 per annum.

           Total inventory costs are thereby reduced by £1,000 per annum.

           Assuming that Hexicon plc pays tax in the same year as it earns profits the present value of the proposal is found by comparing the outflow cost with the discounted after tax savings over the eight-year life of the proposal (using a 12% discount rate).

           Discounted savings:

£1,000 × 67% (1 - tax rate) × 12% annuity factor - 8 years			£
= £670	×	4.968 =	3,329

           Cost of reorganisation (tax deductible)

= £4,000 × 67% (1 - tax rate)		=	(2,680)
Net benefit			£649

           As the present value of the proposal is positive it is worthwhile.

(c)   The main objective of Just In Time (JIT) purchasing is to match the delivery of components from suppliers to their usage in production. If this is achieved there are significant benefits to be gained by both the supplier and the customer.

The customer is likely to use only one supplier for each component and to build up a relationship with the supplier which encourages communication thus enabling the supplier to benefit from advanced production planning and economies of scale. To enhance this relationship the customer makes a long-term commitment to future orders.

The supplier guarantees to deliver goods of an appropriate quality in accordance with an agreed delivery schedule. The benefit to the customer is thereby a reduction(or elimination) of stockholding and significant cost savings. These arise in both holding costs and also in materials handling, because goods are transferred directly from goods inwards to production.

19   HN LTD

(a)   (Note that all the figures refer to £000s)

With an opening overdraft of £(12), if the month 1 cash outflow is £(55), (a 20% probability), then this will increase the overdraft to £(67), keeping the cash balance at the minimum £20. In this case, using joint probabilities, there is a 4% chance that this will be followed by a cash inflow in month 2 of £20 so that the overdraft is reduced to £(47). There is a 2% chance that this will be followed in month 3 by a cash inflow of £25, thereby reducing the overdraft to £(22) and a 2% chance of a cash inflow of £15 which will reduce the overdraft to £(32).

These joint probabilities, cash flows (CFs) and resulting overdrafts (O/Ds) and cash float (Bal) can be summarised in the following table. Note that as soon as the overdraft reaches the maximum permitted £(80), any further deficit must be taken from the cash float (Bal).

	Month 1				Month 2				Month 3		
p	CF	O/D	Bal	jt p	CF	O/D	Bal	jt p	CF	O/D	Bal
.20	(55)	(67)	20	.04	20	(47)	20	.02	25	(22)	20
								.02	15	(32)	20
				.10	10	(57)	20	.05	5	(52)	20
								.05	(5)	(62)	20
				.06	5	(62)	20	.03	(5)	(67)	20
								.03	(10)	(72)	20
.50	(65)	(77)	20	.10	10	(67)	20	.05	5	(62)	20
								.05	0	(67)	20
				.25	(5)	(80)	18	.125	0	(80)	18
								.125	(5)	(80)	13
				.15	(10)	(80)	13	.075	(10)	(80)	3
								.075	(15)	(80)	(2)

	Month 1				Month 2				Month 3		
p	CF	O/D	Bal	jt p	CF	O/D	Bal	jt p	CF	O/D	Bal
.30	(72)	(80)	16	.06	0	(80)	16	.03	0	(80)	16
								.03	(10)	(80)	6
				.15	(10)	(80)	6	.075	(10)	(80)	(4)
								.075	(20)	(80)	(14)
				.09	(15)	(80)	1	.045	(20)	(80)	(19)
								.045	(30)	(80)	(29)

The probability of keeping the float at £20,000 in month 1 is 50% + 20% = 70%. The same calculation for month 2 is (4% + 10% + 6%) + 10% = 30%. For month 3 it is (2% + 2% + 5% + 5% + 3% + 3%) + 5% + 5% = 30%.

(b)   The probability of running out of cash (including spending even the £20,000 float) is zero for months 1 and 2. The probability of running out of cash in month 3 is (7.5%) + (7.5% + 7.5% + 4.5% + 4.5%) = 31.5%

(c)   Possible alternatives for a cash surplus are:

(i)   repaying loans

(ii)   redeeming shares

(iii)   paying higher wages

(iv)   increasing social or other 'high profile' expenditure such as sponsorships, advertising or donations to charity

(v)   financial investments on the money and capital markets.

20   COMFYLOT PLC

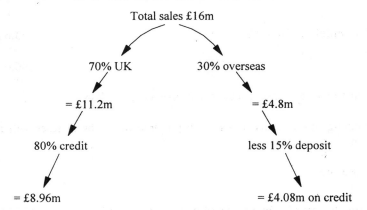

(1)   The costs and savings of domestic factoring can be identified as follows:

Costs of using the factor

	£
Factor charges service fee of 1.5% of all £8.96m credit sales	134,400
Redundancy payments	15,000

80% of the debts are factored at 15.5% The loans only last whilst the debt is outstanding (average 57 days).

The cost of this is therefore:

	£
80% × £8.96m × 15.5% × 57/365	173,505
Investment in the remaining 20% debtors has an opportunity cost (15%) = 20% × £8.96m × 15% × 57/365	41,977
Total cost	364,882

Savings from using the factor

	£
Administration	85,000
Bad debts (0.75% × £8.96m) (the factoring is non-recourse)	67,200
Current opportunity cost of debtors £8.96m × 57/365 × 15%	209,885
	362,085

The net cost of domestic factoring will be £2,797 next year. But redundancy is a non-recurring cost so savings would be expected thereafter.

(2)   The costs and savings associated with the cash discount can be identified as follows:

Costs	£
Administration	25,000
Cost of the discount itself (£8.96m × 0.4 × 0.015)	53,760
	78,760

Savings	
Reduction in bad debts 0.25% × £8.96m	22,400

The discount results in some earlier payment which will reduce the overall level of debtors from the existing (£8.96m × 57/365 =) £1,399,233 to (£8.96m × 40% × 7/365) + (£8.96m × 60% × 57/365) = £908,274.

The opportunity cost of this reduction in the level of debtors of:

	£
£490,959 is multiplied by 15%	73,644
	96,044

The introduction of this cash discount will save a net £17,284

(3)   The cost/saving implications of all three possible increases in sales will provide the most useful information.

Existing costs are:

	£
The opportunity cost of debtors = £4.08m × 75/365 × 15% =	125,753
Bad debts = £4.08m × 1.25% =	51,000
	176,753

Calculations of the net benefit or loss under each projected possible increase in sales are as follows:

	20%	*25%*	*30%*
Sales	£4.896m	£5.1m	£5.304m
Opportunity cost of debtors[1]	160,964	167,671	174,378
Bad debts[2]	73,440	76,500	79,560
	234,1404	244,171	253,938
Less: Current cost (see above)	176,753	176,753	176,753
Net extra costs	57,651	67,418	77,185
Extra administration	30,000	40,000	50,000
Advertising	300,000	300,000	300,000
Total extra cost	387,651	407,418	427,185
Extra contribution			
£960,000 × .35	336,000		
£1.2m × .35		420,000	
£1.44m × .35			504,000
Net benefit (loss)	(51,651)[3]	12,582	76,815

Notes:

(1)   Multiply 80/365 × 15% × £4.896m for 20% sales
                       × £5.1m for 25% sales
                       × £5.304m for 30% sales

(2)   Multiply the sales figures by 1.5%.

(3)   But the benefits of this year's advertising expenditure may spill over and increase next year's contribution.

Marking note: Plan your approach before answering this type of question. A little thought would help you to identify and quantify the costs and financial benefits of each option.

21   ENGOT PLC

Answer Plan

(a)   Different measures of financial gearing.

(b)   Importance of financial gearing: risk, interest payments have to be made.

(c)   Limiting factors on the amount of debt finance: existing covenants, available cashflows and interest cover, security to be offered, effect on cost of capital.

(d)   Meaning of mezzanine finance: halfway between senior debt and equity.

(a)   Financial gearing is a measure of the proportionate relationship between a company's borrowings and its equity finance, ie, it is a measure of capital structure. There are a number of ways in which gearing may be calculated: either expressing debt as a proportion of total finance or as a proportion of equity, and either using book values or market values of the capital. In addition, the debt may be calculated to include all borrowings, or simply, those that are deemed to be part of the company's long-term financing.

The three gearing ratios stated in the question have been calculated in the following ways.

Mr R: Ratio based on market values and including all borrowings.

$$\frac{5,600 + 1,800 \times 1.08 + 1,000 \times 0.98 + 2,800}{20,680(\text{W1})} = 55\%$$

(W1)   Market value of equity   = Number of shares × share price

$$= \frac{£2,200,000}{£0.10} \times £0.94$$

$$= £20,680,000.$$

The market value of equity includes all shareholders' funds and therefore the share premium account and retained profit should not be added.

Mr Y: Ratio based on book values and excluding short-term borrowings.

$$\frac{5,600 + 1,800}{8,330} = 89\%$$

Mr Z: Ratio based on book values and including all borrowings.

$$\frac{5,600 + 1,800 + 1,000 + 2,800}{8,330} = 134\%$$

Book values are constant over time and therefore give a constant gearing ratio. In the case of debt finance it is probably acceptable to use book values, since generally they do not deviate dramatically from market value. However, the book value of equity often considerably distorts the true value of shareholders' funds and consequently distorts the gearing ratio. For this reason, therefore, it is preferable to use market values.

On the issue of borrowings, the criterion relates to which borrowings actually contribute to the long-term financing of the company. A bank overdraft, although strictly short-term and repayable on demand often is an important source of long-term finance for many companies. Therefore it is reasonable to include the bank loans and overdrafts in the figure for borrowings. The 8% loan stock is classified as a short-term liability since it is due for redemption in a year's time. However, presumably it will need to be replaced by a new issue or some other form of finance, in which case it also should be included as debt, if the gearing ratio is to be meaningful.

Based on the above reasoning the preferred ratio would be 55% based on market values and all borrowings. However, it may be argued the book values are preferable since they do not alter and that current liabilities should be excluded since they fluctuate. Such might be the arguments of Mr Y and Mr Z.

(b)   Financial gearing might be important to a company for the following reasons.

   (i)   High gearing increases the risk perceived by ordinary shareholders, since interest payments are paid first from operating profits and thus cause earnings attributable to ordinary shareholders to fluctuate more significantly. In addition, in the event of liquidation debt holders have priority over the assets of the company.

   (ii)   A company which has a high level of debt may encounter difficulties in raising further finance.

   (iii)   At very high levels of gearing the risk of default on interest payments or redemption becomes greater with the associated risk of bankruptcy.

   (iv)   The company's weighted average cost of capital is likely to increase at very high levels of gearing, due to the factors described above and therefore the company value will fall.

(c)   Factors which might limit the amount of debt finance that a company uses may include the following:

   (i)   Existing loan covenants or clauses in the company's articles of association may limit further borrowing.

   (ii)   Inadequate cashflows and interest cover may prevent lenders from being willing to subscribe to further debt.

   (iii)   The company may have no further assets to offer as security for debt.

   (iv)   Higher risk is associated with high gearing and therefore new borrowings may demand a return which is too high for the company to afford.

(d)   Mezzanine finance is a type of funding which may be categorised between debt and equity. It is usually unsecured and has a claim on profits after interest has been paid on 'senior' debt but its return is made by way of interest. To compensate investors for this higher risk it normally has an enhanced coupon rate and may also participate to a certain extent in the equity of the business, perhaps only at a future date by the current issue of a warrant.

Mezzanine finance is used in the following situations:

   (i)   In management buyouts or takeovers which are financed by a high proportion of debt, mezzanine finance is a popular option by which to attract investors. In the case of a management buyout where the management team wishes to retain control of the company through their equity stake and yet are unable to raise further debt for their financing requirements, mezzanine finance may represent an intermediate solution.

   (ii)   In circumstances of corporate restructuring, mezzanine finance may be a useful tool.

22   ARMADA LEISURE

Answer Plan

(a)   Cost; risk, flexibility; matching.

(b)   Definition; arguments in favour; arguments against.

(c)   Definitions; merits of leasing; merits of hire-purchase

(a)   (i)   The overall cost of long-term and short-term capital borrowing must be considered. The difference in the rates of interest will be affected by the lender's perception of the economy and interest rates, but it is generally accepted that longer-term rates will be higher than shorter term rates for the same level of security. However, shorter term borrowing will require more frequent re-negotiation leading to costs in both management time and arrangement fees.

(ii)   The need to re-negotiate finance is a risk for the company because it may occur at a time when the financial picture of the company is unsuitable for such negotiations. As a consequence there is a greater risk with short-term borrowing, and any failure to re-arrange the finance will merely increase the business' problems.

(iii)   The early repayment of long-term debt usually incurs a penalty, so the use of short-term debt is more flexible in this respect. The use of short-term debt may avoid entering into long-term debt arrangements at unfavourable high interest rates, and give flexibility to switch into longer term debt when interest rates improve. Temporary finance needs can often be serviced by an overdraft facility whereby interest is only charged on finance actually used.

(iv)   A common objective is to match the financing of long-term assets to long-term debt, and to use short-term debt for short-life assets and working capital. This is to avoid the problems of having to repay debt when the asset it was used to acquire is in a non-liquid form. If more funds cannot be found to repay the debt then there is a risk of the company being made insolvent.

(b)   (i)   A rights issue is an offer made to existing shareholders to purchase additional shares in proportion to their existing holding. It is usually underwritten by an issuing house.

(ii)   The following arguments may be made in favour of a rights issue:

(1)   The finance is guaranteed if it is fully underwritten by the issuing house

(2)   There will be no change in the members of the company or their relative voting powers provided the existing members subscribe for the shares.

(3)   As the stock market is rising investors will be seeking to buy shares, therefore the rights issue should be sold with relative ease.

(4)   The rights issue being equity finance will lower the gearing ratio, thereby reducing the debt risk of the company.

(iii)   The following arguments may be used against the making of a rights issue:

(1)   The fees of the underwriters and other issuing costs may be expensive depending upon the underwriter's perception of the success or otherwise of the rights issue.

(2)   A rights issue forces the existing members to either subscribe for the shares or sell the rights; they may resent having to spend money to maintain their existing percentage holding in the company.

(3)   Rights issues have to be made at a discount to encourage their purchase, this usually reduces the share price initially as there is a time-lag between raising the finance and generating the corresponding increase in earnings.

(4)   As future forecasters are expressing doubts about the economy the issue may not be taken up by the members. This would dilute the control and make subsequent attempts to raise equity finance more difficult.

(c)   (i)   Leasing, referred to in financial accounting as operating leases, is the right to use an asset for a defined period of time, by the payment of a rental over the period of that usage.

Hire purchase however, which in financial accounting is a form of finance lease, is the acquisition of an asset by a series of payments, the last of which confers legal title to the asset.

(ii)   The merits of leasing are:

(1)   There is a clear cashflow advantage as payments are made as the asset is being used, instead of a significant part of the cost being paid on acquisition.

(2)   Leasing assets, especially those which are continually being improved by technological development, reduces the risk of obsolescence.

(3)   The leases are a means of obtaining off-balance sheet finance, although the notes to the accounts must separately identify their operating lease obligations.

(4)   The whole of the rental payment is tax deductible, the lessor retains the right to claim capital allowances. This is more appropriate in companies having relatively low profits and operating in areas where accelerated capital allowances are available.

(iii)   The merits of hire-purchase are:

(1)   The title to the asset eventually passes to the customer, so a tangible benefit is received in respect of the payments.

(2)   The interest element of the hire-purchase payment is tax deductible, and the customer may claim capital allowances on the cost of the asset.

23   AMBLE PLC

(a)   The operating cash flows of Amble

Year	0	1	2	3	4
		£'000	£'000	£'000	£'000
Sales		1,320	2,021	2,183	2,355
Less cash operating costs:					
Direct labour		354	553	608	668
Material Z		102	161	174	188
Component P		173	265	286	308
Component Q		77	118	127	137
Other variables		25	39	42	45
Management salaries		67	72	77	82
Selling expenses		166	174	183	192
Rent		120	126	132	139
Incremental overheads		50	53	55	58
		1,134	1,561	1,684	1,817
Sales less cash operating costs		186	460	499	538
Tax (paid) saved		9	(86)	(100)	(114)
Purchase and sale of machine	(864)				12
Net cash flows	(864)	195	374	399	436

Using linear interpolation to find the IRR of these cash flows:

(i)   with a discount rate of 18% NPV = 38
(ii)   with a discount rate of 22% NPV = (36).

Therefore the IRR is 18% + [(38/(38 + 36)](22% - 18%) = 20.1%

Notes to the calculation:

Year	1	2	3	4
Sales				
Price (£)	110	115.5	121.3	127.3
Units	12,000	17,500	18,000	18,500
Total (£000)	1,320	2,021	2,183	2,355
Direct labour				
Cost (£)	29.50	31.60	33.80	36.10
Units	12,000	17,500	18,000	18,500
Total (£000)	354	553	608	668

Material Z

Year 1 requires 12,000 units × 6 kg = 72,000 kg. The cost of this is:

the opportunity cost of using the existing 70,000 units	99,000
+ purchase 2,000 units × £1.46	2,920
	£101,920

Year 2 requires 17,500 units × 6 kg = 105,000 kg
× inflating £1.46 by 5% £1.53

£160,650

Year 3 requires 18,000 units × 6 kg = 108,000 kg
£1.53 × 1.05 £1.61

£173,880

Year 4 requires 18,500 units × 6 kg = 111,000 kg
£1.61 × 1.05 £1.69

£187,590

Management salaries and rent

Both of these require opportunity costs. The best way to find these is to use this formula:

opportunity cost = cost with project less cost without project

Management salaries

Cost with project	=	(2 × £25,000)
		+ £20,000
		+ £17,000
	=	£87,000
Cost without project	=	£20,000
Opportunity cost	=	£67,000

Rent

Cost with project	=	£100,000
Cost without project	=	£100,000 *less* income £120,000
	=	net income £20,000
Opportunity cost	=	£120,000

Tax

Capital allowance based upon straight-line depreciation over 4 years = (£864 - £12)/4 = £213 p.a.

Year	1	2	3	4
Sales less cash operating costs	186	460	499	538
Capital allowances	213	213	213	213
Taxable cash flows	(27)	247	286	325
Tax (paid) (35%)/saved	9	(86)	(100)	(114)

Marking note: The principles of opportunity cost are being tested. Briefly explain these principles for a couple of marks. Always calculate what is required (in this case the IRR), even if you suspect your cash flows are incorrect. You will get a couple of marks for knowing the calculation.

(b)   Discounting the net cash flows identified above at 17% gives a NPV of £58,000. Included in this calculation, the NPV of the tax paid identified above is (£178,000). The overall NPV of the project will disappear if the NPV of the tax payments increases to (£178,000 + £58,000) = £236,000. The tax rate that produces a NPV for tax payments of £236,000 can either be found by trial and error or by solving for R in the following formula using 17% present value factors for the taxable cash flows:

$$(-27 \times .855 \times R) + (248 \times .731 \times R) + (286 \times .624 \times R) + (325 \times .534 \times R) = 236$$

R = 0.46; this is the break-even tax rate which will produce an overall NPV of zero.

Marking note: Again show the examiner that you know about sensitivity analysis if you find yourself struggling with the calculation.

24   ZEDLAND

(a)   Your report should include the following computations and comments:

There are two investment criteria used by Zedland:

Return on investment

This is defined as: $\dfrac{\text{average after – tax annual profit}}{\text{average investment}}$

Firstly the calculation of the after-tax annual profit;

	t_1 £'000	t_2 £'000	t_3 £'000	t_4 £'000	t_5 £'000
Sales (letters)[1]	2,048	2,867	3,010	3,160	3,318
(parcels)	682	1,075	1,129	1,185	1,244
Total sales	2,730	3,942	4,139	4,345	4,562
Expenses:[2]					
Wages	2,457	2,580	2,709	2,844	2,986
Premises	158	165	174	182	191
Maintenance:					
vans	210	265	333	420	529
trucks	84	106	133	168	212
advertising	525	276			
depreciation	232	232	232	232	232
Total expenses	3,666	3,624	3,581	3,846	4,150
Taxable profit	(936)	318	558	499	412
Tax (40%)[5]	374*	(127)	(223)	(200)	(165)
Profit after tax	(562)	191	335	299	247

* a loss in this service can be set against profits earned elsewhere in the organisation, in other words, a loss here saves tax elsewhere.

The unit used in this answer is £000. This produces an average annual after-tax profit of £102,000. Average investment is £1,160/2 = £580,000. This gives a return on investment of £102/£580 = 17.6% (this definition has excluded financing costs, such as interest, from the profit calculation).

Notes to the calculation

1 Sales (letters) for year 1 = $0.525 × 15,000 × (52 × 5 working days)
   = $2,048

   Sales (letters) for year 2 = ($0.525 × 1.05) × 20,000 × 260
   = $2,867

   There is a 5% p.a. increase after that. Sales (parcels) can be calculated in a similar way.

2 All cost data given are current estimates and so all must be inflated by 5%p.a. to obtain the year 1 expense, for example, year 1 wages = current cost of 180 × $13 = $2,340 × 1.05 to get the t1 figure of $2,457.

3 The five managers would be employed with or without the project, that is the incremental cost to the project is zero.

4 Market research is a committed cost whether the project is carried out or not; it is a sunk cost even if the $50,000 has not actually been paid yet.

5 Since this is an incremental project to the existing business, it is assumed that the existing profits are in excess of $500,000 so that the marginal rate of tax is 40%.

Net present value

Restating the above cash flows for timing, the NPV of this project can be calculated.

	t_0	t_1	t_2	t_3	t_4	t_5	t_6
	£'000	£'000	£'000	£'000	£'000	£'000	£'000
Initial outlay	(1,160)						
Sales Total		2,730	3,942	4,139	4,345	4,562	
Cash Expense[1]		(3,434)	(3,392)	(3,349)	(3,614)	(3,918)	
Tax[2]			374	(127)	(223)	(200)	(165)
Net cash flow	(1,160)	(704)	924	663	508	444	(165)
14% discount factors[3]	1	.877	.769	.675	.592	.519	.456
Present value	(1,160)	(617)	711	448	301	230	(75)
NPV value	(162)						

Notes:

1   These exclude depreciation.
2   Tax is lagged by one year.
3   The discount rate should reflect the required return relative to the risk of the project.

The reason why this project produced a negative NPV despite a relatively high ROI is:

- t_0 and t_1 had net cash outflows

- the cash inflows didn't start till t_2. With a high discount rate, the present value of these inflows is much reduced

- ROI takes no account of the timing of these cash flows.

Thus the project satisfies only one of the investment criteria. NPV could, of course, be increased by raising prices (this is a monopoly) and/or cutting costs. However, as a nationalised service, social and economic factors must be taken into account as well as financial ones, although they will be difficult to quantify.

Thus, the service may be introduced regardless of its existing negative NPV.

Marking note: Examiners will reward candidates who have inflated the figures appropriately and who know which cash flows to discount. A tidy layout will help prevent confusion, and assist the marker. Remember to discuss the 'other' factors involved.

25   BANDEN LTD

(Tutorial note: a fairly straightforward question on investment appraisal, including capital rationing and profitability index. An appreciation of linear and integer programming is also required.)

(a)   (i)   **Calculation of expected Net Present Value**

Project		*NPV*
A. £70,000 × 3.605 - £246,000	=	£6,350
B. £75,000 × 0.893 + £87,000 × 0.797 + £64,000 × 0.712 – £180,000	=	£1,882
C. £48,000 × 0.893 + £48,000 × 0.797 + £63,000 × 0.712 + £73,000 × 0.636 – £175,000	=	(£2,596)

    D. £62,000 × 3.037 – £180,000   =   £8,294

    E. £40,000 × 0.893 + £50,000 × 0.797 + £60,000 × 0.712
        + £70,000 × 0.636 + £40,000 × 0.567 – £180,000   =   £5,490

    F. £35,000 × 0.893 + £82,000 × 0.797 + £82,000 × 0.712 – £150,000   =   £4,993

(ii)   **Calculation of Profitability Index (NPV/£)**

    Present Value of cash inflows/initial outlay:

A. 252,350 / 246,000	=	1.026
B. 181,882 / 180,000	=	1.010
C. 172,404 / 175,000	=	0.985
D. 188,294 / 180,000	=	1.046
E. 185,490 / 180,000	=	1.031
F. 154,993 / 150,000	=	1.033

Ranking	*NPV*	*P.I.*
1	D	D
2	A	F
3	E	E
4	F	A
5	B	B
6	C	C

The rankings differ because NPV is an absolute measure of the benefit from a project, while P.I. is a relative measure, and shows the benefit per £ of outlay. Where the initial outlays vary in size the two methods may give different rankings.

(b)   In a capital rationing situation, the projects should be selected which give the greatest total NPV from the limited outlay available.

A and E are mutually exclusive.
C is not considered as it has a negative NPV.
Total outlay is limited to £620,000.

Possible selections are:

Projects	Expected NPV £	Total NPV £	Outlay £'000
A.B.D.	6,350 + 1,882 + 8,294	16,526	606
A.B.F.	6,350 + 1,882 + 4,993	13,225	576
A.D.F.	6,350 + 8,294 + 4,993	19,637	576
B.D.E.	1,882 + 8,294 + 5,490	15,666	540
B.D.F.	1,882 + 8,294 + 4,993	15,169	510
D.E.F.	8,294 + 5,490 + 4,993	18,777	510

The recommended selection is projects D,A & F.

(Tutorial note: neither the NPV nor P.I. rankings will necessarily be appropriate because of the 'lumpiness' of the investments. In this particular instance, because of the similarity in size of the projects, only three can be undertaken, and the NPV ranking clearly leads to D,A & F. Profitability index will not work if projects are indivisable or where multiple limiting factors exist. The P.I. might lead to the incorrect solution of D,E & F.)

(c)   The director is correct in suggesting that the normal cost of capital might not be appropriate in a capital rationing situation.

In a capital rationing situation, the appropriate discount rate may be the opportunity cost of capital ie, the yield available from the best opportunity foregone.

The appropriate discount rate is therefore the higher of:

(i)   the opportunity cost of capital (ie, the IRR of the marginal project rejected due to the capital constraint); and

(ii)   the company's normal cost of capital.

9 NEW SYLLABUS EXAMINATIONS

JUNE 1994 QUESTIONS

Section A – This question is compulsory and MUST be attempted

26 (Question 1 of examination)

Netherby plc manufactures a range of camping and leisure equipment, including tents. It is currently experiencing severe quality control problems at its existing fully-depreciated factory in the south of England. These difficulties threaten to undermine its reputation for producing high quality products. It has recently been approached by the European Bank for Reconstruction and Development, on behalf of a tent manufacturer in Hungary, which is seeking a UK-based trading partner which will import and distribute its tents. Such a switch would involve shutting down the existing manufacturing operation in the UK and converting it into a distribution depot. The estimated exceptional restructuring costs of £5m would be tax-allowable, but would exert serious strains on cash flow.

Importing, rather than manufacturing tents appears inherently profitable as the buying-in price, when converted into sterling, is less than the present production cost. In addition, Netherby considers that the Hungarian product would result in increased sales, as the existing retail distributors seem impressed with the quality of the samples which they have been shown. It is estimated that for a five-year contract, the annual cash flow benefit would be around £2m pa before tax.

However, the financing of the closure and restructuring costs would involve careful consideration of the financing options. Some directors argue that dividends could be reduced as several competing companies have already done a similar thing, while other directors argue for a rights issue. Alternatively, the project could be financed by an issue of long-term loan stock at a fixed rate of 12%.

The most recent balance sheet shows £5m of issued share capital (par value 50p), while the market price per share is currently £3. A leading security analyst has recently described Netherby's gearing ratio as 'adventurous'. Profit-after-tax in the year just ended was £15m and dividends of £10m were paid.

The rate of corporation tax is 33%, payable with a one-year delay. Netherby's reporting year coincides with the calendar year and the factory will be closed at the year end. Closure costs would be incurred shortly before deliveries of the imported product began, and sufficient stocks will be on hand to overcome any initial supply problems. Netherby considers that it should earn a return on new investment projects of 15% pa net of all taxes.

Required

(a)   Is the closure of the existing factory financially worthwhile for Netherby?   **(5 marks)**

(b)   Explain what is meant when the capital market is said to be information-efficient in a semi-strong form.

        If the stock market is semi-strong efficient and without considering the method of finance, calculate the likely impact of acceptance and announcement of the details of this project to the market on Netherby's share price.
                                                                                                          (6 marks)

(c)   Advise the Netherby board as to the relative merits of a rights issue rather than a cut in dividends to finance this project.   **(6 marks)**

(d)   Explain why a rights issue generally results in a fall in the market price of shares.

If a rights issue is undertaken, calculate the resulting impact on the existing share price of issue prices of £1 per share and £2 per share, respectively. (You may ignore issue costs.)   **(6 marks)**

(e)   Assuming the restructuring proposal meets expectations, assess the impact of the project on earnings per share if it is financed by a rights issue at an offer price of £2 per share, and loan stock, respectively.   **(4 marks)**

(Again, you may ignore issue costs.)

(f)   Briefly consider the main operating risks connected with the investment project, and how Netherby might attempt to allow for these.   **(8 marks)**
(Total 35 marks)

27   (Question 2 of examination)

Answer five of the six parts of this question.

(a)   Briefly explain, with examples, the nature and purpose of 'supply-side economic policies'.

(5 marks)

(b)   'The financial manager needs to identify and realise surplus assets.' Explain briefly the benefits to an organisation of adopting this policy.   **(5 marks)**

(c)   Name and comment on the factors which should be considered in the establishment of a normal loss in a process costing environment.   **(5 marks)**

(d)   Explain ways in which the management accountant can monitor the effects of the external environment in which their firm operates.   **(5 marks)**

(e)   'We have a budget of £196,000 for the service which we are providing this year. I propose we put in for that plus the rate of inflation for our next year's budget allocation.' Critically evaluate the above comment and explain briefly how zero-based-budgeting (ZBB) could help to avoid such a situation.   **(5 marks)**

(f)   Explain briefly how time series analysis can assist the management accountant.   **(5 marks)**
(Total 25 marks)

28   (Question 3 of examination)

The Perseus Co Ltd a medium sized company, produces a single product in its one overseas factory. For control purposes, a standard costing system was recently introduced and is now in operation.

The standards set for the month of May were as follows:

Production and sales	16,000 units
Selling price (per unit)	£140

Materials

Material 007	6 kilos per unit at £12.25 per kilo
Material XL90	3 kilos per unit at £3.20 per kilo

Labour

4.5 hours per unit at £8.40 per hour

Overheads (all fixed) £86,400 per month, they are not absorbed into the product costs.

The actual data for the month of May, is as follows:

Produced 15,400 units which were sold at £138.25 each.

Materials

Used 98,560 kilos of material 007 at a total cost of £1,256,640 and used 42,350 kilos of material XL90 at a total cost of £132,979.

Labour

Paid an actual rate of £8.65 per hour to the labour force. The total amount paid out, amounted to £612,766.

Overheads (all fixed)

£96,840

Required

(a)   Prepare a standard costing profit statement, and a profit statement based on actual figures for the month of May.   **(6 marks)**

(b)   Prepare a statement of the variances which reconciles the actual with the standard profit or loss figure.**(9 marks)**

(c)   Explain briefly the possible reasons for inter-relationships between material variances and labour variances.
                                                                                                (5 marks)
                                                                                          (Total 20 marks)

---

29   (Question 4 of examination)

Cepheus Transport Co Ltd currently does around 60% of its work for its holding company and the remainder for a small number of local manufacturers. It operates from a garage and warehouse complex located close to an airport and within two hours drive of the nearest seaport.

Their management accounting information is very limited and what they do have is shown below for the quarter which has just ended:

Type of vehicle	Type F	Type P	Type U	
Number of vehicles owned	8	4	7	
Mileage	*Miles*	*Miles*	*Miles*	
Holding company work	26,000	8,120	12,080	
Work for other companies	14,600	7,400	12,400	
Revenue	£	£	£	£
From holding company	47,450	13,601	14,798	75,849
From other companies	46,720	19,573	23,560	89,853
	94,170	33,174	38,358	165,702

Operating costs

	£	£	£	£
Fuel (diesel at £2 per gallon)	4,368	1,404	1,752	7,524
Drivers' wages				
Fixed	12,800	6,000	10,500	29,300
Variable	7,200	1,625	3,750	12,575
Overtime premium	1,200	250	500	1,950
Other operating costs and				
maintenance costs	4,415	2,371	2,604	9,390
Fixed costs of vehicles				
(including insurance etc.)	3,850	2,142	2,881	8,873
*Depreciation	9,000	3,000	4,000	16,000
	42,833	16,792	25,987	85,612

* Depreciation is charged at 20% of cost per annum, taking a full year's depreciation in the year of purchase and none in the year of sale.

The company's administrative costs, garage and warehouse rent and other fixed overheads amounted to £58,220.

Edith Cepheus, the chief executive, has assured you that this data is quite typical and that to date the company has not experienced any violent fluctuations in trading conditions.

Required

Prepare a report for submission to Mrs Cepheus in which, from the limited supply of data available, you evaluate and comment on current performance and explain how the company can improve its recording system to assist them with planning, control and decision-making.

(20 marks)

---

30   (Question 5 of examination)

Ewden plc is a medium-sized company producing a range of engineering products which it sells to wholesale distributors. Recently, its sales have begun to rise rapidly following a general recovery in the economy as a whole. However, it is concerned about its liquidity position and is contemplating ways of improving its cash flow. Ewden's accounts for the past two years are summarised below.

Profit and loss account for the year ended 31 December

	1992 £'000	1993 £'000
Sales	12,000	16,000
Cost of sales	7,000	9,150
Operating profit	5,000	6,850
Interest	200	250
Profit before tax	4,800	6,600
Taxation*	1,000	1,600
Profit after tax	3,800	5,000
Dividends	1,500	2,000
Retained profit	2,300	3,000

* After capital allowances

Balance sheet as at 31 December

	1992		1993	
	£'000	£'000	£'000	£'000
Fixed assets (net)		9,000		12,000
Current assets				
Stock	1,400		2,200	
Debtors	1,600		2,600	
Cash	1,500		100	
		4,500		4,900
Current liabilities				
Overdraft	–		200	
Trade creditors	1,500		2,000	
Other creditors	500		200	
		(2,000)		(2,400)
10% Loan stock		(2,000)		(2,000)
Net assets		9,500		12,500
Ordinary shares (50p)		3,000		3,000
Profit and loss account		6,500		9,500
Shareholders' funds		9,500		12,500

In order to speed up collection from debtors, Ewden is considering two alternative policies. One option is to offer a 2% discount to customers who settle within 10 days of despatch of invoices rather than the normal 30 days offered. It is estimated that 50% of customers would take advantage of this offer. Alternatively, Ewden can utilise the services of a factor. The factor will operate on a service-only basis, administering and collecting payment from Ewden's customers. This is expected to generate administrative savings of £100,000 pa and, it is hoped, will also shorten the debtor days to an average of 45. The factor will make a service charge of 1.5% of Ewden's turnover. Ewden can borrow from its bankers at an interest rate of 18% pa.

Required

(a) Identify the reasons for the sharp decline in Ewden's liquidity and assess the extent to which the company can be said to be exhibiting the problem of 'overtrading'.

Illustrate your answer by reference to key performance and liquidity ratios computed from Ewden's accounts.

(13 marks)

(Note: it is not necessary to compile a FRS 1 statement.)

(b) Determine the relative costs and benefits of the two methods of reducing debtors, and recommend an appropriate policy.

(7 marks)
(Total 20 marks)

---

31 (Question 6 of examination)

(a) Explain how inflation affects the rate of return required on an investment project, and the distinction between a real and a nominal (or 'money terms') approach to the evaluation of an investment project under inflation.

(4 marks)

(b) Howden plc is contemplating investment in an additional production line to produce its range of compact discs. A market research study, undertaken by a well-known firm of consultants, has revealed scope to sell an additional output of 400,000 units pa. The study cost £0.1 m but the account has not yet been settled.

The price and cost structure of a typical disc (net of royalties), is as follows:

	£	£
Price per unit		12.00
Costs per unit of output		
Material cost per unit	1.50	
Direct labour cost per unit	0.50	
Variable overhead cost per unit	0.50	
Fixed overhead cost per unit	1.50	
		(4.00)
Profit		8.00

The fixed overhead represents an apportionment of central administrative and marketing costs. These are expected to rise in total by £500,000 pa as a result of undertaking this project. The production line is expected to operate for five years and require a total cash outlay of £11m, including £0.5m of materials stocks. The equipment will have a residual value of £2m. Because the company is moving towards a JIT stock management policy, it is expected that this project will involve steadily reducing working capital needs, expected to decline at about 3% pa by volume. The production line will be accommodated in a presently empty building for which an offer of £2m has recently been received from another company. If the building is retained, it is expected that property price inflation will increase its value to £3m after five years.

While the precise rates of price and cost inflation are uncertain, economists in Howden's corporate planning department make the following forecasts for the average annual rates of inflation relevant to the project:

Retail Price Index	6% pa
Disc prices	5% pa
Material prices	3% pa
Direct labour wage rates	7% pa
Variable overhead costs	7% pa
Other overhead costs	5% pa

Note: you may ignore taxes and capital allowances in this question.

Required

Given that Howden's shareholders require a real return of 8.5% for projects of this degree of risk, assess the financial viability of this proposal. **(10 marks)**

(c)   Briefly discuss how inflation may complicate the analysis of business financial decisions.

(6 marks)
(Total 20 marks)

EXAMINER'S COMMENTS

General comments

There were two common reasons why candidates performed badly on this paper: insufficient preparation for the examination; and inability to read and answer the question set. In particular, many candidates were ill-equipped to answer the case study question.

In a large number of cases, candidates were particularly badly prepared for Financial Management topics, even for such a basic building block as investment appraisal.

Question 1: examined various areas connected with the effect of project financing on a company's share price.

In part (a), although there were a relatively easy five marks to be obtained here, many candidates seemed to overlook the word 'financially' in the question, and provided instead a lengthy discussion of the logistic aspects. There was ample indication in the question that an investment appraisal was required. For the majority who did conduct a NPV analysis (some offered payback or ARR), common errors were failure to allow for tax and failure to discount at 15% as instructed, using 12% instead, having apparently assumed debt financing. Where tax was allowed for, many candidates introduced 25% capital allowances. No mention of this was made in the question, and in many answers, the year 6 tax outflow mysteriously disappeared. Many answers attempted to incorporate interest outflows in the cash flow profile, betraying a fundamental misunderstanding of the distinction between an investment, a financial decision and the rationale for DCF analysis.

In part (b), many candidates wasted time by providing lengthy descriptions of all types of market efficiency. There was widespread misunderstanding of the meaning of information-efficient; it means that all publicly available information relevant to a company's future prospects is impounded in today's share price. Many candidates declared that it means that all information is available or that the market uses all available information, suggesting strong-form market efficiency. Candidates who understood the subject went on to explain that, in a semi-strong efficient market, it is impossible to make excess returns by trading on recently released information, and that the announcement of Netherby's new project would tend to raise share price as long as the market agrees with the company's assessment of the project (although this depends on how much information is released).

Too many candidates ignored the instruction in the question to abstract from the method of finance. Very few candidates went on to quantify the likely impact on share price. This would be done by spreading the NPV of the project across the existing number of shares or by applying the existing P/E ratio to the increase in EPS.

In part (c), the question implies an assessment of the case for a rights issue rather than a dividend cut, and hence a discussion of the pros and cons of the former. Many candidates did not understand the definition of a rights issue, confusing it with a scrip issue. Most answers gave only two or three good points, limiting their discussion to the respective implications for control, gearing and share price. Many compared a rights issue to other methods of raising equity, and many said that a rights issue does not affect gearing.

In part (d), the key word in the question is 'generally'. It is true that a rights issue can lead to a higher price if the market views the intended use of the funds with favour. More frequently, the share price falls initially, due to uncertainty over the proposed investment or other use of the funds. The second, and more technical, reason for a share price fall is earnings dilution due to issuing more shares and at a discount to the pre-issue market price which is necessary to make the issue look attractive and ensure its success.

There was widespread failure to identify the correct number of shares, the amount which the company would have to raise (it is clear from the question that any such rights issue would be undertaken to finance the restructuring project) and hence the terms of the issue. Most candidates assumed issue terms (eg,) 1-for-4, and then applied it to both cases. Even candidates who could identify the respective numbers of newly-issued shares were unable to compute the resulting theoretical ex-rights price.

In part (e), many candidates assumed that the project would replace all of Netherby's existing activities and that tent distribution would be the only source of income, an incorrect interpretation of the question. Any resulting calculation would show a dramatic reduction in EPS, although the answer would be consistent with the change in EPS due to the project and its financing, ie, equity financing of the project lowers the EPS by 19p from £1.50 to £1.31, and loan financing raises it by 9p to £1.59. Many answers ignored the impact of the project entirely. Although some credit was given to all these approaches, the highest marks were awarded to those who considered both impacts.

A common failing was to ignore taxation in the computation of the EPS. Another error was to work in terms of dividend per share.

Part (f), in many cases , was a lifeline for weaker candidates, but all too often candidates seemed unable to appreciate the distinction between operating or business risk and financial risk. This is fundamental in Managerial Finance. The former relates to factors which impact on operating profit such as security of supply, exchange rate variations, etc, and the latter to the impact of gearing in the financial structure. Marks were not awarded for discussing financial risk.

It was also important that candidates should offer a brief explanation/discussion of the factors they identified rather than a listing, and also suggest how the various risks may be allowed for, as clearly stated in the question.

Question 2: required 5 short written answers.

Part (a) was not well done. This type of question was clearly flagged in the Examiner's article in the *Students' Newsletter*, March 1994. The clear implication was that candidates have not prepared for the economics element of the syllabus. Of those who did attempt an answer, the vast majority confused supply-side policies with control of the money supply, or wrote vague generalities about supply and demand. Attention to the supply side was a keynote of US and UK economic policies in the 1980s, and has been adopted by many other nations. Candidates must develop a greater awareness of the prevailing economic environment and of government economic policy options and priorities.

In part (b), the majority of candidates performed well. However, some candidates failed to appreciate that there can be surplus fixed assets, current assets and investments and also failed to identify the benefits.

Part (c) was one of the questions where candidates did not answer the question set. The definition of a normal loss and its accounting treatment is covered in Paper 3. This question was an attempt to build on that knowledge and asked about the factors needed to be taken into account when establishing a normal loss in process costing.

In part (d), simply listing the definition of 'the environment' was not enough; the question asked how the management accountant monitors the external environment. For those who included the use of budgets and standards in their answer, it was important also to explain how they could assist in monitoring and possibly provide an example. The same is true of financial ratios, market research etc.

Part (e) required consideration of the two questions; one required a critical view of the existing budgeting system and the other an explanation as to how ZBB could overcome its deficiencies. Many candidates did not do justice to the first part and did not really explain how ZBB could overcome its deficiencies. Again, many candidates did not answer the question set but the one that they hoped would be set.

In part (f), most candidates were awarded approximately two or three marks. Although candidates only had to attempt five out of the six sections, many wasted valuable exam time by attempting all six parts. Another cohort of candidates did less than five parts, perhaps because of not revising the areas covered or a shortage of time.

Question 3: required candidates to calculate and comment on the inter-relations of variances in a manufacturing situation.

Overall this question was very well done and candidates did gain high marks.

There were a number of alternative answers which were acceptable eg, using a volume variance in the reconciliation where a flexed budget had not been used in part (a).

However, workings for this type of computational question are important, but it was evident that many candidates lost a lot of valuable exam time by the method they used to compute the variances. Workings for this type of question need to be clear and concise. In part (c), on inter-relationships, many candidates failed to gain marks because they did not look at the inter-relationships between the variances.

Question 4: dealt with interpreting management information.

This was not a very popular question and there were not many answers. Some candidates did not provide their answer in report form. Other failings included: few computations with the figures provided and no attempt to express costs as, for example, a cost per mile; no attempt to discuss the problems being caused by the holding company; and ignoring the request in the question to advise the company as to how it could improve its recording system.

Question 5: concentrated on ratio analysis and the management of working capital.

This question was poorly done, given that ratio analysis is also covered in Paper 1. In part (a), most answers offered a sprinkling of ratios, but often included largely irrelevant ones such as EPS, with little or no attempt to incorporate the figures into the answer. This required an analysis of the company's liquidity problems and an assessment of the extent to which it is overtrading. It was debatable whether many candidates actually understood the meaning of overtrading; relatively few defined, explained or illustrated it, using the figures provided.

Few answers spotted that the increase in fixed assets appeared to have been largely financed out of working capital and that the company now needed to raise long-term finance. The better candidates queried the wisdom of the dividend increase in these circumstances.

In part (b), the main errors were: failure to include the interest savings due to lower debtor levels under one or both options; confining the discount cost to the debtors figure rather than to 50% of the total sales. Few answers offered much in the way of a concluding assessment, although several went to the opposite (and unrewarding) extreme of giving no calculation at all, but providing a lengthy discussion of the pros and cons of each option. Many candidates omitted this section altogether.

Question 6: was concerned with investment appraisal and the impact of inflation upon decision making.

This was considerably less popular than question 5, but for candidates with good knowledge of DCF methods, offered relatively easy marks. In part (a), candidates seemed generally aware of the corrosive impact of inflation, and the need to achieve a higher nominal return, and were often able to reproduce the Fisher equation. However, very few were able to give a coherent distinction between the two approaches to project evaluation under inflation.

In part (b), candidates had some idea how to inflate cash flows. Common errors were: inclusion of the sunk cost; neglect of the opportunity cost of the building; neglect of the residual values of the equipment and/or building; failure to allow for working capital release, either with or without any adjustment; and over-inclusion of fixed overheads. However, the main and most culpable error was incorrect specification of the discount rate, even among those who had specified the Fisher equation correctly in section (a).

In part (c), candidates failed to read the wording of this section. Most answers were applied to investment decisions although this was not specified in the question, the intention being to elicit a broader appreciation of the problems which inflation inflicts on business financial decision-makers in general.

Those who discussed the problems of forecasting general inflation and also rates specific to investment projects were given credit but it was disappointing that so few answers went beyond this and drew to any extent upon knowledge of economics.

ANSWERS TO JUNE 1994 EXAMINATION

26   (Answer 1 of examination)

(a)   Assuming that the restructuring cost is a revenue item, and that all costs are incurred in year 0, the estimated cash flow profile is:

Cash flow profile (£m)

Item	0	1	2	3	4	5	6
Closure costs	(5)						
Tax saving		1.65					
Cash flow increase		2.00	2.00	2.00	2.00	2.00	
Tax payment			(0.66)	(0.66)	(0.66)	(0.66)	(0.66)
	(5)	3.65	1.34	1.34	1.34	1.34	(0.66)

$$\text{NPV (£m)} = -5 + 1.65(\text{PVIF}_{15,1}) + 2(\text{PVIFA}_{15,5}) - 0.66(\text{PVIFA}_{15,6} - \text{PVIFA}_{15,1})$$

$$= -5 + 1.65(0.870) + 2(3.352) - 0.66(3.784 - 0.870)$$

$$= -5 + 1.44 + 6.70 - 1.92 = +1.22 \text{ (ie, } + £1.22\text{m)}$$

Hence, the restructuring appears worthwhile.

(*Tutorial note:* clearly a cash budget form of presentation was inappropriate in this case.)

(b)   A semi-strong efficient capital market is one where security prices reflect all publicly-available information, including both the record of the past pattern of share price movements and all information released to the market about company earnings prospects. In such a market, security prices will rapidly adjust to the advent of new information relevant to the future income-earning capacity of the enterprise concerned, such as a change in its chief executive, or the signing of a new export order. As a result of the speed of the market's reaction to this type of news, it is not possible to make excess gains by trading in the wake of its release. Only market participants lucky enough already to be holding the share in question will achieve super-normal returns.

In the case of Netherby, when it releases information about its change in market-servicing policy, the value of the company should rise by the value of the project, assuming that the market as a whole agrees with the assessment of its net benefits, and is unconcerned by financing implications.

Net present value of the project = £1.22m

Number of 50p ordinary shares in issue = £5m × 2 = 10m shares

Increase in market price = £1.22m/10m = 12.2p per share.

(Alternatively, the answer could be expressed in terms of Netherby's price-earnings ratio. This would necessitate an assumption about Netherby's sustainable future earnings per share after tax).

(c)   Arguments for and against making a rights issue include the following:

For

(i)   A rights issue enables the company to at least maintain its dividends, thus avoiding both upsetting the clientele of shareholders, and also giving negative signals to the market.

(ii)   It may be easy to accomplish on a bull market.

(iii)   A rights issue automatically lowers the company's gearing ratio.

(iv)   The finance is guaranteed if the issue is fully underwritten.

(v)   It has a neutral impact on voting control, unless the underwriters are obliged to purchase significant blocks of shares, and unless existing shareholders sell their rights to other investors.

(vi)   It might give the impression that the company is expanding vigorously, although this appears not to be the case with Netherby.

Against

(i)   Rights issues normally are made at a discount, which usually involves diluting the historic earnings per share of existing shareholders. However, when the possible uses of the proceeds of the issue are considered, the *prospective* EPS could rise by virtue of investment in a worthwhile project, or in the case of a company earning low or no profits, the interest earnings on un-invested capital alone might serve to raise the EPS.

(ii)   Underwriters' fees and other administrative expenses of the issue may be costly, although the latter may be avoided by applying a sufficiently deep discount.

(iii)   The market is often sceptical about the reason for a rights issue, tending to assume that the company is desperate for cash. The deeper the discount involved, the greater the degree of scepticism.

(iv)   It is difficult to make a rights issue on a bear market, without leaving some of the shares with the underwriters. A rights issue which 'fails' in this respect is both bad for the company's image and may also result in higher underwriters' fees for any subsequent rights issue.

(v)   A rights issue usually forces shareholders to act, either by subscribing direct or by selling the rights, although the company may undertake to reimburse shareholders not subscribing to the issue for the loss in value of their shares. (This is done by selling the rights on behalf of shareholders and paying over the sum realised, net of dealing costs.)

(d)   (*Note:* candidates are not expected to display a knowledge of FRS 14 which is the province of Paper 10).

A rights issue normally has to be issued at a discount in order, firstly, to make the shares appear attractive, but more importantly, to safeguard against a fall in the market price below the issue price prior to closure of the offer. If this should happen, the issue would fail as investors wishing to increase their stakes in the company could do so more cheaply by buying on the open market. Because of the discount, a rights issue has the effect of diluting the existing earnings per share across a larger number of shares, although the depressing effect on share price is partly countered by the increased cash holdings of the company.

The two possible issue prices are now evaluated:

(i)   *A price of £1*

It is assumed that to raise £5m, the company must issue £5m/£1 = 5m new shares at the issue price of £1.

In practice, it is possible that the number of new shares required might be lower than this, as the post-tax cost of the project is less than £5m due to the (delayed) tax savings generated. The company might elect to use short-term borrowing to bridge the delay in receiving these tax savings, thus obviating the need for the full £5m.

Ignoring this argument, the terms of the issue would be '1-for-2' ie, for every two shares currently held, owners are offered the right to purchase one new share at the deeply-discounted price of £1.

The ex-rights price will be:

[Market value of 2 shares before the issue + cash consideration]/3

= [(2 × £3) + £1]/3 = £7/3 = £2.33

(ii)   *Similarly, if the issue price is £2*, the required number of new shares = £5m/£2 = 2.5m, and the terms will have to be '1 -for-4'

The ex-rights price will be [(4 × £3) + £2]/5 = £14/5 = £2.80.

Clearly, the smaller the discount to the market price, the higher the ex-rights price.

(e)   Ignoring the impact of the benefits of the new project:

The rights issue at £2 involves 2.5m new shares.

The EPS was £15m/10m = £1.50p per share.

Hence, EPS becomes $\dfrac{£15m}{10m + 2.5m} = £1.20$

With the debt financing, the interest charge net of tax = [12% × £5m] [1 − 33%] = £0.40m

Hence, EPS becomes $\dfrac{£15m − £0.40m}{10m} = £1.46$

Allowing for the benefits of the new project

The annual profit yielded by the proposal, after tax at 33% = (£2m × 0.67) = £1.34m, although the cash flow benefit in the first year is £2m due to the tax delay.

After the rights issue, the prospective EPS will become:

[£15m + £1.34m]/12.5m = £1.31 per share

With debt finance, the financing cost, net of tax relief, of £0.40m pa reduces the net return from the project to (£1.34m − £0.40m) = £0.94m pa.

(In the first year, the cash flow cost will be the full pre-tax interest payment. Thereafter, Netherby will receive annual cash flow benefits from the series of tax savings.)

The EPS will be: £15.94m/10m = £1.59 per share.

Therefore, in terms of the effect on EPS, the debt-financing alternative is preferable, although it may increase financial risk.

(f)   A range of factors could be listed here. Among the major sources of risk are the following:

(i)   *Reliability of supply.* This can be secured by inclusion of penalty clauses in the contract, although these will have to be enforceable. The intermediation of the European Bank for Reconstruction and Development may enhance this.

(ii)   *The quality of the product.* Again, a penalty clause may assist, although a more constructive approach might be to assign a UK-trained total quality management (TQM) expert to the Hungarian operation to oversee quality control.

(iii)   *Market resistance to an imported product.* This seems less of a risk, if retailers are genuinely impressed with the product, and especially as there are doubts over the quality of the existing product.

(iv)   *Exchange rate variations.* Netherby is exposed to the risk of sterling depreciating against the Hungarian currency, thus increasing the sterling cost of the product. There are various ways of hedging against foreign exchange risk, of which use of the forward market is probably the simplest. Alternatively, Netherby could try to match the risk by finding a Hungarian customer for its other goods.

(v)   *Renewal of the contract.* What is likely to happen after five years? To obtain a two-way protection, Netherby might write into the contract an option to renew after five years. If the product requires re-design, Netherby could offer to finance part of the costs in exchange for this option.

27   (Answer 2 of examination)

(a)   As the difficulties of aggregate demand management (eg, crowding out of the private sector by the public sector, and the inflationary dangers of financing a state deficit) have become more apparent, governments have increasingly turned to 'Monetarist' policy nostrums, which, *inter alia,* urge the removal of barriers to the free flow of resources between alternative uses. So-called supply-side policies are designed to allow the supply of goods and services to adjust rapidly and smoothly to alterations in the pattern of demand, as expressed by the signals emitted by freely-functioning markets ie, prices.

Monetarists argue that a dynamic economy can only operate efficiently if market prices offer clear signals to resource owners regarding their most profitable uses. Rather than using budgetary policies to manage demand, they argue that the authorities should create a stable, non-inflationary economic framework to allow the economy to reach its own natural equilibrium. In their view, the role of the state should be merely to ensure that impediments to the free flow of resources, including labour, should be minimised.

Examples of measures to improve the efficiency of the market system are re-training schemes and mobility allowances to enable workers to switch between alternative occupations and locations, and abolition of minimum wage legislation, which, by artificially inflating wages above the market level, may have prevented some firms from offering more employment.

(b)   A vast amount of finance can be tied up in surplus assets. Surplus assets can be unwanted fixed assets such as plant, machinery, fixtures, equipment etc, or unwanted current assets eg, stocks of finished goods, components, fuels and raw materials.

If such assets can be identified and disposed of the cash which is generated can be used to purchase fixed assets or to finance working capital or to buy stocks and shares.

However, the disposal of surplus assets does provide other benefits. The space used for the fixed assets or inventory can be used for other purposes or even sub-let or sold. Thus the company could expand its operations without having to find more premises. Also, if inventory levels are reduced certain holding costs eg, insurance will tend to decrease.

The down side to this strategy is, firstly, it is difficult to identify surplus assets and secondly, it is not always easy to find a buyer.

(c)   The computation of a 'normal loss' is not an easy task. It is quite difficult to define in quantitative terms what is normal and acceptable.

The 'normal loss' is the loss which is expected to occur under normal operating conditions.

The computation of the normal loss will involve a certain degree of subjective judgement and take account of past performance and future expectations regarding:

–   the expected level of activity
–   the efficiency of the equipment used
–   the competence of the labour force
–   the quality of the materials etc.

The normal loss, because it is expected, is regarded as part of the cost of the process to which it relates. It is therefore valued at nil and the cost of the normal loss units absorbed by the good units. The effect being to increase the cost per unit.

(d)   The management accountant has to make assumptions about the external environment in which the firm operates eg, for the purpose of setting budgets and standards. The management accountant can monitor the following areas of the external environment:

  –   political factors eg, proposed legislation
  –   social influences eg, 'green issues'
  –   economic considerations eg, fiscal policy
  –   technological developments eg, new equipment,

using a variety of sources of data eg, TV, quality newspapers, professional and trade journals, government statistics and information from Chambers of Commerce etc.

In addition, there is also the need to monitor factor markets, product markets and competitors eg, changes in the availability of certain sources of finance and/or changes in the pricing policies of competitors.

A change in the external environment can dramatically affect the budgets, standards and other information generated by the management accounting function. Such monitoring may also help to highlight threats and opportunities and thus contribute towards the firm's long-term survival.

(e)   The statement made indicates that the organisation concerned is currently using an incremental budgeting approach. This approach can in addition to taking into account the previous year's figures plus inflation, also take account of anticipated changes.

This cannot be regarded as a satisfactory way of setting targets. One of the aims of budgetary control is to set targets against which actual performance can be measured. Thus, the targets set should be realistic, fair and achievable.

Zero-based-budgeting (ZBB) attempts to change the attitudes of managers, from the expectation of receiving an incremental increase each year to one of justifying why they need the budget. In ZBB, managers have to assign priorities and justify each activity/programme. The overall aim is to increase efficiency by obtaining better value for money eg,. by getting rid of obsolete activities, thus making better use of scarce resources between competing factions. However, it should be noted that the introduction of ZBB could prove to be quite costly.

(f)   The management accountant can use time series analysis to help make assumptions about the future. It can be particularly helpful during the budget preparation period eg, sales forecasting, predicting future product demand. However, the use of time series data rests on the assumption that the historical relationships between past and future sales will continue.

It can enable the management accountant to detect/identify trends eg, by using graphical representations and/or moving averages. These can be classified into:

  –   seasonal trends ie, those fluctuations which change each year, and
  –   cyclical trends ie, changes which take place every so many years eg, every five years.
  –   abnormal, irregular or erratic fluctuations ie, 'one off happenings.'

28   (Answer 3 of examination)

(a)   **Profit statements**

*(15,400 units)**	Standard		Actual	
	£	£	£	£
Sales (at £140)		2,156,000	(at £138.25)	2,129,050
Less: Costs				
Materials				
Mat. 007				
(6 kilos × 15,400)				
= 92,400 × £12.25	1,131,900		1,256,640	
			(given)	

Mat. XL90 (3 kilos × 15,400) = 46,200 × £3.20	147,840	132,979 (given)
Labour (4.5 hours × 15,400) = 69,300 × £8.40	582,120	612,766 (given)
Fixed overheads	86,400 (given)	96,840 (given)
	1,948,260	2,099,225
Profit	207,740	29,825

* A standard based on the original budget of 16,000 units could have been used in part (a) and then adjusted by means of a sales volume variance in part (b).

(b)   **Reconciliation**

			£
Standard profit on 15,400 units (as above)			207,740

Variance	£	*(+)* *Favourable* £	*(−)* *Adverse* £
Sales price Standard − Actual (£2,156,000 − £2,129,050)			26,950
Materials			
Mat. 007 usage (Standard − Actual) × Standard price (92,400 − 98,560) × £12.25**			75,460
Mat. XL90 usage (Standard − Actual) × Standard price (46,200 − 42,350) × £3.20		12,320	
Mat. 007 Price (Actual quantity × Actual price) (Actual quantity × Standard price)	1,256,640 1,207,360		
			49,280
Mat. XL90 Price (Actual quantity × Actual price) (Actual quantity × Standard price)	132,979 135,520		
		2,541	
Labour			
Efficiency Standard hours − Actual hours* (69,300 − 70,840) = 1,540 × Standard rate £8.40			12,936
Rate Standard − Actual (£8.40 − 8.65) = £0.25 × Actual hours 70,840			17,710

Overheads

Fixed overheads
  Standard – Actual
  (£86,400 – £96,840)   10,440

                                        14,861   192,776   (177,915) (A)

Actual profit   29,825

* $\dfrac{£612,766}{£8.65}$ = 70,840 hours

** Note that it was not really necessary to do a material mix and material yield variance, but provided they added back to the material usage variances they were acceptable.

(c)   Variances may be inter-related eg, the reason why one variance is favourable could also help explain why another variance is adverse.

Using poor quality materials could result in a favourable price variance because of paying a lower price. The poor quality material could be the cause of an adverse material usage variance and an adverse labour efficiency variance eg, materials more difficult to work with, more rejects/spoilt work, more waste.

If a higher grade of labour was used, compared with that which was planned, there would most certainly be an adverse labour rate variance. The higher skill level employed could well be the reason for a favourable labour efficiency variance and a favourable material usage variance eg, a lower number of rejects and less waste of materials.

29   (Answer 4 of examination)

REPORT

To: Mrs Cepheus   15 January 19X5
             Chief Executive
             Cepheus Transport Co Ltd

An evaluation of current performance and the management accounting information

I have now completed my evaluation of the data which you supplied on 5 January 19X5. From the limited amount of data which you provided, it can be observed that currently, your company is making an overall profit of £21,870 which is computed as follows:

	£
Revenue received	165,702
Less: Operating costs (including depreciation)	85,612
Gross profit	80,090
Less: Administration costs and other fixed overheads (including rent)	58,220
Net profit	21,870

The revenue generated *per mile* is:

Type of vehicle	Type F	Type P	Type U
From holding company	£1.825	£1.675	£1.225
From other companies	£3.200	£2.645	£1.900
Operating cost (per mile) (including depreciation)	£1.055	£1.082	£1.062

The revenue per mile for each type of vehicle is in excess of the operating cost per mile. However, the revenue per mile from the holding company is well below that which is generated from dealing with other companies. This will have the effect of increasing the holding company's own profits, because they are apparently paying below market rates for the service which you provide, and reducing your own profits. If you are to be judged on your performance, it is important that you take up this matter with the holding company. If the holding company can pay rates which are nearer to the market rates this will raise your profits and provide you with funds for the expansion of your business and for the replacement of motor vehicles and other fixed assets.

Depreciation policy

In my opinion, in view of the high cost of motor vehicles, it would be fairer to compute your depreciation using the 'time apportionment' basis ie, you charge depreciation on say a month-by-month basis, from the date of purchase to the date of disposal.

Information needed

Should you wish me to do a more in depth appraisal of your performance I would need copies of your published accounts and access to your financial accounting recording system.

Pricing policy

There was also insufficient data relating to your pricing policy. However, I must stress the need for you to monitor:

– your costs;

– your competitors eg, their prices and services;

– the economic environment eg, social factors, legislation etc. which may have a direct impact on your business.

Improvements to the management accounting information system

I suggest that you consider giving a higher priority to management accounting, so that you may receive information which is up-to-date, and relevant, information which will help you with planning, control and decision-making. I propose that you consider making the following improvements:

More detailed records for each individual motor vehicle of:

– the revenue, analysed between the holding company and others;
– their operating costs in terms of fuel, wages, insurance, etc;
– the amount spent on repairs and maintenance;
– the depreciation charged to date, using the time apportionment basis;
– the mileage;
– an analysis of waiting time;
– the revenue per mile, cost per mile, fuel consumption per mile etc.

At the moment, the fuel consumption can only be calculated for each group of vehicles, as follows:

Vehicle	Type F	Type P	Type U
Diesel (gallons) (Fuel cost ÷ 2)	2,184	702	876
Miles	40,600	15,520	24,480
Miles per gallon	18.59	22.11	27.95

The information above provides the average miles per gallon for each class of motor vehicle. Hidden in the average, could be one or more vehicles which for various reasons are performing badly. The information needed to produce this analysis can be extracted from the log sheets/records which are kept by the drivers.

Using budgetary control

Budgets will provide the company with targets for revenues and costs and provide a means of control via the frequent comparison of budgeted and actual figures. This should help the company to take appropriate corrective action to put right that which is not going according to plan. All the aspects of the business would be taken into account in producing the 'master budget' ie, a budgeted trading and profit and loss account, balance sheet and cash budget.

To illustrate the need for budgeting, consider its application to the repairs and maintenance of vehicles expenditure. The budgeting process will require planning of what maintenance is to be done and when it is to be done for each vehicle. Spending targets will be compared with actuals on say, a monthly basis, and significant adverse variances highlighted on reports and investigated so that management can decide upon what action needs to be taken.

Devoting more time/resources to the management accounting activities

You need information for planning, control and decision-making purposes. You need information which can help you:

- make vehicle-by-vehicle internal comparisons;
- to decide whether or not to use a sub-contractor;
- to compare buying vehicles with leasing vehicles;
- to review the possibility of using other forms of transport eg, rail, air, sea;
- to evaluate the cost of carrying out your own maintenance of vehicles with the cost of using a garage;
- to formulate your pricing policy;
- to assess the performance of vehicles loaned to you for testing purposes.

Improving efficiency

Other areas which you will need to look at are:

- route planning, to avoid hold-ups that could cost you time and money;
- scheduling, to make the best possible use of vehicles in terms of capacity, loading etc;
- monitoring the efficiency of keeping to delivery times;
- making use of idle capacity, especially on return journeys.

Fixed costs

One final observation which needs to be drawn to your attention is the high level of fixed costs which you have to recover. The fixed costs make up around 63% of the operating costs, excluding the overtime premium and the fixed element, if any, included in the operating and maintenance costs. The company's current break-even point, based on the above assumptions, may be computed as follows:

	£'000
Revenue	166
Less: Variable costs	31
Contribution	135 (81 % of the revenue)

$$\text{Fixed costs } £54,000 \times \frac{100}{81} = £67,000 \text{ break-even point (40\% of revenue)}$$

To break even, the company needs to operate at around 40% of current capacity. In the event of a downturn in the economy causing the company's operations to fall below its break-even point, a loss-making situation would arise.

Conclusions and recommendations

One of the principal findings to the lower earnings made was in connection with the work performed for the holding company. If you are to stand on your own feet and be responsible for your own performance, you need to be able to charge the holding company a fair price. This should enable you to generate more funds for re-investment and make you better able to assess your profitability.

More resources need to be devoted to the provision/ supply of management accounting information which will assist you to plan and control the company more effectively and help you with your decision-making. This includes introducing a system of budgetary control which provides targets for both costs and revenues, and by continuous comparison with actuals, provides an 'early warning' of where things are going wrong.

In view of the limited amount of data which was provided, and the wide scope of this report, I will be pleased to discuss any of the above matters with you personally in greater detail.

Philip Ness FCCA

---

30   **(Answer 5 of examination)**

(a)   Comparison of the two balance sheets reveals that Ewden has suffered a significant fall in liquidity – cash balances have fallen sharply from £1.5m (probably an unnecessarily high level) in 1992 to just £0.1m in 1993 while an overdraft of £0.2m has appeared, reflecting a reduction in net cash resources of £1.6m. However, company profitability remains satisfactory, indicating that the run-down in liquidity has been required to finance the acquisition of assets.

Analysis of the financial statements reveals that Ewden has been able to reinvest £3.0m of retained earnings (plus an unspecified amount of depreciation provisions) in order to fund a substantial net increase in fixed assets of £3.0m, presumably to support an output expansion. It is possible that this significant capacity increase might have been obtained via acquisition of another company. Such a large increase implies that during the past recession, Ewden had cut back its capacity in order to reduce costs.

But as well as an increase in fixed assets, Ewden has invested £0.8m in stocks and £1.0m in debtors. This substantial investment in working capital is partially offset by an increase in trade and other creditors of £0.2m making a total increase in working capital of £1.6m.

No additional external long-term finance has been raised, so the increased investment in fixed assets and working capital has had to be financed by a significant reduction in cash balances and the opening-up of a bank overdraft, resulting in a heavy net outflow of liquid resources of £1.6m.

Overtrading is the term applied to a company which rapidly increases its turnover without having sufficient capital backing, hence the alternative term 'under-capitalisation'. Output increases are often obtained by more intensive utilisation of existing fixed assets, and growth tends to be financed by more intensive use of working capital. Overtrading companies are often unable or unwilling to raise long-term capital and thus tend to rely more heavily on short-term sources such as creditors and bank overdrafts. Debtors usually increase sharply as the company follows a more generous trade credit policy in order to win sales, while stocks tend to increase as the company attempts to produce at a faster rate ahead of increases in demand. Overtrading is thus characterised by rising borrowings and a declining liquidity position in terms of the quick ratio, if not always according to the current ratio.

The accounts indicate some of the signs of overtrading, although the case is not proven.

Checking Ewden's ratios against the common symptoms of overtrading:

(i)   Fall in the liquidity ratios. For Ewden, the current ratio falls from 2.25 to 2.04, which does not seem to indicate a serious decline in liquidity, although the extent of the decline in the quick ratio, (ie, excluding stocks), from 1.55 to 1.13, might give more cause for concern, especially as the bulk of its quick assets (96%) are in the form of debtors.

(ii)   Rapid increase in turnover – 33% for Ewden.

(iii)   Sharp increase in the sales-to-fixed assets ratio. For Ewden, this has remained steady at 1.33 because the increase in sales has been supported by an increase in fixed assets, suggesting that the output increase was well-planned.

(iv)   Increase in stocks in relation to turnover. For Ewden, the increase is from 11.7% (43 days) to 13.8% (50 days), which is marked but hardly dramatic.

           Measured against cost of sales, the equivalent figures are 20% (73 days) for 1992 and 24% (88 days) for 1993, a more pronounced increase in stockholding.

(v)   Increase in debtors. Ewden's accounts receivable rise as a percentage of sales from 13.3% (49 days) to 16.3% (59 days). This does seem to represent a significant loosening of control over debtors.

(vi)   Increase in the trade credit period. The ratio of trade creditors to cost of goods sold rises slightly from 21.4% (78 days) to 21.8% (80 days). The trade credit period is considerably longer (80 days versus 59 days) than the debtor collection period, suggesting that the company is exploiting the generosity of suppliers in order to enhance sales.

(vii)   Increase in short-term borrowing and a decline in cash balances. Clearly, this has happened to Ewden.

(viii) Increase in gearing. Taking the ratio of long and short-term debt-to-equity as the appropriate measure, gearing has actually fallen (from a relatively low level of 21% to 18%) despite the opening of the overdraft, primarily due to the increase in equity via retentions.

(ix)   Fall in the profit margin. In terms of its gross profit margin (operating profit-to-sales), Ewden actually achieves an increase from 42% to 43%, although there is a marginal fall in the ratio of profit after tax-to-sales from 31.7% to 31.3%. This does not suggest that Ewden is using aggressive price discounting in an attempt to increase sales.

It seems that Ewden's liquidity is under pressure but the company displays by no means all the classic signs of overtrading. Ewden might consider issuing further long-term securities if it wishes to support a further sales surge. If sales are expected to stabilise, the recent increase in capacity should be sufficient to produce the desired output, enabling the liquidity position to be repaired via cash flow, which was substantial in 1993, before allowing for the financing of the capital investment.

(b)   **The discount**

At December 1993, debtors were £2.6m. The debtor collection period was: £2.6m/£16m × 365 = 59 days.

The 2% discount would lower this to 10 days for 50% of customers reducing average debtor days to:

$(50\% \times 59) + (50\% \times 10) = 34.5$ days

The cost of the discount (ignoring any beneficial impact on sales volume) would be:

$(2\% \times 50\% \times £16m) = £160,000$

The revised sales value estimate would be $(£16m - £160,000) = £15.84m$

Average debtors would become $\dfrac{34.5}{365} \times £15.84m = £1,497,206$

The interest saving would be $18\% \times (£2.6m - £1.497m) = £198,540$

Set against the cost of the discount, the net benefit would be:

$(£198,540 - £160,000) = £38,540$

Factoring

Reduction in debtor days = (59 – 45)	=	14 days
Reduction in debtors = $\dfrac{14}{365} \times £16m$	=	£613,699
Interest saving = (18% × £613,698)	=	£110,466
Administrative savings	=	£100,000
Service charge = (1.5% × £16m)	=	£240,000
Net cost = (£240,000) + £100,000 + £110,466	=	(£29,534)

The figures imply that the discount policy is preferable but this relies on the appropriate percentage of customers actually taking up the discount and paying on time. Given that debtor days are currently 59, it seems rather optimistic to expect that half of Ewden's customers will be sufficiently impressed by the discount as to advance their settlement by 49 days. Conversely, the assessment of the value of using the factor depends on the factor successfully lowering Ewden's debtor days. Any tendency for the factor to retain these cash flow benefits for himself, rather than passing them on to Ewden, will further increase the net cost of the factoring option. In this respect, the two parties should clearly specify their expectations and requirements from the factoring arrangement.

31	(Answer 6 of examination)

(a)   Investors advance capital to companies expecting a reward for both the delay in waiting for their returns (time value of money) and also for the risks to which they expose their capital (risk premium). In addition, if prices in general are rising, shareholders require compensation for the erosion in the real value of their capital.

If, for example, in the absence of inflation, shareholders require a company to offer a return of 10%, the need to cover 5% price inflation will raise the overall required return to about 15%. If people in general expect a particular rate of inflation, the structure of interest rates in the capital market will adjust to incorporate these inflationary expectations. This is known as the 'Fisher effect'.

More precisely, the relationship between the real required return (r) and the nominal rate, (m), the rate which includes an allowance for inflation, is given by: $(1 + r) \times (1 + p) = (1 + m)$ where p is the expected rate of inflation.

It is essential when evaluating an investment project under inflation that future expected price level changes are treated in a consistent way. Companies may correctly allow for inflation in two ways each of which computes the real value of an investment project:

(i)   Inflate the future expected cash flows at the expected rate of inflation (allowing for inflation rates specific to the project) and discount at m, the fully-inflated rate – the 'money terms' approach.

(ii)   Strip out the inflation element from the market-determined rate and apply the resulting real rate of return, r, to the stream of cash flows expressed in today's or constant prices – the 'real terms' approach.

(*Tutorial note:* The answer implies that it is possible to determine a 'real' rate of return which can then be adjusted in the light of estimated future rates of inflation. The most likely method of calculating a company's required rate of return will actually produce a 'money cost of capital'. To produce a 'real' cost of capital requires some tinkering with this initial calculation.)

(b)   First, the relevant set-up cost needs identification. The offer of £2m for the building, if rejected, represents an opportunity cost, although this appears to be compensated by its predicted eventual resale value of £3m. The cost of the market research study has to be met irrespective of the decision to proceed with the project or not and is thus not relevant.

Secondly, incremental costs and revenues are identified. All other items are avoidable except the element of apportioned overhead, leaving the incremental overhead alone to include in the evaluation.

Thirdly, all items of incremental cash flow, including this additional overhead, must be adjusted for their respective rates of inflation. Because (with the exception of labour and variable overhead) the inflation rates differ, a disaggregated approach is required.

The appropriate discount rate is given by:

$$(1 + p) \times (1 + r) - 1 = m = (1.06) \times (1.085) - 1 = 15\%$$

Assuming that the inflated costs and prices apply from and including the first year of operation, the cash-flow profile is:

Cash flow profile	(£m)		Time			
Item	0	1	2	3	4	5
Equipment	(10.50)					2.00
Foregone sale of buildings	(2.00)					
Residual value of building						3.00
Working capital*	(0.50)					0.50
Revenue		5.04	5.29	5.56	5.83	6.13
Materials		(0.62)	(0.64)	(0.66)	(0.68)	(0.70)
Labour and variable overhead		(0.43)	(0.46)	(0.49)	(0.52)	(0.56)
Fixed overhead		(0.53)	(0.55)	(0.58)	(0.61)	(0.64)
Net cash flows	(13.00)	3.46	3.64	3.83	4.02	9.73
Present value at 15%	(13.00)	3.01	2.75	2.52	2.30	4.84

NPV = +£2.42m, therefore, the project appears to be acceptable.

However, the financial viability of the project depends quite heavily on the estimate of the residual value of the building and equipment.

Note: the working capital cash recovery towards the end of the project is approximately equal to the initial investment in stocks because the rate of material cost inflation tends to cancel out the JIT-induced reduction in volume, leading to roughly constant stock-holding in value terms throughout most of the project life-span.

(c)   In addition to the problems offered for investment appraisal such as forecasting the various rates of inflation relevant to the project, inflation poses a wider range of difficulties in a variety of business decision areas.

Inflation may pose a problem for businesses if it distorts the signals transmitted by the market. In the absence of inflation, the price system should translate the shifting patterns of consumer demand into price signals to which producers respond in order to plan current and future output levels. If demand for a product rises, the higher price indicates the desirability of switching existing production capacity to producing the good or of laying down new capacity.

Under inflation, however, the producer may lose confidence that the correct signals are being transmitted, especially if the prices of goods and services inflate at different rates. He may thus be inclined to delay undertaking new investment. This applies particularly if price rises are unexpected and erratic.

Equally, it becomes more difficult to evaluate the performance of whole businesses and individual segments when prices are inflating. A poor operating performance may be masked by price inflation, especially if the price of the product sold is increasing at a rate faster than prices in general or if operating costs are inflating more slowly. The rate of return on capital achieved by a business is most usefully expressed in real terms by removing the effect on profits of generally rising prices (or better still, the effect of company-specific inflation). The capital base of the company should also be expressed in meaningful terms. A poor profit result may translate into a high ROI if the capital base is measured in historic terms. Unless these sorts of adjustment are made, inflation hinders the attempt to measure company performance on a consistent basis and thus can cloud the judgement of providers of capital in seeking out the most profitable areas for investment.

DECEMBER 1994 QUESTIONS

Section A – This question is compulsory and MUST be attempted

32   (Question 1 of examination)

The budgeted balance sheet data of Kwan Tong Umbago Ltd is as follows:

1 March 19X5

		Cost £	Depreciation to date £	Net £
Fixed assets				
	Land and buildings	500,000	–	500,000
	Machinery and equipment	124,000	84,500	39,500
	Motor vehicles	42,000	16,400	25,600
		666,000	100,900	565,100

Working capital

Current assets			
	Stock of raw materials (100 units)	4,320	
	Stock of finished goods (110 units)*	10,450	
	Debtors (January £7,680, February £10,400)	18,080	
	Cash and bank	6,790	
		39,640	
Less:	Current liabilities		
	Creditors (raw materials)	3,900	
			35,740
			600,840

Represented by		
	Ordinary share capital (fully paid) £1 shares	500,000
	Share premium	60,000
	Profit and loss account	40,840
		600,840

* The stock of finished goods was valued at marginal cost

The estimates for the next four month period are as follows:

	March	April	May	June
Sales (units)	80	84	96	94
Production (units)	70	75	90	90
Purchases of raw materials (units)	80	80	85	85
Wages and variable overheads at £65 per unit	£4,550	£4,875	£5,850	£5,850
Fixed overheads	£1,200	£1,200	£1,200	£1,200

The company intends to sell each unit for £219 and has estimated that it will have to pay £45 per unit for raw materials. One unit of raw material is needed for each unit of finished product.

All sales and purchases of raw materials are on credit. Debtors are allowed two months' credit and suppliers of raw materials are paid after one month's credit. The wages, variable overheads and fixed overheads are paid in the month in which they are incurred.

Cash from a loan secured on the land and buildings of £120,000 at an interest rate of 7.5% is due to be received on 1 May. Machinery costing £112,000 will be received in May and paid for in June.

The loan interest is payable half yearly from September onwards. An interim dividend to 31 March 19X5 of £12,500 will be paid in June.

Depreciation for the four months, including that on the new machinery is:

- Machinery and equipment £15,733
- Motor vehicles £3,500

The company uses the FIFO method of stock valuation. Ignore taxation.

Required

(a)   Calculate and present the raw materials budget and finished goods budget in terms of units, for each month from March to June inclusive.   **(5 marks)**

(b)   Calculate the corresponding sales budgets, the production cost budgets and the budgeted closing debtors, creditors and stocks in terms of value.   **(5 marks)**

(c)   Prepare and present a cash budget for each of the four months.   **(6 marks)**

(d)   Prepare a master budget ie, a budgeted trading and profit and loss account for the four months to 30 June 19X5, and budgeted balance sheet as at 30 June 19X5.   **(10 marks)**

(e)   Advise the company about possible ways in which it can improve its cash management.

                                                                                            (9 marks)
                                                                                       (Total 35 marks)

Section B - This question is compulsory and MUST be attempted

---

33   (Question 2 of examination)

Answer FIVE of the six parts of this question

(a)   The following two debenture stocks are both traded on the London Stock Exchange:

   (i)   9% debentures issued by Hammer plc, redeemable in early 1996 at their £100 par value. Each debenture is convertible at any time from now onwards into 20 ordinary shares. The current market price per ordinary share is £3.50 (ex dividend).

   (ii) 7% debentures issued by Nail plc, redeemable in five years time at their £100 par value. Each debenture is convertible into 25 ordinary shares in three years time. The current ordinary share price is £4.10 (ex dividend).

   Explain what factors will influence the respective *current* market values of these two convertible stocks.

   (Note: you are not required to perform precise valuations.)   **(5 marks)**

(b)   Briefly explain the methods whereby a company can obtain a quotation for its shares on the London Stock Exchange.   **(5 marks)**

(c)   It is becoming increasingly common for companies to offer their shareholders a choice between a cash dividend or an equivalent scrip issue of shares.

Briefly consider the advantages of scrip dividends from the viewpoint of:

(i)   the company; and
(ii)   the shareholders.   **(5 marks)**

(d)   Distinguish between factoring and invoice discounting, explaining the benefits which companies obtain from each.   **(5 marks)**

(e)   Explain the main *economic* objectives underlying the widespread practice of privatising state-owned companies.   **(5 marks)**

(f)   Explain briefly the relevance of the concepts of 'price elasticity' and the 'cross elasticity' of demand to the product pricing decision.   **(5 marks)**
                                                                                            (Total 25 marks)

Section C - ONE question ONLY to be attempted

34   (Question 3 of examination)

The following budget and actual data relates to Cassiop plc for the past three periods:

Budget	*Period 1*	*Period 2*	*Period 3*
Sales (units)	10,000	14,000	12,200
Production (units)	8,000	14,200	12,400
Fixed overheads	£10,400	£19,170	£17,360
Actual			
Sales (units)	9,600	12,400	10,200
Production (units)	8,400	13,600	9,200
Fixed overheads	£11,200	£18,320	£16,740

The value of the opening and closing stock of the units produced is arrived at by using FIFO. The budgeted and actual opening stock for period 1 was 2,600 units and its valuation included £3,315 of fixed overheads. The company absorbs its fixed overheads via a predetermined fixed overhead rate per unit which is the same for each period. It is assumed that variable costs per unit and selling prices per unit remained the same for each of the periods.

Required

(a)   Calculate the under- or over-recovery of fixed overhead for each period and indicate how it will affect the profit or loss.   **(6 marks)**

(b)   'Absorption costing will produce a higher profit than marginal costing.' Explain why you agree or disagree with this statement, making reference to the data provided above as appropriate.   **(6 marks)**

(c)   Explain briefly why absorption costing is usually considered to be unsuitable as an aid for decision-making. Justify your answer.   **(8 marks)**
                                                                                            (Total 20 marks)

35   (Question 4 of examination)

Your company will shortly be completing its acquisition of a small manufacturing company which is engaged in producing a range of products via a number of processes. The production side of that company is well established. However, its cost and management accounting function is not so well developed. This type of multi-process production system is new to your company.

You are required to:

Prepare a report for management which clearly explains the problems associated with process costing, and which looks particularly at:

–   the treatment of overheads;
–   valuation problems;
–   normal and abnormal gains and losses.

(20 marks)

Section D - ONE question ONLY to be attempted

36   (Question 5 of examination)

Newsam plc is a quoted company which produces a range of branded products all of which are well-established in their respective markets, although overall sales have grown by an average of only 2% per annum over the past decade. The board of directors is currently concerned about the company's level of financial gearing, which although not high by industry standards, is near to breaching the covenants attaching to its 15% debenture issue, made in 1982 at a time of high market interest rates. Issued in order to finance the acquisition of the premises on which it is secured, the debenture is repayable at par value of £100 per unit of stock at any time during the period 1994–1997.

There are two covenants attaching to the debenture, which state:

> 'At no time shall the ratio of debt capital to shareholders' funds exceed 50%. The company shall also maintain a prudent level of liquidity, defined as a current ratio at no time outside the range of the industry average (as published by the corporate credit analysts, Creditex), plus or minus 20%.'

Newsam's most recent set of accounts is shown in summarised form below. The buildings have been depreciated since 1982 at 4% per annum, and most of the machinery is only two or three years old, having been purchased mainly via a bank overdraft. The interest rate payable on the bank overdraft is currently 9%. The finance director argues that Newsam should take advantage of historically low interest rates on the European money markets by issuing a medium-term Eurodollar bond at 5%. The dollar is currently selling at a premium of about 1% on the three-month forward market.

Newsam's ordinary shares currently sell at a P/E ratio of 14, and look unattractive compared to comparable companies in the sector which exhibit an average P/E ratio of 18. According to the latest published credit assessment by Creditex, the average current ratio for the industry is 1.35.

The debentures currently sell in the market at £15 above par.

The summarised financial accounts for Newsam plc for the year ending 30 June 1994 are as follows:

Balance sheet as at 30 June 1994

Assets employed	£m	£m	£m
Fixed (net)			
Land			5.0
Premises			4.0
Machinery and vehicles			11.0
			20.0
Current			
Stocks	2.5		
Debtors	4.0		
Cash	0.5		
		7.0	
Current liabilities			
Creditors	(4.0)		
Bank overdraft	(3.0)		
		(7.0)	
Net current assets			0.0
Total assets less current liabilities			20.0
Long-term creditors			
15% Debentures 1994 – 1997			(5.0)
Net assets			15.0
Financed by			
Ordinary shares (25p par value)			5.0
Reserves			10.0
Shareholders' funds			15.0

Profit and loss account extracts for the year ended 30 June 1994

	£m
Sales	28.00
Operating profit	3.00
Interest payable	(1.00)
Profit before tax	2.00
Taxation	(0.66)
Profit after tax	1.34
Dividend	(0.70)
Retained profit	0.64

Required

(a)   Calculate appropriate gearing ratios for Newsam plc using:

(i)   book values; and
(ii)   market values.   **(3 marks)**

(b)   Assess how close Newsam plc is to breaching the debenture covenants.   **(3 marks)**

(c)   Discuss whether Newsam plc's gearing is in any sense 'dangerous'.   **(4 marks)**

(d)   Discuss what financial policies Newsam plc might adopt:

   (i)   in order to lower its capital gearing; and
   (ii)   to improve its interest cover.   **(10 marks)**
   (Total 20 marks)

---

37   (Question 2 of examination)

(a)   Distinguish between 'hard' and 'soft' capital rationing, explaining why a company may deliberately choose to restrict its capital expenditure.   **(5 marks)**

(b)   Filtrex plc is a medium-sized, all equity-financed, unquoted company which specialises in the development and production of water- and air-filtering devices to reduce the emission of effluents. Its small but ingenious R & D team has recently made a technological breakthrough which has revealed a number of attractive investment opportunities. It has applied for patents to protect its rights in all these areas. However, it lacks the financial resources required to exploit all of these projects, whose required outlays and post-tax NPVs are listed in the table below. Filtrex's managers consider that delaying any of these projects would seriously undermine their profitability, as competitors bring forward their own new developments. All projects are thought to have a similar degree of risk.

Project	Required outlay £	NPV £
A	150,000	65,000
B	120,000	50,000
C	200,000	80,000
D	80,000	30,000
E	400,000	120,000

The NPVs have been calculated using as a discount rate the 18% post-tax rate of return which Filtrex requires for risky R & D ventures. The maximum amount available for this type of investment is £400,000, corresponding to Filtrex's present cash balances, built up over several years' profitable trading. Projects A and C are mutually exclusive and no project can be sub-divided. Any unused capital will either remain invested in short-term deposits or used to purchase marketable securities, both of which offer a return well below 18% post-tax.

Required

   (i)   Advise Filtrex plc, using suitable supporting calculations, which combination of projects should be undertaken in the best interests of shareholders.

   (ii)   Suggest what further information might be obtained to assist a fuller analysis.

    (9 marks)

(c)   Explain how, apart from delaying projects, Filtrex plc could manage to exploit more of these opportunities.
    (6 marks)
    (Total 20 marks)

EXAMINER'S COMMENTS

General comments

There were two striking features about the pattern of marks in this diet. First was the importance of the case-study question, which few students failed, and which often contributed well over half of their overall marks. As with the June 1994 paper, marks on the MA questions were higher than on the FM areas. Once again, it seems that candidates are seeing paper 8 as an exam in MA with a little FM tacked on, and/or are relying on knowledge gained in earlier MA studies to carry them through.

Question 1 part (a): required the calculation of the raw materials budget and finished goods budget in units for each month for a four month period.

Candidates lost marks through not calculating the closing stock of raw materials and finished goods. It was unusual to find some students calculating to closing stocks of raw materials correctly and then calculate the stocks of finished goods incorrectly.

Part (b): required the calculation of sales and production budgets and budgeted closing debtors, creditors and stocks.

Most candidates had no difficulty computing the sales budget. A large number of candidates failed to use FIFO in computing the value of the raw materials used when trying to arrive at the production budget and did not appreciate that stocks were being valued at marginal cost.

Part (c): required the preparation of a cash budget.

Overall, this part of the question was done very well. Those who lost marks, made errors through dealing incorrectly with the periods of credit on debtors and creditors and failed to account for the loan correctly.

Part (d) some candidates re-computed figures, in particular the production costs, which had already been calculated, so wasting valuable examination time. Candidates who did include the production cost, also included the purchase figure, when it was already included in the production cost. Another common error was to exclude the loan interest and to deal incorrectly with the profit and loss appropriations.

In the balance sheet the loan was treated at a current liability falling due within one year by a significant number of candidates and the loan interest outstanding was not included at all.

Part (e): required advice about ways of improving the company's cash management.

In this wide 'open ended' question it was pleasing to see knowledge from other studies being applied, eg, auditing in particular. A lot of the points made needed to be expanded, eg, by explaining why and how such advice would be of benefit and where appropriate giving brief examples.

Question 2 part (a): required assessment of the factors influencing the current market values of two specified convertible debenture stocks.

This question was poorly done, mainly due to neglecting to use the copious information given in the question for answering the question set. The wording of the question clearly referred to 'those two convertible stocks'. Failure to answer the question, however good a survey was provided of the influences on the valuation of convertibles, necessarily restricted maximum marks obtainable.

Part (b): required knowledge of how companies can obtain a listing on the London Stock Exchange.

A straightforward question which was generally well done. Those who did not perform well, wrote about the process of obtaining a listing and/or the listing requirements. The other recurrent error was the inclusion of a rights issue as a method of obtaining a listing.

Part (c): required explanation of the advantages of scrip dividends for both companies and their share-holders.

The wording of this question was carefully phrased to make the distinction between a scrip dividend (which is optional) and a scrip issue (received by all shareholders). Unfortunately, the majority of candidates ignored this distinction, it being clear from their answers that they were writing about the latter. However, many points relating to scrip dividends also apply to scrip issues such as cash flow savings, avoidance of issue costs, reduction in gearing (below what it would otherwise have been). The basic point about scrip dividends is that they offer shareholders a choice and this makes the shares more appealing to a wider clientele of investors.

Part (d): required distinction between factoring and invoice discounting, specifying the advantages of each.

This was quite well done, except for the misconception that invoice discounting is the offer of discounts to customers for prompt payment. Apart from this, the only significant errors were those of omission, eg, failing to explain that factoring normally involves all of a company's sales whereas invoice discounting involves selected invoices (sometimes only one), and failure to explain that factoring will save book-keeping and administration costs, whereas with invoice discounting, the task of collection from customers remains with the company.

Part (e): required explanation of the main economic aims underlying privatisation of state-owned companies.

The key word in the question was 'economic'. Many candidates instead discussed the political aims of promoting wider share ownership. This only scored marks if it was explained that wider share ownership, by encouraging greater interest in share-holding, may augment the flow of new funds onto the capital markets. The core of the answer should have been the impact of privatisation on industrial efficiency, prompted by exposure to new competitive pressures and the opportunity to diversify into areas previously forbidden by statute. The efficiency improvements would thus enhance the technical and allocative efficiency of the nation's industrial structure.

The majority of answers tended to emphasise aims such as; reducing the Public Sector Borrowing Requirement raising revenue and enabling tax cuts, all of which do have economic spin-offs (eg, lower interest rates), but all too often these economic benefits were glossed over. This part of question 2 provided a good example of the need to look beyond the obvious answer.

Part (f): required a brief explanation of the concepts of 'price elasticity' and 'cross elasticity' in relation to the product pricing decision.

A lot of attempts were of a good standard. Weaker answers, either failed to make an mention of 'cross elasticity' or focused on supply and demand.

Question 3 part (a): required the calculation of the under or over recovery of overheads.

Candidates who applied the rules correctly and who demonstrated that they understood the concept of under or over absorption received full marks, provided that they knew the correct treatment in the profit and loss account. On the whole this section was very well done.

Part (b): required an explanation of the statement, 'absorption costing will produce a higher profit than marginal costing'.

Those who agreed and provided some satisfactory reasons as to why, did get some marks. However, a number of candidates did make the point very clearly about fixed production overheads being carried forward in closing stocks and then failed to take account of the fixed production overheads brought into the period via the opening stocks. Many candidates did not make any attempt to relate their answer to or illustrate their answer by reference to the data in part (a) which was asked for in the question. On the whole this part was not answered well.

Part (c): required an explanation as to why absorption costing is usually considered to be unsuitable for decision making.

It was encouraging to find candidates applying terms such as sunk costs, relevant costs and Activity Based Costing in their answers to this question.

Question 4: required a report about process costing with particular emphasis on the treatment of overheads valuation problems and normal/abnormal gains and losses.

Some answers were not in the required report format. Others did not make any recommendations or try to draw any conclusions. Not many candidates attempted this question and from those who did there were not many answers that could be described as being of a high quality.

Question 5: required knowledge of the measurement of gearing, implications of 'excessive' gearing levels, and of policies to reduce both capital and income gearing.

This question was poorly done. It offered a substantial amount of accounting information to enable candidates to illustrate their answers numerically but more importantly, to allow an opportunity to express their expertise in interpreting accounting statements. However, apart from the calculation of gearing ratios, candidates tended to ignore much of the information given. Candidates also seemed unable to work out market values of equity, and even where this was done, a common error was to add on the reserves. The dangers of 'high' gearing and the implications of breaking a debt covenant were not highlighted by many candidates.

Part (d) was generally poorly done, with too many answers consisting of a set of odd jottings without any attempt to explain or justify the suggestions made, or to illustrate them numerically. The opportunity to issue the Eurobond was generally ignored, and those who did recommend it over-looked the exchange rate risk. Finally, whereas it is true that increasing sales/profits and/or reducing costs will likely raise interest cover, the question does specify 'financial policies'.

Question 6: required knowledge of types of capital rationing, of how to evaluate capital expenditure under rationing and of how to exploit the benefits of projects under these conditions.

Most candidates could make the distinction between external and internal rationing, but often could offer no reasons for the latter.

In part (b), a number of candidates seemed to think that mutual exclusivity meant that both projects A and C could be done together or even had to be done together. Others also ignored the information that projects were indivisible. Most students omitted to specify the NPV-preferred project (E), the usual starting point in a rationing exercise, but did calculate the Profitability Indices. Several appeared to think the PI was outlay divided by NPV, and many referred to it as the return on capital, or even more explicitly, as the ROCE. Few candidates seemed to be aware of the role of the IRR in a rationing situation.

Part (c) required a certain amount of creativity – the wording used was 'exploit more of these opportunities', ie, it was intended to point towards avenues other than finding more capital, such as selling the patent, forming a Joint Venture, licensing, etc. Many students simply wrote down a 'shopping list' of points with little or no accompanying explanation. Candidates should remember that the Examiner uses words such as 'discuss' and 'explain' rather than 'list' to encourage analysis and discussion.

ANSWERS TO DECEMBER 1994 EXAMINATION

It should be noted that some of the following answers are perhaps fuller than would be expected from most students under exam conditions. The answers are provided in this degree of detail to offer guidance on the approach required and on the range and depth of knowledge that would be expected from an excellent student.

---

32   (Answer 1 of examination)

		(Units)			
(a)	**Budgets for stocks**	*March*	*April*	*May*	*June*
	Raw materials				
	Opening stock	100	110	115	110
	Add: Purchases	80	80	85	85
		180	190	200	195
	Less: Used in production	70	75	90	90
	Closing stock	110	115	110	105
	Finished production				
	Opening stock	110	100	91	85
	Add: Production	70	75	90	90
		180	175	181	175
	Less: Sales	80	84	96	94
	Closing stock	100	91	85	81

		(Units)				
(b)	**Sales and other budgets**	*March*	*April*	*May*	*June*	*Total*
	Sales					
	(at £219 per unit)	£17,520	£18,396	£21,024	£20,586	£77,526
	Production cost					
	Raw materials (using FIFO)	3,024*	3,321**	4,050	4,050	14,445
	Wages and variable costs	4,550	4,875	5,850	5,850	21,125
		£7,574	£8,196	£9,900	£9,900	£35,570

Debtors

Closing debtors = May + June sales = £41,610

Creditors

June, raw materials = 85 units × £45 = £3,825

$$* \quad \left(£4,320 \times \frac{70}{100} \right) = £3,024$$

$$** \quad \left(£4,320 \times \frac{30}{100} \right) = £1,296 + 45 \text{ units at } £45 = £3,321$$

Closing stocks

Raw materials 105 units × £45 = £4,725
Finished goods 81 units × £110 = £8,910
(Material £45 per unit + Lab & overhead £65 per unit)

(c)   **Cash budget**

	March £	April £	May £	June £
Balance b/f	6,790	4,820	5,545	132,415
Add: Receipts				
Debtors (two months credit)	7,680	10,400	17,520	18,396
Loan	–	–	120,000	–
(A)	14,470	15,220	143,065	150,811
Payments				
Creditors (one month's credit)	3,900	3,600	3,600	3,825
Wages and variable overheads	4,550	4,875	5,850	5,850
Fixed overheads	1,200	1,200	1,200	1,200
Machinery	–	–	–	112,000
Interim dividend	–	–	–	12,500
(B)	9,650	9,675	10,650	135,375
Balance c/f (A) – (B)	4,820	5,545	132,415	£15,436

(d)   **Master budget**

**Budgeted trading and profit and loss account
for the four months to 30 June 19X5**

	£	£
Sales		77,526
Less: Cost of sales		
Opening stock finished goods	10,450	
Add: Production cost	35,570	
	46,020	
Less: Closing stock finished goods	8,910	
		37,110
		40,416
Less: Expenses		
Fixed overheads (4 × £1,200)	4,800	
Depreciation		
Machinery and equipment	15,733	
Motor vehicles	3,500	
Loan interest (two months)	1,500	
		25,533
		14,883
Less: Interim dividends		12,500
		2,383
Add: Profit and loss account balance b/f		40,840
		43,223

Budgeted balance sheet as at 30 June 19X5

Employment of capital	Cost £	Depreciation to date £	Net £
Fixed assets			
Land and buildings	500,000	–	500,000
Machinery and equipment	236,000	100,233	135,767
Motor vehicles	42,000	19,900	22,100
	778,000	120,133	657,867
Working capital			
Current assets			
Stock of raw materials		4,725	
Stock of finished goods		8,910	
Debtors		41,610	
Cash and bank balances		15,436	
		70,681	
Less: Current liabilities			
Creditors	3,825		
Loan interest owing	1,500		
		5,325	
			65,356
			723,223

Capital employed	£
Ordinary share capital £1 shares (fully paid)	500,000
Share premium	60,000
Profit and loss account	43,223
	603,223
Secured loan ($7^1/2$%)	120,000
	723,223

(e)   Possible ways in which the company can improve its cash management are as follows:

– Employing a *treasury function* to invest surplus cash and thereby improving the productivity of the capital employed. Even a small company such as Kwan Tong Umbago Ltd could switch funds from its bank current account to an account on which it can earn some interest. Many businesses fail to make full use of their cash budget, in that it provides them with an indication of when they will have surplus cash in addition to highlighting when they have a shortage.

– Its cash budget can only be as accurate as the data which it uses to estimate the figures. To arrive at more relevant and realistic estimates it may be possible to use computer packages eg, which take account of the numerous variables involved, and statistical techniques such as time series analysis for forecasting sales.

– It may be possible to improve its *credit control*. It currently takes around two months to collect the amounts owing from its debtors whilst paying off its creditors within one month.

It needs to make an effort to collect what is owing more quickly without offering cash discounts which could prove to be expensive eg, by more prompt invoicing and chasing slow payers etc. It could take a little longer to pay creditors provided that it does not lose cash discounts. A small percentage cash discount does have a high implicit annual interest cost!

– It could generate more cash by identifying and disposing of surplus assets eg, unwanted stocks of raw materials and/or finished goods, production and/or office equipment which is no longer required, provided that it can find a buyer. Finding a buyer of the surplus assets may not be easy. Another benefit of disposing of surplus assets which can have a significant impact on cash, is that the disposal may free valuable production, office or storage space. It may also be possible to secure a reduction in insurance premiums at the next renewal date relating to the assets disposed of.

– The company's cash position may also be improved via using more debt financing. The company is low geared and a large proportion of its fixed assets have not already been pledged as security. This should enable it to benefit from low cost financing eg, secured loans or debentures, but would expose it to a higher degree of risk caused by the obligation to make regular payments of capital and interest.

– The management could also consider other ways of financing assets eg, renting or leasing plant and machinery. This should enable them to generate the payments out of the earnings of the plant and machinery concerned.

– Finally, the company could opt to make greater use of sub-contractors which frees it from having to find additional sums for financing the expansion involved. The sub-contractor would have to finance the purchase of the necessary fixed assets, the remuneration of its labour force and the purchase and holding of stocks of raw materials, work in progress and finished goods. The downside from the company's point of view would be the problem of exercising quality control over the supplier.

(*Tutorial note:* The first two of these suggestions are probably inappropriate for the company whose main problem is low profitability - ROCE = 2% - due to an appalling asset turnover ratio.)

33   (Answer 2 of examination)

(a) (i) The market price of Hammer's debentures will be largely determined by their essential debenture characteristics because conversion does not appear to be an attractive proposition. At present, the value of 20 shares is only £70, considerably less than the redemption value of £100. Although there is over a year to go until redemption, the share price would have to rise more than £1.50 (over 40%) over this period to make conversion the better alternative. Consequently, Hammer's stock will be valued as debentures, based on the future interest payments plus the redemption consideration. There will still, however, be some (probably small) option premium to add to this.

     (ii) In the case of Nail's stock, the share conversion value (25 × £4.10 = £102.50) already exceeds the stock redemption value of £100. Conversion is not due for another three years, and although share prices could fall, there is the prospect of further capital gains at conversion. These convertibles will be valued based on the remaining interest payments and the expected ordinary share price at conversion. The critical factors in valuation are thus the actual and expected share price and the length of time to conversion, especially if the share price is volatile.

(b) There are three main ways in which a company can 'come to the market'.

     (i) *Offer for sale by prospectus.* Shares are offered at a fixed price to the public at large, including both investing institutions and private individuals. Application forms and a prospectus, setting out all relevant details of the company's past performance and future prospects, as stipulated by Stock Exchange regulations laid down in 'The Yellow Book', must be published in the national press. An offer for sale is obligatory for issues involving £30m or more.

     A variant on this method is the offer for sale by tender, where no prior issue price is announced, but prospective investors are invited to bid for shares at a price of their choosing. The eventual 'striking price' at which shares are sold is determined by the weight of applications at various prices. Essentially, the final price is set by supply and demand.

(ii)   *A placing* occurs when shares (up to £15m value) are 'placed' or sold to institutional investors, such as pension funds and insurance companies, selected by the merchant bank advising the company, and the company's stockbroker. In a placing, the general public have to wait until official dealing in the shares begins before they, too, can buy the shares.

       An intermediaries' offer is a placing with financial intermediaries, which allows brokers other than the one advising the issuing company to apply for shares. These brokers are allocated shares which they can subsequently distribute to their clients.

(iii)   *Introduction.* In some cases, the proportion of shares held by the public *(25%* for a full listing) may already meet Stock Exchange requirements, and the company is seeking a listing merely to open up a wider market for its shares rather than seeking new capital. No new shares are issued, and new investors can only participate if some of the existing shareholders decide to liquidate their holdings after the listing.

(c)   (i)   From the company's point of view, the scrip alternative preserves liquidity, which may be important at a time of cash shortage and/or high borrowing costs, although it may become committed to a higher level of cash outflows in the future if shareholders revert to a preference for cash. However, having issued more shares, the company's reported financial gearing may be lowered, possibly enhancing borrowing capacity. In this respect, the scrip dividend resembles a rights issue.

       In addition, the company is not required to make an advance corporation tax (ACT) payment to the Inland Revenue. This may be of particular value to companies facing difficulties in 'relieving' ACT ie, offsetting it against mainstream corporation tax (MCT).

       For example, a company which declares cash dividends of £10m (net of tax), and half of whose shareholders choose the scrip alternatives would make the following cash flow savings:

$$[\text{dividend payment saved (£5m) plus ACT saved } (20/80 \times £5m)] = £6.25m$$

       The latter element would be only a temporary saving for a company with a MCT liability. In reality, a considerably lower proportion of shareholders elect for the scrip alternative. This is largely due to the inability of tax-exempt shareholders to reclaim a tax credit, no ACT having been paid by the company in respect of the scrip issue.

(ii)   For shareholders wishing to increase their holdings, the scrip is a cheap way into the company as it avoids dealing fees. The conversion price used to calculate the number of shares receivable is based on the average share price for several trading days after the 'ex dividend day'. Should the market price rise above the conversion price before the date at which shareholders have to declare their choice, there is the prospect of a capital gain, although if the share price appreciation exceeds 15%, any such gain is taxable.

       A scrip dividend has no tax advantages for shareholders as it is treated as income for tax purposes. Nor can a tax credit be reclaimed as no ACT was originally payable.

       If the capital market is efficient, there is no depressing effect on the share price by the scrip dividend through earnings dilution. This is because the scrip simply replaces a cash dividend which would have caused share price to fall anyway due to the 'ex dividend' effect. In other words, shareholder wealth is unchanged.

       However, if the additional capital retained is invested wisely, then share price may be maintained or even rise, although this would depend on the proportion of shareholders who opt for the scrip.

(d)   Factoring and invoice discounting are two ways in which a company can obtain speedier payment in respect of credit sales made to customers. The shorter working capital cycle will quicken the rate of cash flow and in turn enable the company to reduce its reliance on other, perhaps less dependable, sources of short-term finance, such as bank overdrafts.

Factoring is the service provided by a financial institution which will lend the firm up to around 80% of the value of its debtors. The factor will then administer the sales accounts and undertake the collection of the debts. The remaining 20% or so of the value of debtors will be paid over to the client company either when all of the invoices have been settled or after some agreed time period, net of administration fees and interest charges. The service charge will vary between 0.5%–2.5% of turnover, and the interest charge will typically be in the range of 1–3% above base rate.

There is a distinction between 'non-recourse' factoring, whereby bad debts are the responsibility of the factor, and 'with recourse' factoring under which bad debts remain the liability of the client company. An additional fee, typically, 0.5% of turnover, will be required for the factor to provide protection against bad debts.

Sometimes, for reasons of goodwill, a company with a need to quicken its cash flow may not wish to reveal that it has enlisted the aid of a factor, preferring to retain the role as debt collector. In this case, it may utilise *invoice discounting,* a less comprehensive service which involves the financial institution purchasing selected invoices from the client at a discount. The interest cost of this provision of finance is reflected in the discount. For example, if a bundle of invoices with an average maturity of two months were sold at a discount of 2%, the effective interest cost would be $(1.02)^6 = 12.6\%$ (approximately). The administration of the customer accounts remains with the company which settles the debt to the invoice discounter out of the payments duly collected from its customers.

Thus, the main additional benefit provided by full service-and-finance factoring are the administrative costs avoided by not having to operate the credit management function. The factor, perhaps by utilising information about customers obtained from operating the sales accounts of other firms, may also be a more efficient collector of debt than the client company, although there may be adverse goodwill implications.

(e)   The following reasons are often cited to support the *economic* case for privatisation:

To increase competition

Many formerly state-owned firms enjoyed statutory monopoly positions in their respective industries, often for sound reasons, such as to avoid the wasteful duplication of facilities which, say, competing water utilities would entail. Unless closely regulated, monopolies may exploit the consumer by charging high prices. In the UK, several of the statutory monopolies, such as gas, electricity and telephonic communications have now been broken, allowing new firms like Mercury in telecommunications, to compete for a share of the market. Competition of this nature is likely to lead to lower end prices and greater allocative efficiency.

To increase operating efficiency

Monopoly power is said to promote complacency and inertia, allowing excessively bureaucratic management structures to emerge. Exposure to market forces may force managerial economies, as the enterprise is forced to pare its costs in order to compete effectively. This has been seen most dramatically in the case of British Airways, in 1993, the most profitable airline in the world. Even an enterprise which preserves its monopoly is forced to improve its performance relative to other comparable private companies in order to build a stock market rating which ensures access to fresh supplies of capital.

Another way in which efficiency can be improved is by freeing enterprises from government interference in pricing and investment policies and thus allowing managers greater independence to plan effectively for the future. Moreover, enterprises are freer to diversify into other activities eg, some UK water companies have acquired or developed waste management subsidiaries. Some privatised industries are still regulated by the oversight of an industry 'watchdog' such as Oftel, in telecommunications, which by imposing tight pricing formulae, has forced BT to become considerably more cost-conscious.

To reduce the public sector borrowing requirement

The first UK asset sale, in 1977, that of BP shares under pressure from the IMF, was explicitly designed to raise funds for the public purse. The revenue raised from the subsequent and more significant privatisations, such as BT, British Gas and the water companies, made major inroads into the government's borrowing needs, and for a short spell, helped to convert the deficit into a surplus. The rationale behind reducing or eliminating the state's need to borrow is twofold. First, lower state borrowing moderates upward pressure on interest rates, thus reducing the tendency for state expenditure to 'crowd out' private investment expenditure. Secondly, higher state income increases the scope for reduction of taxes in order to raise incentives to work. In these respects, privatisation is part of the monetarist 'supply-side' philosophy.

(f)   The 'elasticity of demand' concept measures the extent to which the demand for a product will respond to a given change in some economic variable eg, price.

If there is a more than proportionate change in demand which results from a price change, ie, the price change has a significant effect on the number of units sold, demand is described as elastic. If the price change has little or no effect on demand ie, a less than proportionate change in the quantity demanded, demand is then described as inelastic. Price elasticity can be calculated as follows:

$$\frac{\% \text{ change in quantity of product demanded}}{\% \text{ change in product's own price}}$$

The concept of 'cross elasticity' describes the situation which exists, where the demand for one product is affected by a change in the price of a related product.

Management would need to monitor very frequently and very carefully, all of their products for which demand is elastic or subject to cross elasticity. This would involve keeping an eye on competitors' pricing and the development of a pricing policy which ensures that a satisfactory contribution is generated and is flexible enough to respond to the activities of competitors. For example, if a substitute made by a competitor is reduced in price, the company will have to decide reasonably quickly as to how it is going to react. Pricing cannot simply be done using cost-plus methods, it has to take account of, the effect it could have on demand and the prices of competitors.

34   (Answer 3 of examination)

(a)   **Calculation of fixed overhead absorption rates**

	Period 1 £	Period 2 £	Period 3 £
Budgeted FOH	10,400	19,170	17,360
Budgeted production (units)	8,000	14,200	12,400
FOH absorption rate (per unit)	1.30	1.35	1.40
Actual production (units)	8,400	13,600	9,200
FOH absorbed (actual units × rate)	10,920	18,360	12,880
Less: Actual FOH	11,200	18,320	16,740
	Under 280	Over 40	Under 3,860
Effect on the profit or loss	Deducted in P&L	Added back in P&L	Deducted in P&L

(Tutorial note: the wording of the question could imply a constant absorption rate across the three periods. This would be £(10,400 + 19,170 + 17,360)/(8,000 + 14,200 + 12,400) = £1.36 per unit. Resulting over/(under) absorptions would then be: Period 1 £224, Period 2 £176, Period 3 (£4,228).*)*

(b)   **The calculation of the closing stock figures (actual)**

	Period 1 (Units)	Period 2 (Units)	Period 3 (Units)
Opening stock	2,600	1,400	2,600
Add: Production	8,400	13,600	9,200
	11,000	15,000	11,800
Less: Sales	9,600	12,400	10,200
Closing stock	1,400	2,600	1,600

Whether or not a profit is higher (or a loss lower) under an absorption costing system compared with a marginal costing system depends on the value of the fixed overheads included in both the opening and closing stocks.

If the closing stock value of FOH is greater than the opening stock value of FOH, the profit will be greater (or loss lower) computed according to absorption costing principles compared with marginal costing, and vice versa.

The differences between the absorption costing profit and the marginal costing profit or loss can be computed as follows:

| | *Period 1* | *Period 2* | *Period 3* |
	£	£	£
Closing stock	1,820	3,510	2,240
	(1,400 × £1.30)	(2,600 × £1.35)	(1,600 × £1.40)
Opening stock (given)	3,315	(Period 1) 1,820	(Period 2) 3,510
	(1,495)	1,690	(1,270)

Absorption profit lower than marginal profit in periods 1 and 3, higher in period 2.

(c) Absorption costing cannot produce costs which are accurate, its principal aim is simply to ensure that all costs are covered. It depends upon a high degree of subjective judgement and thus should not be used for decision-making purposes.

The following areas of absorption costing involve subjective judgement.

− The predetermination of costs and revenues. These take account of perceived assumptions about the environment in which the firm operates.

− Those costs which can be allocated ie, charged direct to cost centres are still only estimates and their division depends upon assumptions eg, the estimated time which factory cleaners spend in each cost centre in which they clean.

− The selection of methods of apportioning overheads to cost centres is at the discretion of the person doing the selecting such as the management accountant. Some overheads could be shared according to floor area, or cubic capacity eg, rent of premises, but yet only one or the other can be used.

− The selection of the method by which the service cost centres are apportioned. Some of the methods favoured have their drawbacks eg, stores cost apportioned according to the number of requisitions take no account of weight, value, handling/storage problems etc.

− The choice of the absorption (recovery) rate eg, direct labour hours, machine hours, percentage of prime cost etc.

− The estimation of the denominator in the absorption rate eg, machine hours, direct labour hours etc.

− The way in which administration, selling and distribution, research and development expenditure will be dealt with ie, will it be absorbed into the product cost or written off to the profit and loss account?

− The treatment of any under- or over-recovery of overheads.

Thus, because of the high degree of subjectivity involved in producing an absorption rate and costs which cannot be classed as accurate, absorption costing is not recommended for decision-making purposes.

35   (Answer 4 of examination)

To the Board of Directors   Date: 18 December 19X4

Report on the problems associated with process costing

I have now completed my review of the problems associated with using process costing and describe my findings below.

My findings have been divided between five principal areas which are:

–   The treatment of overheads

–   Valuation at the point of separation of by-products and joint products

–   Normal and abnormal gains and losses

–   The valuation of work-in-progress and finished good (equivalent units) including the valuation of materials used

–   Others (sub-contractors etc)

The treatment of overheads

Overheads, the indirect expenditure such as non-manufacturing labour and maintenance materials, light and heat etc. has to be included in process costs using marginal costing or absorption costing.

Marginal costing only includes the variable overheads in the process costs ie, those overheads which vary directly with production.

Absorption costing includes all the manufacturing overheads in the process costs. Those overheads which cannot be identified and traced to a specific process are apportioned between the processes according to some arbitrary basis such as floor area, number of employees, etc.

The overheads are then charged to production via a direct labour or machine hour rate. For example, for every direct labour hour worked an amount will be added to the cost of the process to recover the overheads. Costs can only be described as accurate up to the point of their marginal cost. Costs attributed to products via absorption costing can in no way be described as accurate and should not therefore be used for decision-making purposes.

The main problem here is whether to use marginal costing or absorption costing. It must be stressed that if absorption costing is used, the data which it provides should not be used for decision-making purposes.

The valuation at the point of separation

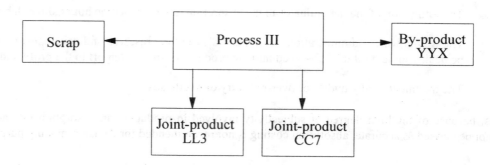

Figure 1: A valuation problem

The above diagram illustrates the problem which has to be faced. How much of process III should be charged, if any, to scrap, the by-product and the two joint products respectively? All three products and the scrap were produced in the same process. There are a number of treatments which can be used. Some examples are:

–   Scrap – of low saleable value, value at nil.

–   The by-product – value it at its selling price. This reduces the process cost.

–   The joint products – share the remaining process cost out in proportion to their weighted selling prices or weighted market values. Sharing the process cost between them using weight alone eg, the process cost per kilo, fails to recognise the fact that the two products are different.

The problem here is that a selection has to be made of the method for valuing the products at the point of separation. It must also be emphasised that the methods used simply share the process costs between the products, and cannot be regarded as accurate.

Normal and abnormal gains and losses

The principle of not charging abnormal losses or including abnormal gains in the process cost is well-established. The key problem to be solved is arriving at what is abnormal. This would involve consultation with the appropriate production personnel and would to a large extent depend upon past experience and future expectations.

The valuation of work-in-progress and finished goods

The valuation depends upon:

–   The estimation of the degree of completion. This should be done by those production personnel who are competent to make such an assessment. The estimation will need to take account of opening stocks, inputs from an earlier process, materials, labour and overheads.

–   The recording of labour for each process and the treatment of idle time, bonus payments and overtime.

–   A selection will also have to be made of the method of valuation of materials which are issued to each process eg, FIFO (first in, first out), LIFO (last in, first out), AVE CO (average cost), STD CO (standard cost) etc. The method adopted could have a significant impact on the process costs eg, FIFO in times of rising prices could in effect be understating the process costs in terms of the material content. The above-mentioned valuation methods also have an impact where stocks are brought forward in cases where there have also been movements in labour rates and overhead rates.

Others

Sub-contractors

The work undertaken by sub-contractors can be included as a direct cost of the next process or the finished product in cases where there is no further processing. The concern here is the maintenance of quality and the keeping of delivery pledges.

Activity-based costing (ABC)

An alternative to the marginal costing and absorption costing approaches is ABC. This method shares out the overheads via 'cost drivers' ie, the reason why the cost has been incurred eg, the number of purchase orders. However, this would need careful consideration and could be the focus of a future report.

Please do not hesitate to consult me should you want more information about the contents of this report.

Margaret Redwick, FCCA

36   (Answer 5 of examination)

(a)   The covenant does not give a precise measure of gearing in so far as it fails to stipulate whether short-term debt should be included in the calculation. It seems prudent to consider gearing measures with and without the bank overdraft.

(i)   **Using book values**

$$\frac{\text{Long - term debt}}{\text{Shareholders' funds}} = £5m/£15m = 33\%$$

$$\frac{\text{Total debt}}{\text{Shareholders' funds}} = £8m/£15m = 53\%$$

(ii)   **Using market values**

The market value of the debentures	=	$1.15 \times £5m = £5.75m$
The price of the ordinary shares	=	P/E ratio × Earnings per share
	=	$14 \times \dfrac{\text{Profit after tax}}{\text{Number of shares}}$
	=	$14 \times \dfrac{£1.34m}{20m} = 14 \times 6.7p = 94p$
Market value of equity	=	$20m \times 94p = £18.8m$

The gearing ratios are:

$$\frac{\text{Long - term debt}}{\text{Shareholders' funds}} = \frac{£5.75m}{£18.8m} = 31\%$$

$$\frac{\text{Total debt}}{\text{Shareholders' funds}} = \frac{£8.75m}{£18.8m} = 47\%$$

(b)   It would seem that, in terms of its borrowing, Newsam has already breached the covenant if a combination of book values and total debt is used, while it is very near to doing so if the market value base is used in conjunction with total indebtedness. It could be argued that short-term creditors also constitute part of Newsam's indebtedness, inclusion of which would increase the gearing measures, but as they are covered by cash and debtors, they have been excluded.

Regarding the liquidity stipulation, at present, Newsam's current ratio is precisely one, compared to a permissible range of (1.35 × 0.8) to (1.35 × 1.2) ie, 1.08 to 1.62. It seems, therefore, that Newsam is also breaching the liquidity requirement in the covenant and will have to take steps to improve its liquidity, especially as the quick ratio is only £4.5m/£7m = 0.64 (although no industry standard is given).

(c)   Financial gearing exposes the company to the risk of inability to meet required interest payments, should the company's profitability falter. If the creditors decide to demand repayment of their capital, the company faces the problem of liquidating assets, and possibly, the whole enterprise, in order to meet these claims. Hence, the first consideration is the degree of safety implied by the firm's interest cover, the ratio of profit before tax and interest to interest payable, in the light of the stability of the firm's sales and profits.

Interest cover is £3m/£1m = 3 times, which might appear low to some analysts, but if the firm's operations are stable, this may be tolerable. In the case of Newsam, although sales growth has been sluggish, its products are branded and well-established, and probably not subject to wide fluctuations. This seems a safe cover.

The second consideration is the value of the firm's assets in relation to the debt capital. In the first instance, the ability to repay the debentures is critical, but if debenture holders demanded repayment, it is inconceivable that Newsam's bankers would not call in the overdraft. Hence, Newsam's ability to repay *all* its debt needs to be assessed.

At book values, fixed assets appear in the accounts at £20m. Whether Newsam could actually achieve this figure in a forced sale is questionable, although it is possible that the value of the land and premises on the open market might exceed their historic cost values. The current state of the property market is important in this respect.

The final consideration is the action which Newsam's debenture holders are empowered to take in the event of breach of covenant, and, more pertinently, what they are *expected* to do in the circumstances. Newsam is likely to have some idea of their probable reaction as precautionary discussions are likely to have taken place already.

(d)   (i)   To lower its gearing ratio, Newsam could adopt a number of policies:

Revalue its fixed assets

Despite the depression in the UK property market in the early 1990s, it is still likely that a revaluation could reveal a surplus. However, this is likely to be a purely cosmetic adjustment – unless the revaluation conveys information which is genuinely new to the market, the share price is unlikely to respond, despite an increase in the book value of assets.

Place a value on its brands

Again, this may be a purely cosmetic exercise, as the market will already have taken into account the value of these brands in setting the share price. Nevertheless, this ploy has been adopted by a number of UK firms.

Tighten working capital management

The bank overdraft could be lowered by a more aggressive working capital management policy. For example, the debtor collection period could be shortened and/or the trade credit period lengthened. There does appear to be some scope regarding debtor days which currently stand at: $4/28 \times 365 = 52$ days which appears quite lengthy, although the trade credit period, currently: $4/20 \times 365 = 73$ days, already is excessively long and would give rise to fears over suppliers' reaction if any further delay was attempted.

The stock turnover at $20/2.5 = 8$ times (or 46 days) may look fairly long and capable of reduction, but overall, the working capital cycle at $(52 + 46) - 73 = 25$ days is quite rapid already.

It may be possible to achieve economies in this area but the scope appears limited.

(Tutorial note: In order to calculate the credit period, you have to assume a reasonable figure for purchases. The examiner has assumed £20 million*).*

Issue more shares

In theory, it should not matter when a rights issue is made, because the share price in an efficient market would always indicate the correct value of the shares, and the only market reaction would be the technical adjustment caused by earnings dilution when shares are sold at a discount. In reality, it is often difficult to convince a flat stock market of the positive reasons for a rights issue. In the present case, the announcement that a moderately performing and poorly-rated company like Newsam was planning to make a rights issue on a weak stock market merely in order to reduce indebtedness would be likely to induce a negative reaction.

This problem could possibly be eased if the company were able to make a placing of new shares with supportive financial institutions after persuading shareholders to forgo pre-emptive rights of purchase.

(ii) To raise the interest cover, Newsam could do the following:

Refinance the debenture with a bank overdraft

The interest saving, assuming no change in the total debt, would be: $(15\% - 9\%) \times £5m = £0.3m$. This would raise the interest cover to $£3.0m/£0.7m = 4.3$ times.

Refinance the debenture with a Eurodollar issue

On the face of it, this alternative appears to offer bigger interest savings – ie, $(15\% - 5\%) \times £5m = £0.5m$, which would raise the interest cover to $£3.0m/£0.5m = 6$ times. However, aside from the issue costs likely to be involved, there are dangers here. The forward market quotation for the dollar suggests that the dollar will appreciate against sterling by 1% over three months, or about 4% over one year. Although it is possible that the dollar could actually depreciate, thus lowering the sterling value of the debt, the foreign exchange market consensus is for a dollar appreciation of sufficient magnitude to eliminate the interest differential between Eurobonds and an overdraft.

In addition, there are dangers in replacing long-term debt with short-term debt. For example, a bank overdraft is, in principle (if not always in practice), repayable on demand, nor is the bank obliged to extend overdraft facilities indefinitely, while the company is exposed to the risk of adverse interest rate movements over the duration of its short-term financing. Newsam must balance these risks and their consequences against the interest cost differential.

37 (Answer 6 of examination)

(a) *Hard capital rationing* applies when a firm is restricted from undertaking all apparently worthwhile investment opportunities by factors external to the company, and over which it has no control. These factors may include government monetary restrictions and the general economic and financial climate, for example, a depressed stock market, precluding a rights issue of ordinary shares.

Soft capital rationing applies when a company decides to limit the amount of capital expenditure which it is prepared to authorise. The capital budget becomes a control variable, which the company may relax if it chooses. Segments of divisionalised companies often have their capital budgets imposed by the main board of directors.

A company may purposely curtail its capital expenditure for a number of reasons:

(i) It may consider that it has insufficient depth of management expertise to exploit all available opportunities without jeopardising the success of both new and ongoing operations.

(ii) It may be deliberate board policy to restrict the capital budget to concentrate managerial attention on generating the very best and most carefully thought out and analysed proposals. In this regard, self-imposed capital rationing may be an exercise in quality control.

(iii) Many companies adopt the policy of restraining capital expenditure to the amounts which can be generated by internal resources ie, retained earnings and depreciation provisions (or in reality, cash flow). This reluctance to use the external capital markets may be due to a risk-averse attitude to financial gearing, possibly because of the operating characteristics of the industry eg, high operating gearing in a cyclical industry. Alternatively, it may be due to reluctance to issue equity in the form of a rights issue, for fear of diluting earnings, or in the case of an unlisted company, reluctance to seek a quotation owing to the time and expense involved and the dilution of ownership.

(b) (i) Assuming Filtrex wishes to maximise the wealth of its shareholders, it will seek the set of investment projects with the highest combined NPVs.

As a first approximation, it may examine the projects ranked according to their estimated NPVs, and select the projects with the highest NPVs, consistent with the budget limitation. However, this approach would confine the programme to project E alone, which apart from losing any benefits of diversification, is a solution which can be improved upon. This is because it overlooks the relationship between the NPV itself and the amount of capital required to yield the estimated NPV. Under capital rationing, it is often considered desirable to examine the productivity of each pound of scarce capital invested in the various projects. This information is given by the profitability index (PI). The ranking of the five projects according to their PIs is:

A	65/150	=	0.43
B	50/120	=	0.42
C	80/200	=	0.40
D	30/80	=	0.37
E	120/400	=	0.30

Moving down the ranking, Filtrex would select projects A and B. but then, due to the indivisibility problem, and also the fact that projects A and C are mutually exclusive, it would have to depart from the rankings and move down as far as D, whereafter the remaining project E is too demanding of capital. The selected programme of ABD would require an outlay of £350,000 and generate an NPV of £145,000. £50,000 of scarce capital would remain unspent and according to the stated policy, would be invested in short-term assets. Although of low risk, these offer a return less than the 18% required by shareholders. Consequently it might be preferable to return this unspent capital to shareholders in the form of a dividend or share repurchase, if shareholders are able to invest for higher returns in alternative activities. Perhaps, closer liaison with major shareholders is required to determine their preferences.

It is possible to improve on both of the previous selections by trial and error, in an attempt to utilise the whole of the capital budget. The optimal selection is BCD which offers a joint NPV of £160,000. However, even this result is suspect as it relies on evaluating the projects at the rate of return required in the absence of rationing, in this case, 18% post-tax. This neglects the impact of capital rationing on the cost of capital – if apparently worthwhile projects are rejected, there is an opportunity cost in the form of the returns otherwise obtainable on the rejected projects. Projects should be evaluated at the discount rate reflecting the rate of return on the best of the rejected projects. Unfortunately, until the evaluation and selection is made, this remains an unknown! Unless project indivisibility is a problem, ranking and selection using the internal rate of return (IRR) will yield the same solution – it would therefore be helpful to find the IRR for each project.

(ii)   In addition to IRRs, other information which may aid the decision-maker might include:

(1)   Whether the rationing is likely to apply over the long-term, in which case,

(2)   The degree of postponability of projects should be more closely assessed ie, whether a project can be postponed and the impact of postponement on its profitability. If projects can be postponed, it may be desirable for Filtrex to select projects in the base period offering a rapid return flow of cash in order to provide funds to enable investment in postponed projects in the next time period. In other words, it would be helpful to examine the cash flow profiles of these projects and hence their rates of payback.

(3)   The respective degrees of risk of these projects. It is implied that all projects have a similar degree of risk which is unlikely in practice, especially for the types of new product development planned by Filtrex. A capital-constrained company may use its limited access to finance to justify rejecting a high risk activity, especially if it is reliant on subsequent cash flows to finance postponed projects.

(4)   The likelihood of obtaining marginal supplies of finance and on what terms.

(*Tutorial note:* The 'profitability index' calculated here is simply the NPV/£ invested in the restricted year, a logical method of tackling single-period capital rationing problems. Students should note that mos authoris [eg, Brealey & Myers and Samuels & Wilkes] use the term profitability index for the ratio of 'gross present value' to investment - PV is NPV - investment in restricted year.)

(c)   There are two basic ways in which a company in Filtrex's position might still manage to exploit more projects. On one hand, it can involve other parties in the project, and on the other, it can resolve to seek outside capital.

Sharing the projects

(i)   To the extent that some part of the project(s) still require further development eg, design and market research, some of this work can be sub-contracted to specialist agencies, who may be able to perform the work at lower cost, or even to take payment out of the project cash flows.

(ii)   The production and/or sale of the products can be licensed or franchised to another party, with Filtrex arranging to receive a royalty or a percentage of sales. This is particularly appropriate for overseas activities.

(iii)   A joint venture could be mounted with a competitor, although for commercial reasons, it is often safer to arrange such alliances with companies outside the industry, or with overseas companies wishing to penetrate the UK market. Clearly, such an agreement would have to be carefully negotiated.

(iv)   The patent rights to one or more products could be sold and the purchaser allowed to develop the projects.

Raising external finance

(i)   A certain amount of marginal finance could be squeezed out of more intensive use of working capital, although this could be counter-productive eg, reducing credit periods for customers may lose sales.

(ii)   Some equipment could be leased.

(iii)   If Filtrex has assets of sufficient quality, it may be possible to raise a mortgage or issue debentures secured on these assets.

(iv)   Alternatively, good quality property assets could be sold to a financial institution and their continued use secured via a leaseback arrangement.

(v)   Filtrex might approach official sources of aid such as a regional development agency, if relevant, or perhaps the European Investment Bank.

(vi)   Filtrex might approach a venture capitalist such as 3i, which specialises in extending development capital to small-to-medium-sized firms. However, they may require an equity stake, and possibly insist on placing an appointee on the Board to monitor their interests.

(vii)   Filtrex may decide to seek a Stock Exchange quotation, either on the main market or the USM. However, this would be time-consuming and costly, and involve releasing at least 25% of the equity (10% for the USM) to a wider body of shareholders.

(Tutorial note: it is now no longer possible to enter the USM, which closed at the end of 1996. The Alternative Investment Market (AIM) was launched in June 1995 to provide a market for the shares of young fast growing companies not yet ready for a full listing; its entry requirements are less onerous than those for the USM.*)*

JUNE 1995 QUESTIONS

Section A – This question is compulsory and MUST be attempted

38   (Question 1 of examination)

(a)   For what *economic* reasons do central governments periodically impose limits on the capital expenditure of regional authorities?   **(5 marks)**

(b)   How does the required return for public sector investment decisions differ from that in the private sector?
                                                                                                    (5 marks)

(c)   The regional authority of Arctica, the most northerly province of Northland, (a member of the European Union which uses sterling as its currency) received many complaints from the general public during the past winter for its poor performance in clearing the local roads in snowy weather conditions. The roads department operates a fleet of five vehicles all beyond their optimum operating lifetimes and consequently having a high rate of breakdowns. Their second-hand value is estimated at £2,000 each. Modern replacements cost £50,000 each. After a life span of six years, it is expected that each vehicle could be resold for £5,000 after overhaul, or for £2,000 as scrap. The vehicles will require overhauls every two years costing £14,000 per vehicle.

A consultant, hired to assess the size of fleet required to provide an acceptable level of service to avoid future complaints, estimates that 10 vehicles would suffice in all but exceptional weather conditions. However, Arctica is concerned about the recent tightening by central government, (on whom regional authorities rely for most of their capital funding), of controls over capital spending. The vehicles would only be needed for the six months from October to March, although they could be hired during the summer months for a maximum of five years to a nearby quarry for a fixed annual contract fee for *all* 10 vehicles of initially £200,000, but declining by £40,000 each year to reflect ageing of the fleet. However, Arctica is concerned that the quarry workings are approaching exhaustion and may be closed in the near future. Indeed, the quarry company will not sign a firm contract for a period exceeding two years out of a similar concern.

During the winter, the 10 vehicles would be kept on stand-by, to be driven, when needed, by refuse disposal truck drivers, assigned from normal duties and paid overtime wage rates if necessary. Incremental operating costs, including salt to treat the roads, will depend on winter weather conditions according to the following probability distribution:

	Cost of drivers' wages, fuel, maintenance and salt	
Winter weather	*Probability*	*Annual cost (£m)*
Severe	0.2	1.5
Average	0.5	0.8
Good	0.3	0.3

Instead of buying 10 vehicles, Arctica is considering contracting-out the whole operation. It has received an unofficial tender from a waste management company, Dumpex plc, which might be willing to perform the required services at an all-in fee of £1m pa, payable at the end of each year.

Central government guidelines require regional authorities to evaluate capital expenditures at a discount rate of 5% expressed in real terms. The real rate of return in the private sector for transport and related activities is currently 8% net of all taxes.

All estimates of costs and benefits have been made in constant price terms. As a public sector organisation, Arctica is not liable to pay taxes.

Required

(i)   Is it financially more worthwhile for Arctica to purchase the new vehicles or to accept the tender from Dumpex?

Explain your answer.   **(11 marks)**

(ii)   What is the maximum annual tender figure at which Arctica would contract out the operation?

Explain your answer.   **(2 marks)**

(d)   Find the break-even value of the annual contract fee payable to Dumpex plc on the assumption that Arctica is unable to conclude any form of contract with the quarry company.

Comment on your results.   **(6 marks)**

(e)   Discuss *three* alternative ways in which Arctica could finance this project.   **(6 marks)**
                                                                                                    (Total 35 marks)

Section B – This question is compulsory and MUST be attempted

39   (Question 2 of examination)

Answer *five* of the six parts of this question. Each part carries five marks.

(a)   Explain the process whereby commercial banks can create the short-term credit required by business and other borrowers, and the constraints on this process.   **(5 marks)**

(b)   'If an organisation applies zero-base budgeting, (ZBB), it is essential that all levels of management understand the 'decision package' concept.'

Explain briefly what the 'decision package concept' is and how it is used in ZBB.   **(5 marks)**

(c)   The following cost information relates to product ZIM 3A, which is produced in one continuous process by Chemacca Ltd:

	£
Actual quantity of materials at standard price	103,500
Actual quantity of materials at actual price	103,250
Actual yield at standard materials cost	102,500
Standard yield from actual input of materials at standard cost	100,000

Required

Calculate and present the following material cost variances:

(i)   price;
(ii)   usage;
(iii)   mix and yield, and

comment briefly on your findings.   **(5 marks)**

(d)   Explain why statistical information is important to the operation of the management accounting function of an organisation.   **(5 marks)**

(e)   Sellmoor plc is considering a proposal to change its credit policy from allowing its debtors a credit period of 50 days, to either 40 days or 60 days, and supplied you with the following data:

	Period of credit allowed to debtors Days	Annual turnover (all on credit) £'000
	50 (current)	420
	40	350 (estimated)
	60	520 (estimated)

The average profit/volume ratio for the company is 22% and the cost of financing debtors is 12%.

Required

Compute and explain briefly what the effect on profit of each proposal would be, if adopted. **(5 marks)**

(f)   Explain briefly the principal steps which management would have to take in order to draw up their capital expenditure budget. **(5 marks)**

(Total 25 marks)

Section C – ONE question ONLY to be attempted

---

40   (Question 3 of examination)

You have been provided with the following operating statement which represents an attempt to compare the actual performance for the quarter which has just ended with the budget:

	Budget	Actual	Variance
Number of units sold ('000)	640	720	80
	£'000	£'000	£'000
Sales	1,024	1,071	47
Cost of sales (all variable)			
Materials	168	144	
Labour	240	288	
Overheads	32	36	
	440	468	(28)
Fixed labour cost	100	94	6
Selling and distribution costs			
Fixed	72	83	(11)
Variable	144	153	(9)
Administration costs			
Fixed	184	176	8
Variable	48	54	(6)
	548	560	(12)
Net profit	36	43	7

Required

(a)   Using a flexible budgeting approach, re-draft the operating statement so as to provide a more realistic indication of the variances, and comment briefly on the possible reasons (other than inflation) why they have occurred. **(12 marks)**

(b)   Explain why the original operating statement was of little use to management. **(2 marks)**

(c)   Discuss the problems associated with the forecasting of figures which are to be used in flexible
       budgeting.

                                                                                                (6 marks)
                                                                                           (Total 20 marks)

---

41   (Question 4 of examination)

The following budgeted information relates to Brunti plc for the forthcoming period:

		Products	
	XYI	YZT	ABW
	('000)	('000)	('000)
Sales and production (units)	50	40	30
	£	£	£
Selling price(per unit)	45	95	73
Prime cost (per unit)	32	84	65
	Hours	Hours	Hours
Machine department (machine hours per unit)	2	5	4
Assembly department (direct labour hours per unit)	7	3	2

Overheads allocated and apportioned to production departments (including service cost centre costs) were to be
recovered in product costs as follows:

      Machine department at £1.20 per machine hour
      Assembly department at £0.825 per direct labour hour

You ascertain that the above overheads could be re-analysed into 'cost pools' as follows:

Cost pool	£'000	Cost driver	Quantity for the period
Machining services	357	Machined hours	420,000
Assembly services	318	Direct labour hours	530,000
Set up costs	26	Set ups	520
Order processing	156	Customer orders	32,000
Purchasing	84	Suppliers' orders	11,200
	941		

You have also been provided with the following estimates for the period:

		Products	
	XYI	YZT	ABW
Number of set-ups	120	200	200
Customer orders	8,000	8,00	16,000
Suppliers' orders	3,000	4,000	4,200

Required

(a)   Prepare and present profit statements using:

      (i)   conventional absorption costing; and   **(5 marks)**
      (ii)   activity-based costing.   **(10 marks)**

(b)   Comment on why activity-based costing is considered to present a fairer valuation of the product cost per unit.

(5 marks)

(Total 20 marks)

Section D – ONE question ONLY to be attempted

| 42   (Question 5 of examination) |

Armcliff Ltd is a division of Shevin plc which requires each of its divisions to achieve a rate of return on capital employed of at least 10% pa. For this purpose, capital employed is defined as fixed capital and investment in stocks. This rate of return is also applied as a hurdle rate for new investment projects. Divisions have limited borrowing powers and all capital projects are centrally funded.

The following is an extract from Armcliff's divisional accounts:

Profit and loss account for the year ended 31 December 1994

	£m
Turnover	120
Cost of sales	(100)
Operating profit	20

Assets employed as at 31 December 1994

	£m	£m
Fixed (net)		75
Current assets (including stocks £25m)	45	
Current liabilities	(32)	
		13
Net capital employed		88

Armcliff's production engineers wish to invest in a new computer-controlled press. The equipment cost is £14m. The residual value is expected to be £2m after four years operation, when the equipment will be shipped to a customer in South America.

The new machine is capable of improving the quality of the existing product and also of producing a higher volume. The firm's marketing team is confident of selling the increased volume by extending the credit period. The expected additional sales are:

Year 1	2,000,000 units
Year 2	1,800,000 units
Year 3	1,600,000 units
Year 4	1,600,000 units

Sales volume is expected to fall over time due to emerging competitive pressures. Competition will also necessitate a reduction in price by £0.5 each year from the £5 per unit proposed in the first year. Operating costs are expected to be steady at £1 per unit, and allocation of overheads (none of which are affected by the new project) by the central finance department is set at £0.75 per unit.

Higher production levels will require additional investment in stocks of £0.5m, which would be held at this level until the final stages of operation of the project. Customers at present settle accounts after 90 days on average.

Required

(a)   Determine whether the proposed capital investment is attractive to Armcliff, using the average rate of return on capital method, as defined as average profit-to-average capital employed, ignoring debtors and creditors.

[*Note:* Ignore taxes]   **(7 marks)**

(b)   (i)   Suggest *three* problems which arise with the use of the average return method for appraising new investment.   **(3 marks)**

       (ii)   In view of the problems associated with the ARR method, why do companies continue to use it in project appraisal?   **(3 marks)**

(c)   Briefly discuss the dangers of offering more generous credit, and suggest ways of assessing customers' creditworthiness.   **(7 marks)**

                                                                                                       (Total 20 marks)

---

43   (Question 6 of examination)

Collingham plc produces electronic measuring instruments for medical research. It has recorded strong and consistent growth during the past 10 years since its present team of managers bought it out from a large multinational corporation. They are now contemplating obtaining a stock market listing.

Collingham's accounting statements for the last financial year are summarised below. Fixed assets, including freehold land and premises, are shown at historic cost net of depreciation. The debenture is redeemable in two years although early redemption without penalty is permissible.

Profit and loss account for the year ended 31 December 1994

	£m
Turnover	80.0
Cost of sales	(70.0)
Operating profit	10.0
Interest charges	(3.0)
Pre-tax profit	7.0
Corporation tax (after capital allowances)	(1.0)
Profits attributable to ordinary shareholders	6.0
Dividends	(0.5)
Retained earnings	5.5

Balance sheet as at 31 December 1994

	£m	£m	£m
Assets employed			
Fixed:			
Land and premises		10.0	
Machinery		20.0	
			30.0
Current:			
Stocks	10.0		
Debtors	10.0		
Cash	3.0		
		23.0	
Current liabilities:			
Trade creditors	(15.0)		
Bank overdraft	(5.0)		
		(20.0)	
Net current assets			3.0
Total assets less current liabilities			33.0
14% Debenture			(5.0)
Net assets			28.0
Financed by:			
Issued share capital (par value 50p)			
Voting shares			2.0
Non-voting 'A' shares			2.0
Profit and loss account			24.0
Shareholders' funds			28.0

The following information is also available regarding key financial indicators for Collingham's industry.

Return on (long-term) capital employed	22% (pre-tax)
Return on equity	14% (post-tax)
Operating profit margin	10%
Current ratio	1.8:1
Acid-test	1.1:1
Gearing (total debt equity)	18%
Interest cover	5.2
Dividend cover	2.6
P/E ratio	13:1

Required

(a) Briefly explain why companies like Collingham seek stock market listings. **(4 marks)**

(b) Discuss the performance and financial health of Collingham in relation to that of the industry as a whole. **(8 marks)**

(c) In what ways would you advise Collingham:

(i) to restructure its balance sheet *prior* to floatation, **(5 marks)**
(ii) to change its financial policy *following* floatation? **(3 marks)**

(Total 20 marks)

ANSWERS TO JUNE 1995 EXAMINATION

It should be noted that the following answers are fuller than would be expected from the average student under exam conditions. Answers are provided in some degree of detail to offer guidance on the approach required, and on the range and depth of knowledge that would be expected from an excellent student.

38   (Answer 1 of examination)

Examiner's comments and marking guide

Question 1: the case study question, centred on a regional authority facing capital spending restrictions imposed by central government, but wishing to invest in new snow-clearing equipment. Essentially a question on project appraisal, but requiring knowledge of the economic context and of sources of finance available to the public sector.

Part (a): many candidates appeared to be unaware of economic principles, and of the role of the state in managing the economy. Most answers were a list of possible reasons for intervention which may or may not have been relevant. These were expressed in vague terms such as 'to control inflation', 'to restrain interest rates', 'to reduce borrowing', etc with little or no attempt to place these points in the context of an economic stabilisation policy. A particular difficulty was a lack of understanding of the interrelationships between the various factors cited. For example, candidates should ask themselves why is it government borrowing may affect interest rates, the exchange rate and perhaps the balance of payments? (There was great confusion between the PSBR and the balance of payments.)

Part (b): the intention of this section was to elicit discussion from candidates of the required rates of return, ie, discount rates, for investment projects, in the public and private sectors respectively. Candidates could also earn some marks (as most did), by talking generally about the nature of the returns in the two sectors, and about respective objectives, ie, profit motive in the private sector and social benefits in the public sector. Few candidates focused on the differential in time horizon risk as between the two sectors, or on the possible risk disparity, although some did focus on the tax aspect.

There was some confusion in the distinction between public and private sector – some candidates read public as 'publicly quoted' and private as 'unquoted'. The correct interpretation should have been clear from the context of the whole question.

Part (c)(i): many different approaches were possible here. For example, the decision problem could be treated in terms of the respective NPVs of the two options, in incremental terms or in terms of Equivalent Annual Costs (EAC). All such approaches would produce the same answer. It was however, essential to use DCF analysis (which was why discount rates were provided) over six years, incorporating Arctica's cut-off rate of 5%. Many candidates attempted to find a one-year cost which included all the initial outlay, for which only limited credit could be offered. Many candidates seemed unsure of how to approach a cost minimisation problem.

Part (c)(ii): this section revealed candidates' lack of knowledge of the EAC concept – a common error was to divide the NPV figure from the previous section by the number of years rather than by the relevant annuity factor.

Part (d) was frequently totally ignored, but for candidates who understood the question, this offered some very easy marks. All that was required was removal of the PV of the hire income and conversion of the resulting higher cost figure into a higher EAC. Many candidates could only associate 'break-even' with cost-volume-profit analysis. Commentary was generally very sparse.

(Candidates can be assured that incorrect answers to earlier sections were not penalised twice – markers applied the 'own answer principle' to give appropriate credit for method even where answers were numerically incorrect.)

In part (e), answers were generally weak. Although the requirement said 'discuss', most responses were little more than lists, often with no acknowledgement of the context of the question. Some answers were completely irrelevant, talking about companies and rights issues, debentures and convertibles, etc. To gain marks, answers had to be relevant to the public sector, and where appropriate, eg, in the case of aspects like government grants or borrowing, to reflect the more stringent regime being applied, ie, the regional authority might have to make a special case to the central authorities to overcome the new restrictions.

			Marks
(a)	Role of discretionary fiscal policy in boom/slump		2
	Importance of forecasting		1
	Relative ease of altering capital budgets, constraints?		2
			—
	Total		5
			—
(b)	Private sector: need to cover opportunity costs		1
	risk		1
	Public sector: longer life of projects - lower rate?		1
	external benefits/costs		1
	opportunity cost arguments		1
			—
	Total		5
			—
(c)	(i)	Calculation of value of offer	2
		EV of operating costs	1
		Residual values/overhaul costs	2
		Contract income	1
		Calculation of PV of cost stream	1
		Discussion/explanation	4
			—
		Total	11
			—
	(ii)	Calculation of equivalent annual contract fee	2
			—
(d)	Removal of contract income		1
	Calculation of resulting PV		1
	Conversion to break-even value		2
	Discussion		2
			—
	Total		6
			—
(e)	Two marks for each suggestion - discussion is essential (suggestions must be relevant to the public sector)		
			—
	Total		6
			—
	Grand total		35
			—

(Step by step answer plan)

Step 1 Read the question again and make sure that you focus on precisely what is required. The bulk of the question concerns investment appraisal - although the words "present value" or "discounted cash flow" were not actually mentioned, this approach was implied by the fact that a discount rate was given.

Step 2 (a) The train of thought required here is (i) what effects may the reduction of authorities' capital expenditure have (on government borrowing, business activity, inflation, etc) and (ii) what economic policy/ objective would these effects fit in with? The latter is what the question is essentially asking.

Step 3   (b)   First ensure you are happy with what is meant by "public sector" and "private sector". In general, parts of case study question are linked, and in this case the main part of the question concerns a regional authority project, which we are told is to be discounted at a lower rate than a similar project that may be undertaken by a private sector company. This should guide you in both the meaning of the sector terminology, and in the likely direction of the difference between the rates. You now have to think why this may be so.

Step 4   (c)   (i)   There is a lot of information here to assimilate. Try to break it down, extracting the essential data in some brief notes:

- Current vehicle fleet - resale values
- Replacement fleet - capital and overhaul costs; resale values (note: a decision needs to be made as to the final overhaul); number of vehicles required; running costs (need an expected value)
- Summer months, hire contract possibility - income
- Alternative option, contracting out - annual fee
- Discount rate - need to choose which is appropriate

Now identify the cash flows (mainly costs) associated with the two options and compare them in present value terms over the same time period. As the examiner says in his comments, there are a variety of possible approaches here. Don't forget to complete the requirement by explaining your answer - interpret the results of your computations in words, and add any other considerations that you think are relevant.

Step 5   (c)   (ii)   The maximum sub-contract fee will be that which makes the PV of the costs of this option equal to that of the in-house option. So look back at your computation for the sub-contract option, substitute "x" for the fee, equate the result to that for the in-house option and solve for x. This is, in fact, finding the equivalent annual cost (EAC) of the in-house option.

Step 6   (d)   Although the terminology used here is different, you are basically repeating the exercise in (c)(ii), with a different PV of costs of the in-house option to aim at. When removing of the contract hire income from the PV computation, don't start again from scratch - start with the net flows for each year and adjust out the income (you could also do this in PV terms).

Step 7   (e)   This is *not* a "write all you know about sources of finance" question. It is very specifically related to the organisation and economic environment in the question. It is simply a waste of time writing about sources that are only open to private sector companies. Note also that "discuss" requires greater explanation than (say) "outline".

Step 8   Now review your answer and ensure that it does precisely answer the question as set.

Items not required by the examiner for this question

- general discussions/lists of sources of finance available to private sector organisations

The examiner's answer

(a)   Central governments apply periodic restrictions on public expenditure, both current and capital, as part of their discretionary fiscal policy. Such intervention in the economy seeks to smooth the oscillations of the business cycle by adjusting the balance between public expenditure and revenue from taxes. Specifically, when an economic downturn is expected, the government will plan to operate a budget deficit ie, spend more than its tax revenue, in order to inject demand into the economy when economic activity is flagging, and conversely, when an economic expansion, with consequent inflationary pressures, is expected.

This contra-cyclical budgetary policy can dampen fluctuations in the economy, thus increasing business confidence and readiness to invest. However, successful operation of this policy requires considerable skill in forecasting future economic trends, perception in recognising the need to act and speed in putting appropriate measures into effect so that they have an impact when required.

When a government wishes to restrict its expenditure it is often easier to cut capital expenditure. Although once approved and begun, capital projects acquire a momentum which is difficult to reverse, design specifications can be changed for subsequent phases of a lengthy project, later phases postponed or cancelled, or projects yet to be undertaken can be delayed indefinitely.

Did you answer the question?

The examiner has initially discussed the purpose of government intervention in general public expenditure, in terms of the required economic effects. He then goes on specifically to address capital expenditure, as the question requires.

(b)   Private sector companies are obliged to earn a return at least as great as the opportunity cost incurred by the owners who subscribe capital to them, that is, to at least match the returns offered by comparable investments in which they might otherwise have invested. This reflects the required compensation to reward the individual for waiting for his money, (his rate of 'time preference'), plus some compensation for risk.

In the public sector, many investments such as civil engineering works, have far longer lives than private sector projects, and may also involve costs and benefits which are not priced by the market – so-called externalities such as pollution or congestion costs. For these reasons, it is often argued that a different discount rate should be applied to public sector projects.

One approach is to adopt the social rate of time preference argument. Society has a longer time horizon than private individuals and to reflect this, a lower rate of discount is warranted, so as not to over-discount the distant benefits which would be valued by future generations.

However, this approach may overlook the opportunity cost incurred by society in undertaking the project in question. Since capital can be invested in a number of ways, it is appropriate to examine what projects and hence what returns are foregone by allocating capital to particular uses. Consequently, the correct discount rate would reflect the rate of return on the best alternative use of public funds, including all externalities – the so-called social opportunity cost return.

(In the Arctica example, the government requires a return of 5% in real terms, below the yield on comparable private sector investments. In the UK in recent years, the Treasury has tended to overlook the externalities argument and focus on the post-tax returns which would otherwise have been achieved in the private sector. In this case, it is more likely that the lower percentage reflects the differential advantage enjoyed by the government in raising capital compared to private sector companies.)

Did you answer the question?

Note the examiner's approach here, which follows a logical analysis of the requirement. First, why should the required rates of return *differ* in general? This involves discussion of the differences in objectives, time horizons, non-financial elements etc. Then, why (as the later part of the question implies) might the public sector required return be generally *lower*?

(c)   (i)   **Evaluation of alternatives**

The optimal course of action from a financial viewpoint is that which minimises the present value of the net costs of meeting the service targets.

The offer

The present value of the annual contract payments sought by Dumpex is found by applying the six-year annuity factor at 5% to the annual payments:

Present value = £1m × PVIFA$_{5,6}$ = £1m × 5.076 = £5.08. (TN 1)

Purchase of new fleet

Expected value of operating costs (£m)

= (0.2 × 1.5) + (0.5 × 0.8) + (0.3 × 0.3) = 0.3 + 0.4 + 0.09 = 0.79

Cash flow profile (£m)

Year

Item	0	1	2	3	4	5	6
Outlay	(0.50)						
Residual values	0.01						0.02
Overhaul*			(0.14)		(0.14)		
Operating costs		(0.79)	(0.79)	(0.79)	(0.79)	(0.79)	(0.79)
Contract income		0.20	0.16	0.12	0.08	0.04	
Net outflows	(0.49)	(0.59)	(0.77)	(0.67)	(0.85)	(0.75)	(0.77)
Discount factor	1.000	0.952	0.907	0.864	0.823	0.784	0.746
Present value	(0.49)	(0.56)	(0.70)	(0.58)	(0.70)	(0.59)	(0.57)

Present value of net outflows = (4.19) (ie, £4.19m).

Note: the overhaul profile recognises that the expenditure in year 6 of £0.14m required to make the vehicles saleable for £5,000 each is uneconomic. The best alternative is to sell for scrap (TN1).

Based upon this information, the in-house option is less costly ie, the net present value of in-house costs is less than the present value of the contracted-out costs. This may be because Dumpex seeks a higher return for an activity of this degree of risk, and/or it must provide for tax liabilities. However, there remains the uncertainty surrounding the period over which Arctica can expect to receive income from the quarry company. In addition, the operating costs are based on expected values – a run of bad winters could result in costs higher than the contracted-out figure.

(ii)   To encourage Arctica to contract out the operation, an annual fee which generates the same or lower present value would have to be offered. The equivalent contract fee is found by dividing the present value of outflows by the appropriate annuity factor ie:

$$£4.19m/5.076 = £0.83m$$

which is considerably below the unofficial offer of £1m.

(d)   There is a distinct danger that the in-house cost is understated as the income from the quarry contract is highly unreliable. As a form of sensitivity analysis, the impact of losing all income from that source can be assessed. The break-even value of the contract fee can be found by removing the given contract income figures from the cash flows, finding the present value of the resulting cost stream and converting it into an equivalent annuity ie, the annual figure which yields the same present value as the series of costs which Arctica expects to incur.

Cash flow profile from part (c) (£m)

Year

	0	1	2	3	4	5	6
Net outflows	(0.49)	(0.59)	(0.77)	(0.67)	(0.85)	(0.75)	(0.77)
Contract income (TN 2)		(0.20)	(0.16)	(0.12)	(0.08)	(0.04)	
Revised net outflows	(0.49)	(0.79)	(0.93)	(0.79)	(0.93)	(0.79)	(0.77)
Discount factor	1.000	0.952	0.907	0.864	0.823	0.784	0.746
Present value	(0.49)	(0.75)	(0.84)	(0.68)	(0.77)	(0.62)	(0.57)

Total present value = (4.72) (ie, £4.72m).

Hence to break even, the fee for the contract with Dumpex would have to be:

[Present value of costs]/PVIFA$_{5,6}$ = £4.72/5.076 = £0.93m.

This means that to cover the risk attaching to the contract with the quarry company, Arctica would have to pay an annual fee to Dumpex of £0.93m, a little below the unofficial tender of £1m. However, it is likely that the latter figure is above the minimum valuation which Dumpex attaches to the contract, being merely an 'opener' in the negotiation process. There seems to be scope for negotiation.

(e) Possible alternative sources of finance including the following:

(i) *Private finance input.* In some countries, (eg, in the UK under the Private Finance Initiative), efforts are being made to involve the private sector in partially or wholly financing public sector investment. This reflects the government's conviction that some services may be more efficiently provided by the private sector. In the case of Arctica, there may be scope for operating a joint venture, sharing control with a private sector company willing to assume a portion of the financial outlay and associated risk in return for a guaranteed service contract.

(ii) *Official aid sources.* If the central government is unwilling to fund the project, Arctica may look to external funding agencies such as the range of loan facilities offered by the European Investment Bank, or grants from the European Union Regional Fund which aims to promote economic development in less-developed areas of the EU.

(iii) *Leasing.* Leasing is a means of transferring expenditure from capital account to revenue account. Instead of incurring a 'lumpy' investment outlay at the outset of the project, the authority may arrange to pay a series of rentals to a leasing company for the use of the asset(s) concerned. With a finance lease, the length of the agreement approximates to the lifetime of the asset(s), and the contract cannot easily be cancelled without prohibitive penalty clauses. Hence, the lessee (user) assumes the risk of equipment obsolescence and idle time. An operating lease is similar to a plant-hire contract whereby the equipment is rented for a limited period corresponding to the requirements of a particular task. Operating leases are usually more expensive than finance leases per period of use, but, as in the case of Arctica, where there are long periods of idle time, they may represent the soundest option.

Did you answer the question?

Note the very narrow scope of this answer - Arctica is a public sector regional authority, operating in circumstances of tightening of controls over governmental capital funding. It requires very careful selection of possible sources of finance to remain relevant.

Tutorial notes

1 The above evaluation ignores the possibility of Arctica still having the benefit of the scrap values of its current fleet if it contracts out the operation. If this was included, it would reduce the PV of the costs of this option by £10,000 to £5.07m. This does not change the conclusion.

2 As there is some doubt about the length of the quarry contract, you may consider only including the first two years' worth. This would increase the PV of costs of this option by £0.20m, ie to £4.39. This would not change the conclusion.

---

39 (Answer 2 of examination)

(**Examiner's comments and marking guide**)

Question 2: part (a) required a knowledge of how commercial banks create credit via the operation of the bank multiplier, and the constraints on the process.

This was very badly done, partly as a result of poor knowledge of Economics and partly due to misinterpretation. The question required explanation of the credit creation process and associated constraints, such as central bank restrictions on reserve ratios. The trigger words should have been 'credit creation' and 'process'. Actual answers ranged from the trivial (such as 'banks receive deposits and lend them out as loans'), through general explanations of the nature of financial intermediation to broad explanations of lending procedures (ie, interviews, credit checks, etc), and/or of the range of bank lending facilities (ie, overdrafts, loans, etc). For properly prepared candidates, interpretation should not have been a problem – the bank multiplier process is commonplace. Responses were especially poor on knowledge of central bank measures to restrict lending.

Part (b) was about 'the decision package concept' in zero-base budgeting.

This part was not answered very well. Many candidates did not answer the question set, instead writing down all they knew about ZBB.

Part (c) required candidates to calculate material variances, including the mix and yield variances from the information supplied and then to comment briefly on their findings.

The majority of candidates made a poor attempt at answering this part. The calculation of the material price variance did not present too much difficulty. However, a large number of candidates scored few or no marks for their calculations of the other material variances. Quite a number of answers described one of the variances as 'the mix and yield variance'. Many of the attempts made no comment at all about their findings.

Part (d). This 'open ended' question asked for an explanation as to why statistical information is important to the management accountant. The majority of candidates did reasonably well here. It was pleasing to find satisfactory explanations of why it is important in areas such as budgeting and decision making and also to find examples of the uses to which the management accountant can put certain statistical techniques/government statistics.

Part (e) concerned the effects on profit of changing the period of credit which is offered to debtors.

Overall this was very well down but quite a number of candidates lost marks by not providing the brief explanation that was required.

Part (f) concerned the steps needed to draw up a 'capital expenditure budget'.

The performance on this part was very mixed. Candidates tending to produce either very good or very poor answers. Quite a number of candidates just wrote about capital investment appraisal eg, NPV, pay-back etc which was just one small component part of the answer. Those who produced better answers looked at inter-relationships with other budgets, financing considerations, alternatives to outright purchase, etc.

		Marks
(a)	Verbal explanation of bank multiplier	1
	Use of numerical example	1
	Limitations on the process:	
	Prudence	
	Monetary policy	
	demand for loans	
	return of cash, etc	
	(½ mark for each point, with an extra ½ for brief explanation)	3
		—
	Total	5
		—
(b)	What decision packages represent/ranking them	1½
	What a typical decision package will indicate	2
	Uses of ZBB/forces managers to state their priorities/secure active participation	1½
		—
	Total	5
		—
(c)	Calculation of material price, usage, cost, mix and yield variances	3½
	Appropriate, brief comments/causes	1½
		—
	Total	5
		—
(d)	1 mark per relevant point which is well explained for this 'open ended' question	5
		—
	Total	5
		—

(e)   Calculation of:

The effect on debtors   2½

The effect on the profit/loss   1½

Brief appropriate comment   1
                                                                                         ———
Total   5
                                                                                         ———

(f)   1 mark per relevant point which is well explained for this 'open ended' question   5
                                                                                         ———
Total   5
                                                                                         ———

The examiner's answer

(a)   The working capital cycle of most companies is financed to some degree by bank loans and overdrafts (advances). To fulfil their function of providers of short-term finance, banks rely on their ability to create money via the bank multiplier process.

The banks are able to create money in the form of credit because they are confident, on the basis of experience, that when a deposit is made, the customer is unlikely to wish to withdraw the whole balance at any one time. However much she/he does withdraw, there is a high probability that she/he will make payments to people who will, in turn, deposit their receipts at the bank. Consequently, bankers know that only a relatively small cash reserve is required to support a given level of deposits so that the remainder can be safely lent to other customers in order to earn interest income.

For instance, if a new customer makes a cash deposit of £1,000 and the bank deems it prudent to retain only 10% of this ie, £100, it can be shown that the deposit can be used to support loans of £9,000. In this case, there is a 'bank deposit multiplier' of 10 at work, given by the reciprocal of the prudential reserve ratio [1/0.1 = 10]. The initial deposit has been multiplied 10 times and new money in the form of credit of £9,000 has been created. There is thus also a *credit* multiplier of nine at work.

Clearly, this process is limited by the banker's own notions of prudence and also by the demand for loans. The reserve ratio may also be controlled by the nation's monetary authorities, who may also impose other restrictions on the structure of banks' balance sheets to limit their ability to lend. The full multiplier also relies on there being no cash leakages from the banking system. If the general public and businesses also require to hold liquid cash reserves, this will dampen the operation of the multiplier- each time an expenditure is made, the recipient will hold back some proportion in cash form before banking the remainder. Such cash leakages may be mitigated by the prevalence of cheque and credit card usage. Finally, if the recipients of loan-financed expenditures deposit their receipts at other banks, the ability of the original lender to create further credit ceases. However, the credit-creating capacity of the banking system as a whole is unimpaired, unless other banks apply stricter reserve requirements to back their own lending.

(b)   In ZBB (zero-base budgeting), past budget allocations are irrelevant and managers are called upon to justify their requests. This means that managers have to produce 'decision packages' and to rank them in their order of importance.

Decision packages represent units of intended activity, such as a proposed new internal transport system or a research and development project.

A typical 'decision package' is a document which will indicate and try to justify, why the proposal is necessary and indicate:

–   the capital and revenue expenditure required
–   details of other resource needs
–   the assumptions which have had to be made eg, the operating level of activity
–   details of alternative courses of action
–   forecasts of income etc
–   the expected benefits

It has been found that ZBB, using its 'decision package concept' has been of particular value in service and support areas. The fact that it calls upon management to justify and explain their claims on the organisation's scarce resources makes it into quite a powerful tool. The ranking process forces managers to state their priorities and enables top management to allocate resources accordingly.

The formulation of 'decision packages' requires the active participation of lower levels of management and subordinates, which should result in more accurate/ realistic information and better co-ordination/communications within the organisation.

(c)   **Product ZIM 3A**

Calculation of variances

			£
(A)	Actual quantity at actual price		103,250
(B)	Actual quantity at standard price		103,500
(C)	Standard yield at standard cost		100,000
(D)	Actual yield at standard cost		102,500

		£
Material: price variance	(A – B)	250 (F)
Usage variance	(B – D)	1,000 (A)
Cost variance	(A – D)	750 (A)

The usage variance is made up of the mix and yield variances as follows:

Mix variance	(B – C)	3,500 (A)
Yield variance	(C – D)	2,500 (F)
		1,000 (A)

The mix and yield variance are the component parts of the adverse material usage variance, which has cost the company more than it planned. The cause needs to be investigated and could be caused by using poor quality materials or the input of a greater than planned proportion of the more expensive materials.

(d)   The role of the management accountant has been described as being that of an 'information manager'. In order to fulfil this role the management accountant must use and provide statistical information. Statistical information is needed to help to:

– set targets eg, information on trends, market research data, inflation rates, etc

– set objectives eg, quantitative information via statistical techniques such as probability and regression analysis

– monitor performance eg, what is happening to stocks, order, prices, etc, and quality measures

– control eg, comparative data, statistical data needed in the setting of standards

– assist with decision making eg, the assessment of risk

– define what the problem is, using statistical data eg, number of customers in restaurant, their average expenditure, consumer spending, etc

– understand their environment eg, economic factors such as supply and demand, etc

– present reports which are supported by facts and appropriate figures/tabulation/ graphs, etc

(e)   **Proposed credit policies**

	40 days £	60 days £
40 days debtors = £350,000 × $40/365$	38,356	
60 days debtors = £520,000 × $60/365$		85,479
Less: Existing debtors £420,000 × $50/365$	57,534	57,534
Effect on debtors	(19,178)	27,945
Cost of debtors (12%)	2,301	(3,353)
Effect on contribution (£70,000)/100,000 × 22%	(15,400)	22,000
Profit/(loss)	(13,099)	18,647

As indicated above, the 40 day policy will result in a reduction of profit and the 60 day policy will result in an increase. However, it should also be noted that the 40 day policy could reduce the level of bad debts and the 60 day policy increase the level of bad debts. It would be advisable also to look at the policy re the payment of creditors at the same time.

(f)   The principal steps which management would have to take in order to produce their capital expenditure budget, could include:

–   The assessment of needs in terms of fixed assets such as buildings, machinery, equipment and fixtures for the short, medium and long terms.

–   The production of a timetable so as to ensure the proper consultation takes place and that the budget is ready for implementation by the due date. The meetings involved should provide the opportunity for participation by the various managerial levels and shop floor representatives.

–   Matching the requirements to the other budgets, as budgets are inter-related eg, the expansion of the production could well involve the acquisition of new fixed assets.

–   Taking the 'principal budget factor' (also called the limiting factor) into account as it places a constraint on the activities of the organisation. If the availability of finance is the 'principal budget factor', the capital expenditure budget will be affected.

–   Appointing someone to co-ordinate the capital expenditure budget eg, the accountant/budget controller. Their role would include communicating with all those involved, providing information/data to assist preparation, chairing meetings, etc.

40   (Answer 3 of examination)

(Examiner's comments and marking guide)

Question 3: involved the calculation of variances using a flexible budgeting approach and commenting briefly on the possible reasons for the variances.

(a)   Many candidates scored well on this question. Those who did not tended either not to flex the budget at all, or flex both variable and fixed costs.

(b)   The majority of candidates had no problem with this part.

(c)   This section was about the problems associated with forecasting the figures which are used in flexible budgeting.

This was not very well answered and represents the area in this question where candidates did not pick up many marks. This was yet another prime example of a question where candidates did not answer the question set. Quite a number of answers were all about the advantages and disadvantages of flexible budgeting or just looked at the problem of distinguishing between fixed and variable costs.

		Marks
(a)	Revised operating statement:	
	An analysis of the variances, plus possible reasons for them up to and including the gross profit	7
	Analysis of other overhead variances, plus possible reasons for them up to and including the net profit	4
	Concluding comment/principal reasons for variances	1
	Total	12
(b)	Comparing 'like with like' explained	1
	Why the statement is not fair	1
	Total	2
(c)	Using historical information/records of materials used	1½
	Separation of fixed and variable costs with brief example	1½
	Step-fixed costs with brief example	1½
	Underlying assumptions on which the budget is based	1½
	Total	6
	Grand total	20

Step by step answer plan

Step 1 Read the question again and make sure that you focus on precisely what is required. Your initial review of the operating statement should have identified a major flaw in its preparation - variances have been extracted with reference to the original budget, incorporating an activity level that turned out to be significantly different from that actually achieved. Comparing actual data to a *flexed* budget (ie standard for *actual* activity level) is a fundamental principle of variance analysis. This is strongly hinted at in the requirement of (a)

Step 2 (a) Having decided that the budget needs flexing, you then have to be careful not to over-complicate matters by flexing fixed costs, which will result in the total variance incorporating a volume variance. The format of the statement in the question is along marginal costing lines (cost of sales are all variable) so stick with this. The re-drafting of the statement should be kept as simple as possible, to allow enough time for comments on possible causes. Note that the examiner has awarded one mark for a general conclusion, in which the major differences are highlighted.

Step 3 (b) Here you are asked to explain the rationale of the adjustments you have made in (a).

Step 4 (c) Many of the general problems in forecasting future costs and revenues are relevant here, but do try to include particular considerations of flexible budgeting, that depends upon a reasonable understanding of the cost behaviours involved.

Step 5 Now review your answer and ensure that it does precisely answer the question as set.

Items not required by the examiner for this question

- Discussion of the advantages and disadvantages of flexible budgeting

(**The examiner's answer**)

(a)　**Revised operating statement based on sales of 720,000 units**

	Budget £'000	Actual £'000	Variance £'000	Possible reasons for the variance
Sales	1,152	1,071	(81)	Sales made to certain segments at lower prices. Bulk discounts given to customers.
Cost of sales				
Materials	189	144	45	Buying in bulk and attracting discount. Buying lower quality materials.
Labour (variable)	270	288	(18)	More time taken to work, lower quality material. More overtime worked to cope with increased volume.
Labour (fixed)	100	94	6	Fixed lower than budget could be caused by employees leaving and not being replaced.
Overheads	36	36	Nil	
	595	562	33	
Gross profit	557	509	(48)	(As above)
Other overheads				
Selling and distribution				
Fixed	72	83	(11)	Additional fixed advertising cost.
Variable	162	153	9	Better vehicle utilisation.
Administration				
Fixed	184	176	8	Staff leave but not replaced
Variable	54	54	Nil	immediately
	472	466	6	
Net profit	85	43	(42)	(As above)

The principal reasons for the variation between budgeted and actual net profits are the sales revenue being lower than planned and the £45,000 less than planned expenditure on materials plus the increased variable labour costs.

Note: The above statement could have used a marginal costing format, and other reasons for variances are possible. (TN1)

(b)　When budget and actual figures are compared, and variances extracted, it is most important that 'like is compared with like' ie, that the budgeted 'level of activity' is the same as the actual 'level of activity'. The statement provided is not a fair and valid comparison, as it is comparing sales and costs for 640,000 units with an actual of 720,000.

(c)　The problems associated with forecasting figures which are to be used in flexible budgeting are:

－　Using past information to forecast the future does not always provide reliable forecasts. What happened in the past does not always hold true for the future eg, records showing how much material was used are just a starting point in the assessment of what quantities should be used.

–   Flexible budgeting relies on being able to separate costs into their fixed and variable elements. This is not always an easy task eg, direct labour can be fixed or variable or a combination of the two such as a fixed salary plus a bonus based on output.

–   The computation of step-fixed costs also needs to be considered. Fixed costs can go up or down as output increases/decreases eg, shedding labour, hiring/renting more machinery and equipment.

–   Another problem is concerned with sorting out the underlying assumptions upon which the budget is to be based eg, the rate of inflation, the level of sales, constraints imposed by limiting factors, judgements re probability, etc.

Tutorial notes

1   All *variable* budget costs/revenues have been flexed by multiplying by a factor of 720/640 = 1.125 and fixed costs are unflexed. As a result the variances calculated are those expected in a marginal costing operating statement, although the layout is more consistent with absorption costing.

---

41   (Answer 4 of examination)

Examiner's comments and marking guide

Question 4: this question looked at activity based costing (ABC).

Most candidates were very well prepared for this question and scored very good marks on both the computational and the written parts.

			Marks
(a)	(i)	Absorption costing profit statement	5
	(ii)	Calculation of cost per machine hour, direct labour hour, per set up, etc.	3
		Activity based costing profit statement	7
	Total		15
(b)		The problems of conventional absorption costing	2
		Relating overheads via cost drivers more accurately to the product/could be significant differences in the information. Supported by a brief example	3
	Total		5
	Grand total		20

Step by step answer plan

Step 1   Read the question again and make sure that you focus on precisely what is required. It is a fairly standard comparison of traditional with activity-based costing absorption methods.

Step 2   (a)   You have already been given the traditional absorption rates , so the main work in (i) is simply converting unit revenues and costs to totals for each product. For (ii) new activity based absorption rates for the individual categories of overheads need to be computed from the cost driver information supplied. These are then applied to products according to their relative use of the cost drivers.

Step 3   (c)   The best answers to this part will be those that draw on information given/derived in (a) to illustrate the points being made. The tendency otherwise may be to talk in vague terms about "more representative cost allocation" without specifically explaining why that is the case.

Step 4   Now review your answer and ensure that it does precisely answer the question as set.

The examiner's answer

(a) (i) **Absorption costing profit statement**

		Products				
		XYI		YZT		ABW
		'000		'000		'000
Sales/production (units)		50		40		30

	£'000	£'000	£'000	£'000	£'000	£'000
Sales		2,250		3,800		2,190
Less: Prime cost	1,600		3,360		1,950	
Overheads						
Machine dept	120		240		144	
Assembly dept	288.75	2,008.75	99	3,699	49.5	2,143.5
Profit (loss)		241.25		101		46.5

Total £388.75

	Cost pools				
	Machining services	Assembly services	Set-ups	Order processing	Purchasing
(£'000)	357	318	26	156	84
Cost drivers	420,000 machine hours	530,000 direct labour hours	520 set-ups	32,000 customer orders	11,200 suppliers' orders
	£0.85 per machine hour	£0.60 per direct labour hour	£50 per set-up	£4.875 per customer order	£7.50 per suppliers' order

(ii) **Activity-based costing profit statement**

		XYI		YZT		ABW
		'000		'000		'000
Sales/production (units)		50		40		30

	£'000	£'000	£'000	£'000	£'000	£'000
Sales		2,250		3,800		2,190
Less: Prime cost	1,600		3,360		1,950	
Cost pools						
Machine dept at 0.85	85		170		102	
Assembly dept at 0.60	210		72		36	
Set-up costs at £50	6		10		10	
Order processing at £4.875	39		39		78	
Purchasing at £7.50	22.5		30		31	
		1,962.5		3,681		2,207.5
Profit/(loss)		287.5		119		(17.5)

Total £389

(b)   Activity-based costing (ABC) is considered to present a fairer valuation of the product cost per unit for the following reasons:

–   It overcomes some of the problems which are associated with conventional absorption costing. In part (a) (i) all of the production overheads and some other overheads had to be allocated or apportioned to the two cost centres, machine department, assembly department and to service cost centres. Those overheads which could not be identified with a particular cost centre would have had to be shared between cost centres using some arbitrary basis such as floor area or the number of employees. In addition, the service department costs would have been apportioned to production cost centres using some arbitrary basis or technical estimates. The total overheads for each production cost centre would then be divided by the estimated number of machine hours or direct labour hours, as appropriate. This meant that costs which could have been more accurately related to the product were not eg, set up costs vary more with the number of set-ups than with the number of machine hours or direct labour hours.

–   In (a) (ii) it can be observed that by having a number of 'cost pools' and dividing them by their 'cost driver' ie, the activity which causes the cost, a more accurate and realistic assessment can be produced. The information so produced using ABC, can be significantly different to that which is generated by traditional absorption costing. The differing levels of activity incurred on behalf of each product in terms of the 'cost drivers' eg, the number of set-ups, customer orders etc, can, and do, have quite a significant impact on the product cost per unit.

42   (Answer 5 of examination)

Examiner's comments and marking guide

Question 5: required calculation of the average rate of return for a new investment project, and discussion of the reasons for and against using this method, then testing knowledge of the dangers of extending additional credit to customers and of ways of screening them for credit-worthiness.

Part (a) seemed to highlight candidates' unease with the whole topic of project appraisal. For example, many candidates elected to conduct an NPV calculation, totally ignoring the thrust of the question. Overheads were often ignored, as is correct for a DCF exercise but not in an ARR calculation, although there were many errors of inconsistency here. Depreciation was frequently ignored, as was the investment in stock required by the new project. Many return on investment calculations were based on initial investment. Although the average could be calculated in several ways, it was important to allow for the residual value, which was deducted by the majority of candidates rather than added.

(The correct calculation of average investment in its simplest form was:

[£14m + £0.5m + £2m] ÷ 2 = £16.5m ÷ 2 =£8.25m or £16m ÷ 2 + £0.5m = £8.5m, ignoring the stock rundown, either being acceptable).

Many answers neglected to indicate whether the project met the 10% required standard, and the vast majority neglected to compare the project's ARR with the divisions's current ROI of 20%, which also has a bearing on project acceptability.

In part (b) too many answers were in bullet point form with little or no explanation. There was considerable repetition eg, candidates saying that the ARR ignored the time value of money and then saying it ignored the timing of cash flows. Few candidates seemed aware of coherent reasons for using ARR beyond its 'simplicity' and 'ease of calculation' and the fact that managers appear to understand it. It is difficult to award marks for such vague answers unsupported by discussion. Candidates should ask themselves questions like 'What is it about the ARR which makes it 'understandable'?'

It was clear that many candidates were referring to the IRR in their answers rather than the ARR.

Part (c) was answered quite well by most candidates, with typical answers displaying good knowledge of the problems involved in extending additional credit. As is common across the board, too many responses to the second part failed to offer any supporting discussion/explanation of credit assessment methods, relying solely on bullet points.

			Marks
(a)		Calculation of present ROCE	1
		Calculation of new sales	1
		operating costs	1
		fixed costs	1
		depreciation	½
		resulting ARR	1
		Discussion	1½
		Total	7
(b)	(i)	Ambiguity/ease of manipulation	1
		Based on accounting profits	1
		Ignores time value of money	1
		Total	3
	(ii)	Use of 'familiar' concepts	1
		Compatibility with performance evaluation measures	1
		Discussion	1
		Total	3
(c)		Risk of default	1
		Slower cash flow	1
		Demand for discounts also	½
		Greater admin expense	½
		Analysis of accounts	1
		credit reports	1
		Prior experience	1
		Cash-only trial	1
		Background information	1
		Total	7
		Grand total	20

Step by step answer plan

Step 1   Read the question again and make sure that you focus on precisely what is required. You are asked to assess a proposed project using the average rate of return (ARR) method - clearly defined - *not* the perhaps expected (and no doubt more familiar) discounted cash flow approach. Whilst the latter is theoretically better, other methods, such as ARR and payback, are still commonly used in practice, and you must be prepared for the examiner to set questions on them.

Step 2   (a)   The first part of the data in the question relates to current operations - try to think why the examiner has given you this. The requirement is to determine whether the proposed project is attractive to *Armcliff* - not the parent company. Presumably what will make a project attractive to a division's management is one that will improve their current performance measure. Thus it is useful to know what the current level of ARR being achieved. This can then be compared with the project ARR.

     Remember that the ARR is a financial accounting based measure - returns are in terms of accounting profits, and investments valued at balance sheet amounts - you must try to put all "relevant cost" principles to the back of your mind. Whilst there are various possible definitions of the ARR (a point that can be raised in (b)) here you are given precise directions, so make sure you follow them. Both average profits and average investment need to be ascertained (ref TN 1)

     Don't forget to conclude by comparison with both current and required rates of return.

| Step 3 | (b) | This part of the question requires you to show both theoretical and practical knowledge about investment appraisal methods. Your points must be made in sufficient depth to convince the examiner you actually understand the relevance of what you are saying. *Why* is the use of accounting profits potentially a problem? |

| Step 4 | (c) | Even though this is a examining a general area of credit management, try wherever you can to relate your points to the business in the question - it is stated that Armcliff intends to extend its credit to improve sales. Again make sure that you explain points enough to get the marks available, whilst still offering sufficient variety. |

| Step 5 | Now review your answer and ensure that it does precisely answer the question as set. |

The examiner's answer

(a)   **Current return on capital employed**

= Operating profit/capital employed = £20m/(£75m + £25m) = £20m/£100m = 20%

Analysis of the project

Project capital requirements are £14m fixed capital plus £0.5m stocks. The annual depreciation charge (straight line) is:

(£14m − expected residual value of £2m)/4 = £3m pa

Profit profile (£m)

Year	1	2	3	4
Sales	(5.00 × 2m) = 10.00	(4.50 × 1.8m) = 8.10	(4.00 × 1.6m) = 6.40	(3.50 × 1.6m) = 5.60
Op. costs	(2.00)	(1.80)	(1.60)	(1.60)
Fixed costs	(1.50)	(1.35)	(1.20)	(1.20)
Depreciation	(3.00)	(3.00)	(3.00)	(3.00)
Profit	3.50	1.95	0.60	(0.20)

Capital employed (start-of-year): (TN 1)

	1	2	3	4
Fixed	14.00	11.00	8.00	5.00
Stocks	0.50	0.50	0.50	0.50
Total	14.50	11.50	8.50	5.50

$$\text{Average rate of return} = \frac{\text{Average profit}}{\text{Average capital employed}} = \frac{£5.85/4}{£40.0/4} = \frac{£1.46}{£10.0} = 14.6\%$$

Note that if debtors were to be included in the definition of capital employed, this would reduce the calculated rate of return, while the inclusion of creditors would have an offsetting effect. However, using the ARR criterion as defined, the proposal has an expected return above the minimum stipulated by Shevin plc. It is unlikely that the managers of Armcliff will propose projects which offer a rate of return below the present 20% even where the expected return exceeds the minimum of 10%. To undertake projects with returns in this range will depress the overall divisional return and cast managerial performance in a weaker light.

However, it is unlikely that the senior managers of the Armcliff subsidiary would want to undertake the project.

(b)   (i)   The ARR can be expressed in a variety of ways, and is therefore susceptible to manipulation. Although the question specifies average profit to average capital employed, many other variants are possible eg, average profit to initial capital, which would raise the computed rate of return. It is also susceptible to variation in accounting policy by the same firm over time, or as between different firms at a point in time. For example, different methods of depreciation produce different profit figures and hence different rates of return.

Perhaps, most fundamentally, it is based on accounting profits expressed net of deduction for depreciation provisions, rather than cash flows. This effectively results in double-counting for the initial outlay ie, the capital cost is allowed for twice over, both in the numerator of the ARR calculation and also in the denominator. This is likely to depress the measured profitability of a project and result in rejection of some worthwhile investment. Finally, because it simply averages the profits, it makes no allowance for the timing of the returns from the project.

(ii)   The continuing use of the ARR method can by explained largely by its utilisation of balance sheet and profit-and-loss-account magnitudes familiar to managers, namely 'profit' and 'capital employed'. In addition, the impact of the project on a company's financial statements can also be specified. Return on capital employed is still the commonest way in which business unit performance is measured and evaluated, and is certainly the most visible to shareholders. It is thus not surprising that some managers may be happiest in expressing project attractiveness in the same terms in which their performance will be reported to shareholders, and according to which they will be evaluated and rewarded.

Did you answer the question?

Note that it is not enough to simply say the popularity of the ARR is due to its simplicity. With the widespread use of sophisticated computer software, this is hardly going to be a major consideration. You are being asked to show your appreciation of the fact that managers will be influenced by methods used for their performance measurement - both internally and externally.

(c)   Armcliff intends to achieve a sales increase by extending its debtor collection period. This policy carries several dangers. It implies that credit will be extended to customers for whom credit is an important determinant of supplier selection, hinting at financial instability on their part. Consequently, the risk of later than expected, or even no payment, is likely to increase. Although losses due to default are limited to the incremental costs of making these sales rather than the invoiced value, Armcliff should recognise that there is an opportunity cost involved in tying up capital for lengthy periods. In addition, companies which are slow payers often attempt to claim discounts to which they are not entitled. Armcliff may then face the difficult choice between acquiescence in such demands versus rejection, in which case, it may lose repeat sales.

Did you answer the question?

Note how the examiner has answered the requirement in the context of the question.

The creditworthiness of customers can be assessed in several ways:

Analysis of accounting statements

In the case of companies which publish their annual accounts, or file them at Companies House, key financial ratios can be examined to assess their financial stability. However, these almost certainly will be provided in arrears and may not give a true indication of the companies' current situation. Some customers may be prepared to supply more up-to-date accounts directly to the seller, although these are unlikely to have been audited.

Analysis of credit reports

It may be possible to obtain detailed assessment of the creditworthiness of customers from other sources, such as their bankers, specialist credit assessment agencies such as Dun & Bradstreet, and from trade sources such as other companies who supply them. These assessments are likely to be more up-to-date than company accounts, but will inevitably be more subjective.

Previous experience

If the firm has supplied the customer in the past, its previous payment record will be available.

Cash-only trial period

If accounting and other data is sparse, and there is no previous trading record with the customer, the seller may offer a trial period over which cash is required, but if the payment record is acceptable (eg, if the customer's cheques always clear quickly), further transactions may be conducted on credit.

Background information

General background information on the industry in which the customer operates will generate insights into the financial health of companies in that sector, and by implication, that of the customer. Many agencies supply such information, although it should only be used as a back-up to other assessments.

Tutorial notes

1   As the examiner says in his report, the average capital employed can perhaps most easily be computed as the average of opening and closing book values, assuming an even reduction in value over the period ie (initial investment + residual value)/2. For the fixed assets, this would give £(14 + 2)m/2 = £8m.

As the stock is said to be held at the higher level until the final stages, it will have a steady value of £0.5m virtually throughout the project, and thus the overall average investment is £(8 + 0.5)m = £8.5m

If the stock is assumed to have been run down to its original levels by the end of the project the average investment would be computed as £([14 + 0.5] + [2 + 0])m = £8.25m

---

43   (Answer 6 of examination)

Examiner's comments and marking guide

Question 6: required knowledge of the reasons why companies seek a stock market quotation, and use of ratio analysis to underpin evaluation of company performance (to judge the attractiveness of the issue), and then how obtaining a quotation might affect company financial policy.

(a)   Few candidates could cite reasons beyond raising new finance and easier access to capital (oddly, borrowed capital was mainly cited) in the future. Some insisted on explaining the drawbacks with obtaining a listing.

(b)   This section, as in previous papers, highlighted candidates' lack of knowledge of basic accounting and ratio analysis. Many curious ratios were given, especially in the areas of ROCE, ROE and dividend and interest cover. Unaccountably, quite a sizeable proportion of candidates chose to ignore Collingham's accounts (and hence the wording of the question) and discussed the industry ratios. Perhaps the main failing was the superficiality of the analysis of the company's 'financial health' in the light of the given and calculated figures.

(c)   The distinction between pre- and post-flotation is somewhat artificial so credit was given for valid points wherever they appeared. Answers were generally disappointing, again showing up lack of basic accounting understanding. A common error was to focus on presentation of the accounts rather than on the underlying financial indicators. Few candidates explained the need to enfranchise the 'A' shares and the desirability of a scrip issue.

Marks

(a)   For each reason cited, ½ a mark plus ½ mark for brief explanation/commentary
(Mere listing of points insufficient to gain full marks)

Total   4

(b)		For each corresponding ratio calculated, ½ a mark	4
		Discussion of relative profitability	1
		liquidity	1
		gearing	1
		dividend policy	1
			—
	Total		8
			—
(c)	(i)	Revaluation of assets	1
		Disposal of surplus assets	1
		Improve liquidity/gearing	1
		Share split	1
		Enfranchise non-voting shares	1
			—
		Total	5
			—
	(ii)	More liberal dividend policy?	1
		Lower reliance on debt finance?	1
		Discussion	1
			—
		Total	3
			—
		Grand total	20
			—

Step by step answer plan

Step 1 Read the question again and make sure that you focus on precisely what is required. It concerns a company that was subject to an MBO 10 years ago and is now considering going public.

Step 2 (a) This is quite a common requirement, and it is well worth having four or five reasons for seeking a listing up your sleeve. However, note that it is not enough simply to cite a reason, without supporting explanation/comment.

Step 3 (b) Your discussion should focus around a comparison of Collingham's ratios with those given for the industry of a whole. However, it is not good enough to simply list the two figures for each ratio with possibly a short comment for each. You need to try to draw an overall picture, by seeing how the ratios may be inter-related, and using any information given to you in the question. You can structure your discussion around profitability (indicating performance), liquidity and capital structure (both contributing to financial health).

Step 4 (c) As the examiner acknowledges, it is somewhat debatable as to when possible changes may be made, so don't worry too much about the exact split between pre and post floatation. The restructuring of the balance sheet looks at how the results of past transactions can be shown in their best light. Remembering what you have just done in (b) should make you think about the possible improvement of ratios as well as just the absolute figures, and their presentation, on the balance sheet. Changes to policy will affect the value of future transactions. "Value" could be said to be in the eye of the beholder, and after floatation the main change is the nature of the shareholder body. Being listed means that any policy that does not suit the company's investors will be immediately, and very publicly, reflected in depressed market prices. You should therefore think about the sort of policies for which institutional investors may be looking. There is also the regulatory point to be made concerning the enfranchising of the "A" shares.

Step 5 Now review your answer and ensure that it does precisely answer the question as set.

Items not required by the examiner for this question

- discussion of problems with obtaining a listing

(**The examiner's answer**)

(a)   Seeking a quotation places many strains on a company, in particular, the need to provide more extensive information about its activities. However, the costs involved in doing this may seem worthwhile in order to pursue the following aims:

(i)   *To obtain more capital to finance growth.* Companies which apply for a market listing are often fast-growing firms which have exhausted their usual supplies of capital. Typically, they rely on retained earnings and borrowing, often on a short-term basis. A quotation opens up access to a wider pool of investors. For example, large financial institutions are more willing to invest in quoted companies whose shares are considerably more marketable than those of unlisted enterprises.

Companies with a listing are often perceived to be financially stronger and hence may enjoy better credit ratings, enabling them to borrow at more favourable interest rates.

(ii)   *To allow owners to realise their assets.* After several years of successful operation, many company founders own considerable wealth on paper. They may wish to liquidify some of their holdings to fund other business ventures or simply for personal reasons, even at the cost of relinquishing some measure of voting power. Most flotations allow existing shareholders to release some of their equity as well as raising new capital.

(iii)   *To make the shares more marketable.* Existing owners may not wish to sell out at present, or to the degree that a floatation may require. A quotation, effected by means of a Stock Exchange introduction, is a device for establishing a market in the equity of a company, allowing owners to realise their wealth as and when they wish.

(iv)   *To enable payment of managers by stock options.* The offer to senior managers of payment partially in the form of stock options may provide powerful incentives to improve performance.

(v)   *To facilitate growth by acquisition.* Companies whose ordinary shares are traded on the stock market are more easily able to offer their own shares (or other traded securities, such as convertibles) in exchange for those of target companies whom they wish to acquire.

(vi)   *To enhance the company's image.* A quotation gives an aura of financial respectability, which may encourage new business contracts. In addition, so long as the company performs well, it will receive free publicity when the financial press reports and discusses its results in future years.

Did you answer the question?

Note that the examiner only considers the potential benefits of being listed, as implied by the requirement.

(b)   The table below compares Collingham's ratios against the industry averages:

	Industry	Collingham		
Return on (long term) capital employed	22%	10/33	=	30.3%
Return on equity	14%	6/28	=	21.4%
Operating profit margin	10%	10/80	=	12.5%
Current ratio	1.8:1	23/20	=	1.15:1
Acid-test	1.1:1	13/20	=	0.65:1
Gearing (total debt/equity)	18%	10/28	=	35.7%
Interest cover	5.2	10/3	=	3.33 times
Dividend cover	2.6	6/0.5	=	12 times

Collingham's profitability, expressed both in terms of ROCE and ROE, compares favourably with the industry average. This may be inflated by the use of a historic cost base, in so far as assets have never been revalued. Although a revaluation might depress these ratios, the company appears attractive compared to its peers. The net profit margin of 12.5% is above that of the overall industry, suggesting a cost advantage, either in production or in operating a flat administrative structure. Alternatively, it may operate in a market niche where it is still exploiting first-comer advantages. In essence, it is this aspect which is likely to appeal to investors.

Set against the apparently strong profitability is the poor level of liquidity. Both the current and the acid-test ratios are well below the industry average, and suggest that the company should be demonstrating tighter working capital management. However, the stock turnover of $(10/70 \times 365) = 52$ days and the debtor days of $(10/80 \times 365) = 46$ days do not appear excessive, although industry averages are not given. It is possible that Collingham has recently been utilising liquid resources to finance fixed investment or to repay past borrowings.

Present borrowings are split equally between short-term and long-term, although the level of gearing is well above the market average. The debenture is due for repayment shortly which will exert further strains on liquidity, unless it can be re-financed. Should interest rates increase in the near future, Collingham is exposed to the risk of having to lock-in higher interest rates on a subsequent long-term loan or pay (perhaps temporarily) a higher interest rate on overdraft. The high gearing is reflected also in low interest cover, markedly below the industry average. In view of high gearing and poor liquidity, it is not surprising that the pay-out ratio is below 10%, although Collingham's managers would presumably prefer to link high retentions to the need to finance ongoing investment and growth rather than to protect liquidity.

Did you answer the question?

Note how the examiner uses a mix of known information (assets valued at historical cost, split of borrowings) and conjecture to give possible explanations for the differences between Collingham's and the industry ratios. he has also computed further ratios if, and only if, he feels they will add to the overall assessment.

(c)   It is common for companies in Collingham's position to attempt to 'strengthen' or to 'tidy up' their balance sheets in order to make the company appear more attractive to investors. Very often, this amounts to 'window dressing', and if the company were already listed, it would have little effect in an information-efficient market. However, for unlisted companies, about whom little is generally known, such devices can improve the financial profile of the company and enhance the prospects of a successful floatation.

(i)   Some changes in the balance sheet that Collingham might consider prior to floatation are:

Revalue those fixed assets which now appear in the accounts at historic cost. The freehold land and premises are likely to be worth more at market values, although the effect of time on second-hand machinery values is more uncertain. If a surplus emerges, a revaluation reserve would be created, thus increasing the book value of shareholders' funds, and hence the net asset value per share. The disadvantage of this would be to lower the ROCE and the return on equity, although these are already well above the industry averages. Asset revaluation would also reduce the gearing ratio.

Dispose of any surplus assets in order to reduce gearing and/or to increase liquidity which is presently low, both absolutely, and also in relation to the industry.

Examine other ways to improve the liquidity position, by reducing stocks, speeding up debtor collection or slowing payment to suppliers, although it already appears to be a slow payer with a trade credit period of $(15/70 \times 365) = 78$ days.

Conduct a share split, because at the existing level of earnings per share, the shares promise to have a 'heavyweight' rating. Applying the industry P/E multiple of 13 to the current EPS of $(£6m/£4m \times 2)$ = 75p, yields a share price of $(13 \times 75p) = £9.75$. While there is little evidence that a heavyweight rating is a deterrent to trading in already listed shares, it is likely that potential investors, certainly small-scale ones, will be deterred from subscribing to a highly-priced new issue. A one-for-one share split whereby the par value is reduced to 25p per share and the number of shares issued correspondingly doubles, would halve the share price, although other configurations are possible.

It will have to enfranchise the non-voting 'A' shares, because, under present Stock Exchange regulations, these are not permitted for companies newly entering the market.

(ii)   Following the floatation, Collingham would probably have to accept that a higher dividend pay-out is required to attract and retain the support of institutional investors. If it wishes to persist with a high level of internal financing, a compromise may be to make scrip issues of shares, especially if the share price remains on the 'heavy' side. Scrip issues are valued by the market because they usually portend higher earnings and dividends in the future.

Finally, if the company has not already done so, it might consider progressively lowering the gearing ratio. It might begin this by using part of the proceeds of the floatation to redeem the debenture early. However, it must avoid the impression that it requires a floatation primarily to repay past borrowings as that might cast doubts on the company's financial stability.

Did you answer the question?

Note that the examiner acknowledges that the split between pre- and post-floatation is somewhat arbitrary, and credit is given for valid points wherever made.

DECEMBER 1995 QUESTIONS

Section A – This question is compulsory and MUST be attempted

44 ✓ (Question 1 of examination)

The YZPK Packing Co Ltd, a family-owned company, has now been trading for six years and has provided you with the following data relating to its last four trading years:

Extracts from its balance sheets

	19X3 £'000	19X4 £'000	19X5 £'000	19X6 £'000
Issued ordinary shares	26	75	75	255
Retained earnings	49	109	396	819
Bank overdraft (secured)	Nil	90	187	94

Extracts from its profit and loss accounts

	19X3 £'000	19X4 £'000	19X5 £'000	19X6 £'000
Turnover	725	1,335	2,496	4,608
Net profit (after tax)	18	48	212	334
Dividends proposed	Nil	Nil	Nil	51

All sales and purchases are made on credit.

Financial analysis

	*Industry	19X3	19X4	19X5	19X6
Current ratio	1.47	1.11	1.02	1.19	1.24
Acid test	0.85	1.03	0.90	0.94	0.95
Debtors, average collection period (days)	51	63	72	76	64
Creditors, period of credit taken (days)	72	103	146	121	118
Stockholding (days)	62	14	22	45	52
Net profit after tax to capital employed	21%	24%	26%	45%	31%

* The industry averages have been around this level for the whole of the four year period.

Required

(a)   Comment on the company's growth in turnover and profits over the four years, and suggest possible problems which such rapid growth may cause. **(4 marks)**

(b)   Suggest reasons why the company's stockholding in days has been less than the industry average. **(6 marks)**

(c)   The board of directors is concerned about the cash flow position of the company. As chief accountant, write a memo to the board setting out various ways in which credit control could be improved and point out the potential threat posed by creditors. **(9 marks)**

(d)   From the additional information supplied below:

    (i)   prepare and present a cash budget and comment briefly on your findings; **(7 marks)**

    (ii) prepare a budgeted profit and loss account, **(5 marks)** for the four months from 1 January 19X7 to 30 April 19X7.

On 1 January 19X7, the bank overdraft amounted to £94,000 and the stock of raw materials amounted to £288,000. All sales and purchases are on credit.

| | *19X6* | | | | *19X7* | | | | Period of |
	Sept £'000	*Oct* £'000	*Nov* £'000	*Dec* £'000	*Jan* £'000	*Feb* £'000	*Mar* £'000	*Apr* £'000	credit
Debtors	420	560	640	250	480	520	500	440	2 months
Creditors	200	220	101	200	210	210	180	190	4 months
Operating expenses	30	30	50	50	30	30	40	40	Nil
Other expenses	36	36	44	40	42	43	41	37	2 months
New equipment					560				2 months
Sale of old equipment					40				3 months
Bank charges				4				2	Nil

An ordinary dividend of £51,000 (ignore ACT), for the year to 31 December 19X6 is due to be paid in April 19X7, and tax for that year amounting to £184,000 is due to be paid in March 19X7.

The closing stock of raw materials amounted to £254,000 as at 30 April 19X7.

The net book value of plant, machinery and motor vehicles etc, at 31 December 19X6 was £426,000. The net book value of the equipment sold was £56,000. Depreciation on these assets is charged at 20% per annum of net book value.

(e)   The company is now considering acquiring more long-term financing and has asked you to comment on the matters which would have to be taken into account by the directors if they converted the company into a plc.

(4 marks)
(Total 35 marks)

Section B – This question is compulsory and MUST be attempted

---
45   (Question 2 of examination)

Answer *five* of the six parts of this question.
Each part carries five marks.

(a)   What is the significance of the forward market for foreign exchange in the management of overseas debtors?

(5 marks)

(b)   Explain the functions of financial intermediaries in bringing together individual savers and borrowers.

(5 marks)

(c)   Identify the major limitations of the payback method of project appraisal and suggest reasons why it is widely used by companies.

(5 marks)

(d)   Briefly explain the purpose and expected benefits of JIT purchasing agreements concluded between the users and suppliers of components and materials.

(5 marks)

(e)   Identify, and briefly explain, the nature of *two* problems associated with the use of fiscal policy to control cyclical variations in the macro-economy.

(5 marks)

(f)   (i)   Explain briefly why forecasting is a very important part of the planning and control process.**(2 marks)**

         (ii)   What information should be considered when producing a sales forecast?

(3 marks)
(Total 25 marks)

Section C – ONE question ONLY to be attempted

46 (Question 3 of examination)

Acca-chem Co plc manufacture a single product, product W, and have provided you with the following information which relates to the period which has just ended:

Standard cost per batch of product W

Materials		Kilos	Price per kilo £	Total £
	F	15	4	60
	G	12	3	36
	H	8	6	48
		35		144
Less:	Standard loss	(3)		
	Standard yield	32		

Labour	Hours	Rate per hour £	
Department P	4	10	40
Department Q	2	6	12
			196

Budgeted sales for the period are 4,096 kilos at £16 per kilo. There were no budgeted opening or closing stocks of product W.

The actual materials and labour used for 120 batches were:

Materials		Kilos	Price per kilo £	Total £
	F	1,680	4.25	7,140
	G	1,650	2.80	4,620
	H	870	6.40	5,568
		4,200		17,328
Less:	Actual loss	(552)		
	Actual yield	3,648		

Labour	Hours	Rate per hour £	
Department P	600	10.60	6,360
Department Q	270	5.60	1,512
			25,200

All of the production of W was sold during the period for £16.75 per kilo.

Required

(a)   Calculate the following material variances:

   (i)   price;
   (ii)   usage;
   (iii)   mix;
   (iv)   yield.   **(5 marks)**

(b)   Prepare an analysis of the material mix and price variances for each of the materials used.

                                                                                 (3 marks)

(c)   Calculate the following labour variances:

   (i)   cost;
   (ii)   efficiency;
   (iii)   rate,

   for each of the production departments.   **(4 marks)**

(d)   Calculate the sales variances.   **(3 marks)**

(e)   Comment on your findings to help explain what has happened to the yield variance.

                                                                                 (5 marks)
                                                                          (Total 20 marks)

---

47   (Question 4 of examination)

(a)   In an attempt to win over key customers in the motor industry and to increase its market share, BIL Motor Components plc have decided to charge a price lower than their normal price for component TD463 when selling to the key customers who are being targeted. Details of component TD463's standard costs are as follows:

Standard cost data   Component TD463
                                                     Batch size 200 units

	Machine Group 1 £	Machine Group 7 £	Machine Group 29 £	Assembly £
Materials (per unit)	26.00	17.00	–	3.00
Labour (per unit)	2.00	1.60	0.75	1.20
Variable overheads (per unit)	0.65	0.72	0.80	0.36
Fixed overheads (per unit)	3.00	2.50	1.50	0.84
	31.65	21.82	3.05	5.40
Setting-up costs per batch of 200 units	£10	£6	£4	–

Required

Compute the lowest selling price at which one batch of 200 units could be offered, and critically evaluate the adoption of such a pricing policy.   **(8 marks)**

(b)   The company is also considering the launch of a new product, component TDX489, and have provided you with the following information.

Product TDX489	*Standard cost per box* £
Variable cost	6.20
Fixed cost	1.60
	7.80

Market research – forecast of demand

Selling price (£)	13	12	11	10	9
Demand (boxes)	5,000	6,000	7,200	11,200	13,400

The company only has enough production capacity to make 7,000 boxes. However, it would be possible to purchase product TDX489 from a sub-contractor at £7.75 per box for orders up to 5,000 boxes, and £7 per box if the orders exceed 5,000 boxes.

Required

Prepare and present a computation which illustrates which price should be selected in order to maximise profits.   **(8 marks)**

(c)   Where production capacity is the limiting factor explain briefly the ways in which management can increase it without having to acquire more plant and machinery.   **(4 marks)**

                                                                                                     (Total 20 marks)

Section D – ONE question ONLY to be attempted

48   (Question 5 of examination)

Burnsall plc is a listed company which manufactures and distributes leisurewear under the brand name Paraffin. It made sales of 10 million units world-wide at an average wholesale price of £10 per unit during its last financial year ending at 30 June 1995. In 1995/96, it is planning to introduce a new brand, Meths, which will be sold at a lower unit price to more price-sensitive market segments. Allowing for negative effects on existing sales of Paraffin, the introduction of the new brand is expected to raise total sales value by 20%

To support greater sales activity, it is expected that additional financing, both capital and working, will be required. Burnsall expects to make capital expenditures of £20m in 1995/96, partly to replace worn-out equipment but largely to support sales expansion. You may assume that, except for taxation, all current assets and current liabilities will vary directly in line with sales.

Burnsall's summarised balance sheet for the financial year ending 30 June 1995 shows the following:

Assets employed	£m	£m	£m
Fixed (net)			120
Current			
Stocks	16		
Debtors	23		
Cash	6		
		45	
Current liabilities			
Corporation tax payable	(5)		
Trade creditors	(18)		
		(23)	
Net current assets			22
Long-term debt at 12%			(20)
Net assets			122
Financed by			
Ordinary shares (50p par value)			60
Reserves			62
Shareholders' funds			122

Burnsall's profit before interest and tax in 1994/95 was 16% of sales, after deducting depreciation of £5m. The depreciation charge for 1995/96 is expected to rise to £9m. Corporation tax is levied at 33%, paid with a one-year delay. Burnsall has an established distribution policy of raising dividends by 10% pa. In 1994/95, it paid dividends of £5m net.

You have been approached to advise on the extra financing required to support the sales expansion. Company policy is to avoid cash balances falling below 6% of sales.

Required

(a)   By projecting its financial statements, calculate how much additional *external* finance Burnsall must raise.

    Notes

    (1)   It is not necessary to present your projection in FRS 1 format.
    (2)   You may ignore advance corporation tax in your answer.
    (3)   You may assume that all depreciation provisions qualify for tax relief.

    (8 marks)

(b)   Evaluate the respective merits of *four* possible external long-term financing options open to Burnsall.

    (12 marks)
    (Total 20 marks)

---

49   (Question 6 of examination)

(a)   The Cleevemoor Water Authority was privatised in 1988, to become Northern Water plc (NW). Apart from political considerations, a major motive for the privatisation was to allow access for NW to private sector supplies of finance. During the 1980s, central government controls on capital expenditure had resulted in relatively low levels of investment, so that considerable investment was required to enable the company to meet more stringent water quality regulations. When privatised, it was valued by the merchant bankers advising on the issue at £100 million and was floated in the form of 100 million ordinary shares (par value

50p), sold fully-paid for £1 each. The shares reached a premium of 60% on the first day of stock market trading.

Required

In what ways might you expect the objectives of an organisation like Cleevemoor/NW to alter following transfer from public to private ownership? **(5 marks)**

(b) Selected *bi-annual* data from NW's accounts are provided below relating to its first six years of operation as a private sector concern. Also shown, for comparison, are the *pro forma* data as included in the privatisation documents. The *pro forma* accounts are notional accounts prepared to show the operating and financial performance of the company in its last year under public ownership as if it had applied private sector accounting conventions. They also incorporate a dividend payment based on the dividend policy declared in the prospectus.

The activities of privatised utilities are scrutinised by a regulatory body which restricts the extent to which prices can be increased. The demand for water in the area served by NW has risen over time at a steady 2% per annum, largely reflecting demographic trends.

Key financial and operating data for year ending 31 December (£m)

	1988 (pro forma)	1990 (actual)	1992 (actual)	1994 (actual)
Turnover	450	480	540	620
Operating profit	26	35	55	75
Taxation	5	6	8	10
Profit after tax	21	29	47	65
Dividends	7	10	15	20
Total assets	100	119	151	191
Capital expenditure	20	30	60	75
Wage bill	100	98	90	86
Directors' emoluments	0.8	2.0	2.3	3.0
Employees (number)	12,000	11,800	10,500	10,000
P/E ratio (average)	–	7.0	8.0	7.5
Retail Price Index	100	102	105	109

Required

Using the data provided, assess the extent to which NW has met the interests of the following groups of stakeholders in its first six years as a privatised enterprise.

If relevant, suggest what other data would be helpful in forming a more balanced view.

(i) shareholders; **(5 marks)**

(ii) consumers; **(2 marks)**

(iii) the workforce; **(4 marks)**

(iv) the government, through NW's contribution to the achievement of macro-economic policies of price stability and economic growth. **(4 marks)**
(Total 20 marks)

ANSWERS TO DECEMBER 1995 EXAMINATION

It should be noted that the following answers are probably fuller than would be expected from the average student under exam conditions. Answers are provided in this degree of detail on the principle of offering guidance on the approach required, and on the range and depth of knowledge that would be expected from an excellent student.

44   (Answer 1 of examination)

Examiner's comments and marking guide

Question 1: this five part mini case study type question provided candidates with a mix of financial management and management accounting material which required them to demonstrate their analytical and comprehensive skills.

(a)   **Required the candidate to comment on the growth in turnover and profits and to suggest possible problems which could be caused by rapid growth.**

Quite a large number of candidates commented on the growth in turnover and profits without making any use of the data which was provided. Some candidates dealt with the growth in turnover and ignored the growth in profits, and others failed to tie up the growth in turnover with the decline in the profit margin. At the other extreme, some candidates went over-board on the growth aspects and did not attempt to answer the second part of this question concerning the problems of rapid growth.

Although 'over-trading' was indeed part of the answer, quite a large number of students focused on this one aspect and ignored the numerous other problems which could have been mentioned.

(b)   **This part asked for reasons why the company's stockholding in days was below the average for the industry.**

JIT (just-in-time) featured in many of the answers which were submitted. A lot of the answers tended to concentrate on the reasons for why the rapid growth in sales had taken place rather than answering the question set which was about the reasons for the low level of stock holding days. The rapid growth in turnover was just one of many possible reasons.

However, it was very pleasing to find answers in which candidates could integrate and display their knowledge of economics and statistical techniques in response to the open-ended question which was set.

(c)   **The question focused on credit control and the threat posed by the creditors.**

This part was answered very well by the majority of candidates. However, some answers failed to focus on the two parts of the question, deviating in all directions, covering inventory control and sources of finance etc.

Although quite a number of candidates answered the credit control part well, many then did not attempt to provide an answer to the other part of the question which concerned the threat posed by the creditors. It was surprising to find a significant number of candidates confusing debtors and creditors. At this level, such confusion should not exist.

(d)   **Required the preparation of a Cash Budget and a Budgeted Profit and Loss Account.**

Overall the candidates did very well on this part and scored high marks. Errors which were made in attempting the cash budget tended to be related to the period of credit, leaving out the opening overdraft (or treating it as a credit balance), calculation errors and failing to include the tax payment.

In the profit and loss account, the calculation of the depreciation and the loss on the disposal, proved to be difficult for a number of candidates.

A number of candidates lost valuable examination time by preparing a cash budget which covered each month from September to April, and others also lost time by preparing a budgeted profit and loss account for each month on an individual basis, rather than for the four month period in total, which is all that was required. Other candidates lost even more time by attempting to prepare a budgeted balance sheet which was also not called for.

(e) **A considerable number of candidates did not focus on the question set, which asked for comments on matters which the directors of the family owned company would have to take into account if they converted their company into a plc.**

A significant number of candidates looked at the various types of long term financing and others described the advantages of becoming a plc which did not match up with the question set. The 'control' aspect, one of the key matters was however, one of the few areas which was picked up and well answered by a pleasing number of candidates.

The overall performance by candidates on question 1 was quite pleasing, particularly in part (d). Certain candidates lost valuable examination time by not answering the question set and/or providing material which was not necessary eg, the budgeted balance sheet mentioned above.

		Marks
(a)	The increase in turnover and profits	1
	Functions keeping pace with growth	1
	Market share at the expense of profitability	1
	Cash flow problems	1
		—
	Total	4
		—
(b)	Observations re stock holding days	1
	Keeping stocks low out of necessity	1
	Tying up a minimum amount of capital	1
	The use of MRP or JIT	1½
	Improvements in stockholding days and the 'trade-offs' involved	1½
		—
	Total	6
		—
(c)	Performance, unexpected	1
	Credit control being given a low priority	1
	Comment re current position	1
	Full review of credit policy, etc	1
	Chasing slow payers, etc	1
	COD (cash on delivery)	½
	Prompt settlement discounts	1
	Liquidity ratios compared with industry figures	½
	Pressure from creditors, dangerous	1
	Conclusions	1
		—
	Total	9
		—
(d) (i)	Cash budget: Inflows	1½
	Outflows and balance	3½
	Comments	2
		—
	Total	7
		—
(ii)	P&L a/c Sales	½
	Cost of sales and gross profit	1½
	Net profit calculation	3
		—
	Total	5
		—

(e)		
	Family company	1
	Become a plc	1½
	Control	1½

	Total	4

	Grand total	35

Step by step answer plan

Step 1   Read the question again and make sure that you focus on precisely what is required. This case study covers aspects of ratio analysis, management of working capital and long term finance. The five parts were self-contained, and could be tackled in any order - but take care not to go overboard on the discussion parts that only carry 4-6 marks.

Step 2   (a)   You have four marks to discuss rates of growth in two figures, and to suggest possible attendant problems. All aspects must be answered, but be concise! Use the data in the question to illustrate your (brief) points concerning growth.

Step 3   (b)   When you have 6 marks for a "suggest reasons why..." you will be expected to produce at least 4 different points - so don't latch onto one and do it to death. It will only get you 1½ marks at the most. Start your answer with a brief summary of the trend in the stockholding days over the period. Tie in your points that follow with earlier parts and/or company/industry specific information given in the question where you can.

Step 4   (c)   Read this requirement carefully - although it mentions the general cash flow position, it specifically requires you to look at credit control (ie debtors) and creditors. Whilst you probably have a lot more to say about the former, don't forget the latter. To focus your discussion, draw on ratios and other data given in the question to get a picture of the apparent current problems with these two elements of working capital; think and discuss how they may fit in with the overall growth situation already identified, then start to get more general in your discussion as to how the situation could be improved.

Step 5   (d)   Again, it is important to read and interpret the requirement carefully to avoid wasting time on these budgets. Although you have data for 8 months, you are only required to prepare a four month cash budget (and *comment*); the profit and loss account will generally be prepared on a less frequent basis than a cash budget, and in this case you were only expected to produce one covering the whole four month period (and *no* balance sheet). Whilst most of the cash information is tabulated for you, take care to look out for other amounts from the paragraphs below the table.

Step 6   (e)   Don't jump into this one as soon as you see the words "long-term financing" and write all you know about that topic. The question is very specifically looking at one possible source - equity, raised from a public issue after conversion to a plc - and is focused more on the actual conversion than the finance itself. Again, look at what you are told about the company's current shareholder base to ensure your answer is context-relevant.

Step 7   Now review your answer and ensure that it does precisely answer the question as set.

Items not required by the examiner for this question

- budgeted balance sheet

The examiner's answer

(a)   YZPK Packing Co Ltd has experienced quite remarkable growth over the past four years in both turnover and profits. Turnover has gone up by over 635% and the net profit after tax has increased by over 1,855%.

A rapid growth company such as this may suffer from the following problems:

–   As a company grows, all business functions do not always keep pace with the growth eg, the management accounting function and the monitoring and control processes.

–   Going for market share and growth in turnover may be at the expense of the productivity of the capital employed eg, using low mark-ups to attract sales volume.

–   Cash flow is a problem. Cash is needed to finance the expansion of both fixed and current assets eg, more machinery, higher stockholdings of raw materials and more debtors. Thus, such companies, high in terms of growth, tend to be faced with cash flow problems.

(b)   **Inventory management**

	Industry average	19X3	19X4	19X5	19X6
Stockholding (days)	62	14	22	45	52

The stocks of raw materials will have grown over the years to support the increased turnover. However, the company's stockholding period is still less than the industry average. The possible reasons for this are:

–   The company being a 'rapid growth company' and in need of all the cash which it generates to help finance its continued expansion, has been keeping stocks low out of necessity.

–   To ensure that a minimum amount of capital is tied up and so avoid expensive holding costs such as interest on loans used to finance the holding of stocks, storage, lighting, heating, insurance, etc.

–   They may be using MRP (material requirements planning) or JIT (Just-in-time) both of which try to ensure that stocks are kept to an acceptable minimum and are used in production very soon after they arrive and that finished goods eg, packing cases, are despatched soon after completion.

The current 52 days may be improved via more use of MRP or JIT and also by searching out and disposing of stock which is obsolete or surplus to requirements.

However, 'trade-offs' and compromises may have to be reviewed/made eg, having lower stock levels but losing discounts for buying in bulk.

Did you answer the question?

Note that the examiner has first looked for reasons that seem particularly relevant to the company in the question, tying up with earlier parts. Then a little imagination is called for to think of more general reasons why a company may wish, or be able, to have low stock levels.

(c)   **Memo to the directors**

Credit control – The management of debtors

	Industry average	19X3	19X4	19X5	19X6
Average collection period (days)	51	63	72	76	64

The performance here is not what one would expect from a 'rapid growth' company ie, being in need of cash flow tends to dictate a better than average performance regarding the average collection period.

It could well be that the credit control function of this company has not been able to keep pace with the growth and is not being seen as a high priority.

The company is currently taking 13 days longer than the industry average. Even though it has improved its performance, it would appear that there is still room for further improvement. They could attempt to improve their credit control by:

–   Making a full review of their credit control system and credit policy and giving the function a higher priority.

–   Chasing slow payers and sending out invoices and statements more promptly eg, telephoning debtors to find out why they haven't paid, or sending invoices along with the goods when they are delivered.

–   Consider a COD (cash on delivery) system for certain types of customer.

–   Investigate prompt settlement discounts. However, this could be expensive. A small discount can have a high APR (annual percentage rate) of interest.

Although the liquidity ratios ie, the current ratio and acid test appear to be satisfactory, when compared with the industry average, this area is a cause for concern. The company is in a dangerous position. It is taking far too long to pay its creditors, currently 118 days compared with an industry average of 72 days. A combination of cash flow problems together with pressure from creditors could bring about the downfall and liquidation of the company.

Once again, 'trade-offs' may be necessary. One of the reasons for the increased turnover could be generous credit terms. If credit terms are reduced, sales could be lost. Improving credit control could release much needed cash which could be used for other purposes eg, paying off creditors and/or reducing the bank overdraft.

Did you answer the question?

Again, the a good answer will combine consideration of points specific to the company in the question - using available data - with general credit control aspects.

(d)   (i)   **Cash budget 19X7**

	Jan £'000	Feb £'000	Mar £'000	Apr £'000
Balance b/f	(94)	272	232	(215)
Inflows				
Debtors	640	250	480	520
Sale of machine	–	–	–	40
(A)	546	522	712	345
Outflows				
Creditors	200	220	101	200
Operating expenses	30	30	40	40
Other expenses	44	40	42	43
Dividends	–	–	–	51
New equipment	–	–	560	–
Taxation	–	–	184	–
Bank charges	–	–	–	2
(B)	274	290	927	336
Balance (A) – (B) c/f	272	232	(215)	9

The cash budget indicates that the overdraft limit will be exceeded in March. The company can, armed with the figures, arrange an increase in the limit with their bankers or take internal action. The internal action could include delaying paying the tax or for the new equipment, or by improving their credit control and collecting their debts more quickly.

(ii)   **Budgeted profit and loss account**

			£'000	£'000
Sales				1,940
Less:	Cost of sales			
	Opening stock		288	
	Add:	Purchases	790	
			1,078	
	Less:	Closing stock	254	
				824
Gross profit (57.53%)				1,116
Operating and other expenses			303	
Bank charges			2	
Depreciation*			62	
Loss on sale of old plant			16	
				383
Net profit (37.78%)				733

*(£426,000 − £56,000 + £560,000) × 20% ÷ 3 = £62,000

(e)   **The ordinary shares**

YZPK Ltd is a family company with the initial share capital subscribed by family friends and relatives. This could also be true of the further injections received in 19X4 and 19X6.

In the future, if more finance is to be raised in this way, the company will most likely have to become a plc so that it can issue shares to the public. However, to be successful in attracting prospective investors, the company will need to have a satisfactory performance record and reasonable future expectations. One of the key issues as to whether or not the company would select this route is the control factor. The existing directors, most probably own a major stake in the shares. To issue lots of shares to the public, could bring about a loss of a controlling interest. To retain control, the directors would have to find funds so that they could buy sufficient shares.

45   (Answer 2 of examination)

Examiner's comments and marking guide

Question 2: (a) this question required explanation of the use of forward markets in managing overseas debtors.

There was considerable confusion in this area, due in large measure to candidates' inability to understand the difference between debtors and creditors, but mainly due to lack of knowledge about currency markets and methods of payment. Many answers declared that the issue concerned fixing prices before the sale, and/or was a way of ensuring payment from customers, suggesting some form of international factoring. Of those who did understand the use of forward contracts (including forward options but not currency options!), most talked of buying currency forward as would be done by an importer wishing to hedge payments to creditors - the question clearly stated debtors.

(b)   **This question required a discussion of the general functions of financial intermediaries.**

Some good answers were given by candidates but many superficial ones. Candidates seemed to grasp the pooling function of intermediaries and how they solve the problem of the double coincidence of wants, but not the more complex functions such as risk spreading. Many answers simply concentrated on a specific institution and described their functions. Banks were a particular favourite, no doubt because credit creation appeared on the previous paper. There was considerable confusion between financial intermediaries and independent financial advisers.

(c)   **This section required a discussion of the problems with the payback method and the reasons for its continued use.**

This was probably the best answered section of question 2. Candidates were generally aware that payback overlooks the time value of money and ignores cash flows beyond the payback point, and that it is simple to use. However, there was some confusion between cash flows and profits revealed in the answers, and relatively few candidates identified the advantages of payback in risky and cash-constrained situations (many said it totally ignored risk).

(d)   **This section required explanation of the purpose of JIT agreements and the benefits to both parties.**

Again, quite well-answered with good awareness of the purpose of JIT and the benefits to the recipient of supplies. However, answers generally neglected the benefits conferred to the sender of supplies. There were widespread assertions that JIT helped the cash flow of the sender by speeding up debtor collection. Although this may be a product of closer relationships between the two parties, it does not follow that it will necessarily happen.

(e)   **This section required an explanation of two problems in the conduct of fiscal policy.**

This part was very poorly-done, reflecting candidates' apparent weakness in the economics area. There was little attempt to answer the question, beyond saying that counter-cyclical policy may create unemployment and sometimes lead to inflation, although discussion in terms of policy conflicts obtained credit. Few candidates really understood what fiscal policy tries to achieve over the business cycle, and many confused it with monetary policy, discussing interest rate changes and monetary contractions/expansions. While it is true that fiscal policy may have monetary implications, it is important to clearly distinguish the two types of policy.

(f)   **This short scenario question was about the importance of forecasting and the information requirements relating to sales forecasts.**

The majority of candidates performed well on both parts to this question. It was again pleasing to see candidates demonstrating their knowledge of economics, statistical techniques and marketing etc in a constructive way to produce numerous and quite different acceptable answers.

		Marks
(a)	Definition of the forward market/forward rate	2
	Problem of FX rate uncertainty facing exporters	1
	Explanation of how the exporter can cover forward	2
	Total	5
(b)	Brief explanation of the broad function of a financial intermediary	1
	Maturity transformation	1
	Risk spreading	1
	Economies of size	1
	Access to managed investment funds	1
	Total	5

(c) Major limitations:
  ignores timing of cash flows   1
  ignores cash flows beyond the payback period   1
  Reasons for using it (any three):
  simple/appealing to firms without financial skills   1
  useful as a communication device   1
  useful as a screening device   1
  helpful under capital rationing   1
  safeguard against risk   1
                                                                        ___
  Total   5
                                                                        ___

(NB. ½ mark for a mention of each point, but a full mark for a modicum of explanation.)

(d) Main aim to shorten time between delivery and use   1
  Requires close cooperation to ensure quality and reliability   1
  Benefit to supplier: guaranteed outlets/production planning   1
  Benefits to users:
  shorter production cycle, bulk-buying economies,   1
  lower stock-holding costs, especially financing costs   1
                                                                        ___
  Total   5
                                                                        ___

(e) Purpose of counter-cyclical fiscal policy   1
  Problems with fiscal policy (any two)
  Financing problems, monetary interactions   2
  Forecasting problems   2
  Time-lags   2
  Crowding-out   2
  (For each point mentioned, half a mark, but up to 2 marks
  per problem, depending on quality of discussion.)
                                                                        ___
  Total   5
                                                                        ___

(f) (i)   The importance of forecasting/example   2
  (ii)   The sales forecast   1
         Industry forecasts   1
         Surveys of buyers' intentions   ½
         Statistical techniques   ½
  (An open ended question, therefore, marking scheme is flexible)   ___
  Total   5
                                                                        ___

  Grand total   25
                                                                        ___

The examiner's answer

(a) The forward exchange market sets a price for delivery of currency at some future specified date, thus providing a mechanism whereby exporters can achieve protection against fluctuations in foreign exchange rates, and hence forecast their future cash inflows more accurately.

A major problem for exporters is uncertainty over future exchange rates and hence over the domestic currency value of goods sold on credit. Even in currency blocks like the Exchange Rate Mechanism, quite sizeable variations are permitted in the relative values of different currencies. One way of avoiding exposure to foreign exchange variability is to insist on payment in one's own currency, thus shifting the exchange risk to the customer. However, this ploy risks loss of competitive advantage to rivals who are willing to shoulder the exchange risk. An alternative policy is to utilise the forward market as explained in the following example.

A UK firm sells goods with a sterling value of £1m on three months credit to a customer in the Netherlands which will pay in Guilders. If the exchange rate at the date of signing the export deal is 2.40 Guilders per pound sterling, the value of the deal is £1m × 2.40 = 2.4m Guilders. The exporter is concerned that sterling will appreciate over the period before settlement thus reducing the sterling value of the Guilders receivable. If after three months, the spot rate moves to 2.80 Guilders per pound. the amount of sterling receivable will have dropped over 14% to 2.4m/2.80 = £857,143 possibly wiping out the profit on the export sale.

Protection can be obtained by hedging on the forward exchange market. Assume that when the export contract is signed, the three-month forward rate for Guilders is 2.45. This is above the spot rate, reflecting the market's expectation that sterling will strengthen. The exporter can lock in this rate by arranging with a bank to deliver Guilders to be exchanged for sterling at 2.45 in three months time, thus yielding sterling proceeds of 2.4m/2.45 = £979,592. This is some 2% lower than the sterling value as at the date of the export order, but it is guaranteed (unless the bank fails) and hence offers protection against more pronounced sterling appreciation. Conversely, if sterling weakens, the exporter is precluded from enjoying the windfall gains accruing to recipients of payments in overseas currency.

(b)   A financial intermediary is an institution which brings together units seeking funds with others wishing to invest surplus funds. Using their size and expertise, they offer important services to the financial system.

Maturity transformation

It would be difficult for individuals wishing to lend capital to find potential borrowers wishing to borrow for the same length of time. By pooling the funds of many individuals, the intermediary can extend loans of varying terms while using its liquidity to safeguard individuals' rights to withdraw their capital.

Risk spreading

Individuals would find it difficult to assess the riskiness of potential borrowers, lacking both the time and resources to undertake a detailed credit evaluation. They would also be wary about over-exposing themselves to risk by lending to small numbers of borrowers. Pooling of funds allows the intermediary not only to specialise in credit risk assessment but also to spread the risk over a large number of clients.

Scale economies

Finding people wanting to borrow can be expensive and time-consuming, so-called 'shoeleather costs'. An institution can utilise its size to exploit economies of scale in marketing its services to a broad range of potential customers.

Access to managed investment portfolios

Some financial institutions, such as unit trusts and investment trusts in the UK, allow investors access to well-diversified portfolios of securities. By pooling the funds of a large number of people, they enable smaller investors to achieve a degree of diversification which they could not otherwise attain due to the transactions costs and the time necessary for active portfolio management. Investors receive returns in the form of regular dividends and capital value appreciation.

(c)   The payback method relies on comparing the period over which the initial outlay of a project is expected to be recovered with some arbitrarily-defined required payback period. If the former period is less than the stipulated time-span, the project is acceptable.

The major limitations of this method are that it does not consider expected cash flows in all future periods, and ignores the timing of cash flows, by failing to discount cash flows to present values. As a result it gives an indication neither of the project's profitability nor the contribution which it is expected to make to shareholders' wealth.

However, it does serve some useful purposes, explaining why so many companies continue to use it:

(i)   It is simple to operate and to understand, and is thus appealing to firms which may lack the resources to conduct more sophisticated analysis.

(ii)   For the same reason, it may be a useful device for communicating information about the minimum requirements for an acceptable project. For example, a minimum required return of 25% approximates to a four-year payback period.

(iii)   It is useful as a screening device to sift out the obviously inappropriate projects from those which merit more detailed scrutiny.

(iv)   Under conditions of capital rationing, it may be desirable to bias project selection in favour of projects which offer a rapid rate of return cash flow in order to provide capital for further investment.

(v)   It is an important safeguard against two forms of risk. First, by minimising the period over which capital is exposed to risk of non-recovery, the firm is better protected against the risks of market failure or entry into its markets by new competitors. Secondly, by favouring projects with a quick and early return and thus enhancing short-term liquidity, it lowers the risk of inability to meet financial obligations as they fall due.

(d)   The main purpose of JIT purchasing is to compress the time period elapsing between delivery and use of materials and components as far as is physically possible. In extreme cases, this can involve new deliveries being transferred direct to the production line from the receiving bay. The concept is not new, having been operated, for example in the delivery of building materials such as ready-mixed concrete for many years. However, JIT has increasingly been applied in recent years to a wider range of manufacturing, assembly and even retail activities. The essence of a JIT arrangement is close cooperation between user and supplier. The supplier is required to guarantee product quality and reliability of delivery while the user offers the assurance of firmer long-term contracts. Users will tend to concentrate their purchasing on fewer (and perhaps only single) suppliers, thus enabling the latter to achieve greater scale economies and efficiency in production planning. The user would expect to achieve savings in materials handling, inventory investment and store-keeping costs since (ideally) supplies will now move directly from unloading bay to the production line. If a JIT system operates efficiently, it effectively precludes the need for stock control although the receiving company must ensure efficiency in the receipt and handling of supplies.

(e)   Economies tend to grow in cyclical fashion, with periods of recession following periods of recovery and prosperity. However, excessive economic instability is considered undesirable. First, slack activity imposes costs in terms of unemployed resources and lost output, and second, overheating at times of rapid expansion imposes costs in terms of inflation and lost international competitiveness. Governments periodically intervene in the economy in order to moderate cyclical fluctuations, raising expenditure and/or cutting taxes at times of recession, and restricting expenditure and/or raising taxes in boom times.

Some problems arising from the use of fiscal policy are:

Forecasting problems

The conduct of fiscal policy requires knowledge of where the economy is now and how it is likely to develop in the future. Forecasting economic trends usually involves the construction of complex economic models which embody assumptions about the relationships between economic magnitudes, based on past behaviour. The validity of the forecast depends on the extent to which such relationships are likely to apply in the future, and also on the volume and reliability of data about the present state of the economy which provides the forecasting base.

Time-lags

Policy-makers are often hampered by inability to recognise the need for action and to assess the scale of the required intervention. Consequently, it is often argued that discretionary fiscal policy can be counter-productive because of the time-lags involved – by the time the policy measures are introduced and begin to impact on people's behaviour, the nature of the problem may have changed.

Crowding-out

Some economists argue that an increase in government expenditure, far from supplementing aggregate demand, will only displace or 'crowd out' private sector expenditure. Increased command over resources by the state may simply lower the ability of firms and individuals to obtain resources. For example, if the state wishes to computerise more of its activities, the increased demand for skilled systems analysts may drive up the salary levels which all organisations will have to pay to recruit and retain such specialists.

Financing problems

A public sector deficit has to be financed in some way. If the state borrows on the financial markets, the resulting increase in demand for funds may raise interest rates, thus dampening the incentive of firms to invest. Alternatively, the government may borrow from the central bank ('printing money'). Because this usually involves an increase in the monetary aggregates, it poses the risk of raising the rate of inflation, although this effect is likely to depend on the current level of unemployed resources.

(f)　(i)　Forecasting is a very important part of the planning and control process. Management in all sectors of the economy need to forecast trends to assist them to plan for the future. They have to make decisions based on the best available information now, on what they expect may happen in the future eg, sales forecasts and cash flow forecasts may affect the labour budget and investment plans.

　　(ii)　In arriving at its sales forecast, a company could review economic trends such as employment levels, interest rates, inflation and those concerned with international trade. For example, high interest rates could affect the company's ability to invest in new projects and also affect demand for its products because of a reduction in disposable income.

　　　　Industry forecasts could also prove to be very useful. The company could, by taking into account its market share and the expected market conditions, produce useful data which would help to forecast sales.

　　　　The sales forecast could also benefit from surveys of buyers' intentions information/feedback from sales personnel and advice from experts.

　　　　Use can also be made of statistical techniques such as index numbers and time-series analysis.

46   (Answer 3 of examination)

Examiner's comments and marking guide

Question 3: candidates were required to calculate and comment on a number of variances.

(a) and (b) The answers submitted were generally very disappointing as a very large proportion of candidates could not calculate the material mix variance and the material yield variance. A significant number of candidates computed the usage variance and the mix variance as the same figure.

(c)　The majority of those who attempted this question performed very well on this part and their answers tended to accord with the published suggested answers. There were other alternative acceptable answers to this part for which marks were awarded.

(d)　The sales variances were reasonably well done. Here also, there were some quite acceptable alternative answers, in addition to those published in the suggested answers for which marks were awarded.

(e)　This tended to be neglected in terms of the time and thought required to produce a sensible answer. Many of the answers submitted failed to explain what had happened to the yield variance and to link it up with the other variances.

			Marks
(a)	Material variances		5
(b)	Analysis of mix variance		1½
	Analysis of price variance		1½
			—
	Total		3
			—
(c)	Labour variances		4
			—
(d)	Sales variances		3
			—
(e)	Using a different combination		1
	Substituting the lower cost material for F and H		1
	Materials of a lower quality		1
	Quality of materials linked to labour efficiency		½
	Motivational aspects		1½
			—
	Total		5
			—
	Grand total		20
			—

Step by step answer plan

Step 1 Read the question again and make sure that you focus on precisely what is required. It is a variance analysis question, concerning a batch manufacturing process. You are asked for specific variances, but are not expected to produce (or indeed have enough information for) a full operating statement. It requires a thorough working knowledge of the topic. There is some debate as to whether the actual level of activity should be measured in number of batches processed, or actual output, and the examiner acknowledges that this gives rise to acceptable alternative answers.

Step 2 (a) (b) Before leaping into the first calculation, think a little about how you can most efficiently process and present the data required to produce all the material variances requested - for example, in a "line-by-line" approach for all of (a). Or you could incorporate (b) as well, by preparing a table that analyses the variances by product right from the start - using total figures for (a), and the individual figures for (b). But ensure you clearly identify your answers.

Step 3 (c) Note that you are asked for the variances for each of the departments - and no mix/yield analysis is required. A tabular approach can again be used to process the information clearly and efficiently. Note that the activity level is measured in terms of batches (TN 2)

Step 4 (d) There is just one product, so the basic sales variances are total, price and volume. Here, in particular, there are different approaches that are equally acceptable to the examiner (TN 3)

Step 5 (e) It is easy to overlook short written parts at the end of a longish computation question, but some of the easiest marks can be gained here. It entails an interpretation of your computations, particularly in (b), to identify possible reasons for the adverse yield variance. As this part comes at the end of the whole question, it may indicate that other aspects may also be relevant - eg the possible link between efficiency of labour and materials usage.

Step 6 Now review your answer and ensure that it does precisely answer the question as set.

(**The examiner's answer**   )

(a)   **Material variances**

(i)   Actual quantity at actual price (given)   £17,328

(ii)   Actual quantity at standard price: £

                F 1,680 × £4   6,720
                G 1,650 × £3   4,950
                H   870 × £6   5,220
                                         £16,890

(iii)   Standard yield × Standard cost (TN 1)
               (32 × 120) × £4.50 (W1)   £17,280

(iv)   Actual yield × Standard cost
               3,648 × £4.50   £16,416

Variances   £

Price   (i) – (ii)   438 A
Usage   (ii) – (iv)   474 A
Cost   (i) – (iv)   £912 A

Mix   (ii) – (iii)   390 F
Yield   (iii) – (iv)   864 A

Usage (as above)   £474 A

WORKINGS

(W1)   Standard cost per kilo = $\dfrac{£144}{32 \text{ kilos}}$ = £4.50

Variances

A = Adverse   F = Favourable

(b)   **Further analysis of material variances**

Mix	*Total*	*F*	*G*	*H*
Standard (kilos)	1,800	1,800	1,440	960
Actual (kilos)	1,680	1,680	1,650	870
		120 F	210 A	90 F
× Standard price (£)		4	3	6
	£390 F	£480 F	£630 A	£540 F

Price	Total	F £	G £	H £
Standard		4.00	3.00	6.00
Actual		4.25	2.80	6.40
		0.25 A	0.20 F	0.40 A
× Actual kilos used		1,680	1,650	870
	£438 A	£420 A	£330 F	£348 A

(c) Labour variances

Cost variances	Total £	Dept P £	Dept Q £
Standard cost (TN 2)	6,240	4,800	1,440
Actual cost	7,872	6,360	1,512
(i)	£1,632 A	£1,560 A	£72 A

Efficiency variances	Total £	Dept P £	Dept Q £
Standard hours		480	240
Actual hours		600	270
		120 A	30 A
× Standard rate per hour (£)		10	6
(ii)	£1,380 A	£1,200 A	£180 A

Rate variances	£	£	£
Standard rate		10.00	6.00
Actual rate		10.60	5.60
		0.60 A	0.40 F
× Actual hours worked		600	270
(iii)	£252A	£360A	£108 F

Proof: (i) = (ii) + (iii)

(d) Sales variances (TN 3)

	£
Budgeted sales for actual level of activity (120 × 32 × £16)	61,440
Actual sales (3,648 × £16.75)	61,104
	£336 A

Made up of:

	£
Volume variance(3,840 − 3,648 kilos) × £16	3,072 A
Price variance (£0.75 × 3,648)	2,736 F
	£336 A

(e)   The actual mix used had the same weight as the standard mix ie, 4,200 kilos but used a different combination to the standard mix [as indicated in (b)]. It used less than planned of materials F and H, and more than planned of material G, a lower cost material. In addition to substituting the lower cost material for F and H which could affect the yield, the adverse yield variance could have also been caused by using materials of a lower quality than that which was planned eg, the lower price per kilo of G gives a favourable price variance, but this could be due to buying a lower quality material. (TN4)

The labour efficiency variance could have been caused by poor quality materials taking longer to process. It could also be caused by a lack of motivation on the part of employees eg, the employees in department Q getting a pay rise lower than expected, could have caused them to work more slowly and to waste more material because of not taking as much care as they should. This could also help to explain the actual yield, 30.4 kilos per batch being lower than the standard yield of 32 kilos per batch.

Tutorial notes

1   Alternatively, this line could be computed as
Actual (input) quantity in standard mix at standard prices

$$4,200 \times \frac{£144\,*}{35} \qquad\qquad £17,280$$

* this is the standard cost per kg input if it is standard mix and at standard prices

2   Note that the actual level of activity used in determining standard cost is in terms of batches processed here (120) rather than actual kg of material output (as used for the material variances). This is on the basis that the labour hours would be expected to vary on the number of batches going through, and would not necessarily be affected by a change in yield for those batches.

3   An acceptable alternative approach for the volume variance, which goes back to the original budgeted volume in terms of total kg, is as follows:

Budgeted sales volume at standard price
(4,096 kg at £16 per kg)   £65,536
Actual sales volume at standard price
(3,648 kg at £16 per kg   £58,368

Sales volume variance   £7,168A

Alternatively the volume variance could be calculated at standard **margin** per unit ($£16 - £^{196}/_{32}$) to give a variance of £4,424 (A)

4   The analysis of the mix variances in (b) suggests that using fewer kg of F (standard cost less than the average cost of material input) is good news and that using more kg of G (also a cheap ingredient) is bad news. This is clearly somewhat incongruous and is the reason why some people compare the standard cost of ingredients with the average cost of input (£144 ÷ 35 = £4.11 per kg). It is also the reason why any attempt to split a mix variance is sometimes deemed a pointless exercise (apart from the 3 marks that it earned in this exam).

---

47   (Answer 4 of examination)

(**Examiner's comments and marking guide**)

Question 4: the first two parts of this question called for the application of marginal costing techniques to help resolve some pricing problems plus some comments relating to the pricing strategy. Part (c) required brief explanations of possible management action which could be taken to increase production capacity.

(a) and (b) Many candidates did not take a marginal costing approach. However, marks were still awarded to those candidates who took and justified taking an absorption costing approach.

It was observed that in part (b), a considerable number of candidates were unable to deal with the 'buying-in' aspect of the question.

This question was not as popular as question three, and parts (a) and (b) were not very well answered. However, part (c) presented few problems to all those who attempted it, and was generally well done.

		Marks
(a)	Calculation of variable cost per unit	1½
	Identification of lowest possible price	1
	Fixed overheads have to be recovered	1
	Competitors prices and market research	1½
	Likely reactions of competitors	1
	Reactions of customers to 'special prices'	1
	Such a strategy takes place	1
		—
	Total	8
		—
(b)	Contributions outputs up to 7,000 units	1
	Contributions outputs over 7,000 units	1
	Total contributions possible for each selling price/brief comments	6
		—
	Total	8
		—
(c)	Up to one mark for each point explained	4
		—
	Grand total	25
		—

Step by step answer plan

Step 1 Read the question again and make sure that you focus on precisely what is required. It is concerned with decision making, employing general marginal costing principles and requiring some practical comments/explanations. Students are sometimes put off this sort of question as it can't be "pigeon-holed", requiring a specific pre-learnt technique (as in, say, variance analysis). But in fact the computations are not complex, and the requirements are quite specific, so it shouldn't be dismissed too soon.

Step 2 (a) When you are asked for "the lowest selling price" at which a product should be offered, you should generally be thinking along marginal/relevant costing lines. Provided it is not the business's only, or main, product, one may assume that non-incremental fixed costs are being covered elsewhere in the business, and thus can be ignored. In this case, the information indicates this scenario (note, it is a price that is only going to be charged to some key customers) and the marginal cost approach was expected. However, the examiner has said that marks were still awarded to those who justified taking a marginal approach.

Once you have tackled the computations, don't forget the critical evaluation. This should be both from the company's point of view, and that of their customers/market.

Step 3 (b) First note that the manufacturing variable cost is less than the buying-in price, so the company will generally want to manufacture up to full capacity before buying in (although you should note the assumptions here - see TN 1). Thus for each demand level given, you need to decide the split between manufacture and buying in, compute the total variable costs and compare with the revenue (using the appropriate price) to get contribution. The level with the highest contribution is then chosen.

Step 4 (c) For 4 marks, you are expected to produce at least four suggestions. Make sure you explain each suggestion sufficiently to show how it helps to increase capacity.

Step 5 Now review your answer and ensure that it does precisely answer the question as set.

The examiner's answer

(a)

Per unit	←	Machine group	→		
	1	*7*	*29*	*Assembly*	*Total*
	£	£	£	£	£
Total cost	31.65	21.82	3.05	5.40	
Less: Fixed overheads	3.00	2.50	1.50	0.84	
	28.65	19.32	1.55	4.56	
Setting	0.05	0.03	0.02	–	
Variable cost	28.70	19.35	1.57	4.56	54.18

The lowest possible price could be (200 × 54.18) = £10,836 per batch of 200 which would cover the whole of the variable cost.

However, the above-mentioned price would not be making any contribution towards the recovery of the fixed overheads. If the company is to make a profit, it has to recover its fixed overheads.

Even in this case, the selling price cannot really be set simply by reference to the variable costs. The prices at which competitors are offering the same product, plus engaging in market research should also be considered. Of particular importance are the likely reactions of competitors eg, if the strategy starts a price war the company could lose more than it gains.

In addition, the company needs to think about what the likely outcome will be if other customers of the product concerned find out about the 'special price'!

Finally, the company must realise that this kind of strategy cannot work overnight, it does take time. It could, in fact, be a number of years before the company can charge the customer the full price.

(b)   **For outputs up to 7,000 units/Sales up to 7,000 units**

	£	£	£	£	£
Selling price	13.00	12.00	11.00	10.00	9.00
Less: Variable cost	6.20	6.20	6.20	6.20	6.20
	6.80	5.80	4.80	3.80	2.80

For outputs and sales over 7,000 units

	£	£	£
Selling price	11.00	10.00	9.00
Less: Bought-out finished price	7.75	7.75	7.00
	3.25	2.25	2.00

Selling price	Volume units	Contribution per unit		Total contribution
£		£	£	£
13	5,000	6.80		34,000
12	6,000	5.80		34,800
11	7,000	4.80	33,600	
	200	3.25	650	
				34,250
10	7,000	3.80	26,600	
	4,200	2.25	9,450	
				36,050
9	7,000	2.80	19,600	
	6,400	2.00	12,800	
				32,400

The price of £10, and sales of 11,200 units would maximise the profit, as illustrated above at £36,050 provided the estimates prove to be correct. (TN 1)

(c)   Management can increase their company's production capacity by:

–   improving product design so that the production process can be simplified and take up less time;

–   improving plant lay-out, production methods and production scheduling, to reduce idle time and avoid bottlenecks;

–   introducing the working of overtime and/or 'shift working', if this has not already been done, to make more production time available;

–   introducing or improving an existing incentive scheme which makes use of the standard costing system, to enhance productivity.

Note

In (c), other ways of overcoming the problem which could be considered are:

–   Buying certain components from outside suppliers rather than manufacturing them, which frees machines and equipment for other purposes.

–   Employing sub-contracting manufacturers to produce completed products which also frees production facilities.

Tutorial notes

1   Note that it has been assumed that the fixed overheads shown in the standard cost card for the TDX489 are an absorption of existing costs rather than incremental costs attributable to the production of that product only. Otherwise the possibility of buying in all the required boxes, thus avoiding the overheads, should be considered.

Also note that it is assumed in the above answer that where there is scope for manufacturing to full capacity, the company would want to do this. Otherwise, a higher contribution could be obtained at the £10 price by buying in 5,001 (at cost of £7 and contribution of £3) and manufacturing 6,199 (at a cost of £6.2 to give a contribution of £3.80) This would yield a total contribution of £38,559.20.

48   (Answer 5 of examination)

(Examiner's comments and marking guide)

Question 5: (a) This section required candidates to use a projection of a company's current financial statements to identify the extent to which a proposed capital programme could be funded internally, and hence, how much external finance was required.

This part was done extremely badly by candidates. Candidates failed to recognise the need to predict the operating cash flow to be generated by the company, and the amount of external funding required, despite the strong hint in note 1 to the requirement and the very context of the question. Most candidates tried to project the balance sheet which had some merit if they could then identify an aspect of long-term finance as a balancing item, but such answers came adrift in attempting to measure profits and hence tax liability, which was irrelevant to the question. Once again, it seems that candidates do not appreciate the difference between profits and cash flow. Hence, credit was given to those who did work in cash flow terms, but most answers failed to treat depreciation correctly, or time the tax and dividend payments correctly. Interest payments were generally ignored, and many neglected the need to provide more working capital. A remarkably high proportion failed even to calculate the new level of sales correctly.

(b)   **This section required an evaluation of four long-term financing options relevant to the company in this question.**

This should have been a straightforward elaboration of the respective merits of different financing options applicable to the company. Instead, very few answers gave the remotest acknowledgement to the company, (eg,) recommending debt finance without considering the company (eg,) present capital or income gearing, and advising public issues of shares, oblivious of the fact that the company is already quoted and existing shareholders will have pre-emption rights. Some recommended that it should obtain a stock market quotation and then went through the various methods. Many candidates gave highly repetitive answers eg, debentures/deep discount bonds/zero coupon bonds/convertibles are effectively all variations on the long-term debt theme, similarly, long-term loans from banks. There was little attempt to qualify answers eg, venture capital could have a role to play although it could be argued that the company is too large to qualify.

Many candidates gave methods of short-term finance eg, bank overdrafts, factoring and invoice discounting. Some recommended devices like bonus issues and warrants which do not raise cash, although the former may conserve cash to allow internal financing, which is not relevant to the question, and the latter can only be of relevance for future financing. Inevitably, there were many recommendations to use reserves.

		Marks
(a)	Calculation of working capital needs	1
	Calculation of total capital needs	1
	Calculation of margin	1
	Projection of operating cash inflows	2
	Projection of operating cash outflows	2
	Calculation of external financing needs	1
		—
	Total	8
		—
(b)	3 marks per valid suggestion, depending on quality of discussion, especially the relevance to Burnsall's situation	
		—
	Total	12
		—
	Grand total	20
		—

(Step by step answer plan)

Step 1 Read the question again and make sure that you focus on precisely what is required. The scenario is a company that is seeking finance to fund an expansion. Part (a) needed careful thought to arrive at the right approach; however (b), carrying the majority of marks, was an independent discussion, and could have been tackled first.

Step 2 (a) There are a number of clues to the approach needed here. First the requirement emphasises the word *external*, implying that some of the finance may be raised internally. How? by use of surplus cash arising from operations - you were guided to this by Note (1) that concerns FRS 1 ie cash flow statements. So the approach required is

- calculate the total finance needed (to cover a 20% increase in working capital, plus capital expenditure)

- estimate the net cash inflow to be generated from next year's operations by converting profit information to cash flows, taking account of non-operating liabilities to be paid off from this year's balance sheet

- deduce the shortfall of finance to be funded externally

Even if you don't manage to sort out the cash flows exactly, setting out this approach up front will help to keep you on track and to convince the examiner you appreciate the nature of the problem.

Step 3 (b) It is essential that you tailor your answer to the particular circumstances outlined in the question - it asks for the options open to Burnsall. Look back at the current long-term financing situation: equity - it is a listed company; debt - it already has some debt but at a reasonably low level. Just appreciating these basic facts will help to avoid making inappropriate, and thus time-wasting, suggestions. As the examiner says, your four options should be quite distinct to get full marks.

Step 4 Now review your answer and ensure that it does precisely answer the question as set.

Items not required by the examiner for this question

- discussions of the different methods of making public issues
- discussion of short-term finance methods

(The examiner's answer)

(a) The company will need additional finance to fund both working and fixed capital needs.

As sales are expected to increase by 20%, and since working capital needs are expected to rise in line with sales, the predicted working capital needs will be 20% above the existing working capital level. Ignoring tax liability, this is:

$1.2 \times$ [Stock + Debtors + Cash – Trade creditors]
$= 1.2 \times$ [£16m + £23m + £6m – £18m]
$=$ £32.4m, an increase of £5.4m

Together with the additional capital expenditures of £20m, the total funding requirement:

$=$ [£5.4m + £20m]
$=$ £25.4m

This funding requirement can be met partly by internal finance and partly by new external capital. The internal finance available will derive from depreciation provisions and retained earnings, after accounting for anticipated liabilities, such as taxation, that is, from cash flow.

Note that the profit margin on sales of £100m (£10 × 10m units) before interest and tax was 16% in 1994/95. If depreciation of £5m for 1994/95 is added back, this yields a cash flow cost of sales of £79m (ignoring movements in current assets/liabilities). No further adjustment for depreciation is required.

Using the same margin, and making a simple operating cash flow projection based on the accounts and other information provided:

Inflows	£m	£m
Sales in 1995/96: (£10 × 10m units) + 20%	120.00	
Cost of sales before depreciation: (£79m + 20%)	(94.80)	
Operating cash flow		25.20
Outflows		
Tax liability for 1994/95	(5.00)	
Interest payments: 12% × £20m	(2.40)	
Dividends: 1.1 × £5m	(5.50)	
		(12.90)
Net internal finance generated		12.30
Funding requirements		(25.40)
Net additional external finance required		(13.10)

(b)   A wide variety of financing options is open to Burnsall including the following:

(i)   Some new equipment could be leased via a long-term capital lease. Tax relief is available on rental payments, lowering the effective cost of using the equipment. Lessors may 'tailor' a leasing package to suit Burnsall's specific needs regarding timing of payments and provision of ancillary services. Alternatively, good quality property assets at present owned by Burnsall could be sold to a financial institution and their continued use secured via a leaseback arrangement, although this arrangement usually involves losing any capital appreciation of the assets.

(ii)   If Burnsall's assets are of sufficient quality ie, easily saleable, it may be possible to raise a mortgage secured on them. This enables retention of ownership.

(iii)   Burnsall could make a debenture issue, interest on which would be tax-allowable. The present level of gearing (long-term debt to equity) is relatively low at £20m/£122m = 16%, Burnsall has no short-term debt apart from trade creditors and the Inland Revenue, and its interest cover is healthy at profit before tax and interest divided by interest charges = [16% × £100m]/[12% × £20m] = 6.7 times (even higher on a cashflow basis). It is likely that Burnsall could make a sizeable debt issue without unnerving the market. Any new debenture would be subordinate to the existing long-term debt and probably carry a higher interest rate.

(iv)   An alternative to a debt issue is a rights issue of ordinary shares. Because rights issues are made at a discount to the existing market price, they result in lower EPS and thus market price, although if existing shareholders take up their allocations, neither their wealth nor their control is diluted. If the market approves of the intended use of funds, a capital gain may ensue, although the company and its advisers must carefully manage the issue regarding the declared reasons and its timing in order to avoid unsettling the market.

Examiner's note: only four sources are required for the answer, but other sources of finance may also be mentioned, such as:

(v)   Burnsall could approach a venture capitalist such as 3i, which specialises in extending development capital to small-to-medium-sized firms. However, 3i may require an equity stake, and possibly insist on placing an appointee on the board of directors to monitor its interests.

(vi)   Burnsall could utilise official sources of aid such as a regional development agency depending on its location, or perhaps the European Investment Bank.

Did you answer the question?

Note that the examiner has confined his suggestions to *long term* finance methods that are *relevant to Burnsall*. This precludes any detailed discussion of public issues of shares, as Burnsall is already listed (although a rights issue is possible). Imagination is needed to come up with four distinct options - try to widen your consideration beyond basic debt/equity sources.

---

49   (Answer 6 of examination)

Examiner's comments and marking guide

Question 6: a very topical question which might have led the unwary into quasi political discussion. Fortunately, the vast majority avoided this temptation. However, there was widespread inability to utilise the information contained in the question, even to the extent of calling for information actually given, or easily calculable from that data.

(a)   **This section required discussion of how the aims of a water utility would alter following privatisation.** This section was answered reasonably well in the main, but answers should have gone beyond merely stating the service/profit dichotomy. Issues relevant to objectives which deserved a mention were the dimensions of shareholder aims (profit, EPS, dividends, share price) and removal of much government interference, and the need to serve a new master in the form of the stock exchange, but which opened up new avenues of finance. Nor does it follow that the utility would abandon quality objectives - indeed, the regulators might even tighten up on these. A major deficiency was the weak or lack of emphasis on aims prior to privatisation and hence, discussion of how they had changed.

(b)   **This section sought discussion of the extent to which the utility's performance over time had met the interests of different stakeholders.**

Candidates seemed unaware that most shareholders look for some combination of dividends and capital gain. There was great misunderstanding about the meaning of PE ratios. Movements in these do not tell us much, unless coupled with EPS data, with which we can then derive share prices. All the required information to do this was given in the question. Very little use was made of the information provided to calculate growth rates, either in nominal or real terms.

Candidates seemed unable to appreciate that if volume of output rose by 2% per annum, then the additional turnover growth is probably due to price increases, in this case, well above the movement in the RPI. Candidates seemed incapable of using index numbers to measure this discrepancy. Many said that if volume increased, consumers must have been happy, ignoring the monopoly position of the supplier. There were very few mentions of the role of the regulator. Credit was given for mentions of capital expenditure and presumed improvements in quality.

Candidates seemed happier with discussing labour issues, although few could use the data provided to calculate changes in real pay per head. Most recognised the higher rewards for directors. The contribution of the company to general economic aims was not well understood. Many said that since the RPI went up by some 2% pa, the price stability aim was not satisfied, appearing to blame the company for the movement in the RPI! There was little evidence of understanding that higher capital expenditure and greater efficiency was likely to assist economic growth, although most recognised the unemployment created by the firm, which might detract from growth, especially if it required higher public expenditure. Against this, the utility was generating more and more tax revenue, recognition of which obtained credit.

Marks

(a)   Aims under public ownership:
       operating: safe, reliable supply of water   1
       financial: target return on investment   1
       Problem of political interference, inability to finance required investment   1
       Aims under private ownership:
         target return on investment, cash flow   1
       Possible short-termist bias toward high dividend payout   1
                                                                                    ——

       Total   5
                                                                                    ——

(b)   (i)   *Shareholders*
              Aim to maximise shareholder wealth   1
              Analysis of dividend performance   2
              Analysis of share price performance   2
                                                                                    ——

              Total   5
                                                                                    ——

       (ii)   *Consumers*
              Analysis of price behaviour   1
              Comments on role of regulator   1
                                                                                    ——

              Total   2
                                                                                    ——

       (iii) *Workforce*
              Analysis of payroll numbers   1
              Analysis of average real remuneration   1
              Directors' rewards   1
              Discussion   1
                                                                                    ——

              Total   4
                                                                                    ——

       (iv)   Macro-economic aims
              Price stability: pricing policy   1
                                pay   1
              Economic growth: efficiency   1
                                capital expenditure   1
                                                                                    ——

              Total   4
                                                                                    ——

              Grand total   20
                                                                                    ——

Step by step answer plan

Step 1   Read the question again and make sure that you focus on precisely what is required. It principally concerned the evaluation of the performance a privatised water company from the perspective of various interested parties.

Step 2   (a)   If you are asked to discuss how objectives may change following privatisation, it makes sense to start your answer with a discussion of what they would have been whilst the organisation was still in the public sector. Note that these objectives won't necessarily all change radically on privatisation, they may just change in priority.

Step 3 (b) Use the marks allocated to each party to decide on the depth needed to your answer. For each, decide what factors they would be principally concerned with. You then need to review the data given to ascertain the extent to which these can be measured and assessed. For example, the investment objectives of shareholders should be familiar to you - a balance between income and growth. Whilst income is quite easily evaluated by looking at the dividend stream, capital growth requires some computations involving P/E ratios and EPS. You should have a good working knowledge of these fundamental equity measures.

Parts (ii) and (iii) need less technical knowledge and more practical application, but again use the data wherever you can to illustrate points made.

Part (iv) requires a reasonable grasp of economic principles, particularly relating to economic growth - the ways in which the economy as a whole can benefit from the investment, efficiency and tax payments of the company.

Step 4 Now review your answer and ensure that it does precisely answer the question as set.

The examiner's answer

(a) The main function of public enterprise is to serve the public interest – in the case of a water undertaking, it would be responsible for ensuring a safe and reliable supply of water to households at an affordable price which would also require close attention to control of operating and distribution costs. Prior to privatisation, UK public enterprises were also expected to achieve a target rate of return on capital which struck a balance between the going rate in the private sector and the long-term perspective involved in such operations. The authority would also have faced political constraints on achieving its objectives in the form of pressure to keep water charges down and also periodic restrictions on capital expenditure.

One problem faced by such enterprises was their inability to generate the funds necessary to finance the levels of investment required to maintain water supplies of acceptable quality.

Did you answer the question?

Note that the examiner has started his answer by setting the scene before the change - this then gives a framework for the alterations that follow.

Once privatised, NW would be required to generate returns for shareholders at least as great as comparable enterprises of equivalent risk. Moreover, it would be expected to generate a stream of steadily rising dividends to satisfy its institutional investors with their relatively predictable stream of liabilities.

Any capital committed to fixed investment would have to achieve efficiency in the use of resources and to achieve the level of returns required by the stock market. In the UK, it is alleged that there is an over-concern with short-term results, both to satisfy existing investors and to preserve the stock market rating of the company. Although this may safeguard future supplies of capital, it has militated against infrastructure projects and activities such as R & D, which generate their greatest returns in the more distant future.

(b) (i) **Shareholders**

In financial theory, companies are supposed to maximise the wealth of shareholders, as measured by the stock market value of the equity. In the absence of perfect information, it is not possible to measure the relationship between achieved shareholder wealth and the outright maximum. However, good indicators of the benefits received by shareholders are the returns they obtain in the form of dividend payments and share price appreciation.

Dividends

The pro forma dividend was 7p and by 1994 the dividend per share had grown by 186% to 20p, an average annual growth of around 19%. The pro forma payout ratio was 33%, falling to 31% by 1994. The pro forma EPS was 21p rising by 210% to 65p, an average annual increase of nearly 21%. This suggests that the company wishes to align dividend increases to increases in EPS over time.

Share price

The flotation price was £1, rising to £1.60 on the first day of dealing. By 1990, the EPS had become 29p. Given a P/E ratio of 7, this implies a market price of 203p per share. By 1994, the EPS had risen to 65p, and with a P/E ratio of 7.5, this corresponds to a market price of 488p. Compared to the close of first-day's dealings, the growth rate was 205% (a little over 20% as an annual average) and over the period 1990 – 1994, the growth was 140% (an annual average of about 25%).

Although information about returns in the market in general and those enjoyed by shareholders of comparable companies are not available to act as a yardstick, these figures suggest considerable increases in shareholders' wealth, and at a rate substantially above the increase in the Retail Price Index (RPI).

(ii)   **Consumers**

Although NW's ability to raise prices is ostensibly restrained by the industry regulator, turnover has risen by 38% over the period, an annual average of 5.5%. This is above the rate of inflation over this period (about 2% pa) and also above the trend rate of increase in demand (also 2% pa). This suggests relatively weak regulation, perhaps reflecting the industry's alleged need to earn profits in order to invest, or perhaps that NW has diversified into other, unregulated activities which can sustain higher rates of product price inflation.

However, before accusing NW of exploiting the consumer, one would have to examine whether it did lay down new investment, and also how productive it had been, especially using indicators like purity and reliability of water supply.

(iii)   **Workforce**

Numbers employed have fallen from 12,000 to 10,000 ie, 17%. The average remuneration has risen from £8,333 to £8,600, a mere 1% in nominal terms (TN 1) but about minus 8% in real terms, after allowing for the 9% inflation in retail prices over this period. This suggests a worsening of returns to the labour force, although a shift in the skill mix away from skilled workers and/or a change in conditions of employment away from full-time towards part-time and contract working might explain the figures recorded. Certainly, the efficiency of the labour force as measured by sales per employee (up from £37,500 to £62,000 – an increase of 65%) has outstripped movements in pay. However, apparently greater labour efficiency could be due to product price inflation and/or the impact of new investment.

The directors, however, seem to have benefited greatly. It is not stated whether the number of directors has increased, but as a group, their emoluments have trebled. Arguably, this might have been necessary to bring hitherto depressed levels of public sector rewards into line with remuneration elsewhere in the private sector in order to retain competent executives. Conversely, the actual remuneration may be understated as it does not appear to include non-salary items such as share options, which would presumably be very valuable given the share price appreciation that has occurred over this period.

(iv)   **Macro-economic objectives**

There are numerous indicators whereby NW's contribution to the achievement of macro-economic policies can be assessed. Among these are the following:

(1)   *Price stability*

–   *Via its pricing policy.* As noted NW's revenues have risen by 38% in nominal terms and 29% in real terms. This questions the company's degree of responsibility in cooperating with the government's anti-inflationary policy.

–   *Via its pay policy.* There is evidence that NW has held down rates of pay, but if this has not been reflected in a restrained pricing policy, then the benefits accrue to shareholders rather than to society at large. Moreover, the rapid increase in directors' emoluments is hardly anti-inflationary, providing signals to the labour force which are likely to sour industrial relations.

(2)   *Economic growth*

–   *Via its capital expenditure.* Higher profitability has been implicitly condoned by the regulator in order to allow NW to generate funds for new investment. This appears to have been achieved. Capital expenditure has nearly quadrupled. As well as benefiting the industry itself, this will have provided multiplier effects on the rest of the economy to the extent that equipment has been domestically-sourced.

–   *Via efficiency improvements.* It is not possible to calculate non-financial indicators of efficiency, but there are clear signs of enhanced financial performance. The sharp increase in sales per employee has been noted. In addition, the return on capital as measured by operating profit to total assets has moved steadily upward as follows:

	1988	*1990*	*1992*	*1994*
	26%	29%	36%	39%

Tutorial notes

1   Average remuneration in 1988 $=$ $\dfrac{£100m}{12,000}$ $=$ £8,333

in 1994 $=$ $\dfrac{£86m}{10,000}$ $=$ £8,600

This represents an increase of approximately 3.2% over 6 years. The equivalent annual rate is approximately 0.53% (or 1% to nearest percentage point).

JUNE 1996 QUESTIONS

Section A - This question is compulsory and MUST be attempted

50 (Question 1 of examination)

Behemoth plc is a steel manufacturer which operates the full range of production processes from iron-making to steel-rolling and pressing. Being highly capital-intensive, its cost structure includes a high proportion of fixed costs. It is considering means of making some of its fixed commitments more flexible and thus converting certain fixed costs into variable costs. In particular, it is proposing to overhaul its input supply systems and transfer its labour force on to more flexible contracts.

The managers of Behemoth are unsure about the overall effect of these measures, partly because they are unclear about the precise behaviour of costs as output is varied, using the existing procedures and contracts. However, they believe that, at current output levels, about 75% of its total costs are fixed.

Behemoth hires a consultancy firm to investigate the present relationship between cost and output and also to advise on the likely impact of the proposed changes on the cost structure. The consultants have studied cost-output data for the past five years, and using a linear regression model, estimate the following line of best fit:

$$TC = 1,400 + 46V$$

where

TC	=	Total operating cost in £m per annum
V	=	Volume of production per annum (millions of tonnes of steel)

The consultants estimate that the proposed changes will require an outlay of £100m to lower fixed costs to £1,300m per annum and raise variable costs to £50 per tonne, but will not affect the total capacity, reckoned to be 12m tonnes per annum. Some directors argue that these developments should be financed by borrowing at a fixed rate of 8%, interest rates having fallen during the recent recession. The expenditure can be wholly written off for tax purposes in one year. The rate of corporation tax is 33%, payable a year in arrears.

In 1995, a year of economic recovery, Behemoth produced an output of 10m tonnes of steel products at an average price of £200 per tonne. It expects to average an output of 11m tonnes per annum over the whole economic cycle. Behemoth's shareholders have instructed its managers to pursue a target rate of return of 15% on the book value of equity.

Behemoth's accounting statements for the most recent period are shown

Profit and loss account for year ended 31 December 1995

	£m
Sales	2,000
Operating costs	(1,920)
Operating profit	80
Interest charges	(8)
Earnings before tax	72
Corporation tax payable	(10)
Profit after tax	62

Balance sheet as at 31 December 1995

	£m
Fixed assets	1,800
Net current assets	300
10% Loan stock	(80)
Net assets	2,020
Issued share capital	800
Reserves	1,200
Shareholders' funds	2,020

Required

(a)   Explain the difference between operating and financial gearing.   **(5 marks)**

(b)   Explain why a steel producer such as Behemoth should be concerned about its levels of operating and financial gearing.   **(5 marks)**

(c)   Interpret the meaning of the regression equation obtained by the consultant, and discuss any reservations you would have about relying on it for decision-making.

Make use of the profit and loss account in your answer in order to check the validity of the estimated cost function.   **(8 marks)**

(d)   Assume that the management of Behemoth accept the validity of the consultant's computations.

Advise the board as to the desirability of the proposed measures, taking into account:

(i)   the payback period
(ii)   the effect on the break-even point
(iii)   the effect on financial gearing.

Carefully specify any assumptions you make.   **(12 marks)**

(e)   What volume of output should Behemoth produce in order to meet the specified rate of return?

Comment on the feasibility of this target.   **(5 marks)**
          (Total 35 marks)

Section B - This question is compulsory and MUST be attempted

51   (Question 2 of examination)

Answer FIVE of the six parts of this question
Each part carries five marks

(a)   (i)   Briefly explain why 'Monetarist' economists argue against using short-term variations in the money supply to influence the economy.

(ii)   How do such variations affect company decisions?   **(5 marks)**

(b)   Describe briefly what a 'rights issue' is and explain why such issues are a common way of raising additional finance.   **(5 marks)**

(c)   Explain briefly the possible advantages of having worker representatives and junior management participating in the budget preparation process.   **(5 marks)**

(d)   You are provided with the following information:

	Budget	Actual
Sales (units)	72,000	64,000
Selling price	£10 per unit	£8.40 per unit
Variable cost	£6 per unit	£6.20 per unit

Using a contribution approach, calculate appropriate variances and comment briefly on the possible causes of those variances.   **(5 marks)**

(e)   ZXC plc operates a process costing system. Discuss briefly the issues which need to be considered in valuing materials to be included in work in progress.   **(5 marks)**

(f)   Discuss briefly the options available to a company to utilise its idle production capacity, and identify the associated financial benefits.   **(5 marks)**
                                                                                                            (Total 25 marks)

Section C - ONE question ONLY to be attempted

| **52** | **(Question 3 of examination)** |

(a)   Discuss the advantages and disadvantages of using the 'full cost' (absorption costing) method for dealing with the costs of internal services. Include in your answer comments on the motivational aspects of this method of costing.   **(7 marks)**

(b)   Describe the factors which affect the choice of bases of apportionment by which internal services are to be apportioned.   **(5 marks)**

(c)   JR Co Ltd's budgeted overheads for the forthcoming period applicable to its production departments, are as follows:

	£'000
1	870
2	690

The budgeted total costs for the forthcoming period for the service departments, are as follows:

	£'000
G	160
H	82

The use made of each of the service has been estimated as follows:

	Production department		Service department	
	1	*2*	*G*	*H*
G (%)	60	30	-	10
H (%)	50	30	20	-

Required

Apportion the service department costs to production departments:

(i)   using the step-wise ('elimination') method, starting with G, and
(ii)   the reciprocal (simultaneous-equation) method, and
(iii)   comment briefly on your figures.
                                                                                                            (8 marks)
                                                                                                            (Total 20 marks)

53   (Question 4 of examination)

Sychwedd plc manufacture and sell three products R, S, and T which make use of two machine groups, 1 and 2. The budget for period 1, the first quarter of their next accounting year, includes the following information:

	Machine Group	
Fixed overhead absorption rates:	*1*	*2*
Rate per machine hour	£10	£11.20

	Product R	*Product S*	*Product T*
Sales (kilos)	12,000	25,000	40,000
	£	£	£
Sales	120,000	250,000	360,000
Variable costs	73,560	164,250	284,400
Fixed overheads	19,752	38,300	42,400
Budgeted net profit	26,688	47,450	33,200

For the second quarter (period 2), it is estimated that the budgeted machine hours and direct labour hours needed to produce 1,000 kilos of each of the products are:

	Machine Group	
Machine hours	*1*	*2*
Product		
R	75	80
S	30	110
T	50	50
Direct labour hours		
Product		
R	30	40
S	10	50
T	20	20
Budgeted fixed overheads (to be absorbed using a machine hour rate)	£40,800	£68,365
Budgeted variable labour and overheads, rate per direct labour hour	£7.50	£8.50

	Product R	*Product S*	*Product T*
Budgeted material costs per 1,000 kilos	£4,508	£5,096	£6,125
Expected sales (kilos)	10,000	25,000	50,000
Planned price changes Compared with period 1	10% increase	no change	no change

A sales commission of 4% of the sales value will be paid.

There are no budgeted opening or closing stocks ie, all production is expected to be sold.

Required

(a)   Compute the machine hour rate for each machine group for period 2.

(3 marks)

(b)   Calculate the budgeted contribution and net profit for each of the three products for period 2.

(9 marks)

(c)   Assuming that the sales trend shown over the two periods is forecast to continue, comment briefly on the figures and advise management accordingly.

(8 marks)

(Total 20 marks)

Section D - ONE question ONLY to be attempted

54   (Question 5 of examination)

(a)   Discuss:

(i)   the significance of trade creditors in a firm's working capital cycle, and

(4 marks)

(ii)   the dangers of over-reliance on trade credit as a source of finance.

(4 marks)

(b)   Keswick plc traditionally follows a highly aggressive working capital policy, with no long-term borrowing. Key details from its recently compiled accounts appear below:

	£m
Sales (all on credit)	10.00
Earnings before interest and tax (EBIT)	2.00
Interest payments for the year	0.50
Shareholders' funds	2.00
(comprising £1m issued share capital, par value 25p, and £1m revenue reserves)	
Debtors	0.40
Stocks	0.70
Trade creditors	1.50
Bank overdraft	3.00

A major supplier which accounts for 50% of Keswick's cost of sales, is highly concerned about Keswick's policy of taking extended trade credit. The supplier offers Keswick the opportunity to pay for supplies within 15 days in return for a discount of 5% on the invoiced value.

Keswick holds no cash balances but is able to borrow on overdraft from its bank at 12%. Tax on corporate profit is paid at 33%.

Required

Determine the costs and benefits to Keswick of making this arrangement with its supplier, and recommend whether Keswick should accept the offer.

Your answer should include the effects on:

-     The working capital cycle
-     Interest cover
-     Profits after tax
-     Earnings per share
-     Return on equity
-     Capital gearing.

(12 marks)

(Total 20 marks)

55   (Question 6 of examination)

(a)   Briefly explain the main features of the following:

-    Sale-and-leaseback
-    Hire-purchase
-    Financial leasing

(6 marks)

(b)   Howgill Ltd is the leasing subsidiary of a major commercial bank. It is approached by Clint plc, a company entirely financed by equity, which operates in the pharmaceutical industry, with a request to arrange a lease contract to acquire new computer-controlled manufacturing equipment to further automate its production line. The outlay involved is £20m. The equipment will have only a four-year operating life due to the fast rate of technical change in this industry, and no residual worth. The basic project has a positive net present value when operating cash flows are discounted at the shareholders' required rate of return.

Howgill would finance the purchase of the machinery by borrowing at a pre-tax annual interest rate of 15%. The purchase would be completed on the final day of its accounting year, when it would also require the first of the annual rental payments. Howgill currently pays tax at 33%, 12 months after its financial year end. A writing-down allowance is available based on a 25% reducing balance.

Under the terms of the lease contract, Howgill would also provide maintenance services, valued by Clint at £750,000 pa. These would be supplied by Howgill's computer maintenance sub-division at no incremental cost as it currently has spare capacity which is expected to persist for the foreseeable future.

Clint has the same financial year as Howgill, also pays tax at 33% and its own bank will lend at 18% before tax.

Required

Calculate the minimum rental which Howgill would have to charge in order to just break-even on the lease contract.

(Note: you may assume that the rental is wholly tax-allowable as a business expense.)

(6 marks)

(c)   Assume that Howgill does proceed with the contract and charges an annual rental of £7m.

Calculate whether, on purely financial criteria, Clint should lease the asset or borrow in order to purchase it outright:

(i)   ignoring the benefit to Clint of the maintenance savings   **(6 marks)**
(ii)   allowing for the maintenance savings.   **(2 marks)**
(Total 20 marks)

ANSWERS TO JUNE 1996 EXAMINATION

It should be noted that the following answers are probably fuller than would be expected from the average candidate under exam conditions. Answers are provided in this degree of detail on the principle of offering guidance on the approach required, and on the range and depth of knowledge that would be expected from an excellent candidate.

50   (Answer 1 of examination)

Examiner's comments and marking guide

Question 1: the case study was particularly poorly done. It required candidates to examine the financing decision of a company in the context of its operating environment and its existing financial structure. As such, the question was testing knowledge and understanding from Section 7 of the syllabus. Candidates must appreciate that it is not enough simply to be able to describe different types of finance - they have to understand when to utilise them and the effect which they have on key indicators. In particular, the question required knowledge of operating gearing and cost-volume profit analysis. These should be familiar concepts and are not peculiar to financial management.

Part (a) required a distinction between operating and financial gearing.

This caused great difficulties. Remarkably few candidates were able to give a coherent explanation of financial gearing or operating gearing. Most had little idea about the latter, discussing various irrelevant issues. The better answers tried to relate to the question, and used the figures provided to illustrate the ratios.

Part (b) required an explanation of why a highly capital intensive company should worry about each type of gearing.

This invited explicit reference to the context of the question ie, the company is highly capital intensive with, therefore, a high break-even point, and thus is highly exposed to cyclical variations in volume. Since adding a layer of financial gearing worsens this exposure, it should be very wary of debt financing because it raises the break-even volume. This line of argument was missed by most candidates, although some marks were available for descriptions of general problems related to debt financing.

Part (c) required ability to interpret a linear regression equation, and to explain its limitations.

Candidates were mainly able to identify the fixed and variable components of the cost function, and to apply them in some fashion to the Profit and Loss data provided. However, such comparisons were usually let down by not comparing like with like ie, by using different volumes. The limitations of linear regression were not generally appreciated. Comments demonstrating candidates' lack of understanding and confusion with linear programming were very common.

Part (d) required an assessment of the effect of a proposed internal restructuring on break-even point and financial gearing and also calculation of a pay back period for the project.

The majority of candidates did not realise that this was a straightforward cost-saving exercise, with an initial outlay generating higher variable costs and lower fixed costs. Many answers were in the form of a projected Profit and Loss statement or a cash flow forecast over many periods instead of a one-line answer. Many candidates undertook DCF calculations, most omitted the effect of tax and many included interest charges. Many candidates confused break-even analysis with payback analysis - they are similar in concept but the former identifies a break-even volume and the latter a point in time when cash outlay is recovered. Interest charges should, however, appear in a break-even calculation - this aspect was usually omitted. Most attempts at the gearing component of this section were reasonable.

Part (e) required assessment of the required volume to achieve a specified return on equity.

The majority of candidates omitted this section, although there were easy marks obtainable. It simply required an additional break-even calculation, introducing a required return on investment ie, an additional fixed charge. Many candidates related the required return to the issued share capital rather than to equity and most also ignored the tax charge.

		Marks
(a)	Explanation of operating gearing	1½
	Effect on volatility of EBIT	1
	Explanation of financial gearing	1½
	Effect on volatility of shareholder earnings	1
	Total	5
(b)	Exposure to cyclicality	1
	Capital intensive nature/high operating gearing	1
	Further effect on risk of financial gearing	1
	Overall effect on break-even point	2
	Total	5
(c)	Explanation of FC and VC terms	2
	Reservations:	
	Correlation	1
	May not be linear	1
	Validity over other output ranges	1
	Based on past data	1
	Inclusion of allocated costs	1
	Max	4
	Cross-check with P&L account	2
	Total	8
(d)	Payback: reduction in FC, increase in VC	1
	effect on cash flow	1
	computation	1
	Break-even: calculation of present break-even volume	2
	incorporation of debt interest	1
	calculation of new break-even volume	2
	Change in capital gearing	2
	interest cover	1
	Comment	1
	Total	12

(Alternatively, the answer may incorporate cost data from the regression equation)

(e)	Calculation of present ROE	1
	Calculation of target profit	1
	Calculation of new break-even volume	2
	Comment	1
	Total	5
	Grand total	35

Step by step answer plan

Step 1   Read the question again and make sure that you focus on precisely what is required. This case study is set in the environment of a steel manufacturer that is considering investment in a project to lower its operating gearing. It covers a wide variety of topics from both the FM and MA areas of the syllabus.

Step 2   (a)   Financial gearing may be more familiar to you than operating gearing. As the names imply, the first relates to fixed financial charges, the latter to fixed operating charges. Even if you have not come across operational gearing much before, the main context of the question could have given you a clue - written parts of questions, in particular case studies, are very rarely unrelated to the circumstances of the question. Indeed, it is a good idea to use data from the question to illustrate the measures.

Step 3   (b)   Having defined the two types of gearing in (a), you now have to specifically relate them to the company in the question. If you are more familiar with financial gearing, start with this aspect and see if you can apply the same principles to operating costs. The principal problem with increasing financial gearing levels is that it increases risk to equity earnings by "amplifying" the effects of fluctuating operating profits. In turn, the fluctuations of operating profits, brought about by oscillating volumes, will be accentuated by high levels of fixed costs.

Your answer will be completed by the addition of a reference to information specific to Behemoth - that it operates in an industry that is known to fluctuate more than average, and that it is highly capital-intensive.

Step 4   (c)   Three requirements here: - interpretation of the regression equation (showing the familiar straight line cost function); discussion of its reservations and checking its validity using the P&L account. It is the second of these that attracts most marks - showing the very common desire of the examiner to ensure that accountants appreciate the assumptions and limitations of models that may be used to help manage a business.

Step 5   (d)   To tackle the computations required here efficiently and accurately, you need to appreciate the simplicity of the situation presented. By spending a lump sum now, future fixed costs per annum will decrease and variable costs per unit will increase, with a net cash flow benefit. In order to evaluate the effects of this as required, you then need to make decisions such as the volume to use, the timings of cash flows, and whether and how to incorporate tax and interest. On their own, each of these mainstream measures shouldn't normally cause you too many problems - putting them together in the same question doesn't make them more difficult.

Step 6   (e)   This is similar to a "target profit" contribution analysis problem (where target volume = [fixed costs + target profit]/contribution per unit) except that the target is given in relative terms rather than absolute. Thus an extra step is required, to turn the relative target to an actual, pre-tax (since all other elements of the calculation are pre-tax) profit figure.

Step 7   Now review your answer and ensure that it does precisely answer the question as set.

The examiner's answer

(a)   Most businesses operate with a mixture of variable and fixed factors of production, giving rise to variable and fixed production costs, respectively. Operating gearing refers to the relative importance of fixed costs in the firm's cost structure, costs which have to be met regardless of the firm's level of output and sales revenue. In general, the higher the proportion of fixed-to-variable costs, the higher is the firm's break-even volume of output. As sales expand beyond the break-even point, profits before interest and tax, and shareholder earnings, will rise by a greater proportion.

Financial gearing refers to the proportion of debt finance in the firm's capital structure (capital gearing) and also to the proportion of earnings which are pre-empted by prior interest charges (income gearing). It is obligatory to meet interest payments, irrespective of the level of sales revenue and operating profits. Generally, introducing financial gearing into the capital structure will raise earnings per ordinary share and generate a multiplier effect on shareholder earnings as sales increase. However, since this effect also operates in a downward direction, a geared capital structure increases the likely variability in shareholder earnings. It also raises the probability of financial failure should the company be unable to meet interest charges in a poor trading year.

(b)   Behemoth operates in a highly cyclical industry, producing a basic product whose demand tends to fluctuate to a greater degree than the overall economy. Steel usually leads the economy into recession and is one of the last sectors to recover.

Capital-intensive firms like Behemoth have a high level of operating gearing. As a result, they are especially prone to the impact of oscillations in the business cycle. As their output volume decreases, their earnings before interest and tax decline sharply and vice versa. Therefore, such companies are regarded as relatively risky and the stock market attaches a low price-earnings ratio to their earnings. In other words, investors tend to seek a relatively higher return from holding their shares to compensate for the greater variability in earnings and the potential loss. The addition of a second tier of risk in the form of financial gearing serves to accentuate the risk of inability to meet prior charges. Given the need to meet these interest charges, the effect of financial gearing is to raise the firm's break-even point. Generally speaking, companies with high operating gearing should not over-rely on debt finance.

Did you answer the question?

The examiner had developed a careful line of argument here that links the general problems of high operating and financial gearing levels with the particular, highly capital intensive industry within which Behemoth operates.

(c)   The regression equation suggests that total production cost comprises a fixed element (the intercept of the line, £1,400m) and a variable element, as given by the slope of the line fitted. It appears that for every unit produced, variable cost increases by £46 ie, the average variable (or unit variable) cost is £46.

However, there are many drawbacks with this method of modelling which may undermine its usefulness as a decision guide.

(i)   We are not told the correlation coefficient and thus do not know how close a fit the line is to the observations. If the correlation is low, then the fitted line may be unreliable.

(ii)   Even though we may obtain a good correlation for a linear relationship, it is possible that the true relationship contains elements of curvature.

(iii)   The relationship derived, even if correctly-shaped, is only valid over the observed ranges of output. In other words, when extended to higher or lower output ranges, the shape of the relationship may be different. For example, it is likely that at very low outputs, operating costs fall sharply due to the exploitation of indivisibilities, while at high outputs, they may rise sharply due to pressures on capacity leading to more breakdowns and idle time, etc.

(iv)   The relationship is based on past data. One imagines that the analyst would have corrected for inflation over the study period, but it is possible that his results are still contaminated by structural changes like the coming on-stream of new equipment, changes in product quality and changes in working practices. His results are only an average relationship over a lengthy period. However, to take a shorter period could expose the model to the undue influence of random events.

(v)   The underlying data may be biased by the inclusion in fixed costs of allocated cots, such as head office expenses. The focus should be solely on costs incurred at this particular operating unit.

Notwithstanding these reservations, it is possible to obtain a rough cross-check on the validity of the regression line by inspection of the accounts. The total cost of operation is reckoned to split into 75% fixed and 25% variable. Of the operating costs of £1,920m, this would correspond to £1,440m fixed and £480m variable. Given an output volume of 10m tonnes, this yields a per unit variable cost of £48, similar to the estimate obtained by the consultants.

(d)   **Payback**

1995 was a year of economic recovery, during which Behemoth produced 10m tonnes against a capacity of 12m tonnes. Accepting the consultants' estimate and assuming an average output over the cycle of 11m tonnes, the project will generate annual savings of:

[reduction in fixed cost of £1,400m - £1,300m]
    - [increase in variable cost of 11m × £4 per unit]
        = [£100m - £44m] = £56m

Assuming Behemoth's profitability recovers sufficiently to absorb the tax relief on the expenditure, the annual cash flows associated with the new expenditure are:

Item (£m)/Year	0	1	2	3	etc
Outlay	(100)				
Tax saving		33			
Net cash saving		56	56	56	etc
Tax at 33%			(18)	(18)	etc
Net cash flows	(100)	89	38	38	etc

Clearly, on these assumptions, the outlay generates a very rapid payback of just over one year. Inability to claim the tax relief immediately would slow down the payback, while a lower output figure could improve it, since variable costs are now higher.

Break-even

The break-even volume at present can be deducted by inspection of the accounts*. Fixed costs are £1,440m and variable costs per unit are £48. With a product price of £200 per tonne, and allowing for interest charges, this gives break-even at:

$$\frac{£1,440m + £8m}{£200 - £48} = \frac{£1,448m}{£152} = 9.53m \text{ units (TN 1)}$$

This corresponds to 79% of the full capacity of 12m units.

With the new production arrangements, and assuming debt financing, generating additional interest charges of (£100m × 8%) = £8m, the new break-even volume would be:

$$\frac{£1,300m + £8m + £8m}{£200 - £50} = \frac{£1,316m}{£150} = 8.77m \text{ units}$$

This corresponds to 73% of the full capacity of 12m units.

However, these calculations assume a given product price of £200. In reality, steel prices vary substantially over the trade cycle. In addition, variations in the product mix would influence the average price.

*   Alternatively, the answer may incorporate cost data from the regression equation. (TN 1)

Financial gearing

(i)   Capital gearing. Behemoth already has £80m/£2,020m = 4%. Financing the project with debt would raise the long-term debt by £100m to £180m, and ignoring the eventual beneficial impact of the project's returns on retained earnings and equity, the capital gearing would rise to £180m/£2,020m = 9%.

(ii)   Interest cover. Initially, the interest cover is high at £80m/£8m = 10 times. The additional interest charges of £8m would lower this to £80m/£16m = 5 times, again ignoring the cash flow and profit benefit of the new expenditure.

Despite the high operating gearing, the additional risks posed by financial gearing do not look excessive. The directors will have to take a view on this, bearing in mind the stage of the economic cycle and the likelihood of keeping operating profits above £16m, the minimum level required to cover the new total interest charges.

(e)   Shareholders require a return of 15% on the book value of their equity. Behemoth currently achieves profits after tax of just £62m on an equity base of £2,020m ie, ROE = £62m/£2,020m = 3.1%. The target profit after tax is (15% × £2,020m) = £303m. This is equivalent to approximately [£303m/1 - 33%] = £452m pre tax. This can be treated as tantamount to an additional fixed charge. In all, fixed charges become:

Fixed production costs + Interest charges + Profit target
= £1,300m + £16m + £452m = £1,768m

With an average product price of £200 and the new unit variable cost of £50, this suggests a required volume of:

$$\frac{£1,768m}{£200 - £50} = 11.8m \text{ tonnes}$$

This output corresponds to virtually full production capacity, seemingly a formidable target.

Tutorial notes

1   If the consultant's figures are used, the break-even would be

$$\frac{£1,400m + £8m}{£200 - £46} = \frac{£1,408m}{£154} = \quad 9.14m \text{ units}$$

---

51   (Answer 2 of examination)

> **Examiner's comments and marking guide**

Question 2: Part (a) required candidates to discuss problems with monetary policy from a Monetarist perspective, and to explain the problems which short-term monetary variations present to firms.

This question was not popular and was very badly done, reflecting candidates' habitual unease with issues of economics. Few answered the question set, preferring to outline the Quantity Theory and specifying the impacts of monetary variations on prices and interest rates, neglecting to mention problem areas such as time lags and perverse longer-term effects. Some did mention the link between interest rate movements and investment and financing decisions but very few understood that greater price uncertainty hinders firms' attempts to plan production and investment.

(b)   **This section called upon candidates to describe a 'rights issue' and to explain why such issues are in common use.** On the whole, the description was very well done. However, a number of candidates often confused 'rights issues' with 'bonus issues'. The reasons why 'rights issues' are used was also very well done by a considerable number of candidates. The weaker answers were those that were very thin and lacked full explanation of the reasons why they were used.

(c)   **This open ended short scenario question concerned the benefits of worker and junior management participation in the budget preparation process.** An encouraging number of candidates received very good marks for this question. However many candidates did not answer the question set, in whole or part. For example some candidates included a lot of irrelevant detail when describing budgets or the benefits of budgeting.

(d)   **The candidates were required to demonstrate and apply their knowledge of standard costing to a simple marginal costing contribution variance analysis and discussion of the situation.** Many candidates failed to calculate the contribution variance and many did not offer any suggested reasons as to why the adverse variances may have occurred.

(e)   **This question required candidates to discuss the issues relating to the valuation of materials to be included in the work in progress by a company using a process costing system.** A considerable number of candidates focused on one aspect only and excluded various other aspects.

Some candidates merely gave a list of bullet points which limits marks available when the question specifically asks for a discussion or description.

(f)   **This question called for a discussion of how to utilise idle production capacity and the identification of the financial benefits.** Many candidates gave sensible acceptable answers for the first part of the question. Practical sensible suggestions were awarded marks. A large number of candidates did however, fail to spell out the financial benefits which could result from their suggestions. A number of candidates did not answer the question set, and offered a description of the causes of 'idle time' with a particular emphasis on labour problems.

		Marks
(a)	Forecasting problems	1½
	Measurement problems	1½
	Disruption of expectations/impact on decisions	2
	max	5

(b)	What is a 'rights issue'?	
	- at the discretion of directors, etc	1
	- existing shareholders maintain control	1
	(Reasons why they are offered up to a max of 1½ marks per point which is well explained and illustrated, as appropriate)	3
	Total	5

(c)	- drawing on their knowledge and experience	
	- in contact with the workforce	
	- participation, junior managers etc more committed to the achievement of plans/objectives	
	- improvements in communications	
	- constructive comments, etc.	
	(Up to a max of 1½ marks for each point which is well explained and illustrated as appropriate)	5

(d)	Calculation of the variances in the contributions	2
	Calculation of the variances for sales	1
	Brief/relevant comments eg, competition, large bulk orders, etc	1
	labour mix, etc	1
	Total	5

(e)	WIP complete for input from previous process	½
	The method of valuation used	1
	The degree of completion	2½
	The treatment of losses	½
	Other considerations	½
	(Flexible)	5

(f)	½ or 1 mark per valid point explained and illustrated, as appropriate, eg, increasing the profitability of capital employed; marketing effort, special orders, moving plant and machinery about; reducing stocks etc, identify surplus assets	5
	Total	25

The examiner's answer

(a)   (i)   'Monetarist' economists are very sceptical about the ability of governments to successfully fine-tune the economy using either fiscal or monetary means. Two major problems in using short-term variations in the money supply are:

        1.   **Forecasting difficulties**

        When using any policy instrument to control economic fluctuations, policy-makers need information about the present state of the economy and in which direction it is tending. This requires timely collection of economic data and accurate forecasting for the need to act to be recognised. Monetarists emphasise problems of data-gathering and forecasting, inevitably based on past data, suggesting that delays in these areas are likely to have a perverse impact. Instead of short-term monetary manipulation, they stress the need to allow the money stock to grow in line with the overall economy.

        2.   **Measurement difficulties**

        To control any economic magnitude, it is useful to be able to measure it. Over time, new, widely-acceptable methods of payment have become available, and until they are built into definitions of money, they have the capacity to distort measurement of the 'true' stock of spending power. Experience has shown that when economic authorities attempt to restrict monetary growth, new forms of money emerge at a quicker rate.

    (ii)   Company decision-makers value stable economic conditions because stability aids forward planning. If the rate of monetary expansion is broadly known, they will accommodate their economic actions to suit the expected rate of inflation. If the government begins to increase monetary growth, people cannot predict the upward movement in the rate of inflation. Such an increase in uncertainty is likely to dislocate their decision-making in important ways. For example, they may apply price increases above the current rate of inflation, thus exacerbating the inflationary process. In addition, they may postpone replacement investments or forgo new capital expenditure, thus reducing their ability to respond to future increases in demand.

(b)   A rights issue can be made at the discretion of the directors and does not have to be approved by the company in general meeting. It can be made by a company whose shares are listed on the Stock Exchange and provides existing shareholders with an invitation to subscribe for shares usually at a price which is below the current market price. This allows the existing shareholders to maintain their current level, of control eg, in respect of voting rights. The ex-rights share price, will however depend on the market's reaction and expectations.

The reasons why such issues are very common are:

-    They provide the shareholders with some flexibility. They can either sell their rights in the market or keep them and pay for them in full. This means that such issues usually succeed as they in effect force shareholders to go one way or the other, ie, keep the shares or assign some/all of them.

-    The costs of a rights issue, for example when compared with a new issue of equity finance tends to be much cheaper with lower administrative costs and lower under-writing fees. The company making the issue will have to produce a brochure eg, with details, terms, capital structure data, future prospects, and dividend prospects etc, but, provided that the issue is for less than 10% of the class of shares concerned, the company does not have the expense of having to produce and issue a prospectus.

-    Companies may use a rights issue to reduce their gearing in book value terms by increasing the ordinary share capital, and may also use some of the cash received to pay off some/all of their long-term debt which could reduce the gearing, in market value terms, all other things remaining equal.

(c)   The possible benefits of involving worker representatives and junior management in the budget preparation process are:

-    They know their area and being able to draw upon their knowledge and experience could save their organisation a lot of money. For example, they could point out that if their organisation was to invest in a new machine which was being proposed by senior management, that it would also be necessary to buy certain additional equipment, in order to be able to carry out all of the functions for which it is being acquired.

-    They are in regular contact with the workers and know what can and cannot be done eg, if a target is set too high this may cause a reduction in motivation and lead to poor industrial relations. Thus, they can make a valuable input which should help ensure that targets set are fair, reasonable and attainable.

-    Those junior managers who have to put the plans into practice, will be more committed to doing so if they were actively involved in the budget preparation process. For example it is difficult for them to be 'fully accountable' if they were not a party to the discussion which helped to formulate the plans.

-    Being involved in various budget committee meetings by such personnel could also help improve communications. For example, if the organisation does not spell out its objectives and plans clearly, those not involved in the meetings will either tend to follow their own personal objectives or formulate their own perceived objectives for their organisation.

-    Participation by worker representatives and junior management should enable them to make their views known and prompt them to make constructive comments/recommendations and propose realistic plans.

(d)   The variance between the budgeted contribution (for the actual level of activity) and the actual contribution is:

	Selling price £	Variable cost £	Contribution £	Contribution for 64,000 units £
Budget	10.00	6.00	4.00	256,000
Actual	8.40	6.20	2.20	140,800
Variance	(1.60)	(0.20)	(1.80)	(115,200)

The contribution variance is made up of		£
Sales price variance	£1.60 × 64,000	(102,400)
Variable cost variance	£0.20 × 64,000	(12,800)
Contribution variance		(115,200)

The sales variances are:		£
Total variance:	Budget (£10 × 72,000)	720,000
	Actual (£8.40 × 64,000)	537,600
		(182,400)

This is made up of:

	£
Sales volume variance	
(Budget 72,000 units - Actual 64,000 units × £10)	(80,000)
Sales price variance (as above)	(102,400)
	(182,400)

or the sales volume variance could be calculated as:

	£
Actual quantity at standard contribution 64,000 × (£10 − £6) =	256,000
Budgeted quantity at standard contribution 72,000 × (£10 − £6) =	288,000
Sales quantity variance	£32,000 A

and the total sales variance is:

	£
Actual sales at actual price and standard variable cost	
64,000 × (£8.40 − £6)	153,600
Budgeted sales at standard contribution	
72,000 × (£10 − £6)	288,000
Total sales variance	134,400 A

The reasons for the adverse variances could have been caused by a combination of factors such as:

- Competition at home and overseas forcing selling prices down and/or accepting a number of large bulk orders, but still necessitating a reduction in demand/market share.

- Changes in technology/life-styles etc. This could also reduce demand for the product.

- The adverse variance in the variable costs could have been caused by using a different labour-mix in terms of skill levels and/or using materials of a higher quality than that which was planned.

- Additionally, the assumptions on which the budget was based, could have changed during the budget period and the budget not revised.

(e) The work in progress will be 100% complete for the input received into the process from the immediately preceding process for materials, layout and overheads.

The value of the material content of work in progress will depend on:

The method of valuation used

The method used to price the materials issued to the process eg, FIFO (first in, first out), LIFO (last in, first out), AVECO (average cost), or standard cost could have a significant impact on the valuation.

Estimating the degree of completion

Unlike labour and overheads which can be semi-complete, the work in progress will be 100% complete for all material which has been used in the process up to the date of valuation.

For example, if the work in progress is estimated to be 70% complete, all the material from the preceding process will be included and so will:

- any material added at the start of the processing, and

- any material added to the processing before it reaches the 70% degree of completion stage, but material which would be added after the 70% completion stage or at the end of processing would be excluded.

The treatment of losses

In the above example if a loss happens before the 70% completion stage then it should be accounted for and will have an impact on the value of work in progress, and vice versa.

Other considerations

Materials returned and not used in the processing should be adjusted for in the valuation. Also, the value of work in progress could be reduced by a proportion of the sales of scrap which could be credited to the process account.

Note: in addition to the above, answers could have also included a paragraph about the problems of dealing with *normal and abnormal losses.*

(f)   If idle production capacity such as idle plant and machinery can be utilised it could help to improve the profitability of the capital employed in the following ways:

- increasing the marketing effort to bring about an increase in demand for existing products eg, via pricing policies, special promotions, advertising, etc.

- accepting special orders which make a contribution towards the recovery of fixed overheads by making use of the idle capacity, however, the contribution generated must be greater than any reduction in fixed overheads which may have taken place if the idle capacity was not used, or greater than any increase in the fixed overheads if the idle capacity is used.

- moving idle plant and machinery to another department or another factory could reduce the amount which has to be expended on new plant and machinery and the associated interest charges etc on the financing of such assets.

- better labour and material utilisation eg, materials which are already in stock could be used on one of the special orders which brings about savings in holding costs

- identifying surplus assets which could either be sold off to improve cash flow and create space or sub-let to a third-party.

---

52   (Answer 3 of examination)

> **Examiner's comments and marking guide**

Question 3: (a) and (b) required a discussion of the advantages and disadvantages of absorption costing for dealing with internal services, comments on motivational aspects and the factors affecting the choice of the bases by which internal services are apportioned.

Candidates who scored low marks, did so because they could not write much at all about the subject and failed to discuss the matter, as applied to internal services and/or motivational aspects.

(c) (i) AND (ii) Only a very small number of candidates were able to work out (ii) using the simultaneous equation method. If candidates used the repeated distribution method and gave good reason why, marks were awarded.

(iii)   Sensible comments were rewarded. A considerable number of candidates did not attempt this part of the question.

		Marks
(a)	Up to a max of 1½ per valid point which is well explained and illustrated, as appropriate, could include: (also applies to part b)	
	Full cost method attempts to ensure that all internal services costs are recovered	1
	Encourages managers to consider support costs	1
	Costs outside a manager's control	1
	Link with SSAP 9	1
	Motivational points	3
	Total	7

(b)	Services provided to each other service cost centre	½
	Selection of the base of apportionment	1
	No. of departments	½
	Realistic technical estimates	½
	Cost/benefit	½
	Critical comments re the methods of apportioning internal services and the ranking process	2
		—
	Total	5
		—
(c)	'Step-wise' calculation	1½
	Reciprocal method, calculation of x and y	2
	Calculation of the (£'000) 1,028 and 774	1½
	Comments on the two methods (1 mark max per point explained)	3
		—
	Total	8
		—
	Grand total	20
		—

Step by step answer plan

Step 1   Read the question again and make sure that you focus on precisely what is required. It examines the treatment of service department costs, both by discussion and computation.

Step 2   (a)   This part considers the application of the full cost method to service department costs - ie recharging them to production departments, even though they don't necessarily vary with production activity. Make sure you attempt all three parts of the requirement - advantages, disadvantages and motivational aspects - even if you can't think of very much to say on each.

Step 3   (b)   Service department costs should ideally be apportioned according to the relative level of service provided to the user departments. This entails identification of the service provided and a suitable "cost driver" for that service. This will get you the first 2 or 3 marks. To gain more marks, consideration should be made of the practicalities / materiality / cost v benefit aspects.

Step 4   (c)   These re-apportionment methods should be familiar to you. The step-wise method gives partial recognition to intra-service department service - so G's costs are apportioned across the other three departments, including H. However, H's costs are only apportioned across the production departments, despite the element of its service provided to G. The reciprocal method gives both intra-service department elements full recognition. If you can't remember how to set up the equations for this, the examiner said he would give marks for the more laborious repeated distribution method (often quicker and safer). Don't forget the comment - use the results of your computations to illustrate where appropriate.

Step 5   Now review your answer and ensure that it does precisely answer the question as set.

The examiner's answer

(a)   The advantages and disadvantages (including the motivational aspects) of using the 'full cost' method for dealing with internal service department costs are:

The full cost method is worthy of consideration because it does attempt to ensure that all/most of our internal services costs are recovered in product costs. It also encourages managers to consider the support costs which affect their area of activity and that production is charged with a 'fair share' of the costs.

However, problems can arise from the adoption of such a system particularly where the costs for which managers are responsible are outside their control.

The system can help to motivate managers by making them aware of what such support costs consist of and encourages them to assist services departments in controlling their costs.

However, the motivation of managers could suffer as a result of using such a system where:

-    their department/cost centre is revenue earning and their profits distorted because of the subjective nature of the cost apportionments

-    they are held responsible for costs over which they have no control

-    competition between departments/costs centres could produce conflict as a direct result of 'unfair' allocations/apportionments of expenditure.

Examiner's note: (not part of the answer). This 'open-ended' question could include other factors eg, the link with SSAP 9.

(b)   The factors which affect the selection of the bases of apportionment for the costs of internal services, are as follows:

-    The service which each service department provides to each other and to each production department.

-    Selecting an appropriate base of apportionment eg, number of employees, value of purchase orders, number of stores issue notes, direct labour hours etc.

-    The number of departments which have to be serviced and the amount of the overhead expenditure involved.

-    Being able to produce realistic technical estimates about the usage of the service.

-    The cost/benefit, in terms of the amount of work involved in implementing the system.

It must be noted that certain methods of apportioning internal services do ignore the services provided to other services eg, the 'elimination' (or 'two step') method. Even if the ranking used in these methods is done very carefully the effect on the costs which are apportioned could be quite significant.

Did you answer the question?

Note that this answer includes consideration of the practicalities that may lead to simple, blanket bases being used for apportionment, where the costs of devising and implementing a "better" system would outweigh any benefit accruing - particularly for less significant (immaterial) elements of cost.

(c)   (i)   The 'step-wise' ('elimination') method

| | Production depts | | Internal services | |
| | 1 | 2 | G | H |
	£'000	£'000	£'000	£'000
Overheads	870	690	160	82
G apportioned	96	48	-160	16
				98
H apportioned	61	37		-98
	1,027	775		

(ii)   The reciprocal (simultaneous equation) method

let x = costs of department G
and y = costs of department H

x = 160 + 0.2y
y =   82 + 0.1x
multiply by 10, to eliminate decimals, gives:

£'000
$$10x - 2y = \quad 1,600 \ (1)$$
$$-x + 10y = \quad 820 \ (2)$$
multiply equation (1) by 5, and add to equation (2), will give:

£'000

		£'000
$50x - 10y$	=	8,000
$-x + 10y$	=	820
$49x$	=	8,820

$$\therefore \ x \quad = \frac{8,820}{49} = \qquad 180$$

$$\text{and } y \quad = \frac{820 + 180}{10} = \qquad 100$$

			Production depts	
Internal		*Total*	*1*	*2*
Services		£'000	£'000	£'000
G	(180 × 90%)	162	($\frac{6}{9}$) 108	($\frac{3}{9}$) 54
H	(100 × 80%)	80	($\frac{5}{8}$) 50	($\frac{3}{8}$) 30
		242	158	84
Overheads (given)			870	690
			1,028	774

(iii) The step-wise method is simple to compute. Given that the figures are budgeted figures ie, estimates. The degree of accuracy is questionable, whichever method is used. However, the 'step-wise' method ignores the services provided to other services which have been cleared ie, the service provided by G to H is taken into account but, the service provided by H to G is ignored.

The calculations in this computation are only £1,000 different but, there could be much wider differences. The reciprocal method, does take into account the services provided by internal services to each other and could therefore be considered the more equitable of the two methods.

---

53   (Answer 4 of examination)

(**Examiner's comments and marking guide**)

Question 4: (a) this part of the question required the calculation of a machine hour rate, and was generally answered well by candidates.

(b)   This part required a lot of workings, and many candidates obtained good marks for this part.

(c)   Candidates should have noted that eight marks had been allocated to this part of the question. The performance for part (c) was very disappointing particularly in the light of pleasing answers to parts (a) and (b); some did not even bother to attempt this part of the question at all, thus throwing away the 8 marks that it carried.

		Marks
(a)	Budgeted machine hours	2
	Machine hour rate calculation	1
		—
	Total	3
		—
(b)	Product profitability analysis (including workings)	8
	Critical comments	2
		—
	Total	10
		—
(c)	Budgets, just estimates/contribution approach/product life cycles	1
	Comments on each product eg, product R in decline, etc	4
	The very high proportion of material costs, explained	2
		—
	Total	7
		—
	Grand total	20
		—

Step by step answer plan

Step 1   Read the question again and make sure that you focus on precisely what is required. It first requires some fairly standard absorption rate and budgeted contribution/profit computations; the remaining 40% of the marks are awarded for analysis of the figures produced, comment and advice.

Step 2   (a)   A machine hour rate needs total budgeted overheads for the period (given in the question) and total machine hours budgeted to be worked. The latter is determined from budgeted product activity levels (here, production = sales) and machine hours by products (here given in terms of hours per 1,000 kg).

Step 3   (b)   The computations required here are not complex, but there are a lot of numbers to work through. You need to make sure you set out your answer in such a way that the examiner can award marks for method even if you make the odd slip here and there. Set up a proforma statement first, ensuring you can identify the contribution line as well as profit, then use separate workings where necessary to compute the figures. These should be referenced in to your statement.

Step 4   (c)   It is a temptation to think that by the time you have worked your way through the data for the first two parts, you're virtually there, and it need only a quick note or two for this part. When there are this many marks involved, this is a dangerous strategy. At the very least, as the question specifically refers to the sales trend, you can assess what is happening to each product in this respect. Consider both the sales volumes and the resulting contributions, as you have this information for both periods. On the whole, you should be ignoring fixed costs in your analysis as they are absorbed on a relatively arbitrary basis. Then look for any other points worthy of mention - eg the high proportion of material costs.

Step 5   Now review your answer and ensure that it does precisely answer the question as set.

The examiner's answer

(a)

		Machine group	
Period 2		*1*	*2*
Product			
R (10 × machine hours per 1,000)		750	800
S (25 × machine hours per 1,000)		750	2,750
T (50 × machine hours per 1,000)		2,500	2,500
Budgeted machine hours		4,000	6,050
Overheads (given)		£40,800	£68,365
Machine hour rate		£10.20	£11.30

(b)

		Product Profitability Analysis		
Period 2		*Product R*	*Product S*	*Product T*
	Kilos	10,000	25,000	50,000
		£	£	£
Sales	(A)	110,000	250,000	450,000
Direct materials		45,080	127,400	306,250
Variable labour and overheads		5,650	12,500	16,000
	(see W1)			
Sales commission at 4%		4,400	10,000	18,000
Variable cost	(B)	55,130	149,900	340,250
Contribution	(A)-(B)	54,870	100,100	109,750
Fixed overheads	(W2)	16,690	38,725	53,750
Budgeted net profit		38,180	61,375	56,000

WORKINGS

(W1)

Variable labour and overheads

Machine Group hours:	Direct labour			Labour and Overhead rate per hour	Products		
	R	S	T		R £	S £	T £
1	30 :	10 :	20	£7.50	225	75	150
2	40 :	50 :	20	£8.50	340	425	170
					565	500	320
Number of batches					10	25	50
					5,650	12,500	16,000

(W2)

Fixed overheads

Machine Group	Machine hours			Machine hour rate	Products R £	Products S £	Products T £
	R	S	T				
1	75 :	30 :	50	£10.20	765	306	510
2	80 :	110 :	50	£11.30	904	1,243	565
					1,669	1,549	1,075
Number of batches					10	25	50
					16,690	38,725	53,750

The net profit figures have been calculated using absorption costing ie, absorbing fixed overheads into the product costs via arbitrary bases such as floor area, number of employees etc, in addition to the variable costs.

The fixed overhead recovery rate uses machine hours ie, an output based measure, when in fact a lot of the fixed overheads will tend to vary more with time than output. Absorption costing is an attempt to ensure that costs are recovered. It does not attempt to provide accurate and realistic product costs. The marginal costing contribution approach, only includes those costs which vary with output ie, the variable costs, and by indicating the amount which each product contributes towards the recovery of the fixed overheads and profit, is considered to be the more appropriate method for decision-making purposes.

Did you answer the question?

The above comment is not an actual requirement of this part of the question and, despite the original marking guide, would not have earned marks in (b) but might have earned marks in part (c).

(c)   At the outset it should be noted that the budgets are only estimates and that the assumptions on which they were based could change. They provide targets against which the actual performance can be compared as and when the information becomes available.

For decision-making purposes management need to use a contribution approach and also assess where the product is in its life cycle.

The sales of product R are expected to fall. If this continues in the future, the product will be in the decline stage of its *life cycle* and a time could come when its contribution would not cover the fixed overheads assigned to it, meaning that they would have to be recovered out of the contributions generated by the other products.

Product S, if it continues to remain static in terms of the sales demand would appear to have reached its peak. However, there should be a significant increase in period two in its contribution, possibly resulting from increased efficiency, improved productivity and cost reductions.

Product T could well be into its growth stage with an anticipated 25% increase in volume planned for period two. Here also the selling price is expected to remain unchanged and increases in efficiency etc should help to increase the contribution per kilo from £1.89 to around £2.20.

The management need to consider what action they can take to reverse the trends in products S and T and search for new products.

Management also needs to be made aware of the very high proportion of material costs eg, material cost for all products as a percentage of the total cost is over 73%. This high level of investment in materials should make inventory management a very high priority. In order to reduce material costs and expensive holding costs, management will need to monitor and review the situation at frequent intervals. They could consider actions which would reduce waste eg, better design/production methods, or reduce the cost eg, by using substitutes.

Examiner's note: it is not necessary to mention and use the keywords relating to the product life cycle in the answer.

---

54 (Answer 5 of examination)

Examiner's comments and marking guide

Question 5: part (a) required a discussion of the significance of trade creditors in the working capital cycle, and of the dangers of over-reliance on trade credit.

This was generally quite well done, offering relatively easy marks for the well-prepared candidate. There was some confusion between debtors and creditors and a pronounced tendency not to fully explain the points made, especially with regard to short and long-term liquidity implications.

Part (b) required analysis of selected accounts data to assess the effects of a new credit arrangement with suppliers on key financial indicators.

This was not well done. Many candidates opted for a discursive approach, often preferring to ignore totally the information provided, thus disqualifying themselves from the higher marks. It appeared that some might have been puzzled by the absence of a separate figure for purchases, although the question clearly stated that the supplier accounted for 50% of the cost of sales. Assuming no stock movements, it follows that purchases from this supplier are 50% of the difference between sales and the EBIT, ie, 50% × [£10m - £2m] = £4m. Using sales as a proxy was acceptable although not for full marks. Candidates have to read the question carefully and utilise the information provided, specifying any assumptions.

Even if candidates did fail to proceed along the expected lines, there were opportunities for easy marks obtainable from calculating accounting indicators. However, presentation was particularly poor, with relatively few systematic attempts to answer the question in a structured way. Although the question clearly required a 'before and after' approach, remarkably few candidates could supply the correct starting figures. There were many basic errors in calculation of PAT (eg, failure to allow for tax-deductibility of interest). EPS (eg, using profit before tax, incorrect calculation of the number of shares), and ROI (eg, using only issued share capital as the denominator). Calculations of profit and interest cover also tended to neglect the beneficial effect of the discount offered, which applied to a full year's supplies rather than to outstanding balances.

			Marks
(a)	(i)	Definition/explanation of working capital	1
		Definition/explanation of trade credit period	1
		Role in the cash conversion cycle	2
			──
		Total	4
			──
	(ii)	Cost of giving up discounts	1
		Reactions of upset suppliers	2
		Image/goodwill problems	1
			──
		Total	4
			──

(b)   Calculation of ratios and cycle time   2
       Effect of discount on credit period and cycle time   1
       Calculation of interest cover without/with discount   2
       Calculation of changes in:
         PAT   3
         EPS   1
         ROE   1
         Capital gearing   1
       Comment   1
                                                                             ———
       Total   12

       Grand total   20
                                                                             ———

Step by step answer plan

Step 1   Read the question again and make sure that you focus on precisely what is required. It is essentially a management of working capital question, but also considers profitability and gearing aspects.

Step 2   (a)   This part carries 8 marks for discussion of the use of trade creditors (note that (ii) is referring to creditors, as it refers to a *source* of finance). take care not to overlap your answers to the two parts. Part (i) basically requires an explanation of the working capital cycle, a definition of the creditors payment period and an explanation of how this period fits into, and affects, the working capital cycle. You can use the data from the question to illustrate (note you are going to have to compute the current period and cycle as part of your answer to (b)).

              Part (ii) concerns the possible consequences of extending the credit period, both financial and otherwise.

Step 3   (b)   The requirement is very specific as to the aspects you should include in your determination of costs and benefits. The financial effects of the supplier arrangement are the discount (a benefit) and the early payment (a cost in terms of interest). You should therefore initially compute the "before" and "after" figures for the six measures, taking account of these factors. Make simplifications or assumptions if necessary to enable a quick comparison to be made - there are not many marks available for each. For example, if you cannot see how to get purchases or cost of sales, then use of sales would earn some marks. Then (and importantly) you need to comment, both on the individual effects and the overall picture. Finally, give a recommendation.

Step 4   Now review your answer and ensure that it does precisely answer the question as set.

The examiner's answer

(a)   (i)   For many firms, trade creditors - suppliers of goods and services - represent the major component of current liabilities, the amounts owed by the company which have to be repaid within the next accounting period. Together with current assets - cash, stock and debtors - current liabilities determine the firm's net working capital position ie, the net sum it invests in working capital.

              Different suppliers will operate different credit periods, but the average trade credit period in days can be calculated as follows:

              Trade creditors/Credit purchases × 365

              Sometimes, it is expressed in terms of total purchases and sometimes in terms of overall cost of sales. The length of the trade credit period depends partly on competitive relationships among suppliers and partly on the firm's own working capital policy.

              The trade credit period is an important element in a company's cash conversion cycle - the length of time between a firm making payment for its purchases of materials and labour and receiving payment for its sales. The time period over which net current assets have to be financed depends not only on policy towards suppliers but also on debtor management and stock control policy:

Cash conversion cycle =
[Debtor days + stock period] − [trade credit period]

(ii)   In effect, because trade credit represents temporary borrowing from suppliers until invoices are paid, it becomes an important method of financing the firm's investment in current assets. Firms may be tempted to view trade creditors as a cheap source of finance, especially as in the UK at least, it is currently interest-free. Having a debtors collection period shorter than the trade collection period may be taken as a sign of efficient working capital management. However, trade credit is not free.

First, by delaying payment of accounts due, the company may be passing up valuable discounts, thus effectively increasing the cost of goods sold.

Second, excessive delay in the settlement of invoices can undermine the existence of the business in a number of ways. Existing suppliers may be unwilling to extend more credit until existing accounts are settled, they may begin to attach a lower priority to future orders placed, they may raise prices in the future or simply not supply at all. In addition, if the firm acquires a reputation among the business community as a bad payer, its relationships with other suppliers may be soured.

(b)   **Working capital cycle**

At present the working capital cycle is:

Debtor days:	£0.4m/£10m	×	365	=	15 days
Stock days:	£0.7m/£8m	×	365	=	32 days (cost of sales = £10m - £2m)
Creditor days:	£1.5m/£8m	×	365	=	(68 days)
		Total			(21 days)

Clearly, Keswick is exceptionally efficient in its use of working capital. (TN1)

The proposed arrangement would shorten creditor days in relation to half of cost of sales to 15 days. The effect is to lower the average to:
$$(\tfrac{1}{2} \times 68 \text{ days}) + (\tfrac{1}{2} \times 15 \text{ days}) = 41.5 \text{ days}$$

Overall, this will increase cycle time to:
$$[15 + 32 - 41.5 \text{ days}] \text{ ie, to 5.5 days}$$

Interest cover

At present, interest cover (earnings before interest and tax divided by interest) is:
= £2m/£0.5m = 4.0 times, which is not unduly low.

The advanced payment will raise interest costs but will generate savings via the discount. The discount applies to half of cost of sales, ie, $\tfrac{1}{2} \times$ £8m × 5% = £0.2m. The EBIT will increase accordingly.

The net advanced payment of (£4m − £0.2m) = £3.8m will have to be financed for an extra (68 − 15) days, generating interest costs of:
$$[\text{£3.8m} \times 12\% \times \tfrac{53}{365}] = \text{£66,214}$$

The interest cover slightly declines to:
$$[\text{£2.0m} + \text{£0.2m}]/[\text{£0.50m} + \text{£0.066m}] = 3.89 \text{ times}$$

Profit after tax, ROE and EPS

The 'before' and 'after' profit and loss accounts appear thus:

	£m *No discount*	£m *With discount*
Sales	10.000	10.000
Cost of sales	(8.000)	(7.800)
Earnings before interest and tax	2.000	2.200
Interest	(0.500)	(0.566)
Taxable profit	1.500	1.634
Tax at 33%	(0.495)	(0.539)
Profit after tax	1.005	1.095

$$\text{ROE} = \frac{£1.005\text{m}}{£2\text{m}} = 50.3\% \qquad\qquad \frac{£1.095\text{m}}{£2\text{m}} = 54.8\%$$

$$\text{EPS} = \frac{£1.005\text{m}}{£1\text{m} \times 4} = 25.1\text{p} \qquad\qquad \frac{£1.095\text{m}}{4\text{m}} = 27.4\text{p}$$

The proposal appears beneficial to Keswick in terms of the effect on profitability measures ie, EBIT, PAT, EPS, and ROE. However, it does have a marginally harmful effect on its interest cover. It also lengthens its working capital cycle and turns it into a net demander of working capital. This suggests an increase in its capital gearing.

Before the adjustment, gearing at book values (overdraft/shareholder's funds) was:
$$£3.0\text{m}/£2\text{m} = 150\%$$

The overdraft will increase by:
$$[£3.8\text{m} \times {}^{53}\!/_{365}] = £0.55\text{m}$$

Ignoring the beneficial effect on equity, gearing after the adjustment becomes:

$$£3.55\text{m}/£2\text{m} = 178\%$$

This looks rather perilous, considering the short-term nature of much of the debt, and Keswick's low liquidity. Perhaps Keswick should reconsider its policy regarding long-term borrowing, although whether prospective lenders would oblige is probably doubtful.

Tutorial note

1   The limited information about cost of sales upset students and tutors alike when this question was set. You should notice what the examiner has done (sales − EBIT = cost of goods sold) as an example of using some figure, however inappropriate, to demonstrate your knowledge. State an assumption and plough on.

---

55   (Answer 6 of examination)

Examiner's comments and marking guide

Question 6: part (a) required explanations of sale and leaseback (SAL), HP and financial leasing.

This was generally quite well done. However, there were recurrent errors. For example, the impression that with a SAL, the asset is purchased then immediately resold for cash (in which case, why bother?), confusion between operating and financial leasing, and statements to the effect that a financial lease is off-balance sheet and 'normally' involves an option to buy.

Part (b) and (c) required a lease evaluation from both lessor's (b) and lessee's (c) perspectives.

There was much confusion here, leaving the impression that too few candidates understood the distinction between the two parties and their roles. Answers were poorly presented, and rarely offered an actual solution, indicating a poor understanding of the significance of the numerical data derived. The analysis required a standard DCF lease evaluation, although many answers were given in undiscounted form. Many candidates threw in the maintenance charge for the lessor, ignoring its non incremental nature, many candidates who did do a DCF analysis included interest in the cash flows and most omitted the lessor's liability to tax on rentals. In calculating the lessee's break-even rental, most candidates failed to appreciate that an annuity application was required, simply dividing by the number of years. The bright spot was in calculating the WDAs and subsequent tax savings (yet often with insufficient years and often ignoring the balancing allowance). Astute candidates realised that this operation could be utilised again in evaluating the lessee's lease-or-buy decision. The few who offered coherently structured answers, appreciating the different positions of the two parties, scored high marks.

		Marks
(a)	Definition/explanation of: Sale-and-leaseback	2
	HP	2
	Finance leasing*	2
		—
	Total	6
		—
(b)	Calculation of stream of tax savings	3
	Effect of tax on discount rate	1
	Break-even calculation	3
		—
	Total	7
		—
(c)	Specification of: post-tax cash flows	2
	borrowing cash flows	1
	Effect of tax on discount rate	1
	Calculation of NPV and decision	1
	Incorporation of maintenance/calculation	1
	Decision plus comment	1
		—
	Total	7
	* Note: non-UK specific answers are acceptable)	—
	Grand total	20
		—

Step by step answer plan

Step 1   Read the question again and make sure that you focus on precisely what is required. It looks at various methods of capital expenditure finance, concentrating particularly on leasing.

Step 2   (a)   You have 2 marks for your description of each finance method given. Note that "features" will include both a description of how the method actually works (the logistics) and the consequences/benefits of the method.

Step 3 (b)   Here you are looking at a lease from the *lessor's* point of view. The relevant cash flows will therefore be rental income; cost of equipment and their tax consequences (tax *charge* on income, tax *relief* on capital allowances). The lessor will "break-even" when the *net present value* of the cash flows from this project is exactly zero. The requirement to employ discounted cash flow techniques is indicated by the inclusion of a cost of capital (interest rate, which needs to be adjusted for tax) - and the basic knowledge that it is on this basis that lessors will actually compute their rental charges (including a profit element).

There are various ways you can set out the workings to this part. The basic approach is to set up a normal NPV computation, slot in the cash flows you know, put an unknown R for the rental income (which will also be incorporated into the tax charge) and put in the discount factors. Set the whole thing equal to 0 and solve for R.

Bear in mind when you are setting out your workings that some may be of use in (c).

Step 4 (c)   You are now looking at the lease from the other side - the *lessee's* viewpoint - in comparison with borrow and buy. Again, you can approach this in different ways, but the flows to be compared, on an incremental or absolute basis, are *Lease:* rental, tax relief, (+ maintenance savings for (ii)); *Borrow and buy:* capital cost, tax relief on CA's (as computed in (b)).Note that the discount rate differs from that of the lessor.

Step 5   Now review your answer and ensure that it does precisely answer the question as set.

The examiner's answer

(a)   **Sale and leaseback (SAL)**

SAL is an arrangement whereby a firm sells an asset, usually land or a building, to a financial institution and simultaneously enters an agreement to lease the property back form the purchaser. The seller receives the purchase price almost at once, but is committed to a series of rental payments over an agreed period, long enough for the purchaser to recoup his initial outlay plus an element of profit. The main advantage to the vendor is the rapidity with which otherwise illiquid assets can be converted into cash. SAL is therefore suitable for capital-rationed companies who are eager to finance expansion programmes before perceived market opportunities evaporate.

The main disadvantage for the vendor of the asset is the loss of participation in any capital appreciation. A further disadvantage is the reduction in the balance sheet value of *owned* assets and hence possible reduction in the company's future capacity to borrow.

Hire purchase (HP)

In an HP contract, equipment is purchased on behalf of the intended user by a finance house, usually a subsidiary of a bank. The user pays a periodic hire charge, commonly monthly. This includes both an interest element on the initial outlay plus recovery of capital. The ownership of the asset passes to the user at the end of the contract period, unless the user defaults on the payment schedule, in which case, the owner can re-possess the asset. To ensure that the asset is worth re-possessing, the hire period is always set at less than the expected useful life of the asset. A feature of an HP contract is that the user, ie, future owner, can claim capital allowances on the initial cost of the asset.

Financial leasing

A finance lease is a contract where equipment is purchased by a leasing company, often a subsidiary of a bank, for long-term hire. The hire period corresponds to the expected lifetime of the asset, and, in most cases, the ownership of the asset does not pass to the user. In the UK, capital allowances are available to the purchaser, and may be passed on to the user in the form of a reduced rental charge. If the owner does relinquish ownership, these capital allowances are clawed back by the tax authorities. In the UK, both the leased asset and the corresponding stream of rental liabilities have to appear on the user's balance sheet. As a result, finance leasing cannot be used to disguise gearing but it is helpful to the capital-rationed firm, and also considerably cheaper than HP.

Did you answer the question?

Note that the mechanics of each method has first been described, followed by a brief discussion of the effects of such a method on cash flow, gearing, asset worth, etc

(b)   For Howgill to break-even, the present value of its after-tax rental receipts must equal the present value of its costs. The cost incurred is the initial outlay on the asset, net of the present value of capital allowances. Given spare capacity in the computer maintenance division, the opportunity cost of using these facilities is zero.

Consider the present value of the tax savings. It is assumed that Howgill can begin to set off the available allowances against profits immediately, ie, beginning in 1996, the financial year in which the acquisition takes place.

				(£m)		
Year	*0*	*1*	*2*	*3*	*4*	*5*
Written-down value	15.00	11.25	8.44	6.33	0	
Allowance claimed	5.00	3.75	2.81	2.11	6.33	
Tax saving at 33%		1.65	1.24	0.93	0.70	2.09
Discount factor at 10%*		0.909	0.826	0.751	0.683	0.621
Present value		1.50	1.02	0.70	0.48	1.30

Present Value of tax savings = 5.00 ie, £5.00m
* Note: This discount rate is found as follows:
    15% [1 – 33%] = 10%
(Strictly speaking, the tax delay should also be allowed for. This reduces the effective tax rate to 28.7%, thus yielding a discount rate of about 10.5%.

This effect is not incorporated in this solution but either approach is acceptable.)

The tax savings have a total value of £5m, reducing the effective cost of the equipment to £15m. The present value of the after-tax rentals must therefore at least cover this amount. The rentals are payable from year 0 to year 3 inclusive, while the tax payable on this income will become due at the end of year 1 - 4 inclusive.

Denoting the rental payment as R, we need to solve the following expression (denominated in £m):

15 = R + [3-year annuity at 10% of R] less [4-year annuity at 10% of R times 33%]

ie,

        15 = R + R [2.487] – R (33%) [3.170]
        15 = R [1 + 2.487 – 1.046]
        15 = 2.441R
whence   R = 6.15 ie, £6.15m is the required annual rental.

(c)   To evaluate the lease decision from Clint's viewpoint, it is necessary to compare the cashflows associated with leasing with those connected with borrowing-in-order-to-buy, using Clint's borrowing cost of 18% adjusted for tax. In incremental terms:

			(all figs in £m)			
Year	*0*	*1*	*2*	*3*	*4*	*5*
Lease						
Rentals	(7.00)	(7.00)	(7.00)	(7.00)		
Tax savings		2.31	2.31	2.31	2.31	
Net (L)	(7.00)	(4.69)	(4.69)	(4.69)	2.31	
Borrow-to-buy						
Outlay (TN 6.1)	(20.00)					
Tax savings		1.65	1.24	0.93	0.70	2.09
Net (B)	(20.00)	1.65	1.24	0.93	0.70	2.09

Incremental cash flows [L-B]:

	13.00	(6.34)	(5.93)	(5.62)	1.61	(2.09)
Discount factor at 12%*	1.000	0.893	0.797	0.712	0.636	0.567
PV	13.000	(5.66)	(4.73)	(4.00)	1.02	(1.19)

Net present value = (£1.56m) which argues against leasing.

Note: this discount rate is found as follows:

$$18\% [1 - 33\%] = 12\%.$$

(If the tax delay is incorporated, the discount rate, becomes around 12.8%. Either approach is acceptable).

However, this result overlooks the value of the maintenance costs, which lessees often have to bear themselves. The savings comprise a four-year annuity of £0.75m less a four year annuity of tax payments, but delayed by a year. These have a present value of:

PV of cost savings (£m) at 12%:

= 0.75 [3.037] − 0.75 [(33%) (3.037)]/1.12

= (2.28 − 0.67) = 1.61 (ie) £1.61m

These cost savings have the effect of reversing the decision ie, they make the lease worthwhile, viz:

PV of cost savings	=	£1.61m
NPV of lease decision	=	£(1.56m)
Revised value of lease	=	+ £0.05m

However, the decision to lease is highly marginal.

Tutorial notes

Note that the actual cash flows for the 'borrow' option will be the interest payments, tax relief on same, and the loan repayments. However, when these are discounted at the post-tax cost of borrowing, they will have a present value equal to the original loan - ie, the cost of the asset.

DECEMBER 1996 QUESTIONS

Section A - This question is compulsory and MUST be attempted

56   (Question 1 of examination)

LKL plc is a manufacturer of sports equipment and is proposing to start project VZ, a new product line. This project would be for the four years from the start of year 19X1 to the end of 19X4. There would be no production of the new product after 19X4.

You have recently joined the company's accounting and finance team and have been provided with the following information relating to the project:

Capital expenditure

A feasibility study costing £45,000 was completed and paid for last year. This study recommended that the company buy new plant and machinery costing £1,640,000 to be paid for at the start of the project. The machinery and plant would be depreciated at 20% of cost per annum and sold during year 19X5 for £242,000 receivable at the end of 19X5.

As a result of the proposed project it was also recommended that an old machine be sold for cash at the start of the project for its book value of £16,000. This machine had been scheduled to be sold for cash at the end of 19X2 for its book value of £12,000.

Other data relating to the new product line:

	19X1	19X2	19X3	19X4
	£'000	£'000	£'000	£'000
Sales	1,000	1,300	1,500	1,800
Debtors (at the year end)	84	115	140	160
Lost contribution				
on existing products	30	40	40	36
Purchases	400	500	580	620
Creditors (at the year end)	80	100	110	120
Payments to sub-contractors,	60	90	80	80
including prepayments of	5	10	8	8
Net tax payable				
associated with this project	96	142	174	275
Fixed overheads and advertising:				
With new line	1,330	1,100	990	900
Without new line	1,200	1,000	900	800

Notes

-       The year-end debtors and creditors are received and paid in the following year.

-       The net tax payable has taken into account the effect of any capital allowances. There is a one year time-lag in the payment of tax.

-       The company's cost of capital is a constant 10% per annum.

-       It can be assumed that operating cash flows occur at the year end.

-       Apart from the data and information supplied there are no other financial implications after 19X4.

Labour costs

From the start of the project, three employees currently working in another department and earning £12,000 each would be transferred to work on the new product line, and an employee currently earning £20,000 would be promoted to work on the new line at a salary of £30,000 per annum. The effect of the transfer of employees from the other department to the project is included in the lost contribution figures given above.

As a direct result of introducing the new product line, four employees in another department currently earning £10,000 each would have to be made redundant at the end of 19X1 and paid redundancy pay of £15,500 each at the end of 19X2.

Agreement had been reached with the trade unions for wages and salaries to be increased by 5% each year from the start of 19X2.

Material costs

Material XNT which is already in stock, and for which the company has no other use, cost the company £6,400 last year, and can be used in the manufacture of the new product. If it is not used the company would have to dispose of it at a cost to the company of £2,000 in 19X1.

Material XPZ is also in stock and will be used on the new line. It cost the company £11,500 some years ago. The company has no other use for it, but could sell it on the open market for £3,000 in 19X1.

Required

(a)   Prepare and present a cash flow budget for project VZ, for the period 19X1 to 19X5 and calculate the net present value of the project.

(14 marks)

(b)   Write a short report for the board of directors which:

(i)   explains why certain figures which were provided in (a) were excluded from your cash flow budget, and

(ii)   advises them on whether or not the project should be undertaken, and lists other factors which would also need to be considered.

(7 marks)

(c)   LKL needs to raise £5 million to finance project VZ, and other new projects. The proposed investment of the £5 million is expected to yield pre-tax profits of £2 million per annum. Earnings on existing investments are expected to remain at their current level. From the data supplied below:

Balance Sheet (extract from last year):

	£'000
Authorised share capital Ordinary shares of 50p each	20,000
Issued ordinary share capital, Shares of 50p each	2,500
Reserves	4,000
10% Debentures (20X4)	2,000
Bank Overdraft (secured)	2,000
	10,500

Other information:	£'000
Turnover	55,000
Net profit after interest and tax	3,000
Interest paid	200
Dividends paid and proposed	800

The 50p ordinary shares are currently quoted at £2.25 per share. The company's tax rate is 33%. The average gearing percentage for the industry in which the company operates is 35% (computed as debt as a percentage of debt plus equity, based on book values, and excluding bank overdrafts).

(i)   Calculate and comment briefly on the company's current capital gearing.

Discuss briefly the effect on gearing and EPS at the end of the first full year following the new investment if the £5 million new finance is raised in each of the following ways;

(ii)   By issuing ordinary shares at £2 each.

(iii)   By issuing 5% convertible loan stock, convertible in 20X4. The conversion ratio is 40 shares per £100 of loan stock.

(iv)   By issuing 7.5% undated debentures.

(You should ignore issue costs in your answers to parts ii - iv)

(14 marks)
(Total: 35 marks)

Section B. - This question is compulsory and MUST be attempted

| 57   (Question 2 of examination) |

Answer FIVE of the six parts of this question

(a)   Explain the purpose of cartels such as OPEC, and why they are inherently unstable arrangements.

(5 marks)

(b)   Briefly explain why companies issue share warrants and why they may be attractive to investors.

(5 marks)

(c)   For what reasons may a small but rapidly growing company prefer to borrow via a term loan rather than an overdraft?

(5 marks)

(d)   Identify the effects on private sector businesses of a significant public sector budget deficit.

(5 marks)

(e)   Briefly explain the relationship which you would normally expect to find in an information-efficient capital market between relative yields on the following types of security:

-       preference shares
-       corporate bonds
-       equities
-       government stock   **(5 marks)**

(f)   Briefly explain the relevance of three measures which may be used to assess performance in public sector services which provide education.

(5 marks)
(Total: 25 marks)

Section C - ONE question ONLY to be attempted

58   (Question 3 of examination)

A manufacturing company has provided you with the following data which relates to component RYX, for the period which has just ended:

	Budget	Actual
Number of labour hours	8,400	7,980
Production units	1,200	1,100
Overhead cost (all fixed)	£22,260	£25,536

Overheads are absorbed at a rate per standard labour hour.

Required:

(a)   (i)   Calculate the fixed production overhead cost variance and the following subsidiary variances:

- expenditure
- efficiency
- capacity

(ii)   Provide a summary statement of these four variances.

(7 marks)

(b)   Briefly discuss the possible reasons why adverse fixed production overhead expenditure, efficiency and capacity variances occur.

(10 marks)

(c)   Briefly discuss two examples of inter-relationships between the fixed production overhead efficiency variances and the material and labour variances.

(3 marks)
(Total: 20 marks)

59   (Question 4 of examination)

The following information relates to product J, for quarter three, which has just ended:

	Production (units)	Sales (units)	Fixed Overheads £'000	Variable costs £'000
Budget	40,000	38,000	300	1,800
Actual	46,000	42,000	318	2,070

The selling price of product J was £72 per unit.

The fixed overheads were absorbed at a predetermined rate per unit. At the beginning of quarter three, there was an opening stock of product J of 2,000 units valued at £25 per unit variable costs and £5 per unit fixed overheads.

Required:

(a)   (i)   Calculate the fixed overhead absorption rate per unit for the last quarter, and

                 Present profit statements using FIFO (first in, first out) using:

        (ii)   absorption costing, and

        (iii)   marginal costing, and

        (iv)   reconcile and explain the difference between the profits or losses.

                                                                     (12 marks)

(b)   Using the same data present similar statements to those required in part (a), using the AVECO (average cost) method of valuation, reconcile the profit or loss figures, and comment briefly on the variations between the profits or losses in (a) and (b).

                                                              (8 marks)
                                                         (Total: 20 marks)

Section D - ONE question ONLY to be attempted.

60   (Question 5 of examination)

(a)   The Treasurer of Ripley plc is contemplating a change in financial policy. At present, Ripley's balance sheet shows that fixed assets are of equal magnitude to the amount of long-term debt and equity financing. It is proposed to take advantage of a recent fall in interest rates by replacing the long-term debt capital with an overdraft. In addition, the Treasurer wants to speed up debtor collection by offering early payment discounts to customers and to slow down the rate of payment to creditors.

    As his assistant, you are required to write a brief memorandum to other Board members explaining the rationales of the old and new policies and pin-pointing the factors to be considered in making such a switch of policy.

                                                              (6 marks)

(b)   Bramham plc, which currently has negligible cash holdings, expects to have to make a series of cash payments (P) of £1.5m over the forthcoming year. These will become due at a steady rate. It has two alternative ways of meeting this liability.

    Firstly, it can make periodic sales from existing holdings of short-term securities. According to Bramham's financial advisers, the most likely average percentage rate of return (i) on these securities is 12% over the forthcoming year, although this estimate is highly uncertain. Whenever Bramham sells securities, it incurs a transaction fee (T) of £25, and places the proceeds on short-term deposit at 5% per annum interest until needed. The following formula specifies the optimal amount of cash raised (Q) for each sale of securities:

$$Q = \sqrt{\frac{2 \times P \times T}{i}}$$

    The second policy involves taking a secured loan for the full £1.5m over one year at an interest rate of 14% based on the initial balance of the loan. The lender also imposes a flat arrangement fee of £5,000, which could be met out of existing balances. The sum borrowed would be placed in a notice deposit at 9% and drawn down at no cost as and when required.

    Bramham's Treasurer believes that cash balances will be run down at an even rate throughout the year.

Required:

Advise Bramham as to the most beneficial cash management policy.

Note: ignore tax and the time value of money in your answer.

(9 marks)

(c)   Discuss the limitations of the model of cash management used in part (b).

(5 marks)
(Total: 20 marks)

61	(Question 6 of examination)

(a)   Burley plc, a manufacturer of building products, mainly supplies the wholesale trade. It has recently suffered falling demand due to economic recession, and thus has spare capacity. It now perceives an opportunity to produce designer ceramic tiles for the home improvement market. It has already paid £0.5m for development expenditure, market research and a feasibility study.

The initial analysis reveals scope for selling 150,000 boxes per annum over a five-year period at a price of £20 per box. Estimated operating costs, largely based on experience, are as follows:

Cost per box of tiles (£) (at today's prices):

Material cost	8.00
Direct labour	2.00
Variable overhead	1.50
Fixed overhead (allocated)	1.50
Distribution, etc.	2.00

Production can take place in existing facilities although initial re-design and set-up costs would be £2m after allowing for all relevant tax reliefs. Returns from the project would be taxed at 33%.

Burley's shareholders require a nominal return of 14% per annum after tax, which includes allowance for generally-expected inflation of 5.5% per annum. It can be assumed that all operating cash flows occur at year ends.

Required:

Assess the financial desirability of this venture in *real* terms, finding both the Net Present Value and the Internal Rate of Return (to the nearest 1%) offered by the project.

Note: Assume no tax delay.

(7 marks)

(b)   Briefly explain the purpose of sensitivity analysis in relation to project appraisal, indicating the drawbacks with this procedure.

(6 marks)

(c)   Determine the values of

(i)   price
(ii)   volume

at which the project's NPV becomes zero.

Discuss your results, suggesting appropriate management action.

(7 marks)
(Total: 20 marks)

ANSWERS TO DECEMBER 1996 EXAMINATION

It should be noted that the following answers are probably fuller than would be expected from the average candidate under exam conditions. Answers are provided in this degree of detail on the principle of offering guidance on the approach required, and on the range and depth of knowledge that would be expected from an excellent candidate.

56   (Answer 1 of examination)

Examiner's comments and marking guide

Question 1: The objectives of this question were to prepare and discuss the concept of incremental/relevant cash flows (parts (a) and (b)), and to calculate and comment upon proposed alternative ways of raising finance on the gearing and EPS.

There was some confusion on the part of some candidates between whether to attempt to do a cash budget or an incremental cash flow budget, and the marking team were sympathetic in cases where this had occurred. Candidates do need to appreciate that for calculating an NPV, it should be the incremental/relevant cash flows that are used. The candidates who performed well in this area were those who demonstrated a good understanding of the subject in the report which was called for in part (b). However, although many candidates were able to explain why sunk costs, depreciation and the feasibility study were not relevant costs they were unable to apply the same kind of logic to some of the other costs. In the computation section (part (a)) some candidates did not attempt to calculate the amount of cash from sales or paid out for purchases.

A number of candidates did not make any attempt at part (c), the gearing/EPS/sources of finance question. Many of those who did attempt the question did not include the additional income generated when calculating the EPS and/or did not illustrate what would happen to the EPS if the holders of the 5% Convertible Loan Stock converted their holdings into Ordinary Shares.

		Marks
(a)	Workings, cash from sales and cash for purchases	3
	Computing/tabulating the cash inflows	2½
	Computing/tabulating the cash outflows	6
	Computing/tabulating the net present value	2½
	Total	14
(b)	The report - the heading, introduction and concluding statement, etc	1½
	Making the point about the incremental cash flows arising only if the project goes ahead	1
	Items which were excluded - feasibility study, depreciation, the three employees, materials XNT and XPZ, and the prepayments (½ mark each, but to include very brief comment on each)	2½
	Comments on NPV e.g. wealth creating, risk, etc.	1
	Brief description of other factors which will have to be taken into account	1
	Total	7

(c)	(i)	Gearing calculation/s and comments	2
	(ii)	Earnings per share calculation	1½
		Gearing calculation and comment	1
		Effect of scheme on EPS and the control factor	1
	(iii)	Calculation of undiluted EPS and comments	3
		Calculation of fully diluted EPS and comments	3
	(iv)	Calculation/comments re the EPS	2½
			——
		Total	14
			——
		Grand total	35

Step by step answer plan

Step 1 Read the question again and make sure that you focus on precisely what is required. This case study involves a manufacturing company considering a new investment project. You are required to evaluate the project on a DCF basis, and assess the effects of various methods of finance on key indicators.

Step 2 (a) To determine the relevant cash flows for inclusion in the cash budget and NPV computation, you need to work carefully through the data to identify the *incremental, future, cash* receipts and payments. So, for example, sales need to be converted to cash receipts using opening and closing debtors; tax paid is one year later than payable; only the extra fixed costs should be included, and feasibility study costs are excluded. Whilst doing this, note the figures that you decide to exclude, for part (b).

Step 3 (b) As well as the contents specified, your report must include a proper heading, introduction and conclusion (there are 1½ marks for this). Start the main explanation by summarising the criteria for inclusion of a figure in the cash flow budget. Then go through the specific examples from the question where a figure has been excluded, to show the respect in which they don't meet those criteria. When advising on the acceptability of the project, make a brief comment on the use of the NPV technique. As the requirement is to "list" other factors to be considered, you don't need much more than two or three words one each factor.

Step 4 (c) (i) The question now moves to the long term finance part of the syllabus. When computing the company's current gearing, ensure you use the same basis as that used for the industry average (although it is worth commenting on the relatively large overdraft). You also need to compute the current EPS for the remaining parts of the question.

Step 5 (c) (ii)-(iv) Here, you need to assess the effect of the project and its finance on gearing and EPS. The main effects to take account of are the increase in earnings (pre-tax profits of project, net of any extra interest and the extra tax charge that will arise), any increase in the number of shares, and the changes in capital structure. Go through each finance method in turn, incorporating the relevant changes in to the two measures, and make sure you comment on the result.

Although the requirement was to consider the effects at the end of the first year of investment, where you have convertible loan stock it is always worth considering the fully diluted situation, as is required for financial reporting.

Step 6 Now review your answer and ensure that it does precisely answer the question as set.

The examiner's answer

Project VZ

(a)   Budgeted Incremental Cash Flows

Inflows:	19X1 £'000	19X2 £'000	19X3 £'000	19X4 £'000	19X5 £'000
Sales (W1)	916	1,269	1,475	1,780	160
Savings, employees made redundant		42	44.1	46.3	
Residual value new machine					242
Material XNT, saving on cost of disposal	2				
(A)	918	1,311	1,519.1	1,826.3	402

Outflows:					
Purchases (W2)	320	480	570	610	120
Sale of old machine not received		12			
Labour:					
Employee promoted	10	10.5	11.03	11.58	
Redundancy pay		62			
Materials:					
Material XPZ, lost residual value	3				
Sub-contractors	60	90	80	80	
Lost contribution from existing product	30	40	40	36	
Overheads and advertising	130	100	90	100	
Taxation		96	142	174	275
(B)	553	890.5	933.03	1,011.58	395

Incremental Cash flow (A - B) (TN1)	365	420.5	586.07	814.72	7

Workings

(W1)

	19X1 £'000	19X2 £'000	19X3 £'000	19X4 £'000	19X5 £'000
Opening debtors	-	84	115	140	160
Add sales	1,000	1,300	1,500	1,800	-
	1,000	1,384	1,615	1,940	160
Less closing debtors	84	115	140	160	-
Cash from sales	916	1,269	1,475	1,780	160

(W2)

Opening creditors	-	80	100	110	120
Add purchases	400	500	580	620	-
	400	580	680	730	120
Less closing creditors	80	100	110	120	-
Cash from purchases	320	480	570	610	120

The net present value of Project VZ

Year	Cash Flow £'000	PV at 10%	P.V. £'000
19X1	365.0	.909	331.8
19X2	420.5	.826	347.3
19X3	586.0	.751	440.1
19X4	814.7	.683	556.5
19X5	7.0	.621	4.3
			1,680.0
Less Initial investment (1,640 - 16)			1,624.0
Net present value			56.0

(b)

3rd October, 19X0

To The Board of Directors of LKL plc
From R.U. Tre-Vere, Accounting and Finance team

Preliminary Report Re-The New Product Line
I have now prepared the cash flow budget enclosed herewith, and computed the net present value of the project.

The cash flows

The principal reason why certain figures were not included in the cash flows is that they are **incremental cash flows** and only include the income and expenditure which will arise **only if the project goes ahead.**

The following figures were not included in the incremental cash flows:

- the feasibility study which cost £45,000 had to be paid out whether or not the project went ahead.

- the depreciation is a non-cash movement item. The cash expended on the asset moves when it is paid over to the vendor.

- the three employees paid £12,000 each would continue to receive that amount whether or not the project goes ahead.

- the cost of the materials XNT and XPZ was paid out some time ago and is not therefore a relevant cash flow.

- the prepayments were already included in the amounts paid to the sub-contractors and did not require any adjustment to the cash flows. The relevant figures are the actual cash to be paid to them each year, e.g. 19X1 £60,000, and so on.

The net present value (NPV)

The NPV of the project is a positive £56,000. This indicates, that using our cost of capital 10% as our discount rate, the project is wealth creating. However, if the project is considered to be high risk, then the cash flows will need to be discounted at a higher rate to take this into account.

In addition to looking at the cash flows and net present value, other factors will also need to be considered such as: servicing and maintenance, reliability of the plant and machinery, availability of spare parts, retraining of operatives, importing and foreign exchange problems if it is being supplied from another country etc.

Please do not hesitate to contact me should you require further information.

R. U. Tre-Vere ACCA

(TN4)

(c)   (i)   The company's current gearing *(£'000s)*

$$\frac{£2,000}{£8,500} \times 100 = 23.53\%$$

The current gearing position is on the low side, particularly when compared with the industry average of 35%. This provides an indication that the company still has the scope and capacity to attract more debt.

There is however, a large secured bank overdraft, and it is quite likely that quite a high proportion of it represents hard-core debt. It is also most unlikely that the bankers would call in such a large overdraft at short notice. If the overdraft were included in the gearing calculation, and treated as debt, the gearing ratio 38.1% is a little above the industry average.

Current earning per share (£'000)

$$EPS \quad \frac{£3,000}{5,000} = 60p \text{ per share}$$

(ii)   *An issue of ordinary shares*

$$\text{Number of new shares} = \frac{£5,000,000}{£2} = 2,500,000 \text{ shares}$$

Earnings		£'000
Current net profit after interest and tax		3,000
	£'000	
Additional earnings	2,000	
Less tax at 33%	660	1,340
		4,340

$$EPS \quad \frac{£4,340}{7,500} = 58p \text{ per share}$$

$$\text{Gearing} \quad \frac{2,000}{13,500} \times 100 = 14.81\%$$

More equity would reduce the gearing further. The gearing in the future would also tend to fall due to increases in reserves via retained earnings.

The scheme would reduce the EPS by 2p per share when compared with current earnings. Other considerations which should be looked at are:

- the control factor i.e. those shareholders who currently control the company could lose control unless they buy some of the shares being offered.

(iii)   *5% convertible loan stock earnings*

	£'000	£'000
Current (as above)		3,000
Plus Additional earnings	2,000	
Less Loan stock interest at 5%	250	
	1,750	
Less tax at 33%	578	1,172
		£4,172

Undiluted EPS $\dfrac{£4,172}{5,000}$ = 83p per share

The gearing at the time of issuing the convertible loan stock would be:

$$\frac{£7,000}{13,500} \times 100 = 51.85\%$$

This figure would be expected to decrease in future years as a result of 'ploughing back' profits by way of retained earnings i.e. increasing the equity. On conversion the gearing percentage should fall quite significantly. This would be affected by the retained earnings, new loans taken out and old loans paid off.

The fully diluted earnings per share i.e. where all the holders convert, would be:

Earnings £4,340 as per scheme (i)

EPS $\dfrac{£4,340}{7,000 \text{ shares}}$ = 62p per share

For the period in which the holders cannot or do not convert the undiluted EPS, (provided earnings remain at this level and tax rates do not change), is much greater, at 83p per share as indicated above.

If and when the holders convert a dilution of earnings will take place and the control of the company may be affected. If the interest rate is fixed, the company would appear to have locked in to quite a low rate compared with the 7½% debentures i.e. the convertibles have a low service cost. The gearing would be well above the current industry average, but on conversion would fall well below it.

(iv)   *7½% debentures*

	£'000	£'000
Earnings		
Current		3,000
Add Additional	2,000	
Less Interest at 7½%	375	
	1,625	
Less tax at 33%	536	1,089
		£4,089

$$\text{EPS} = \frac{£4,089}{5,000} = 82\text{p per share}$$

The EPS again illustrates that using more debt i.e. becoming more highly geared, can increase the earnings of the Ordinary Shareholders i.e. EPS 82p per share compared with current earnings of 60p per share. However, the increase in gearing, (TN 3) which would be higher than the industry average, does place the increased risk of insolvency on the company. If trading conditions are bad, the company still has to pay the interest on the debentures.

Examiners note (not part of the answer)

Marks would be awarded to those candidates who comment on and/or provide gearing calculations which increase the equity via the estimated retained earnings resulting from investing the £5 million. (TN5)

Tutorial notes

1   Note that the initial cash flows relating to the purchase of the new machine (£1.64m) and the sale of the old (£16,000) arising at the *beginning* of 19X1 have been omitted from the cash flow budget (although they are brought into the NPV calculation. If they are included in the budget, care must be taken to distinguish between these and the flows that are assumed to arise at the *end* of 19X1, as they will be treated differently in the NPV computation. It is much better practice to head up cash budgets Time, 0, 1, 2, etc, rather than Year 0, 1, 2, etc.

It could be argued that if the lost contribution figures of £30,000, etc are shown after charging the cost of three employees each earning £12,000 who will be paid whether or not the project goes ahead, this cost should be added back to the lost contribution.

There is also some doubt over the relevant cash flows regarding the four employees made redundant. One extra year's savings could be included.

2   The conversion terms are 40 shares per £100 of loan stock. If £5m is raised, this is convertible into £5m/£100 x 40 = 2 million shares. Thus the new total would be 7 million shares.

3   The gearing change for the 7.5% debentures will be the same as that for the %5 convertible loan stock, before conversion.

4   It is not a good idea to spend time in the exam thinking up clever names and certainly do not write your own name.

5   A table showing the effect on earnings per share of each option would have saved some time in this section.

57   (Answer 2 of examination)

Examiner's comments and marking guide

Question 2: (a) This question required an explanation of the nature and purpose of cartel agreements, and why they are inherently unstable.

Most candidates were able to explain the essential features of a cartel, (although some confused it with a customs union), and its role in promoting profits for members. Answers were less satisfactory when it came to explaining why cartel members are motivated to undermine the cartel, and hence, the need for effective policing of the agreement.

(b)   **This question required candidates to explain why companies issue share warrants, and why they may be attractive to investors.**

This question was poorly answered, many candidates produced a list of security attributes, some of which happened to apply to warrants. In addition, many candidates equated warrants with convertible loan stock, and proceeded to expound the characteristics of these. Better answers explained that warrants are attached to loan stock (usually, non-convertible) and sometimes to equities (eg, Eurotunnel), and discussed the warrants independently of the parent security, as required. Other common errors were to confuse warrants with rights issues, and less frequently, with scrip issues and scrip dividends.

There was sparse mention of the high potential rewards from holding and then exercising warrants via the gearing mechanism.

(c)   **This question required explanation of why a fast-growing small firm may prefer a term loan to overdraft finance.**

A very popular question, and quite well done. Most candidates were able to identify the desirable properties of a term loan in relation to an overdraft, especially the security from recall of the facility, the common freedom from exposure to interest rate fluctuations and the forward planning benefits. Relatively few mentioned the possibility of 'tailor-making' loan terms according to the needs of the client and its cash flow profile. However, many did mention the desirability of matching long-term finance to long term assets, for a company investing in plant and equipment.

Candidates were equally divided as to which facility was cheaper. In principle, according to the yield curve idea, short-term finance is cheaper, but in practice, this relationship depends on factors such as the security which the borrower is able to provide, and its track record and prospects, issues omitted in most answers.

(d)   **This question required candidates to explain the effects of public sector deficits on private sector businesses.**

This question was poorly answered indicating that many candidates misunderstood the term 'public sector deficit'. Some identified the public sector as state-owned enterprise, while others confused the public sector deficit with the balance of payments deficit. The majority of answers chose to assume that the government wished to close the deficit, and dwelt on ways of doing this eg, tax increases and their consequences. This tended to overlook the reasons for opening a deficit in the first place, and the benefits for aggregate demand and employment. Most answers only mentioned the impact on interest rates in passing, although better answers explained the crowding-out effect of rising interest rates, and the possible inflationary consequences of deficit financing.

Only rarely did candidates discuss the impact on the overseas sector eg, rising interest rates pushing up the value of sterling to the detriment of exporters.

(e)   **This question required candidates to discuss the relative risk-return attributes of specified securities in an efficient capital market.**

Answers to this question were disappointing. A great number of candidates appeared not to read the question properly, mistakenly taking it to require discussion of how the advent of new information affects the price of each of these securities. Few candidates mentioned the relative riskiness of the securities, or made any attempt to rank them by risk and return attributes. There was little apparent understanding of the distinction between the absolute return on a security and its yield in relation to market price. Unfortunately, many candidates appeared to lack knowledge of basic stock market terminology and the concept of the risk-return trade-off.

(f)   **This short scenario question required the candidate to explain performance measures which may be used in public sector education.**

This question proved popular with candidates most of whom produced reasonable answers.

Note: quite a number of candidates attempted all six questions rather than the five required. This loses valuable examination time.

		Marks
(a)	Explanation of purpose of cartels:	
	i.e. to increase joint profits e.g. by supply restriction	2
	Reasons for instability:	
	inadequately specified and policed agreement	1
	clandestine output increases	1
	inability to control entry	1
		—
	Total	5
		—
(b)	Explanation of features and purpose of warrants	2
	Attraction to investors:	
	separately tradable	1
	prospect of capital gain	1
	mention of gearing effect	1
		—
	Total	5
		—
(c)	Problems with overdrafts:	
	easily recalled by bank	1
	possible inability to renew facility	½
	variable interest rate	1
	Advantages of loans:	
	fixed term and conditions/easier cash flow planning	1½
	can be 'tailor-made'	1
		—
	Total	5
		—
(d)	Appeal of deficits:	
	higher spending/profits in directly-benefiting sectors	½
	multiplier effects on rest of economy	½
	Problems:	
	effect on interest rates with explanation	2
	effect on exchange rate/impact on exporters and importers	1
	impact on expenditure generally	1
		—
	Total	5
		—
(e)	Concept of risk-return trade off	½
	Components of overall returns	½
	Explanation of risk-return characteristics of each security	4
		—
	Total	5
		—

(f)   1 mark per point explained:
The use of scarce resources; measures/cost units in education;
how the measures can be used e.g. services at a lower cost/
for political purposes; meals service example; library example

Total   5

Grand total   25

The examiner's answer

(a)   Cartels are formal agreements among producers, usually of commodities and other homogeneous goods, which are designed to restrict competition in order to yield sustained super-normal profits. Cartels can take various forms, for example, agreements to set a common price and agreements to share out a given market, often on a regional basis. The more comprehensive the agreement, the more closely the behaviour of the industry resembles that of monopoly. Because prices are generally higher and output volumes generally lower than under outright competition, cartels are regarded as potentially contrary to the interests of consumers, if not totally illegal, and thus liable to scrutiny by the competition authorities. The recent investigation of the steel price-fixing cartel by the European competition authorities resulted in heavy fines for several major producers.

In order to operate effectively, a cartel should involve a clearly-specified contract between all suppliers of the product(s) which specifies mutually advantageous prices and volumes. However, lack of information, often deliberately withheld by members, may prevent the cartel arrangement from perfectly replicating the monopolist. In addition to a formal agreement, the cartel needs a policing mechanism to ensure that members adhere to these arrangements. If a member firm believes that it can increase sales volume without fear of discovery, it may hope to increase profits if the market price holds. Generally, however, in markets for homogeneous goods, greater supply will exert downward pressure on the market price and fracture the cohesion of the cartel. The inability to enforce agreed output quotas of member firms plus increased supply from non-OPEC producers, explains why OPEC has been unable to control the world price of oil in recent years.

The experience of OPEC suggests that unless a cartel arrangement is tightly specified and vigorously policed, it is unlikely to offer member firms persistently higher profits than under outright competition.

(b)   A share warrant is an option to purchase ordinary shares, usually attached to issues of fixed interest loan stock. The warrant holder has the right to buy a specific number of shares at a specified price at, or leading up to, a specific date (apart from perpetual warrants which have no time limit).

Warrants have attractions to both companies and investors. They offer investors an opportunity to share in the future prosperity of the company and perhaps make a capital gain should the market price exceed the conversion price at the relevant date. For this reason, the loan stock to which they are attached can often be issued at a coupon rate lower than the going rate for bonds of the appropriate risk. When warrants are exercised by investors other than existing ordinary shareholders, this dilutes the control and earnings of the existing owners. Hence, apart from any interest savings, warrants may not be popular with existing shareholders.

Warrants can be traded separately from the securities to which they are originally attached. They are sometimes called 'geared plays', because variations in market share prices cause more than proportional variations in the market price of warrants. For example, assume that the ordinary shares of ABC plc are trading at £2 each, and that existing warrants entitle the holders to exercise at a price of £1.50. The value of each warrant should thus be £0.50. If the market price per ordinary share rises by 10% to £2.20, the market value of each warrant should rise by (£0.20/£0.50) = 40% to £0.70, the prospective gain on conversion.

(c)   Small firms are often unable to provide suitable security to satisfy lenders' requirements for long-term lending. Consequently, they are forced into using overdraft facilities to a greater degree than larger, more established firms. Overdraft finance has the advantage of incurring interest on a daily basis on the overdrawn balance only, but suffers from certain inherent disadvantages. The attractions of a term loan may best be appreciated by considering these drawbacks.

First, overdrafts are granted for relatively short periods, perhaps six months to a year, and although they may be extended, renewal is not guaranteed. Second, the advance is repayable at very short notice, technically on demand. Demands by the bank to repay at short notice or to accelerate the repayment schedule, may exert intolerable strains on a company's cash flow. Third, they carry variable rates of interest, thereby exposing the company to economic risks outside its control.

By contrast, a loan can be arranged over a term to suit the borrower's needs. So long as the borrower meets the agreed repayment profile (and, in practice, certain other restrictions imposed by the lender), it enjoys unhindered access to the finance for the agreed term, without fear of sudden recall. In addition, the repayment profile may be negotiable to suit the expected cash flow profile of the company. For example, the growing company may be unable to exploit tax reliefs on interest payments in its early years, thus raising the effective cost of finance. In such cases, the bank may consent to an interest holiday, whereby interest is 'rolled up' into the debt. Similar arrangements can be made regarding repayment of capital, ranging from an equal periodic profile to repayment mainly or wholly at the termination of the loan.

Finally, the interest rate can often be fixed, although banks may apply a premium over the overdraft rate for this facility. This has significant advantages for cash flow forecasting. Conversely, if the company is quite well-established and can offer attractive security, the rate of interest may be lower than on an overdraft.

In summary, the advantages of a term loan hinge on its reliability and its versatility regarding initial arrangements.

(d)   Many businesses benefit directly from higher public sector deficits. If these are caused by higher public spending (rather than lower tax revenues), then the sectors where this expenditure is targeted will benefit. Eventually, firms in most sectors of the economy will achieve higher sales, as the multiplier effects spread out across the economy. However, when public sector tax revenue falls short of public expenditure, this creates a need to borrow, termed in the UK, the Public Sector Borrowing Requirement (PSBR).

Among the ways in which the government can finance a PSBR are borrowing from the central bank ('printing money'), borrowing directly from the banking system, or by issuing government securities. These are usually sold by the nation's central bank acting on behalf of the government.

In the UK, Government stock has traditionally been issued on the open market, although since 1995, more reliance has been placed on a system of auctions. In order to pay for stock, individuals and institutions write cheques payable to the Bank of England (BOE), drawn on their own bank accounts, thus establishing a liability for their banks to the BOE. These liabilities are normally settled by the BOE reducing the bankers' operational balances of cash and liquid assets which it holds. As these are not allowed to fall below a defined level, a sufficiently large sale of government stock can exert such pressure on banks' liquidity as to force them to rein back their lending and/or sell securities in the money market to raise cash. An increase in the supply of securities offered to the market will lower their prices and thus increase their yields (assuming they carry a fixed nominal interest rate). These adjustments will cause chain reactions throughout the various sectors of the short-term money market exerting upward pressure on short-term interest rates, and normally, on long-term interest rates as well. Hence, 'the term structure of interest rates' or 'yield curve', will be shifted upwards.

Thus, an increase in public expenditure financed by borrowing raises interest rates generally, thus raising the cost of debt for business borrowers, the higher interest payments eventually worsening their cash flow. It may also cause a fall in share prices which will reduce the ability of companies to raise new equity capital. If, as monetarists believe, the important components of national expenditure are interest-elastic, the increase in interest rates will dampen consumer and business expenditure, thus reducing business turnover and profits. Monetarists also argue that if the additional demand created by the government worsens inflationary expectations, this could cause people to contract economic activity e.g. lower investment expenditure.

In addition, a higher interest rate is likely to strengthen the exchange rate making exports more expensive for overseas buyers and imports cheaper on the domestic market. Hence, exporters will suffer but importers will gain.

(e)   Generally, risk and return are positively related via 'the risk-return trade off' - to encourage rational investors to incur greater risks, they have to be offered the inducement of higher potential returns. In an information-efficient capital market, securities will be priced so as to reflect their relative risks. The current market value of a security is found by discounting the future expected stream of returns at a rate suitably adjusted for risk. Put alternatively, the market price at any time will reflect the required return or yield on that security. It is important to recognise that the yield has two components, the flat yield (the annual payment divided by the present market price), and the potential capital gain. In the case of fixed interest securities, the former tends to be more important, but as the overall risk of the security increases, the potential capital gain tends to assume greater significance. However, there are exceptions e.g. in the case of 'junk bonds' where capital gains are not often expected but the return has to be high to compensate for lack of security.

The securities cited in the question are listed below in descending order of safety i.e. going down the list, the risk, and therefore the required return, increases.

- Government stock - these are virtually free of default risk as few governments renege on their debt obligations, although the risk of interest rate changes, with the resulting impact on capital values, increases with time. Thus the yield on long-dated government stock is usually greater than on short-dated stock. Given the low degree of risk, the yield on government stock tends to set the benchmark for other yields in the market.

- Corporate bonds - these do carry default risk, but are usually secured on specific corporate assets (or carry a floating charge).

- Preference shares - these come in various forms, but generally offer a fixed percentage dividend based on the par value of the share. Sometimes, the holders can participate further in profits if earnings exceed a certain level, and sometimes, the dividend can be passed if company earnings are exceptionally depressed. The precise yield will depend on the type of preference share, but generally they are regarded as more risky than corporate bonds - they have an inferior claim over both company earnings and distribution of the proceeds of a liquidation.

- Equities - the most risky of all securities, since dividends are a payment out of residual earnings, which are subject to greatest fluctuation. This is due to the effect of inherent business fluctuations and financial gearing (although many companies attempt to 'smooth' dividend payments).

(f) To ensure that the scarce resources which have been placed at their disposal are used efficiently and effectively, public sector services such as education need to place a high priority on their financial control and performance. There has always been a quest for 'yard sticks' in such organisations i.e. ways in which performance can be measured, compared and evaluated.

One of the measures which tends to be used in education is the amount spent on each pupil/student, i.e. the cost per pupil/student, for each school or college etc. It should be noted however, that the amount spent per head is no indication that the amount involved has been spent wisely and is not necessarily a measure of efficiency. It can be used in two ways:

1. To support the view that it is possible to provide a similar service at a lower cost, or

2. By political parties who point to the fact that in their areas of influence, more is spent per pupil/student on education.

Where the educational establishment provides a meals service, comparisons can be made using the cost of each meal served or on a cost per pupil/student basis. Such comparisons would only be valid if the meals mix and volume of meals served were similar. Where the meals service was revenue earning performance could also be evaluated using ratios for profitability etc.

In cases where the educational establishment provides a library, cost comparisons could be made with similar sized libraries using the cost per book, or cost per pupil or cost of new books.

Examiner's Note (not part of the answer)

Other appropriate measures/cost units could be used e.g. the cost per successful student.

58	(Answer 3 of examination)

Examiner's comments and marking guide

Question 3: This question required the candidates to calculate fixed overhead variances and to discuss possible causes of those variances, and then to discuss the inter-relationship of the fixed overhead efficiency variances material and labour variances.

This question was generally well answered. However, many of the candidates were confused as to which variance was which eg, they mixed up the efficiency and capacity variances. Many candidates under performed on the discussion part because they either repeated themselves or did not write enough. The examiners were pleased to see that many candidates had a good idea of the reasons for the inter-relationships of variances.

		Marks
(a)	Calculations	
	Budgeted FOH rate and standard labour hours per unit	1½
	Standard labour hours	½
	Production FOH cost variance	1
	FOH expenditure variance	1
	FOH efficiency variance	1
	FOH capacity variance	1
	Proof	1
		—
	Total	7
		—
(b)	Production FOH expenditure variance ½ to 1 mark per point explained e.g. definition; what an adverse variance indicates; causes of adverse variances; etc.	4
	Production FOH efficiency variance ½ to 1 mark per point explained e.g. what it compares; what an adverse variance indicates plus examples.	3
	Production FOH capacity variance ½ to 1 mark per point explained e.g. what it compares; causes and examples of adverse variances	3
		—
	Total	10
		—
(c)	1½ points per example of the inter-relationships between the FOH efficiency and labour and material variances.	3
		—
		3
		—
	Grand total	20
		—

Step by step answer plan

Step 1 Read the question again and make sure that you focus on precisely what is required. It is a variance analysis question, concentrating on fixed overhead variances. Whilst you may be quite happy with the computations, note that 13 of the 20 marks are for discussion - before you decide to do this question, you must make sure you have enough to say on these parts.

Step 2 (a) Depending upon the way you compute variances, you may compute all four in one working (eg using the "line by line" method) or separately (using formulae etc). Whichever method, make sure you clearly identify the variances required - making sure you get the efficiency and capacity variances the right way round (these being a split of the volume variance). The summary statement required should show how the three subsidiary variances add up to the overall cost variance. Note that (b) tells you that these should all be adverse.

Step 3   (b)   This part is testing your understanding of the relevance of the figures you have just computed, and carries half the marks of the question - do not underestimate it! The best approach is, for each variance, start by defining the variance itself - ie how it is calculated. Then you have to look for possible causes of an *adverse* result. Give specific examples of events that may have contributed - don't just talk vaguely of "over-spending" or "inefficiency".

Step 4   (c)   The inter-relationships again need specific examples for illustration. Since overhead efficiency variances are computed on the same basis as labour efficiency, once you have linked the material and labour variances, the overhead variance should follow.

Step 5   Now review your answer and ensure that it does precisely answer the question as set.

The examiner's answer

(a)   Budgeted fixed overhead rate

$$\frac{£22,260}{8,400 \text{ hours}} = £2.65 \text{ per hour}$$

Standard labour hours per unit of production

$$\frac{8,400}{1,200} = 7 \text{ hours per unit}$$

Production fixed overhead cost variance:

Standard labour hours for actual production $1,100 \times 7 = \underline{7,700}$ standard hours

	£
Actual cost	25,536
Less Standard cost (7,700 × £2.65)	20,405
	5,131 (A)*

Fixed production overhead expenditure variance:

	£
Actual cost	25,536
Less Standard cost as per budget	22,260
	3,276 (A)

Fixed production overhead efficiency variance:

Actual hours	7,980
Less Standard hours	7,700
	280 × £2.65 = <u>742</u> (A)

Fixed production overhead capacity variance:

Actual hours	7,980
Less Budgeted standard hours	8,400
	420 × £2.65 = £<u>1,113</u> (A)

* (A) = Adverse
  (F) = Favourable

Proof   *Production fixed overhead variances:*

	£
Expenditure variance	3,276 (A)
Efficiency variance	742 (A)
Capacity variance	1,113 (A)
Cost variance	£5,131 (A)

(b)   *The production fixed overhead expenditure variance.* This is the difference between the budgeted and actual overhead for the period and provides an indication of the efficiency in keeping to the spending targets which are set.

An adverse variance is an indication of over-spending in one or more of the component parts which make up the overhead cost e.g. rent of premises, light and heat, insurance of buildings etc. The causes of such variances could have been a higher than planned inflation rate, an unexpected outcome to a rent review, colder weather, the area in which the firm is situated becoming a higher risk area for insurance purposes, etc.

However, it should be noted that under-spending is not always an indication of efficiency and should be investigated.

The production fixed overhead efficiency variance compares standard and actual efficiency in terms of hours, multiplied by the standard rate applicable to the actual production. An adverse variance means that more hours than planned were taken because of, for example: using different skill levels of labour, poor quality materials which take longer to work on or result in more spoilt work, poor training, poor motivation/morale, poor working conditions, poor supervision, etc.

The production fixed overhead capacity variance compares the actual and planned capacity and is the difference between the budgeted and actual levels of activity, valued at the standard overhead rate. Adverse variances could be caused by a failure to attract orders e.g. because of a poor assessment of demand and/or not monitoring competitors. It could have also been caused by machines breaking down e.g. as a result of poor servicing and maintenance, or using defective or poor quality materials, power failures, or labour disputes, etc.

Did you answer the question?

Note that for the marks available, the examiner is expecting quite a detailed analysis of possible factors contributing to the adverse variances; this is best achieved by giving specific examples of possible circumstances in which these variances may arise.

(c)   Two examples of the inter-relationships between the overhead efficiency variances and the labour and material variances are as follows:

Using an unskilled or semi-skilled worker to do the work usually performed by a skilled worker will tend to lead to a favourable labour rate variance, an adverse labour efficiency variance and an adverse material usage variance and an adverse overhead efficiency variance.

Using defective or poor quality materials could lead to an adverse material usage variance, an adverse labour efficiency variance and an adverse overhead efficiency variance, and in some cases a favourable material price variance.

59	(Answer 4 of examination)

Examiner's comments and marking guide

Question 4: The question looked at absorption and marginal costing profit statements using FIFO and AVECO.

In part (a), most candidates performed very well. The errors and omissions tended to be in the valuation of stock and the under/over absorption of overheads.

Numerous candidates were prepared to spend little or no time at all on the discussion part of the question. Candidates at this level need to appreciate that the numerical type questions do tend to have a number of marks awarded for the comments/discussion parts of questions, and prepare accordingly.

The Examiner was concerned that some candidates ignored part (b) altogether.

			Marks
(a)	(i)	Calculation of FOH absorption rate	1
	(ii)	Absorption costing (FIFO) profit statement including the workings	5
	(iii)	Marginal costing (FIFO) profit statement	2½
	(iv)	Reconciliation	1
		Explanations:	
		½ mark per point explained e.g. why the higher profit with absorption FIFO? rate depends on estimates of production units and FOH; adjustment needed for over-absorption; treatment of FOH in marginal costing; etc.	2½
		Total	12
(b)		Absorption profit statement (AVECO)	3
		Marginal costing profit statement (AVECO)	2½
		Reconciliation	1½
		Brief comment re the causes of variations in profits using the two valuation methods (FIFO and AVECO)	1
		Total	8
		Grand total	20

Step by step answer plan

Step 1   Read the question again and make sure that you focus on precisely what is required. The marginal and absorption costing systems are being examined, with elements of overhead absorption and stock valuation. As usual, the computations were supported by discursive elements to ensure you understand the significance of the figures you have produced.

Step 2   (a)   Unless told otherwise, you should assume that profit statements will be based upon actual information rather than budgeted. You are given budgeted information to calculate the pre-determined absorption rate. The use of this may lead to under/over absorption of fixed costs in the absorption method, which could be recognised in your statement. The key difference between the two costing methods is in the stock valuation, and this is what is brought out in the reconciliation. In this case it is not just a question of changes in volumes of stock but also the rate at which fixed overheads have been absorbed into the stock.

The requirement to "reconcile and explain" means show some numbers, then explain what is happening in words.

Step 3 (b) This repeats much of the work in (a), with a different stock valuation method. Having already sorted out layouts etc in (a) this should be a lot quicker. You are required to briefly comment on the effect the change of stock valuation method on the profits - an easy mark if not ignored!

Step 4 Now review your answer and ensure that it does precisely answer the question as set.

The examiner's answer

(a) (i) Fixed overhead absorption rate per unit

$$\frac{\text{Budgeted FOH}}{\text{Budgeted Production}} \qquad \frac{£300,000}{40,000} = £\underline{7.5}$$

(ii) *Absorption Costing (FIFO) Profit Statement*

	£'000	£'000
Sales 42,000 × £72		3,024
Less cost of sales:		
Opening stock 2,000 × £30	60	
Add Production 46,000 × £52.5 (W1)	2,415	
	2,475	
Less Closing Stock 6,000 × £52.5	315	2,160
		864
Add Over-absorption (W2)		27
Profit		891

Workings

		Per unit £
W1	Variable Cost	$45 \left(\text{ie, } \dfrac{£1,800,000}{40,000} \right)$
	Fixed O.H. (as above)	7.5
		52.5

W2	Fixed Overhead absorbed	46,000 × £7.5 = 345,000
	Less Actual	318,000
		£27,000

(TN1)

(iii) *Marginal Costing (FIFO) Profit Statement*

	£'000	£'000
Sales (as above)		3,024
Less cost of sales		
Opening stock 2,000 × £25	50	
Add Production 46,000 × £45 (W1)	2,070	
	2,120	
Less Closing Stock 6,000 × £45	270	

	1,850
Contribution	1,174
Less fixed overheads (actual)	318
Profit	856

(iv) *Reconciliation*   *Profit*

Absorption	891
Marginal	856
	35

Fixed overheads in Closing stock	
6,000 × £7.50	45
Less Opening stock 2,000 × £5.00	10
	35

The difference is explained by the fixed overheads being carried forward in stock valuations.

The figures presented using absorption costing (FIFO) give a higher profit because more of the fixed overheads are carried forward into the next accounting period than were brought forward from the last accounting period. The fixed overhead absorption rate is dependent on the estimation of both the production units and the fixed overheads, and as illustrated both may vary when the actual figures are known. Thus, it can be seen that in the absorption costing statement the over-absorption of the fixed overheads have to be adjusted for at the end of the period. In the marginal cost statements the fixed overheads are treated as 'period costs' and not carried forward in stock valuations to the next accounting period. The question of under- or over-absorption does not arise in marginal costing. Marginal costing by using only the variable costs shows how much contribution is being made, and is regarded as giving a more useful set of figures for decision making purposes.

(b) *Absorption Costing (AVECO) Profit Statement*

	£'000	£'000
Sales		3,024
Less: Cost of sales		
Opening stock plus production (48,000 × £51.56) (TN2)	2,475	
Less Closing stock (6,000 × £51.56)	309	2,166
		858
Plus Over-absorption		27
Profit		885

Marginal Costing (AVECO) Profit Statement

	£'000	£'000
Sales		3,024
Less cost of sales		
Opening stock plus production (48,000 at £44.17) (TN2)	2,120	
Less Closing stock 6,000 × £44.17	265	1,855
Contribution		1,169
Less Fixed overheads		318
Profit		851

Reconciliation

Difference in profits		34
		——
Absorption closing stock =	309	
Less Marginal closing stock =	265	44
	——	
Less Fixed costs in absorption opening stock		10
		——
		34
		——

The variations in the profits in (a) and (b) of £6,000 and £5,000 respectively are caused by using the two different methods of valuation (FIFO and AVECO). The method of valuation can affect the profit and losses for both the absorption and the marginal approaches, and could lead to much wider variations than those illustrated.

Tutorial notes

1   It is common to see a profit and loss account that first records the wrong fixed overhead figure which then needs to be corrected by including an under-/over-absorption of overheads. One would hope that full marks would be obtained if the correct fixed overheads figure was stated in the first place making the subsequent need for an adjustment unnecessary.

2   The average cost of stock =

	Units	absorption	marginal
Opening stock (as in (a))	*2,000*	£60,000	£50,000
Production	*46,000*	£2,415,000	£2,070,000
	——	——	——
Totals	*48,000*	£2,475,000	£2,120,000
Average		£51.5625	£44.1667

---

60   (Answer 5 of examination)

Examiner's comments and marking guide

Question 5: (a) This section required a discussion in report format of the pros and cons of adopting certain changes in financial policy.

Most answers were presented well, although only a few candidates were able to identify the old and new strategies as conservative and aggressive respectively. Most candidates examined each of the three proposed policy changes in isolation rather than discussing them in broader context, or indeed, considering the external reaction to this policy shift. Nevertheless, discussion of the individual areas was often quite creditable.

(b)   **This section required calculation of the relative costs of two specified policies for meeting a series of payments.**

Candidates made a reasonable attempt at the calculation but a disappointing number got the units wrong or input an incorrect interest rate. In calculating interest benefits many candidates failed to realise that the relevant principal is the average balance rather than the initial balance. Comparisons of policies were invariably flawed. Many compared the optimal transaction *amount* (rather than cost) of option one with the transaction costs of option two. Also, very few candidates considered the opportunity costs of the two policies, especially the foregone returns in option one.

(c)   **This section required a discussion of the limitations of the Baumol model of cash management specified in Section (b).**

Generally, answers lacked sufficient details to obtain good marks. Few got beyond a discussion of the uncertainty of the interest rates used. The majority tended to focus more on the context of the problem ie, commenting on Bramham's perception of the two alternative policies, rather than critiquing the actual model.

		Marks
(a)	Explanation of matching strategy	2
	Explanation of aggressive policy	2
	For each valid issue raised, ½ mark up to max of	2
	Total	6
(b)	Policy 1:	
	Use of square root formula	2
	Calculation of transaction costs	1
	Calculation of interest income	1
	Policy 2:	
	Calculation of net interest costs	1
	Comparison of policies with discussions and recommendations:	
	Simple comparison of cash management costs	1
	Recognition of overall net benefits	3
	Total	9
(c)	For each valid difficulty raised, up to one mark	
	(but each requires an element of explanation) max	5
	Grand total	20

Step by step answer plan

Step 1   Read the question again and make sure that you focus on precisely what is required. It considers various treasury policies, concerning finance, credit and cash management.

Step 2   (a)   You have 6 marks to discuss three separate requirements here - two explanations and a discussion of further factors. None can be covered in great depth (and you really need to look at the changes as a whole rather than individually) but you do need to bring out the contrast between the safer but possibly expensive "matching" policy with the higher risk, more actively managed "aggressive" policy.

Step 3   (b)   You need to think carefully about your approach before launching into computations here. It is a situation that is in many ways analogous to the optimum stock policy problem, and the formula given is the equivalent of the EOQ formula. The approach is to compare the two options on an annual cost basis.

The first option is to use the company's existing stocks of securities to meet the payments, by realising regular "optimal" amounts. This method incurs transaction costs, partly offset by short-term interest earned on the cash whilst it held, and loses interest from the securities realised.

The second option leaves the existing securities intact and meets the payments from a loan. The associated costs are the arrangement fee and the loan interest (again, partially offset by short-term interest earned on cash whilst it is held) - but no interest is lost from the securities.

Having worked through the numbers, don't forget that the aim is to advise - and you should consider other factors in addition to the cost comparison.

Step 4   (c)   You should recognise the model as the equivalent of the EOQ formula used in stock management. The limitations are thus the same, with appropriate translations of terms and costs.

Step 5   Now review your answer and ensure that it does precisely answer the question as set.

The examiner's answer

(a)   Memo to: Ripley plc Main Board
      From: An(n) Accountant
      Subject: Alternative Financial Strategies

The present policy is termed a 'matching' financial policy. This attempts to match the maturity of financial liabilities to the lifetime of the assets acquired with this finance. It involves financing long-term assets with long-term finance such as equity or loan stock and financing short-term assets with short-term finance such as trade credit or bank overdrafts. This avoids the potential wastefulness of over-capitalisation whereby short-term assets are purchased with long-term finance i.e. the company having to service finance not continuously invested in income-earning assets. It also avoids the dangers of under-capitalisation which entails exposure to finance being withdrawn when the company is not easily able to liquidate its assets. In practice, some short-term assets may be regarded as permanent and it may be thought sensible to finance these by long-term finance and the fluctuating remainder by short-term finance.

The proposed policy is an 'aggressive policy' which involves far heavier reliance on short-term finance, thus attempting to minimise long-term financing costs. This requires very careful manipulation of the relationship between creditors and debtors (maximising trade creditors and minimising debtors), and highly efficient stock control and cash management. While it may offer financial savings, it exposes the company to the risk of illiquidity and hence possible failure to meet financial obligations. In addition, it involves greater exposure to interest rate risk. The company should be mindful of the inverse relationship between interest rate changes and the value of its assets and liabilities.

Did you answer the question?

These first two paragraphs have addressed the first two requirements - the explanation of the rationales of the old and new policies. This includes both the general aims and mechanics of the policies, and the potential consequences. The remaining part of the requirement is covered by the following paragraph.

Before embarking on such an aggressive policy, the Board should consider the following factors:

-        How good are we at forecasting cash inflows and outflows? How volatile is our net cash flow? Is there any seasonal pattern evident?

-        How efficiently do we manage our cash balances? Do we ever have excessive cash holdings which can be reduced by careful and active management?

-        Do we have suitable information systems to provide early warnings of illiquidity?

-        Do we have any holdings of marketable securities that can be realised if we run into unexpected liquidity problems?

-        How liquid are our fixed assets? Can any of these be converted into cash without unduly disrupting productive operations?

-        Do we have any unused long- or short-term credit lines? These may have to be utilised if we meet liquidity problems.

-        How will the stock market perceive our switch towards a more aggressive and less liquid financial policy?

Did you answer the question?

The examiner was expecting at least four different points to be made here.

(b)   To determine the net benefits of each policy, both cash costs and opportunity costs have to be considered.

First, consider the cash management costs expected from each policy over the course of the forthcoming year.

Policy 1 Selling securities

The cash transaction costs are partly offset by small interest earnings on the average cash balance held. Transactions costs:

Optimal proceeds per sale:	$Q = \sqrt{\dfrac{2 \times £1.5m \times £25}{0.12}}$ = £25,000	
No of sales	= £1.5m/£25,000	= 60
Transaction costs	= 60 × £25	= £1,500
Average cash balances:	= £25,000/2	= £12,500

Interest on short-term deposits:			
Av cash balance × 5%	= £12,500 × 5%	=	(£625)
			———
Total management costs			£875
(TN1)			

Policy 2 Secured loan facility

Assuming an even run-down in cash balances:

Interest charges	= £1.5m × 14%	=	£210,000
Offsetting interest receipts:			
(= average balance × 9%)	$= \dfrac{£1.5m}{2} \times 9\%$	=	(£67,500)
Arrangement fee:		=	£5,000
			———
Total management costs			£147,500

Hence, the policy of periodic security sales appears greatly superior in cost terms by [£147,500 - £875] = £146,625. However, this simple comparison ignores the income likely to be received from the portfolio of securities under each policy. By taking the secured loan, the company preserves intact its expected returns of [12% × £1.5m = £180,000] from the portfolio. Conversely, making periodic sales from the portfolio during the year lowers the returns to: [average holding of securities × 12%] = £1.5m/2 × 12% = £90,000.

The net benefits from the two policies can be shown thus:

Security sales			
Income from portfolio	£90,000		
Net management costs	(£875)	Net income	£89,125
Loan alternative			
Income from portfolio	£180,000		
Net management costs	(£147,500)	Net income	£32,500
			———
		Difference	£56,625

The policy of periodic security sales thus offers greater benefits. However, it is necessary to consider also the company's net worth position at the end of the year ahead. By relying on security sales, the company would avoid the need to repay a loan at the end of the year, but, against this, will have no holdings of securities to fall back on. Moreover, the capital value of this portfolio is uncertain, due to exposure to variation in the return from the portfolio. For example, if money market rates rose over the year, the capital value of the portfolio would probably fall, although the extent of the decrease in value would depend on the nearness to maturity of the securities.

(c) Some limitations of the simple cash inventory model are:

- It assumes a steady run-down in cash holdings between successive security sales. In reality, the pattern of cash holdings is likely to be far more erratic, with exceptional demands for cash punctuated by periods of excessive liquidity. However, the period between sales is short enough and the transaction cost low enough to allow flexibility in cash management.

- It allows for no buffer stock of cash. In reality, security sales are unlikely to be made when cash balances drop to zero, but when they fall to a level deemed to be the safe minimum.

- It uses a 'highly uncertain' estimate of the return from the portfolio. Bramham should investigate the implications of assuming alternative (higher and lower) rates, and perhaps determine a 'break-even rate' at which the two policies are equally attractive. In this example, the actual rate would have to be well above 12% to achieve this result.

- There may be economies in bulk-selling of securities, although exploiting these would increase the holding cost.

Tutorial notes

1   Some would argue eg, Samuels & Wilkes, that the net loss of interest (12% − 5% = 7%) should be used in the EOQ formula.

---

61   (Answer 6 of examination)

Examiner's comments and marking guide

Question 6: (a) this section asked candidates to compute the NPV and IRR of a new investment proposal.

Common errors were to include the sunk cost in the evaluation, to discount profit rather than cash flow (ie, the allocated fixed overhead should have been deleted), to build in a tax delay, to apply tax reliefs and/or capital allowances to the initial outlay, or total omission of tax.

More fundamentally, only a small proportion of candidates appeared to understand the difference between a real terms and a money terms evaluation (despite this having appeared in a previous paper). The question was quite specific - the analysis was to be done in real terms, which involved deflating the given money-terms discount rate and applying to the uninflated cash flows. Most answers applied the 14% discount rate to either uninflated cash flows or to inflated cash flows (which had some merit, but meant that annuity factors could not be used in the evaluation).

Attempts to calculate an IRR were generally good, although there was some confusion between the IRR and the ARR. Linear interpolation is a technique quite well understood.

Many candidates penalised themselves by writing out the discount factors in their answers and by neglecting to use the annuity tables provided where appropriate. Layout and presentation of calculations was often very poor.

(b)   **This section required candidates to explain the purpose of sensitivity analysis in relation to project appraisal and to discuss its limitations.**

Most candidates were able to offer an acceptable definition of sensitivity analysis, although few really appreciated the managerial implications of the procedure ie, to identify critical variables with a view to focusing attention on achieving favourable outcomes in these areas. Few were able to specify problems of the technique besides its single variable focus, often claiming instead that it was too complex or difficult for managers to comprehend, or that it ignored risk and uncertainty.

Some answers missed the point entirely by talking about linear programming, or making a comparison between the NPV and IRR methods of appraisal.

(c)   **This section required application of sensitivity analysis to obtain the break-even values of price and volume respectively.**

Candidates performed poorly in this section with many unable to apply the technique in a meaningful way. Many attempted to apply the CVP formula, entirely neglecting tax and the time factor. Although marks were awarded for reasonable attempts, few candidates were able to build upon their answers by discussing the implications of their findings for managerial action.

			Marks
(a)	Specification of discount rate		1
	Specification of relevant operating cost		1
	Reconciliation of sunk cost		1
	Calculation of (after-tax) NPV		2
	Calculation of IRR		2
			—
	Total		7
			—
(b)	Explanation of role of sensitivity analysis		2
	For each valid difficulty raised, up to one mark,		
	(but each requires an element of explanation)	max	4
			—
	Total		6
			—
(c)	Calculation of break-even values at 1.5 marks each		3
	Recognition of critical factor		1
	Discussion of implications for management action		3
			—
	Total		7
			—
	Grand total		20
			—

Step by step answer plan

Step 1   Read the question again and make sure that you focus on precisely what is required. The topic is investment appraisal, using DCF techniques and incorporating aspects of inflation and sensitivity analysis.

Step 2   (a)   For the DCF techniques, you first need to identify the relevant cash flows, using the usual principles. These will include tax effects (with no delay, you are told to assume, and the capital allowance effects have already been accounted for). However, before discounting these for the NPV, you must adjust the discount rate as it is given as a nominal (or money) rate - ie incorporating inflation - and the cash flows and evaluation are in real terms, excluding inflation.

Step 3   The simple annuity nature of the project means that the IRR can be estimated using annuity tables, rather than the less accurate interpolation formula. The latter is acceptable, but is more time consuming.

Step 4   (b)   Your answer should start with an explanation of the aims and mechanics of sensitivity analysis, as applied to project appraisal. Then try to think of as many problems as you can with the procedure - the examiner was expecting at least 4. Think about how things may change/fluctuate in practice and whether the procedure can properly deal with these.

Step 5 (c) This part requires an application of sensitivity analysis to two particular factors in your NPV computation. The basic approach is to go back to your computation, substitute a variable for the element now being varied, and find the value for which the NPV becomes 0. In order to comment sensibly on your results, it is more useful to evaluate the relative (%) change this represents. This will allow you to identify the more critical of the two factors, and your advice should focus around its management.

Step 6 Now review your answer and ensure that it does precisely answer the question as set.

Items not required by the examiner for this question

- computation of the ARR
- computations of discount factors (supplied)
- discussions concerning sensitivity analysis in the context of linear programming
- a comparison between the NPV and IRR methods of appraisal

The examiner's answer

(a) In a real-terms analysis, the real rate of return required by shareholders has to be used. This is found as follows:

$$\frac{1 + \text{nominal rate}}{1 + \text{inflation rate}} - 1 = (1.14/1.055) - 1 = 8\%$$

The relevant operating costs per box, after removing the allocated overhead are $(8.00 + 2.00 + 1.50 + 2.00) =$ £13.50. The costs of the initial research etc are not relevant as they are sunk. The set-up cost has already been adjusted for tax reliefs but the annual cash flows will be taxed at 33%.

The NPV of the project is given by:

$$
\begin{aligned}
\text{NPV}(£) \quad &= \quad [\text{PV of after-tax cash inflows}] - [\text{set-up costs}] \\
&= \quad 0.15\text{m} [20 - 13.50] (1 - 33\%) \text{PVIFA}_{8.5} - 2\text{m} \\
&= \quad 0.65\text{m} (3.993) - 2\text{m} \\
&= \quad +2.6\text{m} - 2\text{m} \\
&= \quad +0.6\text{m ie, } +£0.6\text{m}
\end{aligned}
$$

Hence, the project is attractive according to the NPV criterion.

The IRR is simply the discount rate, R, which generates a zero NPV ie, the solution to the expression:

NPV = 0 = 0.65m (PVIFA$_{R.5}$) − 2m
whence PVIFA$_{R.5}$ = 2m/0.65 = 3.077

To the nearest 1%, IRR = 19%. Since this exceeds the required return of 8% in real terms, the project is acceptable.

(b) A sensitivity analysis examines the impact of specified variations in key factors on the initially-calculated NPV. The starting point for a sensitivity analysis is the NPV using the 'most likely' value or 'best estimate' for each key variable. Taking the resulting 'base case' NPV as a reference point, the aim is to identify those factors which have the greatest impact on the profitability of the project if their realised values deviate from expectations. This intelligence signals to managers where they should arrange to focus resources in order to secure favourable outcomes.

Problems with sensitivity analysis include the following:

- It deals with changes in isolation, and tends to ignore interactions between variables. For example, advertising may alter the volume of output as well as influencing price, and price and volume are usually related.

- It assumes that specified changes persist throughout the project lifetime - e.g. a postulated 10% change in volume may be projected for each year of operation. In reality, variations in key factors tend to fluctuate randomly.

- It may reveal as critical, factors over which managers have no control, thus offering no guide to action. Nonetheless, it may still help to clarify the risks to which the project is exposed.

- It does not provide a decision rule e.g. it does not indicate the maximum acceptable levels of sensitivity.

- It gives no indication of the likelihood of the variations under consideration. Variations in a factor which are potentially devastating but have a minimal chance of occurring provide little cause for concern.

(c)   The values for which NPV becomes zero are found by calculating the break-even values for the selected variables. Once determined, these give an indication of the sensitivity of the NPV to changes in these factors

  (i)   Price (P)

$$
\begin{aligned}
\text{NPV} \ = \ & 0 \ = 0.15m\,[P - 13.50]\,(1 - 33\%)\,(\text{PVIFA}_{8,5}) - 2m \\
\text{whence} = \ & 0 \ = [0.15mP - 2.025]\,(2.675) - 2m \\
& 0 \ = 0.4P - 5.42m - 2m \\
& 0.4P \ = 7.42m \\
& P \ = \pounds18.55
\end{aligned}
$$

This means price can drop by $[\pounds20 - \pounds18.55]/\pounds20 = 7\%$ from the level assumed in the initial evaluation without making the NPV negative.

  (ii)   Volume (V)

Using a similar procedure:

$$
\begin{aligned}
\text{NPV} \ = \ & 0 \ = V[20 - 13.50]\,(1 - 33\%)\,(\text{PVIFA}_{8,5}) - 2m \\
& 0 \ = V\,[17.39m] - 2m \\
& V \ = 2m/17.39m \\
& \ = 115{,}000
\end{aligned}
$$

This means volume can drop by $[150{,}000 - 115{,}000]/150{,}000 = 23\%$ from the level assumed in the initial evaluation without making the NPV negative.

The results suggest that the NPV of the project is more sensitive to price variations than to changes in volume. Since price seems to be the more critical factor, management might plan to engage in price support measures like advertising and promotional expenditure. It might also attempt to obtain exclusive supply contracts with retailers, although these could violate competition regulations. Measures such as these are likely to be costly, in turn reducing the NPV of the project. It is possible that by making such adjustments, other variables become more critical, necessitating further analysis. At this stage, we might infer that, given the project has a positive NPV of £0.6m, Burley could afford to engage in promotional activity with a present value marginally below this amount over the lifetime of the project.

Did you answer the question?

Note that the examiner centred his advice around the management of sales price, since this was identified as the more sensitive of the two factors. He is looking for your ability to use calculated information to focus management attention - giving equal time to the consideration of volume control would rather lose the point of the computations. However price and volume are likely to be interlinked - a point which a fuller answer might have covered.

JUNE 1997 QUESTIONS

Section A - This question is compulsory and MUST be attempted

62   (Question 1 of examination)

Bardsey plc operates a chain of city centre furniture stores, specialising in high quality items. It is 60% owned by the original family founders. Its sales over the past decade have never grown faster than 5% in any one year, even falling during a recent recession. No growth is expected from existing operations in the next few years despite continuing to offer generous credit to customers.

In order to achieve faster growth, it is considering the development of a number of 'out of town' sites, adjacent to giant supermarkets and DIY stores. During 1997, this would involve a capital outlay of £50m plus additional working capital requirements of £20m in order to finance stock-building. In recent years, Bardsey's capital expenditure, mainly store refurbishments and vehicle replacements, and averaging around £10m per annum, has been financed entirely from cash flow. This category of investment will continue at about the same level in 1997. Bardsey's fixed assets were revalued two years ago.

Bardsey's accounting statements for the last financial year are summarised in Exhibit A, and Exhibit B gives information on key financial indicators for the stores sector as a whole (listed companies only).

Bardsey's debentures currently sell on the stock market at £130 per £100 nominal. The current bank base rate is 8%, and economists expect interest rates in general to fall over the next few years. The stock market currently applies a price: earnings ratio of 11:1 to Bardsey's shares.

Required:

As Bardsey's chief accountant, you are instructed to:

(a)   Calculate Bardsey's expected net cash flow in 1997 without the investment, assuming no changes in the level of net working capital.

(5 marks)

(*Note:* A statement in FRS 1 format is not required.)

(b)   Prepare a report, containing suitable reservations about the use of ratio analysis, which compares Bardsey's financial performance and health with the stores sector as a whole.

(15 marks)

(c)   Advise the board of Bardsey as to how the proposed investment programme might be financed. You should refer to possible economic reasons why interest rates may fall, and to the possible implications for Bardsey's financing decision.

(12 marks)

(d)   Suggest other possible uses of the increasing cash balances if Bardsey rejects the proposed investment.

(8 marks)

(Total: 40 marks)

Exhibit A: Bardsey's financial statements
Profit and loss account for the year ended 31 December 1996

	£m
Turnover	150.0
Cost of sales*	(90.0)
Operating profit	60.0
Interest charges	(15.0)
Pre-tax profit	45.0
Corporation tax	(12.0)
Profits after tax	33.0
Dividends proposed	(20.0)
Retained earnings	13.0

Balance sheet as at 31 December 1996

Assets employed	£m	£m	£m
Fixed (net):			
Land and premises		200	
Fixtures and fittings		50	
Vehicles		50	300
Current:			
Stocks	60		
Debtors	100		
Cash	40	200	
Current liabilities:			
Trade creditors	(85)		
Dividends payable	(20)		
Tax payable	(12)	(117)	
Net current assets			83
Total assets less current liabilities			383
15% Debentures 2010-12			(100)
Net assets			283
Financed by:			
Issued share capital (par value 25p):			100
Revaluation reserve			60
Profit and loss account			123
Shareholders' funds			283

* This includes depreciation of £8m

Exhibit B: Selected ratios for the stores sector

Return on (long-term) capital employed	14.3% (pre-tax)
Return on equity	15.3% (post-tax)
Operating profit margin	26.2%
Fixed asset turnover (sales/fixed assets)	1.2 times
Stock period	180 days
Debtor days	132 days
Gearing (total debt/equity)	42%
Interest cover	3.2 times
Dividend cover	2.1 times
P/E ratio	15:1

Section B - ONE question ONLY to be attempted

63   (Question 2 of examination)

You are the chief accountant of Deighton plc, which manufactures a wide range of building and plumbing fittings. It has recently taken over a smaller unquoted competitor, Linton Ltd. Deighton is currently checking through various documents at Linton's head office, including a number of investment appraisals. One of these, a recently rejected application involving an outlay on equipment of £900,000, is reproduced below. It was rejected because it failed to offer Linton's target return on investment of 25% (average profit-to-initial investment outlay). Closer inspection reveals several errors in the appraisal.

Evaluation of profitability of proposed project NT17
(all values in current year prices)

Item (£'000)	0	1	2	3	4
Sales		1,400	1,600	1,800	1,000
Materials		(400)	(450)	(500)	(250)
Direct labour		(400)	(450)	(500)	(250)
Overheads		(100)	(100)	(100)	(100)
Interest		(120)	(120)	(120)	(120)
Depreciation		(225)	(225)	(225)	(225)
Profit pre-tax		155	255	355	55
Tax at 33%		(51)	(84)	(117)	(18)
Post-tax profit		104	171	238	37

Outlay	
Stock	(100)
Equipment	(900)
Market research	(200)
	(1,200)

$$\text{Rate of return} = \frac{\text{Average profit}}{\text{Investment}} = \frac{£138}{£1,200} = 11.5\%$$

You discover the following further details:

1. Linton's policy was to finance both working capital and fixed investment by a bank overdraft. A 12% interest rate applied at the time of the evaluation.

2. A 25% writing down allowance (WDA) on a reducing balance basis is offered for new investment. Linton's profits are sufficient to utilise fully this allowance throughout the project.

3. Corporate tax is paid a year in arrears.

4. Of the overhead charge, about half reflects absorption of existing overhead costs.

5.   The market research was actually undertaken to investigate two proposals, the other project also having been rejected. The total bill for all this research has already been paid.

6.   Deighton itself requires a nominal return on new projects of 20% after taxes, is currently ungeared and has no plans to use any debt finance in the future.

Required:

Write a report to the finance director in which you:

(a)   Identify the mistakes made in Linton's evaluation.

(10 marks)

(b)   Restate the investment appraisal in terms of the post-tax net present value to Deighton, recommending whether the project should be undertaken or not.

(10 marks)
(Total: 20 marks)

---

64   (Question 3 of examination)

Whirlygig plc manufactures and markets automatic dish washing machines. Among the components which it purchases each year from external suppliers for assembly into the finished article are window units, of which it uses 20,000 units per annum.

It is considering buying in larger amounts in order to claim quantity discounts. This will lower the number of orders placed but raise the administrative and other costs of placing and receiving orders. Details of actual and expected ordering and carrying costs are given in the table below:

			Actual	*Proposed*
O	=	Ordering cost per order	£31.25	£120
P	=	Purchase price per item	£6.25	£6.00
I	=	(annual) Inventory holding cost		
		(as a percentage of the purchase price)	20%	20%

To implement the new arrangements will require reorganisation costs estimated at £10,000 which can be wholly claimed as a business expense for tax purposes in the tax year before the system comes into operation. The rate of corporate tax is 33%, payable with a one-year delay.

Required:

(a)   Determine the change in the economic order quantity (EOQ) caused by the new system.

Note: EOQ is given by $Q = \sqrt{\dfrac{2 \times D \times O}{I \times P}}$

where D = demand, or usage.

(4 marks)

(b)   Calculate the payback period for the proposal and comment on your results.

(10 marks)

(c)   Briefly discuss the suitability of the payback method for evaluating investments of this nature.

(6 marks)
(Total: 20 marks)

65   (Question 4 of examination)

A UK site of a chemical company has a number of semi-automated plants which specialise in individual products. One product, Alpha, has an annual budgeted volume of 240,000kg for which equal amounts of production and sales are planned in each of 12 reporting periods. The budgeted/standard manufacturing and selling costs for period 1 are shown below:

	Per kg £	Total P1 £
Manufacturing		
Material	3.50	70,000
Labour and variable overhead	2.50	50,000
Fixed overhead		100,000
		————
Total manufacturing cost		220,000
Variable selling overhead	1.50	30,000
Fixed selling overhead		40,000
		————
		70,000

1.   The standard selling price is £17 per kg.

2.   Variable selling overheads are incurred in proportion to units sold.

3.   Manufacturing overheads are recovered based on the budgeted volume levels.

For reporting purposes and identifying stock values the company operates a standard absorption costing system. For P1 the production was 18,400kg, however sales amounted to only 12,400kg.

In order to undertake some basic sales and marketing planning the accountant analyses costs into variable and fixed elements in order to compute the break-even point and profits at various sales volumes. The sales manager had calculated the break-even point as 14,737kg and for 12,400kg sales he predicts a loss. He was mildly surprised therefore to see the profit statement which was produced for the period to reveal a small profit as follows:

Product Alpha
Profit Statement P1

Production	18,400 kg		
Sales	12,400 kg		
		£	£
Sales			208,800
Manufacturing costs			
Standard cost of sales			
12,400 × £11		136,400	
Add Manufacturing variances			
Volume		8,000	
All other expenditure		5,500	
		————	
		149,900	
Actual selling overheads			
Variable		17,500	
Fixed		38,300	
		————	
			205,700
Actual net profit			3,100

Required:

(a)   Analyse the budgeted costs into fixed and variable elements and calculate both the break-even point and the budgeted profit/loss based on the actual kg sold where a marginal cost system is in use.

(3 marks)

(b)   (i)   Demonstrate how the value of the manufacturing volume variance has been computed and briefly explain its significance.

(5 marks)

         (ii)   Calculate the variances which apply to the variable and fixed selling overheads.

(3 marks)

(c)   Reconcile the profit/loss from (a) above with the actual net profit given in the question showing all relevant variances. Briefly explain how a profit is revealed when a loss was anticipated by the sales manager.

(9 marks)
(Total: 20 marks)

---

66   (Question 5 of examination)

ABC plc, a group operating retail stores, is compiling its budget statements for 1998. In this exercise revenues and costs at each store A, B and C are predicted. Additionally, all central costs of warehousing and a head office are allocated across the three stores in order to arrive at a total cost and net profit of each store operation.

In earlier years the central costs were allocated in total based on the total sales value of each store. But as a result of dissatisfaction expressed by some store managers alternative methods are to be evaluated.

The predicted results before any re-allocation of central costs are as follows:

	A £'000	B £'000	C £'000
Sales	5,000	4,000	3,000
Costs of sales	2,800	2,300	1,900
Gross margin	2,200	1,700	1,100
Local operating expenses			
Variable	660	730	310
Fixed	700	600	500
Operating profit	840	370	290

The central costs which are to be allocated are:

	£'000
Warehouse costs:	
Depreciation	100
Storage	80
Operating and despatch	120
Delivery	300
Head office:	
Salaries	200
Advertising	80
Establishment	120
Total	1,000

The management accountant has carried out discussions with staff at all locations in order to identify more suitable 'cost drivers' of some of the central costs. So far the following has been revealed.

	A	B	C
Number of despatches	550	450	520
Total delivery distances (thousand miles)	70	50	90
Storage space occupied (%)	40	30	30

1. An analysis of senior management time revealed that 10% of their time was devoted to warehouse issues with the remainder shared equally between the three stores.

2. It was agreed that the only basis on which to allocate the advertising costs was sales revenue.

3. Establishment costs were mainly occupancy costs of senior management.

This analysis has been carried out against a background of developments in the company, for example, automated warehousing and greater integration with suppliers.

Required:

(a) As the management accountant prepare a report for the management of the group which:

(i) Computes the budgeted net profit of each store based on the *sales value* allocation base originally adopted *and* explains 'cost driver', 'volume' and 'complexity' issues in relation to cost allocation commenting on the possible implications of the dissatisfaction expressed.

(6 marks)

(ii) Computes the budgeted net profit of each store using the additional information provided, discusses the extent to which an improvement has been achieved in the information on the costs and profitability of running the stores and comments on the results.

(11 marks)

(b) Explain briefly how regression analysis and coefficient of determination (r^2) could be used in confirming the delivery mileage allocation method used in (a) above.

(3 marks)
(Total: 20 marks)

---

67   (Question 6 of examination)

(a) Three of the various uses of budgets are performance evaluation, resource allocation and authorisation. Demonstrate your understanding of each of these in the contexts given below, providing an example in each case:

(i) performance evaluation, in the context of a private sector manufacturing company

(ii) resource allocation, in the context of a private sector service company

(iii) authorisation, in the context of a public sector organisation.

(12 marks)

(b) Assess what benefits may be achieved by an organisation adopting a zero-based approach in its budgetary process and what difficulties may be encountered.

(8 marks)
(Total: 20 marks)

ANSWERS TO JUNE 1997 EXAMINATION

62   (Answer 1 of examination)

Examiner's comments and marking guide

Question 1: (a) This question required candidates to calculate a company's expected cash flow figure (but not in FRS 1 format).

This section should have offered an easy five marks for well-prepared candidates, although many omitted it entirely. The main errors were omission of important items, and inclusion of irrelevant data eg, debtors and creditors (despite the clear instruction given in the question). Many chose to inflate some or all of the data despite the clear signal that 'no growth is expected'. It seems that some candidates are determined to make life more complicated than necessary!

(b)   **This question required candidates to prepare a report, using ratio analysis regarding a company's financial performance and health.**

This part was poorly attempted. Most answers, often long and rambling, amounted to little more than checklists of the company's ratios against those of the sector, with little or no attempt to interpret and explain their meaning. As a result of neglect of important contextual material eg, nature of the product, recent asset revaluation, marks tended to be low. They were very low for those candidates who omitted to calculate ratios at all, or who chose to comment only on the ratios for the industry sector. A large number of candidates neglected to offer any reservations about the use of ratio analysis, as was required.

(c)   **This question required candidates to advise a company as to suitable methods of financing an investment programme.**

The key to this section was use of the contextual material provided, in conjunction with data calculated in the earlier sections. Where candidates recognised the importance of answering the question in context, answers were good. Often, however, they were simply 'shopping lists' of all possible means of financing regardless of relevance eg, it is hard to see why a venture capitalist should be interested in such a company, or why the company should want a flotation when its shares are already quoted on the stock market! It seems that too few candidates read questions with appropriate care. A reflection of this problem was the common neglect to consider why interest rates should fall, and to consider the implications for financing.

It is a matter of great concern that so many prospective accountants think that reserves/retained earnings from previous years can be used to finance new investment, and that debentures, shown as a liability on a balance sheet, can be sold to raise cash.

(d)   **This question required candidates to suggest alternative uses of a mounting cash pile.**

Failure to read the question appeared to be responsible fro the widespread problems here, many candidates simply giving additional means of financing omitted from part (c). Some answers showed great (and creditable) originally in their suggestions, although a large proportion simply offered various forms of short-term deposits and money market instruments.

		Marks
(a)	Cash generation. The errors here are most likely to be of omission. One mark deducted per omission	5
	Total	5
(b)	Calculation of each relevant ratio, with discussion as to why the company may under/over-perform the sector (rather than mere comparison with the sector): one per ratio	Max 9
	Identification of drawbacks with ratio analysis: one per valid point plus element of explanation	Max 4
	General comments about Bardsey's over-capitalisation	2
	Total	15
(c)	Financing. For each plausible financing alternative discussed, two marks up to max of:	8
	Discussion of reasons for interest rate reduction	2
	Comments on implications for Bardsey's financing	2
	Total	12
(d)	For discussion of each plausible alternative: two marks up to	8
	Total	8
	Grand total	40

Step by step answer plan

Step 1 Read the question again and make sure that you focus on precisely what is required. This case study question concerned a business with fairly static operations at present, which generate a steady positive cash flow. It is considering expansion by investment.

Step 2 (a) You are required to compute cash flow for the coming year. As the main cash flow will be from operations, the starting point is last year's operating profit. The key to earning full marks here was the careful reading of information given in the question and requirement - this served to considerably simplify the computations (see examiner's comments). The only adjustment to last year's operating profit to get it to this year's operating cash flow was thus depreciation. This then needs adjustment for *cash payments* to be made next year in respect of this year's tax and dividend creditors, and next year's interest and investment.

Step 3 (b) Although the requirement for the report seems quite general, both the information supplied and the requirement itself drop heavy hints as to what is expected. The requirement mentions ratio analysis - so this should clearly be part of your answer. Which ratios? You are given a list relating to the stores sector, so these are the main ones to consider (although you may feel others are also relevant). The question also specifically requires comparison of Bardsey's ratios with those of the sector (this means both in numbers *and* comment) and discussion of the limitations of such an analysis. Once you have identified these elements, think about how you are going to structure your answer. Although you are likely to do the computations first, these could be put in an appendix at the end of your report. Once you have the numbers, look for clues form the question as to possible reasons for differences between Bardsey and the sector, the "contextual material" referred to in the examiner's comments. Once all specific requirements of the question have been met, you should draw a short conclusion as to the overall picture drawn from your analysis.

Step 4 (c)   As the examiner says, it is essential that you focus on the business and market defined in the question in order to avoid making irrelevant, impractical or inappropriate comments. Look at the type and size of business it is, the market in which it is operating, the picture given by its financial statements and the information you have derived in earlier parts (including, in particular, the amount of external finance that will be required). This should restrict your discussion of sources of finance to those that are actually of practical application to Bardsey (note the marking guide implies at least four are to be suggested). You can be more general when discussing interest rates.

Step 5 (d)   The first thing to check is that you have understood the requirement. In contrast to (c), where the aim was to *raise* additional finance, here we are looking at ways to *invest* surplus cash. The same contextual focus is required, as in (c), an sufficient variety (again, at least four distinct uses).

Step 6   Now review your answer and ensure that it does precisely answer the question as set.

(The examiner's answer)

(It should be noted that the following answers are probably fuller than would be expected from the average candidate under exam conditions. Answers are provided in some degree of detail to offer guidance on the approach required, and on the range and depth of knowledge that would be expected from an excellent candidate.)

(a)   Bardsey appears to be a strong generator of cash. Ongoing investment needs are partly met out of depreciation provisions, a deduction before calculating operating profit. Assuming no changes in operating activity or in the net working capital position, cash generation for 1997 is likely to be as follows:

	£m
Operating profit	60
plus	
Depreciation	8
Working capital	-
Operating cash flow	68
Less	
Replacement investment	(10)
Interest due for 1997	(15)
Taxation due from 1996	(12)
Dividends due from 1996	(20)
Net cash flow	11

(b)   Report on Bardsey plc's financial health and performance

This report focuses mainly on the financial ratios which can be calculated from the accounts and the industrial comparators given, but it is important to acknowledge the drawbacks with this form of performance appraisal:

-   it is usually desirable to examine ratios over a series of years, long enough to iron out any random influences but short enough not to be distorted by structural changes such as divestment.

-   it is important to recognise that the end-of-year accounts may not be representative either of the trading year concerned, given the tendency to 'window dress' accounts at year end (eg, speeding up debtors collection), or of current trading circumstances, given the delay in preparation of accounts.

-   Other companies may prepare accounts on different bases, using different policies and over different financial years.

-   In practice, it is difficult to define the boundaries of an industry given the differences in product offerings and product mixes produced and sold by companies.

- It is often not sufficient to examine financial ratios alone. A more balanced approach to performance appraisal might focus on aspects such as customer satisfaction and rate of innovation.

Did you answer the question?

This discussion of reservations about the use of ratio analysis was a specific requirement of the question. You can choose to deal with it up-front, as here, or after your analysis, possibly linking it to specific ratios used.

---

1. The company is achieving a pre-tax return on long-term capital of £60m/[£283m + £100m] = 15.7%, which compares well enough with the industry as a whole. In fact, given the recent asset revaluation, this may indicate better than average performance if other companies have not conducted similar revaluations.

2. The return on equity at £33m/£283m = 11.7% is well below that of the industry, probably reflecting a higher equity base following the recent revaluation. Alternatively, other companies may operate at higher gearing ratios, thus increasing their ROEs if the interest cost of debt is lower than the ROE. This is borne out by examination of the industry gearing figures.

3. Bardsey trades with an operating profit margin of £60m/£150m = 40%, well in excess of the sector. This could suggest a number of things. Perhaps Bardsey is more efficient than its competitors, perhaps it applies higher prices, competing on quality of service, or maybe it sells higher quality products which appeal to a more affluent clientele.

4. The fixed asset turnover ratio is often taken as an indicator of efficiency. At just £150m/£300m = 0.5 for Bardsey, this compares unfavourably with the sector average of 1.2, but this is probably partly explained by the asset revaluation.

5. Lengthy stock periods are common in the furniture trade, which often holds high value-added goods for display purposes. Bardsey's stock period (stocks/cost of sales as the figure for purchases is not given) is £60m/£90m × 365 = 243 days, well in excess of the industry figure of 180 days, although if it is serving a higher quality market segment, this might be expected. Against this, if the industry figure is based on purchases, the two figures are not directly comparable.

6. As suggested above, Bardsey's capital gearing (£100m/£283m = 35% at book values) is lower than that of the sector, although the sector figure cited includes short-term debt which Bardsey does not presently use.

7. Interest cover at £60m/£15m = 4 appears safe, implying that profits could drop substantially without endangering Bardsey's ability to pay interest. However, the issue is really much more complex than this, depending on the balance of fixed and variable costs ie, operating gearing, which is probably quite high in this sector.

8. Dividend cover at £33m/£20m = 1.65 is low, perhaps reflecting pressure by the dominant shareholders to pay high dividends. Alternatively, this ratio could be inflated by temporarily low profits as Bardsey emerges from recession. Besides, there is no problem in financing a high payout given Bardsey's substantial cash holdings and strong cash flow.

9   In addition, the liquidity ratios appear satisfactory at £200m/£117m = 1.71 for the current ratio and £140m/£117m = 1.20 for the acid test. However, debtors are very high at £100m, with debtor days of £100m/£150 × 365 = 243 days probably reflecting the impact of special offers such as lengthy interest-free credit periods. However, no industry comparators are given.

Did you answer the question?

Note that the examiner has three elements relating to each ratio - the computation of Bardsey's ratios (which could be in an appendix), how it compares with the sector ratio **and** possible reasons for the difference, using information from the question where relevant. All three must be present in your answer to gain full marks. Alternative answers (ratios) are possible eg, excluding depreciation from cost of sales in (5) when finding a stock period.

Overall, Bardsey presents a picture of sluggish performance in the mature market of retailing quality products, continued demand for which ensures adequate profitability and strong cash flow. The relatively low P:E ratio suggests the market is not expecting substantial growth from Bardsey, nor, given the concentration of shareholders, it is likely to be subject to a take-over.

Without attempting to diversify into new markets and products, there is probably a case for paying even higher dividends to prevent even greater over-capitalisation.

(c)   Bardsey requires finance of (£50m plus £20m) for its new developments. £11m of this can be internally financed, leaving a substantial net external financing requirement of (£70m less £11m) = £59m. Some possible financing alternatives are:

Run down cash holdings

Bardsey is currently holding substantial cash balances, which would largely cover the additional financing needs. However, some degree of liquidity may be thought desirable as protection from adverse contingencies. There are no 'rules' in this respect, but a buffer stock of highly liquid assets held in cash and/or money market investments would be prudent.

Rights issue

Bardsey appears currently to be over-capitalised. There is little point in issuing more equity in this situation, especially as the current ROE is relatively weak, and the relatively low P/E ratio already applied by the market hints at a possibly unfavourable reaction.

Short-term borrowing

On the 'matching' principle, it looks sensible to undertake short-term financing for at least part of the working capital requirements. Short-term overdraft financing is usually cheaper than equity financing, especially allowing for tax relief on debt interest (the 'tax shield'). Given Bardsey's strong asset backing, a modest increase in gearing does not seem risky. Even without the benefits from the new projects, borrowing perhaps £10m at say, 3% above base rate ie, 11%, thus imposing extra interest charges of (11% × £10m) = £1.1m, would lower interest cover only to £60m/[£15m + £1.1m] = 3.7 times.

Long-term borrowing

There is considerable scope for increasing gearing, as noted, but whether it is wise to increase long-term borrowing is doubtful unless this can be achieved on a variable rate basis, given that interest rates are expected to fall. If not, it seems better to use short-term debt pending the fall in interest rates, and then to re-finance with long-term debt as and when rates fall. If anything, there seems a case for repaying some of the existing long-term debt (if permitted) given that it costs 15% (before tax relief) to finance.

Sale-and-leaseback (SAL)

SAL involves selling 'quality' assets (usually property in 'good' sites, which command high rents and are likely to increase in value) to a financial institution in exchange for the right of continued occupation. It seems likely that many of Bardsey's assets would qualify, but if 'out-of-town' developments are taking sales from city centres, this could already be undermining property values in some locations.

Did you answer the question?

Having identified the amount of external finance needed, the examiner has limited his discussion to those sources that are appropriate for this amount and the circumstances of the company itself.

Interest rates

A critical element in the financing decision is expectations about the future course of interest rates and the economic determinants of interest rate changes. In this case, people are expecting falling rates. Among the possible reasons for a fall in interest rates are the following:

(i)   lower government borrowing, thus reducing downward pressure on the price of 'gilts' (government stock)

(ii)   lower demand for investment funds by the private sector

(iii)   an unexpected fall in the actual rate of price inflation

(iv)   a fall in the expected rate of inflation, caused perhaps by upward adjustment of the exchange rate, or a fall in the national level of wage settlements

(v)   looser regulation of the monetary system, for example, a decrease in prudential ratios, enhancing the ability of banks to lend using the bank multiplier effect

(vi)   less need for the monetary authorities to intervene to dampen speculative pressure on the exchange rate.

Clearly, Bardsey will have to take a view on the reasons why, in the current context, people expect a cut in interest rates, and the likelihood of these events occurring. Indeed, if the money market is efficient, it might be argued that expected lower rates are *already* factored into the existing term structure of interest rates.

Lower future rates may provide an opportunity to borrow long-term on a fixed rate basis thus locking into a historically low interest rate. Conversely, short-term financing at a variable interest rate may be a good hedge against further falls in rates. Lower interest rates also tend to favour running down cash holdings and short-term financing, and will increase asset values, which favours a SAL. Against this, if the inflation rate is falling, the borrower does not enjoy the benefit of the falling real value of debts.

(d)   **Possible uses of 'spare' cash include:**

Pay out higher dividends

Dividend cover at £33m/£20m = 1.65 times is below the sector average of 2.1 times, reducing scope for higher distribution. However, this would be preferable to investing in projects with dubious prospects of generating adequate returns and would presumably impress those institutional shareholders seeking income rather than capital appreciation, especially if they can reclaim tax credits.

Paying higher dividends also promotes expectations of at least the same level of dividends in the future, expectations which Bardsey may have difficulty in meeting, given its present sluggish performance. For these reasons, temporarily cash-rich companies often pay a 'Special Dividend', emphasising their 'one-off' nature.

However, the ownership structure of Bardsey is important here. Arguably, a family-dominated company might want to avoid yet higher dividends which may not be tax-efficient for some members paying higher rate tax. These could prefer capital gains on which tax can be deferred. In addition, there is a higher tax threshold on capital gains compared to that on income, and gains can also be indexed.

Take-overs

Spare cash could be used to acquire other companies. This is a short-cut to growth but requires specialised skills in valuing the target(s) and integrating newly-acquired companies. There is a danger of over-paying for the target company, especially in the excitement of a contested bid. Much will depend on the track record of Bardsey in this respect. If it has not previously acquired other companies, attempting to do so at this juncture could well provoke adverse market reaction.

Share repurchase

Under certain conditions, UK companies are allowed to buy back a certain proportion of their shares on the market. This tends to raise EPS, and exerts upward pressure on share price. It could be interpreted adversely as a signal that the company has exhausted ideas for profitable expansion, as seems likely in the case of Bardsey.

Repay debt

Bardsey has £100m of debentures outstanding, with a coupon rate of 15%. Allowing for tax, this requires a cash outflow of £15m (1-33%) = £10.05m per annum ie, an effective cost of about 10% (although lower than this when expressed at market values). The ROE is currently only just above this, so unless Bardsey expects to improve its ROE, it may be desirable to lower long-term indebtedness. This may depend also on the attitudes to risk of the predominant shareholders.

Social responsibility

Bardsey could take the opportunity to improve its public image by increased 'social expenditure'. For example, it might upgrade the health, welfare and sporting facilities provided for its employees. It could also adopt policies designed to promote the welfare of the community at large eg, sports sponsorship, provision of educational endowments and environmental programmes. Such policies generally have a beneficial effect on a company's standing in the community which may translate into improved sales and profitability, although this is difficult to quantify in practice.

Did you answer the question?

Note that the examiner has not confined himself to uses that involve profitable investment for the business. Where there are limited such opportunities available, giving cash back to shareholders, employees or the community may be considered.

---

63   (Answer 2 of examination)

Examiner's comments and marking guide

Question 2: (a) This question required candidates to report to senior management on the mistake in a previous investment appraisal.

This was generally well done, candidates appearing well-prepared and knowledgeable about the standard 'traps', in project appraisal. There was some tendency not to answer this section from a discounted cash flow (DCF) context, merely focusing on errors in the accounting rate of return per se. Although the requirement should have been clear from the context and the wording of part (b), this was taken account of in the marking.

(b)   **This question required candidates to rework the project appraisal using the NPV (net present value) method.** The wording here was categoric - candidates had to use DCF analysis. many answers scored highly and it seems that candidates are now coming to grips with the requirements of DCF evaluation and the taxation complexities. There remained some errors - eg, a tendency to misuse *WDAs (writing down allowances)* by adding them to cash flows with or without any further adjustment for tax savings. Candidates should ensure that they understand the difference between a tax allowance and a tax saving, and the resulting cash flow impact. There was a tendency for candidates to ignore their own earlier recommendations, especially in the area of working capital investment/disinvestment and in the treatment of interest. Many wrongly identified 12% as the appropriate discount rate. Generally, there was little discussion of results beyond a simple yes/no recommendation.

Another persistent problem was candidates, apparent misunderstanding of how to deal with inflation. The information given was perfectly consistent - the returns were expressed in current year prices ie, the prices ruling in each year of the project, thus incorporating inflation, and the 20% discount provided was a nominal rate ie, money rate, which incorporated inflation expectations. There was no need to make further adjustment for inflation.

		Marks
(i)	For specification of errors, with element of explanation:	
	one mark per error up to max of 8	8
	Format of report	2
		—
	Total	10
		—

(ii)	Calculation of WDAs	1
	Determination of tax savings	1
	Beyond this, the errors are most likely to be of omission.	
	One mark deducted per omission or other error of a non-	
	mathematical nature.	6
	Recommendation and comment	2
		——
	Total	10
		——
	Grand total	20
		——

Step by step answer plan

Step 1 Read the question again and make sure that you focus on precisely what is required. This question concerns different methods of investment appraisal, contrasting the profit based accounting rate of return with the theoretically better net present value approach. Whilst the exact requirement of (a) is open to interpretation, part (b) is quite clear in its requirement for a "post-tax net present value". You may have considered tackling this first, as it would highlight the differences between the methods as required in (a). Note that 2 marks are awarded for report format - so think about the structure: headings, introduction, specific requirements of (a) and (b), then a conclusion/recommendation.

Step 2 (a) Linton's evaluation is on the basis of an accounting based return on investment, and you are asked to identify the mistakes in the evaluation. The clues to the "mistakes" lie in both the "further details" given in the question, and the requirement of (b). The examiner was looking for an unfavourable comparison of the ROI with the theoretically sounder DCF approach, using the information to highlight differences re cash flows, timings, appraisal rates, time value etc. However, the examiner allowed the alternative approach of identifying mistakes in the calculation of the ROI itself (although there are fewer points that can be made here, and probably not 8 as implied by the marking guide).

Step 3 (b) A standard NPV requirement here, including tax and inflation (although, as the examiner says, cash flows and discount rate had already been adjusted for the latter, and thus it could be ignored). The layout of the question lends itself to a horizontal approach to tabulation of cash flows (a cash budget), although you can use whichever layout and order of workings you prefer, as long as it is clear. The tax effects of the individual WDA's can, for example, be incorporated within the main NPV computation. Make sure you conclude your computations with a written comment

Step 4 Now review your answer and ensure that it does precisely answer the question as set.

The examiner's answer

Report submitted to:	Finance Director, Deighton plc
From:	An(n) Accountant.
Date:	12th of Never
Subject:	Investment Project NT17

The above investment project was rejected by the former management of Linton Ltd, but it appears that the evaluation (attached) was flawed. This report identifies these flaws and re-evaluates the proposal which appears to be worthwhile. As the market opportunity is still open, I recommend acceptance of the project.

(i)   Mistakes by Linton

1.   The initial investment in working capital should be offset by a working capital release in the final year, assuming a constant level of stock-holding until the last year.

2.   The interest cost, although a cash outflow in reality, should be subsumed in the overall cost of capital. Linton's evaluation confused the investment decision with the financing decision. If the project were evaluated by the new owners, Deighton's required return of 20% would be the correct rate of discount (assuming no impact on Deighton's risk).

3.   No scrap value was shown for either the old equipment, or the new machine at the end of four years.

4.   Depreciation is not a cash outflow. By deducting the depreciation charge, Linton has double-counted for the capital cost.

5.   However, the annual depreciation allowances (WDA) do affect the tax outflows. These were ignored.

6.   No tax delay was allowed for.

7.   The overhead charge was over-stated. Only half of the amount charged appears to be incremental.

8.   The market research cost, whatever it relates to, is irrelevant ie, it is sunk, unless a buyer could be found for the report.

Did you answer the question?

Note that the examiner has first considered the actual figures used in the evaluation for possible omissions/incorrect inclusions - these would apply which ever method is being considered. He has then moved on to talk about DCF principles, and how these also contribute to errors in Linton's evaluation.

(ii)   In the following solution, the tax allowances in relation to the initial outlay on equipment are evaluated separately. (Other approaches are acceptable.)

The tax-adjusted cost of the capital expenditure can be found by deducting the present value of the tax savings generated by exploiting the writing-down allowance from the initial outlay. It is assumed that the available allowances can be set off against profits immediately ie, beginning in the financial year in which the acquisition of the asset occurs. This yields five sets of WDAs as the project straddles five tax years. The solution assumes no scrap values.

Item (£'000)	0	1	2	Year 3	4	5
Allowance claimed at 25%	225	169	127	95	284	
Written-down value	675	506	379	284	0	
Tax saving at 33%		74	56	42	31	94
Discount factor at 20%		0.833	0.694	0.579	0.482	0.402
Present value		62	39	24	15	38

Present value of tax savings = 178 ie, £178,000

The effective cost of the equipment is:

[Nominal outlay   -   present value of tax savings]
  =   [£900,000 - £178,000]
  =   £722,000.

The cash flow profile is: (TN 2)

Item (£'000)	0	1	2	3	4	5
Equipment/scrap (net)	(722)				0	
Sales		1,400	1,600	1,800	1,000	
Materials		(400)	(450)	(500)	(250)	
Direct labour		(400)	(450)	(500)	(250)	
Inc overheads		(50)	(50)	(50)	(50)	
Operating cash flow		550	650	750	450	
Tax at 33%		-	(182)	(215)	(248)	(149)
Working capital	(100)				100	
Net cash flow	(822)	550	468	535	302	(149)
Discount factor at 20%		0.833	0.694	0.579	0.482	0.402
Present value	(822)	458	325	310	146	(60)

NPV = + 357 ie, £357,000

Recommendation

Thus, the equipment purchase is acceptable and should be undertaken, although an analysis of its risk is also recommended.

Tutorial notes

1 Students should recognise this particular examiner's use of the word 'nominal' when describing discount rates. He means money cost of capital.

2 Note that where the original cash flow information is given in £'000, you should keep to this in your computations.

3 Do not follow the example shown here of silly names or dates in reports. It may impress in Paper 8, it will not in other papers and it wastes time.

---

64 (Answer 3 of examination)

(Examiner's comments and marking guide)

Question 3: (a) This question required candidates to calculate the change in the EOQ (Economic Order Quantity) caused by introducing a new stock management system.

This section earned top marks for the many candidates who could use the square root formula provided, although many had trouble with decimal points, and yet more wrongly inserted the data provided in the denominator of the formula.

(b) **This question required candidates to calculate the payback on the investment in the new stock management system.**

After allowing for any errors in (a), this section was a high mark earner for those who appreciated that the principles of investment appraisal are equally applicable to 'revenue' expenditure, and that they were dealing with a cost saving situation. The main, and widespread, error was incorrect computation of the holding cost - this relates to Q/2, rather than D/2. This error revealed whether candidates really understood the use of the EOQ - a moment's reflection should have indicated that, at the EOQ, the order cost equals the holding cost. Other errors centred on omission, or misuse, of the tax information provided. Many candidates who failed to understand the requirement in (b) simply gave up. It is therefore important that candidates carefully select their optional questions.

(c)   **This question required candidates to discuss the suitability of the payback method of investment appraisal.**

Candidates seemed well-versed in the pros and cons of payback although the ability to orient the answers to the context of the question was usually absent. When payback is achieved so quickly and the outlay is small, neglect of the time value of money is probably not a major issue.

		Marks
(a)	EOQ before change in system	2
	EOQ after change in system	2
		—
	Total	4
		—
(b)	Change in order costs	2
	Change in holding costs	2
	Value of discounts	1
	Cash flows after tax	2
	Payback period with comment	1
	Commentary, up to	2
		—
	Total	10
		—
(c)	Why payback is used:	
	One mark per valid comment, with explanation, up to	3
	Criticisms of payback:	
	One mark per valid comment, with explanation, up to	3
		—
		6
		—
	Grand total	20
		—

(**Step by step answer plan**)

Step 1   Read the question again and make sure that you focus on precisely what is required. Whilst this question is set in the context of stock management, its main subject matter is an investment appraisal method, the payback period.

Step 2   (a)   This offers an easy 4 marks provided you are careful to use the data accurately in the formula. Don't be put off by the fact that you've no idea when discount operates.

Step 3   (b)   It may seem strange to apply an investment appraisal method to a change in stock ordering system, but it has the required elements - an initial investment (reorganisation costs) with subsequent annual returns (cost savings, net of tax effects). The cost savings are in the annual purchase price of stock - the bulk discount. However, there are also the stock ordering and holding costs to consider, which in fact show a cost increase. This is a logical continuation from (a) - you need to compute total annual holding and order costs with the two different order quantities and associated costs. Once the annual net cost savings have been computed they and their tax effects must be set out in a cash flow table to determine the point at which they repay the initial reorganisation costs. Don't forget to comment upon your results as asked (up to 2 marks are available for this).

Step 4   (c)   The examiner likes discussion of general principles or methods to be answered within the context of the question wherever possible. So, jot down the general points about payback that you (hopefully) have learnt, and try to see if you can illustrate them from the question, or can see which are the most significant in the given circumstances. Try to give a balanced view - advantages or benefits of the method as well as criticisms.

Step 5   Now review your answer and ensure that it does precisely answer the question as set.

> **The examiner's answer**

(a)   The optimal order size is found by applying the EOQ formula:

$$Q = \sqrt{\frac{2 \times \text{Demand} \times \text{Order cost}}{\% \text{ Carrying cost} \times \text{Purchase price}}}$$

Before the change in the process

$$Q = \sqrt{\frac{2 \times 20,000 \times £31.25}{0.2 \times £6.25}} = \sqrt{1m} = 1,000 \text{ units per order}$$

After the change, this becomes

$$Q = \sqrt{\frac{2 \times 20,000 \times £120}{0.2 \times £6.00}} = \sqrt{4m} = 2,000 \text{ units per order}$$

The EOQ will thus increase by 1,000 units, and the number of orders required will reduce from 20 to 10.

(b)   The result of the new system is to raise the order costs

from   20 orders pa at £31.25 per order = £625 (TN 1)
to   10 orders pa at £120 per order = £1,200
          ie, an increase of £575 per annum.

The carrying cost was originally given by:
          (interest costs, etc × purchase price × average stock)
          = 20% × £6.25 × 1,000/2 = £625

With the new system and the EOQ of 2,000 units, this increases to:
          20% × £6.00 × 2,000/2 = £1,200.

The overall effect is to raise inventory costs

from: Order costs + Holding costs =   £625 + £625   =   £1,250 (TN 2)
to   £1,200 + £1,200 =   £2,400

ie, an increase of £1,150.

However, the company will now qualify for quantity discounts of (£6.25 - £6.00) = £0.25 per unit. In total, this will generate cost savings of (£0.25 × 20,000) = £5,000 per annum. The net annual benefit of the system before tax is thus:

(£5,000 - £1,150) = £3,850

Allowing for tax, the cash flow impact of the re-organisation is:

			Year	
Item (£)	*0*	*1*	*2*	*3, etc*
Outlay	(10,000)			
Tax saving		3,300		
Cost saving		3,850	3,850	
Tax at 33%			(1,271)	(1,271)
Net cash flow	(10,000)	7,150	2,579	2,579

For an initial outlay of £10,000, the company obtains payback in a little over two years - the cash flows over the first two years of operation total (£7,150 + £2,579) = £9,729. More precisely, the payback period is:

$$2 \text{ years} + \frac{£10,000 - £9,729}{£2,579}$$

= 2.11 years ie, 2 years and 40 days. (TN 3)

However, it should be noted that this degree of precision is probably spurious as it assumes daily cash flows.

The new policy thus appears beneficial, suggesting a high return on investment, although the savings appear minor in absolute terms. However, if these are replicated across a wide spectrum of supplies, considerably higher profits may be generated.

(c)   The payback method compares the period over which the initial outlay of a project is expected to be recovered with some arbitrarily-defined required payback period. If the former period is less than the stipulated time span, the project is acceptable.

This method, although crude, does serve some useful purposes which explains why so many companies, large and small, continue to use it:

(i)   It is simple to operate and to understand, and is thus appealing in firms lacking the resources to conduct more sophisticated analyses.

(ii)   For the same reason, it may be a useful device for communicating information about the minimum requirements for an acceptable project. For example, a minimum required return of 20% approximates to a five-year payback period.

(iii)   It is useful as a screening device to sift out obviously unfeasible projects from those which merit more detailed scrutiny.

(iv)   Under capital rationing, it may be desirable to bias selection in favour of projects which offer a rapid rate of return cash flow in order to provide capital for later investment projects.

(v)   It is an important safeguard against two forms of risk. First, by minimising the period over which capital is exposed to risk of non-recovery, the firm is better protected against the risks of market failure or entry into its markets by new competitors. Second, by favouring projects with a quick and early return and thus enhancing short-term liquidity, it lowers the risk of inability to meet financial obligations as they fall due.

The major limitations of the payback method are that it does not consider expected cash flows in all future periods, and ignores the timing of cash flows. More specifically, it fails to consider the time value of money. As a result, it gives an indication neither of the project's profitability nor the contribution which it is expected to make to shareholders' wealth. Theoreticians thus prefer the use of discounted cash flow methods, although payback clearly has its uses, especially in simple investment situations such as this.

Did you answer the question?

Note the structure of this answer - an initial description of the method, then a discussion of its merits or uses, followed by its limitations. This gives a balanced answer to the requirement.

Tutorial notes

1   Average stock is half the order size, as stock levels are assumed to fluctuate evenly between this maximum (when an order has just been delivered) to a minimum of zero (just before the order arrives)

2   Note that, for each EOQ, the annual holding costs and order costs are equal - you can use this fact to check your answers.

3 | Whereas it is reasonable to assume that cost savings accrue evenly over a year, tax is a single annual payment. After two years $(10,000 - 9,729) = £271$ is still to be recovered. The annual cost saving is £3,850. The payback period is $2 + \dfrac{271}{3,850} = 2.07$ years.

65 (Answer 4 of examination)

Examiner's comments and marking guide

Question 4: (a) This question required candidates to apply marginal cost principles to calculate the break-even point and budgeted profit for the actual sales volume.

This should not have been too problematic but though most knew the formula candidates failed to gain marks when they used actual contribution or actual fix costs. Similarly, some failed to use the actual sales volume to calculate the budgeted profit or failed to adjust for the stock value and hence failed to gain marks.

(b) **This part required calculation and comment on the manufacturing volume variance, followed by calculation of the variance on selling overheads.**

A number of candidates managed to calculate the variance (most were able to identify the volume difference) but failed to make any comment about the variance, this resulted in failure to pick up all the available marks in part *(i)*. In part *(ii)* most candidates had some idea about these variances but the most common error was attempting to flex the fixed overhead in calculating the expenditure variance and this inevitably cost marks.

(c) **This part involved reconciliation of profits using selected variances.**

Candidates needed to include the appropriate variances from the calculations above, the sales price variance and the difference in the basis of the valuation of stock. The most frequent omission was the stock value difference and was therefore the cause of marks being missed, the sales price variance was quite frequently well spotted, and some expenditure variances were included. Candidates who did not make any attempt to explain the reason for the profit difference failed to gain all the marks available.

This was the least popular question in this section and perhaps the least well done, however, some candidates demonstrated good understanding and earned some useful marks in the question. Some were clearly note confident with the calculations which are fundamental to this paper.

			Marks	
(a)	BEP		1	
	Budgeted profit		2	
	Total		3	
(b)	(i)	MW	2	
		Explain	3	
			5	
	(ii)	1 mark each variance	3	
			3	
(c)		Sales price variance		2
		Stock adjustment		2
		Overall reconciliation		2
		Comment		3
	Total			9
	Grand total			20

(**Step by step answer plan**)

Step 1 Read the question again and make sure that you focus on precisely what is required. This question is an examination of the absorption and marginal costing approaches within the context of a variance analysis exercise.

Step 2 (a) The analysis of costs between fixed and variable elements is basically done for you - it is mainly a question of combining the manufacturing and selling costs for each element, in order to obtain a standard marginal cost of sales per unit and the total period budgeted fixed costs. These are then used in the computation of break-even, and predicted loss for the *actual* sales level.

Step 3 (b) (i) The proof of the volume variance given is fairly straightforward, but 3 out of the 5 marks are for the explanation of its significance - don't miss this out. Just a quick explanation as to how it arises will get some marks, even if you're not sure of how it may be useful information.

Step 4 (b) (ii) The variable selling overhead variance is purely an expenditure (or rate) variance - based upon *actual sales* volume. When considering the fixed overhead variances, this could in fact be restricted to just the expenditure variance (*budget* total cost versus actual) as the profit statement could imply that it is not absorbed into units sold but treated as a period cost. It is, however, possible to compute a volume variance if this is not assumed - and the marks indicate that this is required.

Step 5 (c) This part of the question is the explanation of why a *budgeted* loss, using *marginal costing* principles (calculated in (a)) turns to a profit when *actual* values and *absorption costing* is used. A moment of thought before launching into the mechanics should identify two basic reasons for this - one is the differences between budgeted and actual revenues/costs (as highlighted by variances) and the other is stock valuation (the overriding factor in this case).

You have already got some variances from the question and (b); the only additional variance required is sales price (sales margin volume is not required as you are starting with budgeted loss for *actual* sales), and you also don't need fixed cost volume variances (TN 3). The remaining reconciling item is the difference in stock valuation under marginal and absorption costing. Finally, don't lose the last 3 marks by failing to explain what you have shown (or attempted to show) with your figures.

Step 6 Now review your answer and ensure that it does precisely answer the question as set.

(**The examiner's answer**)

(a) Break-even point (TN 1)

$$= \frac{£140,000}{£17 - £7.50} = \frac{£140,000}{£9.50}$$

$$= 14,737\text{kg}$$

			£
Sales	12,400kg × £17		210,800
Marginal costs	12,400kg × £7.50		93,000
			117,800
Fixed costs			140,000
Loss			22,200

(b)   (i)   Manufacturing volume variance:

Budgeted volume	20,000kg
Actual volume	18,400kg
	1,600kg
Manufacturing fixed overhead rate (TN 3)	£5.00
Volume variance	£8,000

The volume variance is caused by the month's actual production level falling below the volume that was used to compute the fixed overhead recovery rate. It is an under-recovery of fixed overhead, which the company has charged against the profits for period 1. It does not specifically represent an extra cost or a loss to the company as these fixed costs would be incurred anyway. It acts as a convenient reconciliation (a book-keeping bridge) between the budgeted and actual volume of the period. It occurs because an absorption costing system identifies fixed overhead costs with products based on a unit rate.

(ii)   Variable selling overhead:

		£
12,400 × £1.5	=	18,600
Incurred		17,500
Expenditure variance		1,100 Fav.

Fixed selling overhead:
Recovered:

		£
12,400 × £2	=	24,800
Budget		40,000
Volume variance		15,200 Adv.
Budget		40,000
Incurred		38,300
Expenditure variance		1,700 Fav.

NB: Different approaches are acceptable and note that not all of these values are used in part (c).

	£	£
(c) Predicted loss		22,200
Expenditure variances		
Manufacturing	5,500 A	
Variable sales	1,100 F	
Fixed sales	1,700 F	
Selling price variance	2,000 A	
Fixed overhead carried		
forward in stock value	30,000 F	
		25,300
Actual profit		3,100

The reconciliation is achieved when all the differences between the two statements are accounted for. This involves expenditure variances which were not in the budgeted statement (a) but were adjusted in the profit statement given. It is not appropriate to adjust for volume variances as both statements ultimately reflect the actual fixed costs and these are the only costs to which volume variances apply. (TN 3)

The actual profit statement reports the sales value of £208,800 but 12,400 units at a standard price of £17 should return £210,800 so a price variance of £2,000 is deduced.

Finally, and most significantly, a variable costing statement applies variable manufacturing costs only to stock values. An absorption costing statement, which the company uses for reporting purposes, values stock at full manufacturing cost. The production and sales levels for P1 imply 6,000kg were added to stock, therefore a difference between the two stock values accounts for a difference in profit. The absorption costing statement is adjusted (relieved of cost) by the fixed overhead carried forward in the increased stock value. That is 6,000kg at £5 per kg fixed overhead rate, £30,000. By allowing for the direction of these adjustments a reconciliation is achieved.

Did you answer the question?

A third of the marks are for this explanation. All the examiner has done is go through all the adjusting items in the reconciliation statement and explain how they have arisen in words, concentrating on the most significant factor, the stock valuation.

Tutorial notes

1    $\text{Break-even} = \dfrac{\text{Budgeted fixed costs}}{\text{Standard contribution per unit}}$ both elements including selling costs

2    $\text{Manufacturing fixed overhead absorption rate} = \dfrac{\text{Budgeted cost}}{\text{Budgeted production}} = \dfrac{£100,000 = £5}{240,000/12}$

3   The predicted loss has been calculated on a marginal costing basis, thus reflecting the budgeted fixed costs as a lump sum rather than on a cost per unit basis. The volume variance is only required where the absorption costing system is used to predict profit/loss and there is an over/under absorption of fixed costs caused by actual and budgeted production volumes differing. The £30,000 is not really a variance in (c) so much as a difference in stock valuations.

---

66   (Answer 5 of examination)

Question 5: (a) This section involved the calculation and comparison of profit for different sales outlets using different bases of cost allocation.

The calculations were not too challenging given the level of this paper, so that candidates who selected the question were able to gain a considerable proportion of the marks available for this. There was some evidence of poor use of time when candidates used many repetitive calculations to achieve the profit, especially in part *(i)*. However, candidates failed to pick up some of the other marks available because of poor or insufficient explanation, comment and discussion. They had a reasonable explanation of cost driver, though volume and complexity issues were not well understood, relying on general rather than accounting knowledge. In section *(ii)* comment was too brief, relying mainly on commenting that store C had incurred a loss but not developing this point.

(b)   **This section required brief comment on the use of statistical techniques in cost allocation.**

Some candidates ignored this part or explained the technique, where a little thought would have suggested some reasonable ideas for its relevance and application, which was required.

			Marks
(a)	(i)	Calculations	1
		Explain drivers, etc	3
		Comment on result	2
			—
			6
			—

(ii)	Calculations	4
	Improved allocation?	3
	Results (effect on C, etc)	4
		11

(b)	Regression	1
	r^2	1
	Elaboration	1
	Total	3
	Grand total	20

Step by step answer plan

Step 1   Read the question again and make sure that you focus on precisely what is required. It examines the area of overhead allocation bases, comparing a "blanket" allocation basis for all overheads lumped together, with a more "scientific" method, involving looking at the individual component costs and considering how they may be more fairly allocated. It uses principles and terminology that should be familiar from an awareness of activity based costing (ABC), although here we are looking at the initial allocation/apportionment of costs to cost centres, rather than absorption into cost units. Ensure you get the easy marks in (a) by preparing your answer in report format.   The reference to 'cost drivers' is really a red herring - we've got bases for apportioning overheads.

Step 2   (a)   (i)   The computations only account for 1 mark, so don't waste time by repeating detail from the question - start with the operating profit figures given, and deduct the allocated overhead costs as a total figure for each store. Explanation of the term "cost driver" should be reasonably straightforward from a rudimentary knowledge of ABC; for what is required for "volume" and "complexity" in both explanation and comment, you must focus on the area of cost allocation and think how these issues can affect it.

Step 3   (a)   (ii)   The apportionment of individual overhead costs between cost centres on different bases is a procedure that should be familiar to you. The relevant bases are fairly obvious from the cost driver information given in the question, with the exception of warehouse costs (depreciation and part of HO costs). Don't waste time worrying about the "right" basis to use, make a rational decision, jot it down, and carry on. Again, the computations account for a minority of the allocated marks - ensure you allow enough time to consider what the figures show. Try not to be too categorical - "this method now produces the correct allocation of costs and shows that store C is unprofitable and must be closed" - as any method of allocating true central shared costs between units will have some arbitrary element and needs to be used with care in decision making. Remember fixed costs are fixed whatever fancy methods are used to split them.

Step 4   (b)   Do not waste any of the very few marks allocated to this part by explaining the mechanics of the techniques themselves; think how they can be applied in this particular context. Discuss both regression and correlation

Step 5   Now review your answer and ensure that it does precisely answer the question as set.

Items not required by the examiner for this question

- description of the mechanics of the derivation of a regression equation or coefficient of determination in (b)

The examiner's answer

(a)   (i)   From: Management accountant

To: Group management

Subject: Reporting store's profits

This report presents the budgeted profits for 1998 of stores A, B and C based on the method of sharing central costs that was originally employed by the group - sales value. As a result of discussions with management at various levels alternative 'drivers' of these costs have been revealed. This is explained and then applied to the results budgeted for 1998, finally drawing some conclusions.

	A £	B £	C £
Central costs	416,667	333,333	250,000
Operating profit	840,000	370,000	290,000
Net profit	423,333	36,667	40,000

(TN1)

Cost drivers are events or activities which result in the incurrence of a cost. They are commonly used to allocate costs to cost objectives or reported and 'managed' in order to 'manage' the costs they influence. It is argued that in many traditional costing systems the cost drivers or allocation bases which were used had 'volume' implications. For example number of units produced or sold, machine hours worked or in our case, sales value. It is clear that there are many other factors which give rise to costs being incurred or resources consumed. It is not only the volume of business but the way that business is done which causes costs. Dealing with a small volume of business in a complex product or for a difficult customer is sometimes more costly than a large volume in a familiar situation. It is important that cost reports reveal this issue of complexity so that management can take steps to deal with any business issues which arise. In the original allocation it is implied that store A which makes the most sales consumes the greatest proportion of the central resources. This need not be the case, it depends on what and how it sells and how it is served by the central resource.

Our company has used sales value to allocate all central costs. It is unlikely that this accurately reflects the way central resources have been consumed by the three stores. The basis seems to be one which is conveniently available and one which is related more to what each store can 'bear' of the central costs rather than any cost causality. It has a tendency to penalise a store if its sales are high eg, store A, it is therefore a discouragement to a better performing store. Additionally, it may influence the accuracy of the budgets in that stores may deliberately understate their budgets in order to attract a lower overhead charge.

Did you answer the question?

This last paragraph covers the last part of the requirement, which might easily be overlooked - the implications of the dissatisfaction expressed. How might the current allocation system influence the behaviour of the store managers, and possibly the performance of their stores?

(ii)   A revised profit for each store is shown below which uses the information obtained from recent discussions with staff at all locations.

	Total £	W'hse Opns. £	A £	B £	C £
Head office					
Salary	200,000	20,000	60,000	60,000	60,000
Advertising	80,000	-	33,333	26,667	20,000
Establishment	120,000	12,000	36,000	36,000	36,000
		32,000			

Warehouse

Depreciation	100,000	-	40,000	30,000	30,000
Storage	80,000		32,000	24,000	24,000
Opns/Desp	120,000)				
Opns/Desp	32,000)		55,000	45,000	52,000
Delivery	300,000		100,000	71,429	128,571
			356,333	293,096	350,571
Operating profit			840,000	370,000	290,000
Net profit/(loss)			483,667	76,904	(60,571)

The revised calculations show that the costs identified with store C exceed the current level of operating profit and an overall loss is disclosed. A and B show improved results based on these allocations. The bases selected are believed to bear a closer relationship to how the resources are consumed in providing service to the three stores. The allocation reflects the benefit they receive rather than their 'ability to bear' the cost. There are however still some costs which will always prove difficult to identify and these inevitably result in an arbitrary allocation (if management requires them to be allocated) eg, advertising. It is useful for management to be aware of this analysis, though they should use it with care, it does not directly make decisions for them. It does not give any information about the efficiency with which store C is managed nor does it indicate that the company would make more profit by closing store C.

Did you answer the question?

The above paragraph discusses *the extent to which* an improvement in information has been achieved. This implies that the new method has some advantages but is still not perfect - you must try to balance your review in this way.

It would be useful to see a trend of this information over a period of years, likewise it would be important to know the extent of competition in the area and the market being served.

In the current situation it may be uneconomic to service C at its present volume. Having made this point C has the smallest gross margin percentage (37%), compared with A (44%). It has a different sales mix or different pricing structure. From the further statistics it is also a difficult store to support. It requires proportionately more despatches and greater delivery distances to be travelled. This information suggests there is scope to rationalise delivery to reduce costs, consider direct delivery from some suppliers, examine vehicle routing schedules etc.

Further investigation and discussion is required before taking any firm decisions but the information presented above has highlighted issues which would not have been disclosed by the allocation method previously adopted.

Did you answer the question?

The examiner has now addressed the requirement to comment on the results - ie to stand back from the mechanics and get an overall picture of how the information may be used to improve results.

(b)   Regression analysis and the use of r^2 would demonstrate the association between some of the central costs and allocation bases proposed. In the case of delivery miles it would be necessary to accumulate cost of delivery for a number of periods, say quarterly for three years and set these against the miles travelled. The value would require adjusting for accruals and inflation over the three year periods. A regression equation would identify the variable and fixed elements of the cost. The coefficient of determination (r^2) would express the degree of association between the variable cost and the delivery miles. A close association between these would produce a value for r^2 of close to 1.

Did you answer the question?

Note here the examiner is explaining how the statistical techniques can be used in the given context, rather than giving a detailed description of how they are carried out.

Tutorial note

1   Time could be saved by working in £'000. A total column would help.

---

67   (Answer 6 of examination)

(**Examiner's comments and marking guide**)

Question 6: (a) This section involved explanation and illustration of the different uses of budgets in different settings.

The understanding of budgets seemed often limited to planning and control so discussion of the other purposes, at times, did not score highly. Budgets as a basis for performance evaluation were covered with reasonable success but the answers in relation to other purposes failed to pick up marks because candidates did little in their writing to demonstrate understanding of these alternative roles. Some discussion took place of the role but without any reference to budgets in this context. Examples were often quite limited, and public sector was sometimes mistaken for public company, candidates did not therefore score highly.

(b)   **This section involved discussion of the benefits and problems of ZBB (zero based budgeting).**

Candidates who failed to appreciate that ZBB applied most to overhead management in the service and support areas failed to earn marks here. Their responses seemed guessed and often limited to it starting from 'scratch' and being time consuming. These were not enough to gain high marks.

		Marks
(a)	4 marks for each part must be clear explanation and example	12
(b)	ZBB explained	3
	Evidence of evaluation	3
	Conclusion/judgement	2
		—
		8
		—
	Total	20
		—

(**Step by step answer plan**)

Step 1   Read the question again and make sure that you focus on precisely what is required. It is a purely written question on budgets. The requirements are quite precise - their use in three areas, with examples from specified types of organisations, and benefits and difficulties of adopting a zero based budgeting (ZBB) approach. It is essential to marshal and order your thoughts before starting to write the answer, to avoid repetition or irrelevance.

Step 2   (a)   Your answer should consist of descriptions of the use of budgets in these areas of management, with illustrative examples from the specified types of organisation. Try to think about an organisation with which you personally are familiar - this will make examples a lot easier to devise. Marks are split equally between the four parts, so try to write something for each - a page on (i) with (ii) and (iii) omitted can only earn a maximum of 4 marks.

Step 3 (b) For 8 marks, you need to give an answer in reasonable depth here. If you do not really know very much about ZBB, do not waffle. Say what you can and move on (or stop!). Try to discuss, however briefly, both benefits and difficulties to maximise marks.

Step 4 Now review your answer and ensure that it does precisely answer the question as set.

Items not required by the examiner for this question

- discussions of the general roles of performance evaluation, resource allocation and authorisation within organisational management

The examiner's answer

(a) (i) Budgets are plans, they set targets for the organisation or sub-units of it (departments or divisions). The achievement of the budget is often delegated to managers in these departments. It is therefore possible to measure the extent to which budget targets are met by managers and in this way they are measures of the managers' performance. It must be understood that there may be dimensions of performance not captured by the budget, but it is a convenient device and it offers relative ease of measurement. However, this may result in the less easily measured dimensions of performance not being measured.

If a person is to be evaluated using budget data, it is important that they have an opportunity to influence budget content but not to bias it in their favour. A department manager of a manufacturing company will be required to achieve a certain number of units of output with a given expenditure on direct material. The variance between actual material cost and the flexible budget (based on actual output) is one way of evaluating how the department has been supervised, machines been set and material controlled, etc.

(ii) Budgets enable the business to estimate the amount of physical and financial resources available over a future period. Information can also be collected on the environment in which the business operates in order to identify any strengths, opportunities etc, which may exist. It is then possible for managers of the organisation to discuss how these resources can be allocated to different parts of the business in order to create an optimal plan.

The management of a bank engage in resource allocation decisions when they decide to undertake more business by phone/mail from a regional office rather than dealing with customers in their individual branches. In their efforts to reduce costs, perhaps to improve on last year's budget, the relocation of some staff/resources into large regional offices and closure of some small branches is an example of resource allocation in this sector.

(iii) In some budget systems expenditure which has passed through the budget review procedure automatically becomes approved for commitment without additional formality. In other words, the identification of an expense for a particular budget centre is the formal approval that the head of the centre may go ahead and incur such an expense. No further detailed control in relation to this would occur until the actual expenditure was reported as part of the financial control system.

A public sector organisation is, for example, the departments of a local authority, social services, housing, education. When the authority meet to set their annual budget this is often based on their assessment of spending need in each area. Once the budget, and its division into each area is set, the officers of the local authority are in a position to incur expenditure in line with budget. The budget is their authorisation to spend up to that amount in providing services to the community.

Did you answer the question?

The examiner has structured his answer in line with the requirements. For each part, he first discusses the general role of budgets in the area being considered, and then picks an example from the type of organisation specified to illustrate the point. Do not be tempted to give detailed comments on the potential problems that may arise - this is not the thrust of the question. You are simply being asked to demonstrate your understanding of how budgets may be used in these ways.

(b)   Traditional budgeting, sometimes called incremental budgeting, takes a current level of spending almost without examination and discussion takes place on any extra expenditure. Zero-based budgeting (ZBB) is an approach which takes nothing for granted. It requires that each budget centre makes a detailed case for all of its budget allocation each year. As a result all spending is subject to scrutiny, not just incremental spending. This technique would not suit expenditure planning in line departments of a manufacturing company because clear relationships of input and output will exist and be defined by standard values. In less clearly defined areas such as service departments or service orientated industries, both private and public sector, it might have some value if selectively applied.

It is possible that economies and increased efficiency could result if departments were to justify all, not just incremental, expenditure. It is argued that if expenditure were examined on a cost/benefit basis a more rational allocation of resources would take place. Such an approach would force managers to make plans and prioritise their activities before committing themselves to the budget. It should achieve a more structured involvement of departmental management and should improve the quality of decisions and management information.

It could be expensive however, in time and effort to analyse all expenditure and difficult to establish priorities for the activities or decision packages. Managers are often reluctant to commit themselves to it because they believe they already do it. Critics have asserted that no real change in fund allocation takes place as a result of the exercise.

Any system which encourages managers to examine and communicate about their spending and performance levels must be useful providing it does not prevent individuals fulfilling their other duties and responsibilities.

Did you answer the question?

Again, note that the examiner has clearly shown how each requirement is being met by the structure of his answer. The marks allocated allow a brief description of ZBB; this is then followed by the possible benefits that may accrue from its use, with difficulties concluding the discussion.

DECEMBER 1997 QUESTIONS

Section A – This question is compulsory and MUST be attempted

68   (Question 1 of examination)

Marton Ltd produces a range of specialised components, supplying a wide range of UK and overseas customers, all on credit terms. 20% of UK turnover is sold to one firm. Having used generous credit policies to encourage past growth, Marton now has to finance a substantial overdraft and is concerned about its liquidity. Marton borrows from its bank at 13% per annum interest. No further sales growth in volume or value terms is planned for the next year.

In order to speed up collection from UK customers, Marton is considering two alternative policies.

Option one

Factoring on a with-recourse, service only basis, the factor administering and collecting payment from Marton's UK customers. This is expected to generate administrative savings of £200,000 per annum and to lower the average debtor collection period by 15 days. The factor will make a service charge of 1% of Marton's UK turnover and also provide credit insurance facilities for an annual premium of £80,000.

Option two

Offering discounts to UK customers who settle their accounts early. The amount of the discount will depend on speed of payment as follows:

Payment within 10 days of despatch of invoices: 3%

Payment within 20 days of despatch of invoices: 1·5%

It is estimated that UK customers representing 20% and 30% of Marton's sales respectively will take up these offers, the remainder continuing to take their present credit period.

Another opportunity arises to engage in a just-in-time stock delivery arrangement with the main UK customer, which normally takes 90 days to settle accounts with Marton. This involves borrowing £0·5m on overdraft to invest in dedicated handling and transport equipment. This would be depreciated over five years on a straight-line basis. The customer is uninterested in the early payment discount but would be prepared to settle after 60 days and to pay a premium of 5% over the present price in exchange for guarantees regarding product quality and delivery. Marton judges the probability of failing to meet these guarantees in any one year at 5%. Failure would trigger a penalty payment of 10% of the value of total sales to this customer (including the premium).

In addition, Marton is concerned about the risk of its overseas earnings. All overseas customers pay in US dollars and Marton does not hedge currency risk, invoicing at the prevailing spot rate, which is currently US$1·45:£1. It is considering the use of an overseas factor and also hedging its US dollar income on the forward market. Its bank has offered to buy all of its dollar earnings at a fixed rate of US$1·55:£1. Marton's advisers estimate the following chances of various dollar/sterling rates of exchange:

US Dollars per £	Probability
1·60	0·1
1·50	0·2
1·45	0·4
1·40	0·2
1·30	0·1

Extracts from Marton's most recent accounts are given overleaf.

	(£000)	(£000)
Sales (all on credit)		
Home	20,000	
Export	5,000	25,000
Cost of sales		(17,000)
Operating profit		8,000
Current assets:		
Stock	2,500	
Debtors*	4,500	
Cash	–	

*There are no overseas debtors at the year end.

Note: Taxes and inflation can be ignored in this question.

Required:

(a)   Calculate the relative costs and benefits *in terms of annual profit before tax* of each of the two proposed methods of reducing domestic debtors, and recommend the most financially advantageous policy. Comment on your results. **(14 marks)**

(b)   Calculate the improvement *in profits before tax* to be expected in the first trading year after entering into the JIT arrangement. Comment on your results. **(8 marks)**

(c)   Suggest the benefits Marton might expect to derive from a JIT agreement in addition to the benefits specified in the question. **(6 marks)**

(d)   Briefly outline the services provided by an overseas factor. **(4 marks)**

(e)   (i)   Calculate the maximum loss which Marton can sustain through movements in the dollar/sterling exchange rate if it does not hedge overseas sales. **(2 marks)**

        (ii)   Calculate the maximum opportunity cost of selling dollar earnings forward at US\$1·55:£1. **(2 marks)**

        (iii)   Briefly discuss whether Marton should hedge its foreign currency risk. **(4 marks)**

(Total: 40 marks)

Section B – ONE question ONLY to be attempted

69   (Question 2 of examination)

Phoenix plc, which manufactures building products, experienced a sharp increase in pre-tax profits from the £25m level in 1995–6 to £40m in 1996–7 as the economy emerged from recession, and demand for new houses increased. The increase in profits has been entirely due to volume expansion, with margins remaining static. It still has substantial excess capacity and therefore no pressing need to invest, apart from routine replacements.

In the past, Phoenix has followed a rather conservative financial policy, with restricted dividend payouts and relatively low borrowing levels. It now faces the issue of how to utilise an unexpectedly sizeable cash surplus. Directors have made two main suggestions. One is to redeem the £10m secured loan stock issued to finance a capacity increase several years previously, the other is to increase the dividend payment by the same amount.

Phoenix's present capital structure is shown below:

	£m
Issued share capital (25p par value)	70
Reserves	130
Creditors falling due after more than one year:	
7% secured loan stock 2007	10

Further information

(i) Phoenix has not used an overdraft during the two years.

(ii) The rate of corporate tax is 33%.

(iii) The dividend paid by Phoenix in 1995–6 was 1·50 pence per share.

(iv) Sector averages currently stand as follows:

dividend cover	2·6 times
gearing (long-term debt/equity)	45%
interest cover	6·5 times

(v) Advance corporation tax can be ignored in this question.

Required:

(a) Calculate the dividend payout ratios and dividend covers for *both* 1995–6 *and* for the reporting year 1996–7, if the dividend is raised as proposed. **(6 marks)**

(b) You have recently been hired to work as a financial strategist for Phoenix, reporting to the finance director. Using the information provided, write a report to your superior, which identifies and discusses the relative merits of the two proposals for utilising the cash surplus. **(14 marks)**

(Total: 20 marks)

---

70 (Question 3 of examination)

Blackwater plc, a manufacturer of speciality chemicals, has been reported to the anti-pollution authorities on several occasions in recent years, and fined substantial amounts for making excessive toxic discharges into local rivers. Both the environmental lobby and Blackwater's shareholders demand that it clean up its operations.

It is estimated that the total fines it may incur over the next four years can be summarised by the following probability distribution (all figures are expressed in present values):

Level of fine	Probability
£0·5m	0·3
£1·4m	0·5
£2·0m	0·2

Filta & Strayne Ltd (FSL), a firm of environmental consultants, has advised that new equipment costing £1m can be installed to virtually eliminate illegal discharges. Unlike fines, expenditure on pollution control equipment is tax-allowable via a 25% writing-down allowance (reducing balance). The rate of corporate tax is 33%, paid with a one-year delay. The equipment will have no resale value after its expected four-year working life, but can be in full working order immediately prior to Blackwater's next financial year.

A European Union Common Pollution Policy grant of 25% of gross expenditure is available, but with payment delayed by a year. Immediately on receipt of the grant from the EU, Blackwater will pay 20% of the grant to FSL as commission. These transactions have no tax implications for Blackwater.

A disadvantage of the new equipment is that it will raise production costs by £30 per tonne over its operating life. Current production is 10,000 tonnes per annum, but expected to grow by 5% per annum compound. It can be assumed that other production costs and product price are constant over the next four years. No change in working capital is envisaged.

Blackwater applies a discount rate of 12% after all taxes to investment projects of this nature. All cash inflows and outflows occur at year ends.

Required:

(a) Calculate the expected net present value of the investment assuming a four-year operating period. Briefly comment on your results. **(12 marks)**

(b) Write a memorandum to Blackwater's management as to the desirability of the project, taking into account both financial and non-financial criteria. **(8 marks)**

(Total: 20 marks)

Section C – TWO questions ONLY to be attempted

71 (Question 4 of examination)

A company is proposing the introduction of an activity-based costing (ABC) system as a basis for much of its management accounting information.

(a) Briefly describe how ABC is different from a traditional absorption approach to costing and explain why it was developed. **(8 marks)**

(b) Discuss the advantages and limitations of this 'approach based on activities' for management accounting information in the context of:

   (i)   preparing plans and budgets

   (ii) monitoring and controlling operations

   (iii) decision-making, for example, product deletion decisions. **(12 marks)**

(Total: 20 marks)

72 (Question 5 of examination)

A company operates a number of hairdressing establishments which are managed on a franchise arrangement. The franchisor offers support using a PC package which deals with profit budgeting and control information.

Budget extracts of one franchisee for November 1997 are shown below analysed by male and female clients. For the purposes of budget projections average revenue rates are used. At the month end these are compared with the average monthly rates actually achieved using variance analysis. Sales price, sales quantity, sales mix and cost variances are routinely produced in order to compare the budget and actual results.

Staff working in this business are paid on a commission basis in order to act as an incentive to attract and retain clients. The labour rate variance is based on the commission payments, any basic pay is part of the monthly fixed cost.

Budget

	Male	Female
Clients	4,000	1,000
Average revenue (per client)	£ 7·5	£ 18·0
Average commission (per client)	3·0	10·0
Total monthly fixed cost	£20,000	

Actual results

	Male	Female
Clients	2,000	2,000

Average revenue	£	£
(per client)	8·0	20·0
Average commission		
(per client)	3·5	11·0
Total monthly fixed cost	£24,000	

Required:

(a) Reconcile the budgeted and actual profit for November by calculating appropriate price, quantity, mix and cost variances, presenting the information in good form. You should adopt a contribution style, with mix variances based on units (i.e. clients). **(10 marks)**

(b) Write a short memorandum to the manager of the business commenting on the result in (a) above **(4 marks)**

(c) Comment on the limitations associated with generating sales variances as in (a) above. **(6 marks)**

(Total: 20 marks)

---

73 (Question 6 of examination)

A firm manufactures two products EXE and WYE in departments dedicated exclusively to them. There are also three service departments, stores, maintenance and administration. No stocks are held as the products deteriorate rapidly.

Direct costs of the products, which are variable in the context of the whole business, are identified to each department. The step-wise apportionment of service department costs to the manufacturing departments is based on estimates of the usage of the service provided. These are expressed as percentages and assumed to be reliable over the current capacity range. The general factory overheads of £3·6m, which are fixed, are apportioned based on floor space occupied. The company establishes product costs based on budgeted volume and marks up these costs by 25% in order to set target selling prices.

Extracts from the budgets for 1998 are provided below:

	Annual volume (units)	
	EXE	WYE
Max capacity	200,000	100,000
Budget	150,000	70,000

	EXE	*WYE*	*Stores*	*Maintenance*	*Admin*
Costs (£m)					
Material	1·8	0·7	0·1	0·1	
Other variable	0·8	0·5	0·1	0·2	0·2
Departmental usage (%)					
Maintenance	50	25	25		
Administration	40	30	20	10	
Stores	60	40			
Floor space (sq m)					
	640	480	240	80	160

Required:

Workings may be £'000 with unit prices to the nearest penny.

(a)   Calculate the budgeted selling price of one unit of EXE and WYE based on the usual mark up.

(5 marks)

(b)   Discuss how the company may respond to each of the following independent events, which represent additional business opportunities:

(i)   an enquiry from an overseas customer for 3,000 units only of WYE where a price of £35 per unit is offered

(ii)   an enquiry for 50,000 units of WYE to be supplied in full at regular intervals during 1998 at a price which is equivalent to full cost plus 10%

In both cases support your discussion with calculations and comment on any assumptions or matters on which you would seek clarification.   **(11 marks)**

(c)   Explain the implications of preparing product full costs based on maximum capacity rather than annual budget volume.

(4 marks)

(Total: 20 marks)

ANSWERS TO DECEMBER 1997 EXAMINATION

68   (Answer 1 of examination)

Examiner's comments and marking guide

(a) **This question required candidates to compute the relative impact on profitability of two methods of debtor management.**

Candidates often scored good marks on this section, frequently more than half of their tally for the whole question. Common errors were to ignore reduction in debtors entirely, especially regarding the discount option, to fail to convert debtor days reduction into interest savings, and the application of the reduction in debtor days to debtors rather than to sales. The commentary on the results obtained was frequently creditable.

(b) **This question required candidates to calculate the improvement in profits via the introduction of a JIT scheme.**

Although most candidates identified bank overdraft interest and depreciation, most answers were incomplete in some respect – omission of interest savings due to lower debtors being the most frequent missing item. Many lowered debtor days to 30 days rather than by 30 days, and the majority failed to specify the correct penalty payment. Some candidates essayed a DCF approach in defiance of the wording of the question, and some attempted to mix in the JIT savings with the two options in part (a), either in this section itself or in the previous one.

(c) **This question required candidates to suggest benefits which the supplier might gain from JIT.**

This threw most candidates, who took the wrong perspective by listing those benefits likely to be enjoyed by the recipient of goods. Although some marks were awarded for this, little credit could be awarded for simply a standard outline of JIT benefits, unrelated to the question. Even where the supplier's perspective was adopted, most candidates simply repeated the benefits specified in the question itself. Mentions of TQM, enhanced relationships and the opportunity to enhance business with this and other clients were infrequent. Some candidates listed the negative aspects of JIT which were not required.

(d) **This question required an outline of the services of overseas factors.**

While it is true to say that an overseas factor does provide similar services to those of domestic factors (and credit was given for discussing these), the question required mention of services specific to overseas operations in order to achieve the higher marks. Some simply commented on foreign exchange management services.

(e) **This question required candidates to calculate prospective losses/opportunity costs contingent on exchange rate variations, and to advise whether the company in the question should hedge.**

Probably the most important aspect of managing overseas debtors is the problem of exchange rate fluctuations prior to payment. This issue has been flagged up by the examiner on several occasions and students should have had a greater awareness than displayed of both the issue itself and of the nature of a forward contract, perhaps the simplest hedge available. Marks were hard-won, with credit being given to those candidates who showed awareness of the dangers imposed by exchange rate variability and who understood in which direction the risks of losses/opportunity costs lay i.e. in part (i), dollar depreciation is a bad outcome whereas in part (ii), dollar appreciation involves an opportunity cost.

Answers to part (iii) were often totally unrelated to the hedge cited in the question, which looks unattractive compared to expectations about the exchange rate. Better answers pointed to the symmetry of the risks around the central value of the distribution but questioned the reliability of such probabilistic estimates, suggesting that the safest policy for a trading company, as opposed to a profit-seeking currency speculator, is usually to hedge.

		Marks
(a)	*Factoring:*	
	Reduction in debtors	1
	Interest savings	1
	Service charge	1
	Net benefit	2
		5

Discount:

Debtor collection period before and after	2
Average debtors	1
Interest savings	1
Cost of the discount	1
Net benefit	2
	7
Decision/Discussion/Comment	2
	14 marks

(b) *JIT*

New sales level	1
Calculation of interest savings	2
Penalty cost	1
Interest cost	1
Depreciation	1
Net benefit	1
Comment	1
	8 marks

(c) One mark for each substantive point, rising to two marks according to quality of discussion.

6 marks

(d)

Identification of overseas factors	1
Recognition of similar services	1
Provision of advice on creditworthiness	1
Access to open account trading	1
	4 marks

(e) **(i)**

Recognition of direction of danger (i.e.) dollar falls	0·5
Calculation	1·5
	2 marks

(ii)

Recognition of direction of danger (i.e.) dollar rises	0·5
Calculation	1·5
	2 marks

(iii)

Risk symmetry in long term	2
Concern for prudence by small companies/for major risks	2
	4 marks

Total 40 marks

Step by step answer plan

Step 1 Read the question again and make sure that you focus on precisely what is required. In the context of a medium-sized manufacturing company with both UK and export sales, it covers a variety of areas, including: management of debtors, just in time, foreign exchange risk and hedging.

Step 2 (a) These types of evaluations arise quite frequently in this exam, and tend to involve the same basic computations - interest saving from reduced debtors, discount costs, service charges etc. The first of these is often overlooked, although it can be one of the most significant savings arising. The approach is to first ascertain the amount by which (average) debtor days have been reduced, then multiply this by average daily sales to find debtor reduction. The interest saving can then be calculated. When commenting upon your results, state the conclusion based initially on the figures alone, then consider the validity of the assumptions used.

Step 3 (b) This is really just another method of management of debtors, and a very similar approach to that used in (a) should be taken - cost versus benefits. Go through each line of text in the relevant paragraph of the question, noting the general impact on costs or revenues of each piece of information given. Then evaluate them on an expected value basis where necessary, using the interest rates and probabilities provided. In the comments, when computations involve expected values, it is always worth considering the possible impact of the best and/or worst *actual* outcomes arising.

Step 4 (c) You have to stop and think carefully before answering this to avoid wasting time on irrelevancies. The main point to note is that you are looking at this from the *supplier's* viewpoint, rather than the customer's, for which you may have a standard list of benefits.

Step 5 (d) There are two aspects here - 'factor' and 'overseas'. The first requires a brief description of the general services a factor offers, and the second requires specific additional benefits that an overseas factor will bring.

Step 6 (e)(i) Which way will the exchange rate need to move to make a loss? A loss means getting less £ for the $ receipt than currently offered; this means a lower £/$ rate, or a higher $/£ rate. So look at the effects of the highest rate given.

(e)(ii) An opportunity cost will arise if the actual future spot rate is such that it yields a greater £ value for a $ receipt than the forward rate. This will be if the £/$ rate is higher, or the $/£ rate is lower. So here we compare the £ value at 1.55 with that at the lowest rate given.

A good answer to (iii) will consider the specific circumstances of the hedge in the question as well as the general pros and cons of hedging.

Step 7 Now review your answer and ensure that it does precisely answer the question as set.

The examiner's answer

(It should be noted that the following answers are probably fuller than would be expected from the average candidate under exam conditions. Answers are provided in this degree of detail on the principle of offering guidance on the approach required, and on the range and depth of knowledge that would be expected from an excellent candidate).

(a)   The relative costs and benefits of each option are calculated as follows:

Option 1 – Factoring
Reduction in debtor days =   15 days

Reduction in debtors $= \dfrac{15}{365} \times £20m$

$= £821,916$

Effect on profit before tax:

Interest saving	$= (13\% \times £821,916)$	$= £106,849$
Administrative savings		$= £200,000$
Service charge	$= (1\% \times £20m)$	$= (£200,000)$
Insurance premium		$= (£80,000)$
Net profit benefit		$= £26,849$

Option 2 – The discount
With year-end debtors at £4·5m, the debtor collection period was:

£4·5m/£20m × 365 = 82 days.

The scheme of discounts would change this as follows:

10 days for 20% of customers
20 days for 30% of customers
82 days for 50% of customers

Average debtor days becomes:
(20% × 10) + (30% × 20) + (50% × 82) = 49 days
Hence, average debtors would reduce from the present £4·5m to:
49 × £20m/365 = £2,684,932
The interest saving would be:
13% × (£4·5m – £2·685m)   = £235,950
The cost of the discount would be:
(3% × 20% × £20m) + (1·5% × 30% × £20m) = (£210,000)
The net benefit to profit before tax would be:
(£235,950 – £210,000)   = £25,950

The figures imply that factoring is marginally the more attractive but this result relies on the predicted proportions of customers actually taking up the discount and paying on time. It also neglects the possibility that some customers will insist on taking the discount without bringing forward their payments. Marton would have to consider a suitable response to this problem.

Conversely, the assessment of the value of using the factor depends on the factor lowering Marton's debtor days. If the factor retains these benefits for itself, rather than passing them on to Marton, this will raise the cost of the factoring option. The two parties should clearly specify their mutual requirements from the factoring arrangement on a contractual basis.

(b) *The JIT arrangement*

Existing sales to customer	$= 20\% \times £20m$	$= £4m$
Enhanced sales with premium	$= £4m (1 + 5\%)$	$= £4\cdot2m$
Reduction in debtors	$= 30/365 \times £4m$	$= £328,767$
Interest saving $= £328,767 \times 13\%$		$= £42,740$ (a)
Sales increase		$= £200,000$ (b)
Expected value of penalty cost:		
	$= 5\% \times 10\% \times £4\cdot2m$	$= (£21,000)$ (c)
Bank interest	$= 13\% \times £0\cdot5m$	$= (£65,000)$ (d)
Increased depreciation	$= £0\cdot5m/5$	$= (£100,000)$ (e)
Net change in profit (items a − e)		$=$ £56,740

Thus, participation in the JIT arrangement appears to be worthwhile. However, it should be noted that although the chance of having to pay the penalty is low, if it *is* triggered, the resulting penalty of $(10\% \times £4\cdot2m) = £420,000$ represents a sizeable proportion (over 5%) of total profit. It may thus be prudent to insure against this risk, the premium payable lowering the net benefits of JIT.

(c) In addition to a higher price and quicker settlement by its main customer, such a JIT agreement offers several benefits to the supplier of goods. Among these are:

– A guaranteed order from a major customer will facilitate output planning and the ordering of materials as inputs into its own production. Marton may be able to négotiate JIT arrangements with its own suppliers using the experience gained.

– The close cooperation inherent in a JIT agreement may encourage Marton and its customer to engage in joint research and development into planning future products.

– The experience gained in supplying a major customer may give Marton the confidence and reputation to negotiate JIT agreements with other customers.

Did you answer the question?

This answer meets the requirements of the question in three ways – it takes the *supplier's* view, it looks at benefits *other* than those in the question, and does not consider the *disadvantages*.

(d) Many overseas factors are subsidiaries of UK banks or their agents, which offer facilities to companies with export credit sales usually of above £0·25m. Overseas factors perform largely the same range of functions as factors in UK markets, namely debt collection and administration of accounts payable and provision of finance.

An additional and highly valuable service particularly for smaller firms without large overseas forces is the provision of advice on the creditworthiness of overseas customers, using their own experience, or tapping the expertise of agents who act on their behalf in the pursuit of debts.

If factoring is provided on a non-recourse basis, the factor will bear the risk of bad debts, thus enabling the exporter to sell on open account without risk of default. Even allowing for the additional charge made by the factor, this may well be a much cheaper means of arranging overseas transactions than more formal methods such as letters of credit.

(e) (i) From Marton's viewpoint, an adverse outcome is depreciation of the dollar against sterling as this lowers its income when converted into sterling. The worst outcome is thus an exchange rate of US$1·60:£1.

At present, its dollar income is £5m × 1·45 = $7·25m. At US$1·60: £1, its sterling income would fall to $7·25m/1·60 = £4·53m. Hence, the worst outcome is a loss (compared to the current rate) of (£0·47m).

(ii) If Marton hedges all its expected dollar income over the next year at US1\$1·55: £1, this will generate guaranteed (ignoring other sources of risk) sterling income of \$7·25m/1·55 = £4·68m. If the actual rate of exchange moved to US\$1·3: £1, it would have made sterling earnings of £5·58m. This indicates an opportunity cost of hedging of £0·90m.

(iii) In theory, foreign exchange earnings should not be hedged, as the chances of an adverse movement are equivalent to those of a favourable one, so that in the long-term, exporters like Marton should break even. This can be inferred from the figures above – the chances of the dollar appreciating are equal to the chances of it depreciating against sterling (30%).

Did you answer the question?

Note how the examiner has related the answer to the scenario under consideration.

Indeed, when allowance is made for the wider spread between the rates at which banks will buy and sell currency as between spot and forward transactions, use of the forward market is more costly. However, failure to hedge can leave firms exposed to the risk of erratically large adverse currency movements, perhaps large enough to bankrupt the smaller firm. So, although the risks in the long-term are roughly symmetrical, many companies deem it prudent to hedge at least some part of their overseas earnings, especially those relating to major contracts.

69 (Answer 2 of examination)

Examiner's comments and marking guide

(a) **This question required candidates to calculate simple investor ratios before and after a change in dividend policy.**

Considerable latitude was extended in marking this question, according to whether candidates treated the profits figure given as before or after interest payments. Yet despite this, the marks were very poor, as it appears that candidates are simply unable to compute simple ratios. For example, many calculated the payout ratios out of pre-tax profits and many offered a dividend yield based on the par value of the shares or stated the dividend per share. Common errors were not to increase the dividend at all or to double it.

(b) **This question required candidates to write a report to a superior evaluating two proposed changes in financial policy.**

The standard of answer was very disappointing, often extending to little beyond statements such as "gearing will fall", if debt is repaid, or "shareholders will be happy", if dividends are raised. Answers were often not presented in report format as instructed, and the content was invariably superficial. Candidates seemed unaware of the contemporary cash surpluses facing many companies, not just in the UK, and failed to appreciate the options open to such companies. All too frequently, it was difficult to find beyond a handful of marks for those who gave comparative calculations, although even here, candidates often treated the industry ratios given as if they applied to the company in the question.

		Marks
(a)	Calculation of previous dividend	1
	previous PAT	1
	previous cover/payout ratio	1
	new PAT	1
	new cover/payout ratio	1
	Comment	1
		6
(b)	Format	1
	Introductory comments	1
	Dividend increase:	
	for each valid point plus discussion, one mark to	max 5
	Debt repayment:	
	for each valid point plus discussion, one mark to	max 5
	Comment/assessment	2
		14

Total 20 marks

Step by step answer plan

Step 1 Read the question again and make sure that you focus on precisely what is required. This examines the possible uses of a cash surplus, including an increase in dividend.

Step 2 (a) The dividend payout ratio and dividend cover both relate the amount *available* for dividends (post-tax profits) to the amount actually *paid* - one is the inverse of the other. It is not clear whether the pre-tax profit figures given in the question are after interest or not - the examiner was happy with either assumption.

Step 3 (b) First, your answer must be in report format, with appropriate titles for writer and recipient, as indicated in the question. Second, it needs a good structure - introduction, main content, conclusion. Thirdly, it needs to focus on the two uses specified for the cash surplus, and fourthly it needs to incorporate the data given in the question where this supports or adds to the points being made. Try to take a commercial and practical view of the effect, say, of increasing dividends so substantially in the current economic environment and the particular circumstances of Phoenix.

Step 4 Now review your answer and ensure that it does precisely answer the question as set.

The examiner's answer

(a) *Payout ratios/Dividend cover*

In 1995–6, the dividend was 1·50p per share, making a total payout of £70m × 4 × 1·50p = £4·2m. The profit after tax (£m) was:

Operating profit	25·00
Interest	(0·70)
Taxable profit	24·30
Tax at 33%	(8·02)
Profit after tax	16·28

% Payout £4·20m/£16·28m = 26%

Dividend cover   = 3·9 times

If the present cash balances are used to increase the dividend by £10m, making a total dividend of (£4·20m + £10m) = £14·20m, the figures will appear thus:

Operating profit	40·00
Interest	(0·70)
Taxable profit	39·30
Tax at 33%	(12·97)
Profit after tax	26·33

% Payout £14·20m/£26·33m = 54%

Dividend cover   = 1·9 times

This represents a substantial fall in dividend cover, from significantly above the sector average to well below it. Such an apparent shift in dividend policy is bound to provoke comment both from shareholders and also from the market in general.

(b)

Report to:	The Finance Director.
Subject:	Utilisation of excess cash balances.
From:	Financial Strategist.
Date:	Anyday.

1   Introduction

Phoenix has built up significant cash balances over the past year as a result of exceptional growth in sales and profits as the economy has recovered from recession, sparking demand for the high quality building products in which we specialise. There are several possible uses for surplus cash balances such as investment in the short-term money market and acquisition of other companies. However, my remit is to consider only two such uses, firstly, an increase in dividends and secondly, early repayment of the long-term loan stock, repayable in 2007. This report will consider each of these in turn.

2   Dividend increase

The factors which will need to be considered and investigated are as follows:

(i)   *The preferences of our shareholders.* Many shareholders will have purchased Phoenix shares rather than those of competing companies with higher payouts not for dividend payments but for long-term capital growth. In the past, we have served their interests by restricting dividends and ploughing back profits into the business. We will need to consider how they are likely to respond to such a sharp shift in our distribution policy, albeit due to lack of investment opportunities.

(ii)   *Shareholders' tax position.* A major determinant of shareholders' preferences is their liability to tax. Some institutional shareholders enjoy tax advantages from distribution, while some private shareholders, perhaps the majority, prefer capital gains to dividends because of the tax advantages attaching to the former. This factor underlines the need to inspect our shareholder register and to consult with major shareholders.

(iii)   *Actual and expected liquidity.* Phoenix is highly liquid at present and there are no plans to engage in significant capital expenditures. However, it is prudent to examine our medium to long-term capital requirements to ascertain whether the monies concerned are best left on deposit so as to avoid having to mount a major capital-raising exercise in the future. By the same token, group cash flow forecasts will need examination to identify any major demands for cash of a non-capital nature e.g. closure costs, in the foreseeable future.

(iv)   *Loan covenants.* It is proposed to lower dividend cover significantly. Our lawyers will have to inspect the terms of our long-term loan outstanding to discover whether there are any restrictions on dividend payouts.

(v)   *Stock market reaction.* The proposal is to more than triple dividend payments. Clearly, this represents a major departure from past policy and raises several issues. Presumably, we will present this payment as a special dividend of the kind paid by certain UK utility companies in recent years in order to dampen any expectations of similar increases in the future. This would best be done by paying it at a different time to the regular dividend. However, this begs the tactical question of the extent to which the 'normal' final dividend should be raised. If the normal dividend is also raised significantly, this will signal directors' confidence in our ability to sustain future payments and thus exert pressure on the company to meet these expectations. Given that our earnings are cyclical and have recently been depressed, it is important that we settle on a dividend payout policy which we feel confident of maintaining through the various phases of the business cycle. The stock market tends to be unforgiving of companies which cut dividends.

> **Did you answer the question?**
>
> Note how the examiner has made the standard points about changes in dividend policy, but has tailored them to fit with Phoenix's circumstances. You must always try to show how points you make are relevant to the particular company concerned.

3   Repayment of the loan stock

(i)   *Conditions of the loan.* Again, we must scrutinise the terms of the loan to ascertain whether early payment is permitted at all and whether it triggers any penalties.

(ii)   *The tax shield.* If we repay the loan, we will lose the benefit of the tax relief accorded to debt interest payments. Admittedly, the tax saving is not substantial. i.e. $33\% \times 7\% \times £10m = £0.23m$, but it is nevertheless worth while. Given our recent increase in profitability, and assuming this can be sustained, there is a strong case for increasing our gearing rather than reducing it, although this would be contrary to our traditional policy. Our capital gearing (Debt/Equity) is well below, and our interest cover is well above, current industry averages.

	Phoenix	Industry
Capital gearing	£10m/£200m* = 5%	45%

(*ignoring retentions for the current year)

Interest cover	£40m/£0·7m = 57 times	6·5 times

Did you answer the question?

If you have sufficient information, it is always worth making a comparison between "your" company and the industry in which it operates, to highlight areas where it appears to be out of line.

(iii)   *Interest rate expectations.* If we need to borrow sometime in the future, we will lose if future interests rates exceed 7%, since we will have effectively replaced 7% debt by higher cost debt. The reverse argument also applies.

(iv)   *Reaction of the market.* When companies with high gearing levels and thus high levels of financial risk repay debt, there is usually a favourable effect on share price. Given our low level of gearing, it is doubtful that there would be any such benefit. Indeed, the effect could be adverse, if the market perceives the debt retirement as a signal of harder times ahead.

4   *Recommendation*

Subject to the conditions of the existing loan, if we believe that our profitability will remain buoyant, there is a strong case for raising the level of dividends and for increasing our level of financial gearing. The risks seem low, although we will need to consult our major shareholders in order to sound out their potential reactions.

---

70   (Answer 3 of examination)

Examiner's comments and marking guide

(a)   **This question required candidates to calculate the NPV of a cost-saving project, allowing for taxation and investment incentives.**

The calculations were done reasonably well, and it was encouraging to see candidates also scoring marks for presentation and layout. Common errors concerned the timing of tax reliefs and the EU grant (although these were not heavily penalised). More serious were failures to convert tax reliefs into tax savings, and treating these as cash flows, failure to incorporate the balancing allowance, failure to inflate the operating costs properly, and failure to allow for tax relief on these increased costs. Most fundamental failure was to appreciate that the fines were already discounted. Many students failed to understand that if the NPV was negative, the project could still be attractive if it resulted in bigger savings in fines. A lot of answers double-counted the fines by incorporating these into the cash flows and then comparing the resulting NPV with the fines!

(b)   **This question required candidates to present a memorandum regarding the desirability of the proposed project.**

In too many cases, this was taken as an invitation to waffle around green issues (which earned a mark or two), but often the best part of the answer was the format! Few answers focused on the reliability of using probabilities, on the skewed shape of the distribution given, or on the likelihood of harsher treatment by the authorities in the future. Responses to the "financial" aspects usually failed to address the context of the question, talking about general issues such as training, maintenance programmes and so on.

		Marks
(a)	EV of fines	2
	Presentation/Format of calculation	2
	EU grant net of fee	1·5
	Increased cost profile	1
	Tax savings on cost increases	1
	WDA with tax savings	2
	NPV calculation/use of correct discount rate	1
	Assessment of financial value/comment	1·5
		12

(b)

Format	1
Moral/ethical responsibility	1
Discussion of use of probabilities	2
Possibility of increased future fines with reasons	2
Possibility of higher prices	1
Image effects	1
	8
	Total 20 marks

Step by step answer plan

Step 1 Read the question again and make sure that you focus on precisely what is required. It concerns the appraisal of a project using discounted cash flow techniques, and included taxation, grants and some inflation. The basic calculations were straightforward, but care had to be taken to read and assimilate the data correctly.

Step 2 (a) The basic approach here is to compare the costs of purchasing the equipment (as reduced by tax reliefs and grants) with the benefits (the avoidance of fines), on a present value basis. The most important thing to note first is that the latter has virtually been done for you - the possible *total* fine levels are given in present value terms, and a simple expected value computation is all that is needed. The present value of costs (less tax savings etc) needs a bit more work, and a well laid out table will help both you and the examiner work through it. For each cash flow you put in, think what tax effects it has, if any. The grant and fee have none, the capital outlay and increases in costs do. Try not to join the large number of students that treat capital allowances as tax flows themselves.

Step 3 (b) First get the easy marks by giving your answer in memo format. Now sit back and have a think about the distinct points you are going to make, under financial and non-financial headings. The environmental issue is obviously significant but not by any means the only issue. When computations involve expected values, it is always worth looking at the effects of each of the "actual" outcomes occurring - it can bring surprising results, as here.

Step 4 Now review your answer and ensure that it does precisely answer the question as set.

The examiner's answer

(a) The level of fines has an expected present value (£m) of:

$$EV = (0{\cdot}3 \times 0{\cdot}50) + (0{\cdot}5 \times 1{\cdot}40) + (0{\cdot}2 \times 2{\cdot}0)$$

$$= 0{\cdot}15 + 0{\cdot}70 + 0{\cdot}40 = 1{\cdot}25 \text{ (i.e.) } £1{\cdot}25\text{m.}$$

To determine the expected NPV of the project, Blackwater must weigh the present value of the costs incurred i.e. the outlay and the increased production costs, against the benefits in the form of the two sets of tax reliefs relating to the increased operating costs and to the writing-down allowance and also the present value of the fines avoided. These are set out in the following table.

Year						
Item (£m)	0	1	2	3	4	5
Outlay	(1·000)					
EU grant		0·250				
FSL's fee		(0·050)				
Increased costs	–	(0·315)	(0·331)	(0·347)	(0·365)	
Tax saving at 33%	–		0·104	0·109	0·115	0·120
WDA	0·250	0·188	0·141	0·105	0·316	
Tax saving at 33%	–	0·083	0·062	0·047	0·035	0·104
Net cash flows	(1·000)	(0·032)	(0·165)	(0·191)	(0·215)	0·224
Discount factor at 12%	1·000	0·893	0·797	0·712	0·636	0·567
PV	(1·000)	(0·029)	(0·132)	(0·136)	(0·137)	0·127

NPV = (1·307), i.e. (£1·307m)

Since the negative NPV exceeds the expected present value of the fines (£1·250m) over the same period, it appears that the project is not viable in financial terms (i.e.) it is cheaper to risk the fines.

(b) Memo to: Blackwater plc Main Board.

Subject: Proposed Pollution Control Project.

From: Lower down the hierarchy.

Date: That'll be the day.

On purely non-financial criteria, it can be suggested that as a regular violator of the environmental regulation, our company has a moral responsibility to install this equipment, so long as it does not jeopardise the long-term survival of the company.

But the figures appended suggest that the project is not wealth-creating for Blackwater's shareholders as the EV of the fines is less than the expected NPV of the project. However, this conclusion relies on accepting the validity of the probability distribution, which is debatable. Not only are the magnitudes of the fines merely estimates, but the probabilities shown are subjective. Different decision-makers may well arrive at different assessments which could lead to the opposite decision on financial criteria.

More fundamentally, the use of the expected value principle is only reliable when the probability distribution approximates to the normal. In this case, it is slightly skewed toward the lower outcomes. But more significantly, if the distribution itself is examined more closely, it appears to indicate that there is a 70% chance (0·5+0·2) of fines of at least £1·4m, which exceeds the NPV of the costs of the pollution control project. In other words, there is a 70% chance that the project will be worthwhile. It therefore seems perverse to reject it on these figures.

Did you answer the question?

If it seems strange to you that something with an expected value of £1.25m has a 70% chance of exceeding £1.4m, have another look at the probability distribution. The examiner was looking for an appreciation of the potential dangers of using expected values without looking at the real values behind them.

Moreover, given that Blackwater is a persistent offender, and that the green lobby is becoming more influential, there must be a strong likelihood that the level of fines will increase in the future, suggesting that the data given are under-estimates. Higher expected fines would further enhance the appeal of the project.

It is also possible that the company may sell more output, perhaps at a higher price, if it is perceived to be more environmentally friendly and if customers are swayed by this. This may be less likely for industrial companies although it would create opportunities for self-publicity on both sides. In addition, there may be more general image effects which may foster enhanced self-esteem among the workforce, as well as increasing the acceptability of the company in the local community. It is even possible that the company's share price may benefit from managers of 'ethical' investment funds deciding to include Blackwater in their portfolios.

Finally, this may be only a short-term solution. As the operating life of the equipment is only four years, we will face a further investment decision after this period, although technological and legal changes may well have altered the situation by then.

---

71 (Answer 4 of examination)

Examiner's comments and marking guide

Question 4. This question sought to examine candidates' understanding of activity-based costing, in part (a) specifically, how it compared to traditional absorption costing and why it had been developed by some companies. Part (b) widened the scope of coverage to require discussion of whether the 'approach based on activities' was seen as a help in planning, control and decision-making.

In part (a) candidates performed with moderate success. Reasons for some candidates' failure to pick up marks were that some answers were restricted to the mention of a few key terms such as 'cost pool' or 'cost driver'. These terms were generally not well explained, that is, they were not elaborated on. As a result, a description of the differences between the two methods was unclear and consequently candidates did not gain as many marks as they could. In some scripts candidates paid little or no attention to why ABC was developed and hence failed to pick up the marks available here.

Part (b) was not answered well. Marks were available for both an awareness of the value and problems of 'activity based approaches' and for demonstration of understanding of planning, control and decision-making in general (which is mentioned in the syllabus). Candidates failed to achieve marks because there was a need to improve the structure of their answers. There was little discussion by candidates, therefore they did not demonstrate understanding of 'activity-based approaches' or planning, control and decision-making. Often answers were confined to single short and sometimes unrelated sentences, with little reasoning behind them. Some candidates restricted their emphasis to 'costing' when analysis of activities could have been discussed more widely and some simply declared the approach offered improvement but did not back this up by saying why or how. As a result they did not demonstrate the understanding required.

(a) 2 marks for each elaborated point, e.g.
- activities not departments
- different environment
- different overheads
- non-volume basis
- compare with traditional allocation

(b) 4 marks for each section which looks for:
- understanding of planning, control and decision-making (see syllabus)
- coverage of both improvements and limitations

Step by step answer plan

Step 1 Read the question again and make sure that you focus on precisely what is required. You are asked to discuss the merits and limitations of an activity based costing approach to cost management, an area that should be familiar to you. The topic can only become more significant as manufacturing methods develop, and this question is a good indicator of the depth of knowledge the examiner now expects.

Step 2 (a) The question requires an explanation of the factors that led to the development of ABC, and this is a good place to start the discussion. Discuss how the traditional method was once quite a satisfactory method of dealing with fairly insignificant overheads in a highly labour-intensive production process; then move onto a description of more modern methods and how these led to a review of the treatment of overheads. Try to keep your descriptions clear, perhaps by using simple examples, to ensure the distinction between the two methods is obvious.

Step 3 (b) To get a good mark on this part your answer needs to be well structured, and clearly be seen to be addressing the issues required. The question separates out the three areas of cost management, and you should follow this in your answer. Look at each of the areas, and think about what steps/tasks they generally involve. Then think how an activity based approach would impact on these tasks and consider both the advantages and limitations. This requires more than a superficial knowledge of ABC.

Step 4 Now review your answer and ensure that it does precisely answer the question as set.

The examiner's answer

(a) Traditional costing systems were designed many years ago when a narrow range of products existed and overhead costs were a relatively small proportion of total costs. It has been pointed out that there has recently been changes in the business and competitive environment faced by many companies. The way products are manufactured, services delivered and how companies compete has changed significantly, giving attention for example to variety, flexibility and quality. This calls therefore for a re-examination of the traditional way of costing products and services.

Activity-based costing (ABC) is claimed to be different from traditional approaches to costing. It moves away from a tendency to allocate costs or services through the departmental divisions of an organisation. Instead it recognises that costs may be usefully analysed by the activities performed which are not necessarily defined by departmental boundaries. It therefore uses data collected on the activities performed in order to calculate the costs of products or services benefiting from the activities. It is based on the premise that 'activities cause costs' and 'products consume activities' and therefore this is the logical way to carry out product costing.

It has been further pointed out that traditional approaches to costing have tended to penalise products or services that are produced and delivered in high volumes. This is because the traditional bases of applying costs were often volume-based, for example machine hours, labour hours or a constant percentage overhead burden. Labour hours have been shown in the past to be a popular basis of absorbing costs yet in many cases these are now a small proportion of the total costs of an enterprise. Additionally, some activities carried out in organisations are not necessarily associated with the volume of product or service produced. For example, the administration cost of dealing with a customer enquiry is not related to the volume of the transaction and the cost to set-up a machine is not related to the length of the production run.

The nature of some overhead costs have also changed, for example, focusing on the customer or on quality, as indicated above. Rather than just being costs of the manufacturing process there are now more organisational support costs. It is claimed therefore that for many organisations, having a growing burden of these different overheads and fewer volume-based costs, ABC is more appropriate to their needs. Having said this, some commentators suggest that it is simply a more elaborate form of traditional costing.

(b)　(i)　Installing an ABC system involves an analysis of organisational activities, the extent of their occurrence, their relationship to products and services and their cost. Once a company has undertaken this exercise the database thus produced can become the basis for forward planning and budgeting. For example, once the planned scale of production has been established it is possible to translate this into the number of times activities are required to be performed. This will help to define required departmental capacities for machines and for staffing levels. Extending the activities by the cost per activity enables the financial budget for each activity centre to be established. This activity based estimate will be a contribution to budget discussions, though it will not necessarily establish the budget figure. The activity analysis/ABC cost information therefore becomes the basis for the company modelling alternative scenarios before incorporating an agreed position into the master budget statement.

It should be borne in mind that much of this activity information will be historical therefore as systems change or product volumes differ its accuracy may be invalidated. Likewise, the cost per activity could be an historical rate and will need adjustment for any anticipated cost/inflation changes.

Did you answer the question?

In this, and the next two parts of the answer, note that although the majority of discussion focuses on the uses of ABC in these areas, the examiner has also considered the possible drawbacks or problems, as required.

(ii)　Following on from the notion that 'activities cause costs' and 'products consume activities' it is possible to manage cost incurrence through managing the activities underlying them. As overhead burdens in many organisations have grown, the feedback reporting methods that have been traditionally employed may prove to be insufficient. By preparing regular reports on activity volume some attempt can be made to predict and manage the costs involved. It may provide the opportunity to pose questions regarding different ways of carrying out processes in order to reduce the activities and hence the costs incurred. Management should be seeking methods to proactively manage costs through managing the activities.

Additionally, activities reflect the workrate of departments and other organisational subunits. The activities are therefore additional measures of performance of the department, in this way additional opportunities to manage the departmental performance are created. The following diagram will illustrate this point.

Cost Assignment View

It must be noted however, that in many cases the reporting of activity volume is not enough. To control a cost requires managerial intervention regarding a spending decision. That is to say, if a reduced activity volume is achieved in a particular department in itself this may not reduce the cost. Staff may need to be redeployed or machines disposed of before costs are actually reduced. This is pointing out that ABC is a resource consumption model not a spending model. That is, it is fundamentally allocating costs to products or services. There is no direct link between managing the activities and automatic control or management of the cost.

(iii)   Decision making involves the identification of relevant costs for the various decision alternatives. As each decision is unique so the appropriate identification of costs and revenues are unique also. ABC costs are average costs, perhaps more accurate than traditional costs but still average not marginal costs. An ABC based cost cannot be assumed to be a relevant cost for a decision, for example, to delete a product, close a department or expand the same.

For example assuming a product deletion situation some of the costs identified to the product, through ABC, will be removed but not all costs. At a simplistic level the analysis of costs into variable and fixed components might be preferred to an ABC analysis in order to deal with the product deletion.

The way that proponents of ABC have proposed dealing with the situation, or to deal with product profitability generally, has been to suggest a heirarchy of cost classifications. This hierarchy involves identifying activity costs at the unit (individual item) level, the batch level (changing when the number of batches change, e.g. set-up), the product level (which are common to all products within the product line) and facility sustaining (which relate to the whole plant where various product lines are produced). Thus it will help to focus the mind of the manager regarding which parts of the heirarchy are likely to be removed by the particular deletion decision at hand. It has been pointed out that ABC costs represent long-run average costs of a product, such costs are not designed therefore to be used directly for decision making and users should be warned to beware of these basic assumptions before making profitability decisions based on ABC costs.

72   (Answer 5 of examination)

Examiner's comments and marking guide

Question 5. In part (a) this question required the calculation of sales and cost variances and a reconciliation of budget and actual profit using the variances computed. It was to be followed in part (b) by comment on the results disclosed. The question concluded by testing candidates' knowledge of the limitations of sales variances.

Part (a) was answered reasonably well with the exception of the mix variance which a number of candidates had difficulty with. Parts (b) and (c) tended to be very brief and a much poorer performance was revealed. In part (a) candidates failed to pick up marks if they failed to calculate the mix variance or failed to calculate it correctly. Some did not attempt it, substituting, by design or by accident, the volume variance for the mix and quantity variances and as a result they did not pick up all the marks that were available. Other reasons for failure to gain marks were the calculation of total sales revenue variances rather than their contribution margin equivalent and the attempt to compute volume variances for variable costs, which is not a conventional way of 'flexing' the budget.

Solutions to (b) were at times restricted to repeating in the memorandum the variances calculated in (a). Whilst some marks were awarded for this, further comment or interpretation of the variances was required for higher marks.

In part (c) there was scope to discuss the limitations of generating sales volume, price and mix variances generally or applied to the particular setting given in part (a). Marks were available for either or both treatments, however, responses to this part were very brief, at times non-existent. Some candidates seemed to have very limited ideas on the generation of sales variances, this inevitably resulted in them failing to pick up many marks in this section.

		Marks
(a)	budget profit	1
	actual profit	1
	price variances	2
	mix variance	2
	quantity variance	1
	fixed overhead	1
	labour rate	1
	reconciliation	1
		___
		10
(b)	looking for developed points which explain to the manager, 2 marks for each point.	4
(c)	2/3 marks for each clearly discussed limitation which is identified	6
		___

Total 20 marks

Step by step answer plan

Step 1 Read the question again and make sure that you focus on precisely what is required. This is a fairly standard variance analysis problem, set in a slightly unusual business context. The key here is not to get thrown by this, but just to treat it as you would a normal widget-making process.

Step 2 (a) In order to be able to reconcile them you need to first determine what the budgeted and actual profit figures are. Now move onto the variance analysis, treating clients like product units and commissions like variable labour costs. Using a marginal costing approach, as required, results in sales mix and quantity variances being valued at standard contribution (revenue - commission) and there being no fixed overhead volume variance.

Step 3 (b) You've computed the numbers in (a) - now use them to tell a story. State what the figures are showing (not "adverse cost variance" but "costs higher than expected"), then try to suggest a cause. Since the examiner specifically asked for the mix variance, it is important that you comment on it here. Look for links between variances wherever possible.

Step 4 (c) Some of the comments that may be made here relate to all variances, not just sales - inappropriateness of standards, outdated standards etc. But you must quickly focus on the sales aspects, and the relevance of the mix/quantity analysis for possibly unrelated products is an important point to raise. As usual, try to gear your answer to the particular business concerned whenever possible.

Step 5 Now review your answer and ensure that it does precisely answer the question as set.

The examiner's answer

(a)

	Budget	Actual
	£	£
Sales – Male	30,000	16,000
Female	18,000	40,000

Commission – Male	12,000		7,000
Female	10,000		22,000
Fixed costs	20,000		24,000
	————		————
Profit	6,000		3,000

Profit variance £3,000A

		£
Price variances – Male 2,000 (8·0 – 7·5)		1,000F
Female 2,000 (20·0 – 18·0)		4,000F
Mixture variance		4,200F
Quantity variance		5,200A
Fixed overhead expenditure (20,000 – 24,000)		4,000A
Labour rate variance – Male 2,000 × (3·0 – 3·5)		1,000A
Female 2,000 × (10·0 –11·0)		2,000A
		————
		3,000A

Did you answer the question?

Look at your answer. Does it clearly show a set of variances that attempts to explain a (computed) difference in profit, or is it just a string of workings?

Workings – mixture and quantity variances

AV AM SC	AV BM SC	BV BM SC
9,000	14,400	18,000
16,000	6,400	8,000
————	————	————
25,000	20,800	26,000

       mixture   quantity

      £4,200F   £5,200A

AV AM SC is actual volume × actual mix × standard contribution.

    4,000 × 0·5 × £4·5 = £9,000

    4,000 × 0·5 × £8·0 = £16,000

AV BM SC is actual volume × budget mix × standard contribution.

    4,000 × 0·8 × £4·5 = £14,400

    4,000 × 0·2 × £8·0 = £6,400

BV BM SC is budget volume × budget mix × standard contribution

    4,000 × 4·5 = £18,000

    1,000 × 8·0 = £8,000

(b)   Memorandum To: Manager Franchise Ref:

The overall result is below the budget expectations, the variance analysis will help to explore the reasons for this. It appears that it has been possible to put prices up beyond the level that was envisaged, or clients have been requiring different treatments which has lifted the overall price. This applies to both male and female clients, as the price variances are both in the same direction.

The level of business was significantly less than planned, only 80% of the planned number of clients were attracted to the business. There was a significantly favourable move concerning the mix of clients. Far more female clients attended and they had a higher level of contribution than male clients, resulting in a favourable mix variance. In overall terms the effect of the sales side on the profitability of the business was favourable compared to the original budget.

The adverse profit implications came from higher than planned commission rates paid to staff, perhaps this was likely given the higher than average selling prices achieved. The other negative impact reported was the variance on fixed overhead expenditure and further detail is required here before any corrective action can be anticipated. It may be difficult to change fixed overheads and, depending on further analysis, it may be necessary to amend the budget figure.

(c)   When interpreting the disaggregation of the profit variance with particular reference to sales variances various limitations can be suggested. In the particular business environment envisaged it may be difficult to set 'standard' selling prices, so any variances need to be interpreted with care. It may not be possible, for example, to apply the same rigour as in manufacturing situations, however these approximate targets may prove useful.

It should be noted that the actual sales performance is being compared to a budget which may have been set some time ago. In this regard the extent to which it may have become out of date must be considered. A more recently revised forecast could be used as an alternative.

The splitting of price and volume implications in these variances, whilst common in both theory and practice, needs care in interpretation. There is little doubt that in many market situations the prices and quantities are interrelated, one cannot be read without the other. In the example in part (a) it is possible to suggest that the situation represents a move along the demand curve.

Finally, the attempt to report mix and quantity variances may be dubious. A mix variance seems to imply some relationship between the respective products and that this is incorporated in the planning process. To provide management with a mix variance where no relationship exists is spurious, they should perhaps tackle the quantity differences separately. In the simple example produced in part (a) there may be no connection between the change in male/female attendance.

73   (Answer 6 of examination)

Examiner's comments and marking guide

Question 6. This question required, in part (a), the determination of the selling price per unit after apportionment of variable and fixed costs and the use of a budgeted volume and mark-up. The discussion of two independent business opportunities then occurred in part (b), which was to be supported by some calculations. Finally in part (c) the candidates' understanding of product costs based on maximum capacity was examined.

There were some complete and accurate answers to part (a), performance was good here, however candidates should note that it was only the start of the question. In part (b) there was considerably less success. Candidates often compared the product cost in (a) with the offer price in (b) (i). The failure to consider scope for the use of variable cost, the concept of 'contribution', or to support the conclusion with any further calculations resulted in failure to achieve more marks in this section. In (b) (ii) candidates failed to fully develop their responses, on occasions neglecting to acknowledge the new total volume that would be required or the existing business which may be lost if the new business opportunity were to be accepted. This part frequently had no further calculations undertaken to support it and, for example, where calculations were made, the existing total variable costs were divided by the new expanded volume of business. The failure to develop further calculations or discuss some of the matters requiring further clarification resulted in candidates failing to pick up all the marks here.

The main reason that candidates did not gain higher marks in (c) was that they did not develop their explanations sufficiently. Candidates did not seem to have many ideas on the implications of generating product costs using maximum capacity.

			Marks	
(a)	allocation – fixed costs		1	
	reapportionment		2	
	costs and selling prices		2	5
(b) (i)	variable cost		2	
	extra contribution		1	
	comment		2	
(ii)	extra contribution		2	
	assumptions,			
	limitations and			
	comment		4	11

(c) cost change,
motivation, etc.   2
revised value   1
comment   1   4
                                         ___   ___

Total 20 marks

Step by step answer plan

Step 1   Read the question again and make sure that you focus on precisely what is required. It examines the topic of product costing, for the purposes of pricing and decision making. There are some standard calculations that offer easy marks, and some requirements that require a good understanding of the relevance or otherwise of the individual product cost elements.

Step 2   (a) This is a standard apportionment and re-apportionment exercise, using the step-wise method - take care to choose the correct order in which to clear service departments. This part only attracts 5 marks (9 minutes' worth) so don't spend hours on presentation, explanations etc.

Step 3   (b) When advising on the acceptability of accepting additional orders, the main question to ask is - can it be completed using solely spare capacity, or will it necessitate the curtailment of existing business? If the former, then the basic principle is that the order is acceptable provided the price covers the variable cost of manufacture. If the latter, then the opportunity cost of lost contribution from existing business needs to be brought into the equation. In either case, it is *variable* unit cost that is relevant here, and any apportioned fixed costs should be ignored. So your first task is to compute the variable cost per unit of WYE, including its share of the service departments' variable costs.

Step 4   Now use this information to determine the decision in (a) on financial grounds, then comment on other less quantifiable aspects that may need to be brought into the decision.

Step 5   For (ii) you need to recognise that some of the new business would be met from spare capacity, and some by giving up existing business, and an overall gain/loss must be computed (again in contribution terms). Then, stand back from the numbers to make some practical comments on other impacts of accepting this order.

Step 6   The main consequence here is the inevitable under-absorption of overheads resulting in adverse volume variances. Try to think of some positive aspects, too, and bring in numbers (from the previous parts) if you have time and they add to your argument.

Step 7   Now review your answer and ensure that it does precisely answer the question as set.

The examiner's answer

(a)

	EXE	WYE	Stores	Maintenance	Admin
Material	1·800	0·700	0·100	0·100	
Other variable	0·800	0·500	0·100	0·200	0·200
Gen factory	1·440	1·080	0·540	0·180	0·360
					0·560
Admin	0·224	0·168	0·112	0·056	(0·560)
				0·536	
Maintenance	0·268	0·134	0·134	(0·536)	
			0·986		
Stores	0·592	0·394	(0·986)		
	5·124	2·976			
Volume	150,000	70,000			
	£	£			
Full cost	34·16	42·51			
Price	42·70	53·14			

The prices of EXE and WYE based on the target mark up are £42·70 and £53·14 respectively.

(b) (i) The full cost and the cost plus price both include an allocation of fixed overheads. As the company has some spare capacity they should be aware also of the product variable cost to help with this sort of decision. It can be shown that by focusing on the variable cost only an extra unit of WYE costs £20·97, see below:

	EXE	WYE	Stores	Maintenance	Admin
Material	1·800	0·700	0·100	0·100	
Other variable	0·800	0·500	0·100	0·200	0·200
					0·200
Admin	0·080	0·060	0·040	0·020	(0·200)
				0·320	
Maintenance	0·160	0·080	0·080	(0·320)	
			0·320		
Stores	0·192	0·128	(0·320)		
	3·032	1·468			
Volume	150,000	70,000			
	£	£			
Variable cost	20·21	20·97			

The price offered makes some contribution to the fixed costs and profit of the company though not as much as the normal business.

For 3,000 units, the reported profit will increase by 3,000 × (£35 − £20·97)= £42,090. The company should not replace normal business but if this is additional it appears worth while. They should ascertain that it will not affect their relationship with existing customers or the prices they can command in the market, i.e. the markets are segregated. As a loss leader in this market it may create further business opportunities, though sales should not all be at this sort of price level. Even allowing for the approximation involved in some of the budgeted costs and the arbitrariness of some allocations of costs it appears that the extra revenue exceeds the extra cost and for this volume there is a minimal risk.

(ii) Enquiry price £42·51 + 10% = £46·76

Normal price (from a)   = £53·14

Unlike the scenario in (i) above the volume of this potential order is significant. The price being indicated is above the full cost but below the normal selling price. Some extra volume is attractive but to meet this order the company would have to operate at capacity and turn away existing business. A financial evaluation can be made by comparing the contribution from the volume which is the subject of the enquiry at the offer price with that from the business which must be sacrificed at normal price levels.

Gain from new business	50,000 × (£46·76 − £20·97)	= £1,289,500
Existing trade lost	20,000 × (£53·14 − £20·97)	= £ 643,400
Net gain		= £ 646,100

There is a danger of major goodwill implications for the company in their move to refuse some of their existing business for this product, if that is the option they adopt. This may also extend to products other than the one in question here for which we have no detail. The price being suggested of cost plus 10% is a steep change from the normal price of this product and if it applies to a significant volume, it may well alter the market position of the product. We are not however in a position to bring this into any calculation. If they take the order they are also reliant on the business of one customer and will need to consider the chance of repeat orders from this source.

The analysis assumes that the company is comfortable operating at the 100,000 capacity indicated and that the current cost levels apply, that is, the same variable costs and no change in the total fixed costs. Although the increase in contribution/profit for the order looks attractive the company would be advised to look beyond the current year to longer term negotiation on both price and volume. To turn away existing business which may have a future for the one-off enquiry applied to only one year may be inappropriate. If a longer term contract with price terms which may be attractive to both parties could be established, this may encourage the company to invest in order to expand capacity and not lose any business.

(c)   Generally, using a volume base of maximum capacity, rather than budget volume, will result in lower overhead recovery rates per unit. This is caused by the fixed overheads being spread over a greater volume which will inevitably lead to a lower product cost being compiled.

The cost would not be representative of the average actual product cost being achieved in the current year, unless current volumes are the same as the maximum capacity level. The company must expect an adverse volume variance to be reported if such a costing approach is incorporated into a management information system.

This approach will reveal a target product cost which can be achieved if high levels of business volume are achieved. In this way it can be a motivation to management to go out, be more competitive and attract new business. It will show just how low overhead rates and product costs can get.

The revised product cost can be computed by adjusting the fixed overhead component of the product cost for WYE.

	£ per unit
Original full cost	42·51
Variable cost	20·97
Original fixed cost	21·54
Revised fixed cost	15·08*
Add back variable cost	20·97
	36·05

*This is achieved by adjusting the original fixed cost by the proportion 70:100. An alternative would be to re-examine the overhead apportionment, though it would come to the same conclusion.

Management should be aware that full product costs, including as they do arbitrary overhead allocation and volume levels, are approximations. Pricing and other decisions are usefully informed by a range of values which include variable costs and full costs based on alternative approaches. The accountant must ensure however that management are fully aware of the assumptions contained in the cost calculations which he/she presents.

JUNE 1998 QUESTIONS

Section A – This question is compulsory and MUST be attempted

74   (Question 1 of examination)

Stadium Eats is a themed football (soccer) restaurant, seating 150 people, which was set up four years ago by a partnership of two graduate caterers. The restaurant has proved very popular, and sales are now (1998) averaging £8,500 per week for the 50 weeks of the year that the restaurant is open. The average spend per customer is £15 per head on Saturdays and Sundays, and £12 per head on weekdays. The gross profit margin is 20% and the operating profit margin is 11%.

Stadium Eats is now facing the problem of having to turn customers away on Saturdays and Sundays, as demand is starting to exceed the capacity. Customers are finding that they are needing to place bookings around eight weeks ahead in order to be certain of getting a table at the required time on these days.

In order to overcome the capacity problem, and expand the business further, Stadium Eats are planning to open a second restaurant. They have already identified a suitable site, and drawn up a simple forecast profit and loss account for the new outlet for the first year of trading and an end of year balance sheet. The forecasts are *loosely* based on the revenues and costs of the existing outlet, and are detailed below.

Profit and Loss Account forecast for the year ended 30 June 1999

	£'000
Sales	600
Operating Profit	135
Interest Payable	18
Profit Before Tax	117
Taxation	35
Profit After Tax	82

Notes:
1.   In calculating operating profit, the two owners have not allowed for any salary costs for themselves, as they already draw a salary of £22,000 each from the existing business.

2.   The new restaurant will be able to seat 180 people, and will be open 50 weeks of the year.

3.   The tax rate is assumed to be 30%.

4.   After tax profit is shared equally between the two partners, but will be wholly re-invested in the business. To date, the partners have made no drawings other than the salaries indicated above.

5.   The current cash balance in the existing business amounts to £45,000, and it is expected that £25,000 of this will be required for refurbishment of the premises for the new restaurant.

6.   The two partners will own equal shares in the new concern.

Forecast Balance Sheet as at 30 June 1999

	£'000	£'000
Assets employed		
Fixed (net)		
Premises		280
Fixtures and fittings		75
Current		
Food stocks	3	
Debtors	7	
Cash	18	28

Current Liabilities		
Creditors	12	
Net current Assets		16
Total Assets less current liabilities		371
Long-term Creditors		195
		———
Net Assets		176
		═══
Financed by:		
Ordinary shares (25p nominal)		94
Profit & Loss Account		82
		———
		176
		═══

Notes:

1. The long-term creditors would be made up of bank loans and a mortgage against the premises. The mortgage outstanding at 30 June 1999 would be £184,000 and the balance of the long-term creditors represents a bank loan at 10% interest (fixed rate). The loan would be repaid in monthly instalments, and the balance cleared by June 2004.

2. Stadium Eats is currently run as a partnership, but it is intended that the new restaurant will be operated as a private limited company.

3. In order to raise the cash for their equity investment in the new venture, the two partners would need to raise loans totalling £75,000 against their own homes. They have been assured that the loans will be available but are a little concerned at the risk that they may be taking in borrowing so much to invest in a new business.

Required:

(a) State and explain any reservations that you may have regarding the figures in the forecast profit and loss account, and draft a revised version, adjusted to take account of your criticisms.

(10 marks)

(b) A bank may be concerned about the level of gearing in a business which has applied for additional loan finance. Explain the meaning of the term capital gearing, and why a lender/investor should be wary of further borrowing when gearing is already high.

(10 marks)

(c) Calculate and comment on the level of gearing based on the 1999 Forecast Balance Sheet. (Note that this excludes the proposed £75,000 personal loans for the new restaurant). **(4 marks)**

(d) Given that Stadium Eats are already operating successfully, what other sources of long-term finance might be available to the new business? **(8 marks)**

(e) An accountant has advised the partners that it might be best for them to combine the two restaurants under the umbrella of a single company, and seek a flotation on AIM in five year's time.

Explain the role of AIM within the financial markets, and identify the factors to be considered in seeking a stock market quotation.

(8 marks)

(40 marks)

Section B – ONE question ONLY to be attempted

---

75   (Question 2 of examination)

Chromex plc manufactures bicycles for the UK and European markets, and has made a bid of £150 million to take over Bexell plc, their main UK competitor, which is also active in the German market. Chromex currently supplies 24% of the UK market and Bexell has a 10% share of the same market.

Chromex anticipates labour savings of £700,000 per year, created by more efficient production and distribution facilities, if the take-over is completed. In addition, the company intends to sell off surplus land and buildings with a balance sheet value of £15 million, acquired in the course of the take-over.

Total UK bicycle sales for 1997 were £400 million. For the year ended 31 December 1997, Bexell reported an operating profit of £10 million, compared with a figure of £55 million for Chromex. In calculating profits, Bexell included a depreciation charge of £0·5 million.

Note: The take-over is regarded by Chromex in the same way as any other investment, and is appraised accordingly.

Required:

(a) Assuming that the bid is accepted by Bexell, calculate the payback period (pre-tax) for the investment, if the land and buildings are immediately sold for £5 million less than the balance sheet valuation, and Bexell's sales figures remain static.
(3 marks)

(b) Chromex has also appraised the investment in Bexell by calculating the present value of the company's future expected cash flows. What additional information to that required in (a) would have been necessary?
(5 marks)

(c) Explain how and why the UK government might seek to intervene in the take-over bid for Bexell.
(6 marks)

(d) Suggest four ratios, which Chromex might usefully compute in order to compare the financial performance of Bexell with that of companies in the same manufacturing sector. You should include in your answer a justification of your choice of ratios. Briefly explain why it is important to base a comparison on companies in the same sector.
(6 marks)

(20 marks)

---

76   (Question 3 of examination)

Pellas Ltd is a small manufacturing company which specialises in the production of high quality electronic organisers, which are sold direct to the public by mail order. Summary figures from the Profit and Loss account for the last three years are shown below:

	1995	1996	1997
	£m	£m	£m
Sales	1·250	1·500	1·620
Cost of Sales	0·650	0·830	0·967
Operating Profit	0·600	0·670	0·653

Notes

(1) Unit selling price for the electronic organiser has been held fixed by Pellas since 1995. This is in response to low levels of demand in the UK consumer electronics market.

(2) 80% of the cost of sales is accounted for by electronic components purchased from a supplier who has increased prices by 10% in each of the last two years.

Government financial statistics for the same period reveal the following:

Retail price index	*Wholesale price index*
December 1995 150·7	December 1995 132·4
December 1996 154·4	December 1996 134·8
December 1997 159·5	December 1997 137·5

Required:

(a) Briefly outline the causes of inflation.   **(4 marks)**

(b) Calculate and comment on the annual rate of inflation for 1995/6 and 1996/7, as measured by both the retail and wholesale price indices.   **(4 marks)**

(c) In general terms describe how inflation affects companies.

(6 marks)

(d) Write a report for the directors of Pellas, commenting on the way in which they have managed their sales and costs under inflationary conditions.   **(6 marks)**

(20 marks)

Section C – TWO questions ONLY to be attempted

77   (Question 4 of examination)

Management accounting in profit-seeking organisations may be different from that which could apply in non-profit-seeking organisations.

Required:

(a) Briefly outline the role of a management accountant using a profit-seeking organisation as a setting.

(6 marks)

(b) Contrast the main features of a non-profit-seeking organisation, with one that is profit-seeking, which makes management accounting in this environment different.   **(6 marks)**

(c) Discuss how a management accountant may respond to the challenge of providing appropriate information in a non-profit-seeking organisation.   **(8 marks)**

(20 marks)

78   (Question 5 of examination)

A company operates a system of quarterly rolling budgets. Budgets for the next three quarters have been prepared. The figures below reflect the likely cost behaviour of each element of cost. Quarter four is being developed based on these budgets and other information available.

Budget Quarters 1 to 3

	Q1 (000)	Q2 (000)	Q3 (000)
Activity:			
Sales (units)	18	34	30
Production (units)	20	40	30

Costs:	£000	£000	£000
Direct Materials	50	100	75
Production labour	180	280	230
Factory Overheads (excluding indirect labour)	170	200	185
Administration	30	30	30
Selling and Distribution	29	37	35

In the current planning stage for quarter four, flexible budgets are to be developed for low, most likely and high sales volumes (38,000, 44,000 and 50,000 units respectively). The company wishes to have a closing stock (end of quarter four) equal to the opening stock for quarter one. Management will therefore adjust the production levels to fall in line with this policy.

Cost structures as for quarters one to three will apply to quarter four except that:

i.   raw material prices are expected to rise by 10%

ii.   production labour rates will increase by 2.5%. However, management have declared that all labour rate increases must be matched by increased efficiency so that labour costs (both total fixed and variable per unit) are unaltered.

iii. a quarterly bonus payment, of 50% of the variable labour cost per unit, will apply for all production above 40,000 units.

iv.   fixed factory overheads and fixed selling and distribution expenses will rise by 5%.

The expected selling price per unit is £18. Stock is valued at full factory cost of £13 per unit. This has been established using absorption principles and based on long run cost and capacity predictions. Small fluctuations in cost prices or volumes will not cause this unit cost to be amended.

Required:

(a) Explain what is meant by a 'rolling budget' and what additional benefit may be claimed for this compared to the annual style of budget.   **(4 marks)**

(b) Summarise the variable cost per unit and the total fixed cost, for each cost heading, that will apply to quarter four, for production below 40,000 units.   **(4 marks)**

(c) Prepare detailed flexed budget profit statements for quarter four under the separate assumptions of low, most likely and high levels of sales and corresponding production volumes.   **(6 marks)**

(d) Produce in *summary form only* a statement of the likely change in profit for quarter four if management change their policy on stock levels so as to manufacture the same volume as the forecast sales for the quarter.   Comment on the reason for the profit change and how this might motivate management regarding production levels in the future.   **(6 marks)**

(20 marks)

---

79   (Question 6 of examination)

Rayman Company produces three chemical products, J1X, J2Y and B1Z. Raw materials are processed in a single plant to produce two intermediate products, J1 and J2, in fixed proportions. There is no market for these two intermediate products. J1 is processed further through process X to yield the product J1X, product J2 is converted into J2Y by a separate finishing process Y. The Y finishing process produces both J2Y and a waste material, B1, which has no market value. The Rayman Company can convert B1, after additional processing through process Z, into a saleable by-product, B1Z. The company can sell as much B1Z as it can produce at a price of £1·50 per kg.

At normal levels of production and sales, 600,000 kg of the common input material are processed each month. There are 440,000 kg and 110,000 kg respectively, of the intermediate products J1 and J2, produced from this level of input. After the separate finishing processes, fixed proportions of J1X, J2Y and B1Z emerge, as shown below with current market prices (all losses are normal losses):

Product	Quantity kg	Market Price per kg
J1X	400,000	£2·425
J2Y	100,000	£4·50
B1Z	10,000	£1·50

At these normal volumes, materials and processing costs are as follows:

	Common Plant Facility	Separate Finishing Processess		
		X	Y	Z
	£000	£000	£000	£000
Direct materials	320	110	15	1·0
Direct labour	150	225	90	5·5
Variable overhead	30	50	25	0·5
Fixed overhead	50	25	5	3·0
Total	550	410	135	10·0

Selling and administrative costs are entirely fixed and cannot be traced to any of the three products.

Required:

(a) Draw a diagram which shows the flow of these products, through the processes, label the diagram and show the quantities involved in normal operation. **(2 marks)**

(b) Calculate the *cost per unit* of the finished products J1X and J2Y and the *total manufacturing profit*, for the month, attributed to each product assuming all joint costs are allocated based on:

   (i) physical units **(3 marks)**

   (ii) net realisable value **(4 marks)**

   and comment briefly on the two methods. **(3 marks)**

   NB All losses are normal losses.

(c) A new customer has approached Rayman wishing to purchase 10,000 kg of J2Y for £4·00 per kg. This is extra to the present level of business indicated above.

   Advise the management how they may respond to this approach by:

   (i) Developing a financial evaluation of the offer. **(4 marks)**

   (ii) Clarifying any assumptions and further questions which may apply. **(4 marks)**

   (20 marks)

```
ANSWERS TO JUNE 1998 EXAMINATION
```

```
74   (Answer 1 of examination)
```

Examiner's comments and marking guide

Question 1: The case study was mixed in the quality of answers, with some sections being answered better than others. The question sought to test candidates' understanding of the sources of finance available to unquoted companies, and the risks of poor management of financial gearing (Section 7 of the syllabus). Case studies require the thoughtful application of knowledge, and where answers demonstrated such thoughtfulness, high marks were scored. The majority of candidates, however, more or less ignored the scenario, and reproduced textbook style answers.

Part (a) required critical review of the forecast profit and loss account, and this caused difficulties. Most candidates calculated a pro rata figure for sales, based on the relative size of the new outlet, but few then went on to question the feasibility of being able to repeat the success of the first restaurant so quickly. A large number of candidates tried to spot errors in the financial accounting rather than concentrating on the more fundamental issues such as the lack of detail in the forecast, and the assumption of high margins.

Parts (b) and (c) required understanding of financial gearing, and were generally answered well. It was noticeable that in answering (b), candidates tended to focus on the lender's risks arising from high capital gearing. Only a small proportion looked at the equity investor's perspective of the risks. To gain maximum marks, it is important to answer all the parts of a question.

In answering part (d), many candidates simply listed different sources of finance, as per the textbooks, but failed to consider whether such sources were appropriate in the context of the business in question. Zero coupon bonds cannot be issued by a small scale restaurant business.

The element of part (e) on the role of AIM was generally well done. By way of contrast, the factors to be considered in seeking a stock market listing were rather less adequately detailed.

Perhaps the most important factor for candidates to remember in working through the case study question in paper 8 is the need to write answers which are appropriate to the scenario given.

			Marks
1	**(a)** Two marks for each relevant comment:		
	Forecast is only for one year		
	Figures are summaries only, with no detail		
	Sales figures very optimistic		
	Margins appear too high		
	Owners' salaries ignored	7	
	Re-working of figures at more realistic level	3	10
	(b) Definition	4	
	Comment re lender/investor (2 marks each)	6	10
	(c) Calculation	1	
	Commentary (maximum marks only if includes interest cover and remarks on proprietors' risk)	3	4
	(d) Recognition that non-loan finance is sought	2	
	General mention of venture capital	1	
	Detail re specific types of equity finance e.g. business angels	3	
	Other sources e.g. grants	2	8
	(e) Description of AIM and type of companies listed	3	
	Factors to be considered in opting for stock market quotation	5	8
	Total Marks		40

Step by step answer plan

Step 1 Read the question again and make sure that you focus on precisely what is required. In the context of a new venture, the question looks at forecast results, gearing, sources of finance and the AIM.

Step 2 (a) There are 10 marks for this part, so you need to spend a little time thinking of various issues that may be discussed. You have very little detail in the profit and loss account (indeed, this is one point to raise), so you are expected to look at the broad figures - level of turnover, margins etc - and then comment on the feasibility of achieving these for a brand new enterprise, and possible impact on the existing business. Some of your criticisms cannot be taken into account when redrafting the profit and loss, but some sensible assumptions are needed as regards turnover and margins to produce revised (lower) figures.

Step 3 (b) This gives you a chance to display your general knowledge of gearing before having to relate it to the scenario. Don't stint on your explanation of the meaning of capital gearing - the marks allow you to give a little detail about different definitions and which types of debt may be included etc. You then need to consider the impact of high gearing levels on both lenders and equity investors.

Step 4 (c) Now you need to apply what you have discussed in general terms in (b) to the data and circumstances of the question. Make it clear which definition of gearing you are using in your calculations. You cannot come to any firm conclusions without any benchmarks for comparison, but you can discuss particular aspects of the restaurant business that may affect the impact of the gearing level.

Step 5 (d) Here you can initially recall your sources of finance "checklist", but before writing about any of them, you must think whether they will apply in this particular context. And don't forget the all important source - equity - that appears to be perhaps most appropriate in this case.

Step 6 (e) There are two parts to this requirement - a general discussion on the AIM, followed by the specific factors to be considered in obtaining a listing. The latter actually carries more marks, and should not be skimped on.

Step 7 Now review your answer and ensure that it does precisely answer the question as set.

The examiner's answer

(a) The forecast covers only the first trading year. This is unlikely to be representative of the longer term trading position of the business and hence a forecast over a three to five year period would be more appropriate.

The question indicates that the forecast is *loosely* based on the current Stadium Eats figures. There would in fact appear to have been some questionable assumptions made in constructing the forecast.

Firstly, sales of £600,000 (in excess of the current sales of £425,000) may be viewed as rather ambitious for the first year. It is unrealistic to assume sales will be even close to equivalent to those of the original restaurant within such a short time. Furthermore, it may be that some customers simply switch from eating at Stadium Eats to eating at the new location. The forecast makes no mention of the sales for the *overall* operation, and the possible interdependence of sales between the two outlets.

The figures given in the forecast are lacking in any detail. There is insufficient information and no comparative data to show sales trends over time. It is impossible to learn anything about the costs of the restaurant from the information given. A detailed breakdown of costs by type, and over time, would be very helpful. The operating profit margin is difficult to appraise without further information on the average rate for similar restaurant businesses, but seems excessive when compared with the margin currently achieved. A forecast cash flow would also be useful.

The forecast may also be criticised for failing to take account of the likely need to employ new managerial staff to take responsibility for the existing outlet, in order to free up the partners to concentrate on the new site.

Working on sales in Stadium Eats at present, annual turnover is equal to £2,833 per cover. The estimate for the new restaurant is equal to £3,333 per cover per annum. Being pessimistic sales of perhaps £1,500 per cover pa may be assumed, and this would give a turnover of £270,000 instead of the forecast £600,000.

The current operating profit margin is 11%, which against the forecast sales of £600,000 would yield £66,000 before interest, as opposed to the £135,000 suggested figure for operating profit. This figure assumes management drawings are maintained at just £22,000 each.

Re-working the forecast to use an adjusted sales figure, and maintaining the 11% net margin gives:

Sales	£270,000
Operating Profit	£29,700
Less	
Interest	£18,000
PROFIT BEFORE TAX	£11,700

In practice, it is likely that the lower turnover (compared with the existing outlet) will lead to a reduction in net margin, leading to an even lower operating profit and lower profit before tax. If the margin is reduced to 10%, then on sales of £270,000, the operating profit of £27,000 is reduced to just £9,000 profit before tax.

This is a great deal lower than the forecast, and significantly alters the potential viability of the business, hence the need for a longer term forecast set of figures.

(b) The term capital gearing refers to the extent to which a company is funded by fixed return finance as opposed to equity. Two different formulae may be used when measuring capital gearing.

The first is:

Capital gearing = Debt plus preference share capital/Equity

This measures the ratio of fixed return capital to equity finance within a business.

An alternative formula, commonly used, measures the proportion of fixed return capital in relation to the total capital of a business. The formula is as follows:

Capital gearing = Debt + preference share capital/Total long-term capital

In both cases, debt may be measured as either long-term debt, or all interest bearing debt. Clearly the gearing level will vary depending on the formula selected, and the type of debt included, but in all cases the level of gearing rises as the *proportion* of fixed return finance increases. It is not possible to specify a precise dividing line between high gearing and low gearing. Gearing is a relative measure, and should be assessed in terms of the gearing levels of comparable companies in the same business sector. Companies in different industrial sectors may exhibit very different levels of capital gearing.

The level of gearing is of interest to a bank, which is lending to a business, because it reflects the extent to which the owners of the business are risking their own capital relative to that of the bank. At the same time, the bank will recognise that increased loan finance, which is not matched by an increase in equity investment, will lead to an increase in capital gearing. As the level of debt increases, if sales figures decline or are static, businesses may find it increasingly difficult to meet the interest payments due on the debt. The bank will therefore look for an increase in cash flows from operations to help to pay any incremental interest due on new borrowing. One problem, however, is that gearing does not measure cash flows.

The equity investor should be cautious of highly geared companies, because the return on equity in such a business will be very sensitive to changes in profit before interest. When gearing is high, and interest payments are also high, a dramatic fall in the profit before interest figure may result in a collapse in the profit attributable to equity. Equally, a large rise in pre interest profit may lead to a surge in the profit attributable to equity, if earnings were already more than sufficient to meet interest payments. In summary, high gearing is of concern to the equity investor because it increases the volatility of the return on equity.

Did you answer the question?

The question asks why a lender/*investor* should be wary of high gearing - this should prompt you to consider the situation for both a lender (eg the bank) *and* an equity investor, ie a potential shareholder.

(c) Using the first formula for capital gearing,

Long-term Debt/ Equity = 195/176	=	1·108
That is,	=	110·8%
OR		
Interest Bearing Debt/ Equity = 195/176	=	1·108
	=	110·8%

In this case, the absence of short-term interest bearing debt means that the gearing calculation gives the same result for both calculations.

Alternatively, using the second formula,

Long-term Debt/Total Long-term Capital = 195/371 = 0·526

= 52·6%

OR

Interest Bearing Debt/Total Long-term Capital = 195/371 = 0·526

= 52·6%

As before, the fact that long-term debt is the only form of interest bearing debt, results in a common value for the scale of gearing.

The gearing level appears quite high, inasmuch as debt is a significant source of funding for the business, although the bulk of the debt is of a long-term nature and is secured against property. The restaurant business is a volatile one, subject to changing tastes, and sales volatility needs to be taken into account when analysing financial gearing. For most businesses in a volatile market, the risk of falling sales means that high levels of debt can leave a business facing difficulties in meeting its interest payments. The restaurant business, however, is cash generating, when compared with other types of businesses dependent upon credit sales. In view of this, the new restaurant should have fewer problems in servicing interest payments. Nonetheless, if the owners wish to limit their risk it may be advisable to reduce the level of gearing to below one (depending on the formula used), so that a sharp drop in sales would not threaten the long-term survival of the business. It is often the case that banks will only be prepared to lend to small businesses on the basis of 'matching funds' i.e. £100 loan per £100 equity. As the gearing is in this case already over one, the owners would be unable to increase their borrowing if the matched funds approach was used.

Did you answer the question?

Note how the examiner has considered the specific nature of the business in the scenario in answering this part.

The adjusted profit and loss account given in answer to **(a)** shows interest cover is poor. This would serve to confirm that gearing is uncomfortably high.

Furthermore, the figures do not reveal the true level of indebtedness and risk for the proprietors, who are in fact borrowing £75,000 in order to purchase their equity stake. For them the company is a very risky venture.

(d) The accounts clearly indicate that the business would be best suited to seeking out new equity investors, rather than further borrowing, but the access to such investors will depend on the forecast profitability and medium term growth potential. In order to attract investors, Stadium Eats would need to prepare a Business Plan which included detailed Profit and Loss, Balance Sheet and Cash Flow forecasts, together with information on company strategy and marketing plans. Such a plan could then be studied by potential investors, allowing them to make their own estimates of the business' potential, and the risk that they would be taking in buying an equity stake.

Possible sources of such finance might include Business Angels, Venture Capital funds or wealthy relatives/individuals looking to obtain tax relief via the Enterprise Investment Scheme. The latter scheme offers tax relief to individuals investing in a qualifying company, up to a maximum of £100,000; the Stadium Eats project would therefore be well suited to this source of funding. It is possible that it could encourage customers to sign up as investors, in return for discount vouchers on meals. Business Angels may also use the Enterprise Investment Scheme, but they will also be individuals who are used to dealing with small businesses, and may have some expertise to offer. Some Business Angels will request a seat on the Board of Directors in order to monitor the progress of their investment. Venture Capital Funds vary widely in size, from small regional funds (often part financed by local authorities) through to large scale funds which operate as investment trusts, raising money through the issue of shares to the general public.

Equity is not the sole source of funding which might be available. If the restaurant is located in an economic development area, such as an inner city or rural community, then there may be job creation grants/soft loan funds provided by local or central government. In certain areas, a limited amount of grant finance is also available via the European Union.

(e) AIM is the Alternative Investment Market, which was set up in London to replace the Unlisted Securities Market. AIM serves as the market place in which it is possible for smaller companies to raise equity capital. The issue costs and annual registration fees are much lower than for the main stock exchange, and the investors are more likely to be looking for higher risk investments. As relatively new and fast growing businesses, many AIM companies choose to retain a large proportion of their profits, and so they offer low dividend yields to potential investors. The attraction of such investments lies in the potential for substantial capital gains if the business is successful.

Amongst the factors to be considered when seeking a stock market quotation are:

Does the company need a large-scale injection of equity?

Public quotation involves greater reporting requirements and openness.

A listing increases take-over risks.

The owners are likely to see a reduction in the scale of their shareholding, and perhaps lose overall control.

Are growth rates sufficient to give potential investors their required rate of return?

75   (Answer 2 of examination)

Examiner's comments and marking guide

Question 2: This question covered a number of different elements of the syllabus. Parts (a) – (c) clearly caused some difficulties. Part (d) produced much better quality answers.

In calculating payback, a very large number of candidates used profit instead of cash flow to derive an answer. This is basic knowledge and the method of computation should be familiar.

Those who attempted Part (b) of the question attained reasonable marks, although there was some evidence of a failure to think beyond the need for a discount rate. Many candidates simply omitted this section.

Answers to part (c) were mixed. Candidates demonstrated knowledge of the existence of the Monopolies and Mergers Commission, but few knew exactly what its role was. Almost no-one mentioned the regulatory role of the EU.

Part (d) on ratios which might be used to compare financial performance was answered well. There were some very detailed answers which included relevant formulae, as well as explanations for why specific ratios were selected. Weaker answers used several ratios which measured similar trends e.g., profitability. The best answers looked at profitability, liquidity and capital structure.

			Marks
(a)	Calculation (maximum 2 if depreciation is included) No penalty for only one payback calculation which includes labour savings		3
(b)	One mark for each suggested piece of information, where relevant		5
(c)	Recognition of legislation re monopolies	1	
	Description of MMC	1	
	Public interest criteria	2	
	Nature of intervention (investigation)	1	
	EU legislation	1	6
(d)	Ratios and justification	5	
	Commentary	1	6
	Total Marks		20

Step by step answer plan

Step 1 Read the question again and make sure that you focus on precisely what is required. It concerns a possible take-over, and includes investment appraisal techniques, government intervention and performance evaluation.

Step 2 (a) Although there are various methods for calculating payback, they all use cash flows rather than profit, so your first job is to convert the operating profit figure given to a cash flow, as far as the information allows. You then have to decide whether to include the labour savings or not - if you decide not to, briefly explain why, so the examiner will know you haven't just ignored them.

Step 3 (b) You may not have come across this sort of requirement before, but it offers some easy marks. Think of any NPV calculation you've done before and the information/data used - then see what is missing from the information you have here.

Step 4   (c) Even if you don't know much detail about the workings of the Monopolies and Mergers Commission, you should be able to give an outline of its purpose and what it may do. Note the role of the EU in this context.

Step 5   (d) For "financial performance" do not read solely "profitability". This is one aspect, certainly, but liquidity, gearing and shareholder returns are also important. Pick four ratios that cover this range, briefly explaining how they contribute to the evaluation. Note that the balance of the examiner's answer between the ratios and the commentary does not reflect the marking scheme, where only 1 mark is given for the latter. The discussion in the answer is, however, useful for future reference.

Step 6   Now review your answer and ensure that it does precisely answer the question as set.

The examiner's answer

(a)   Payback period should be based on cash flows, that is, the cash generated from operations, and the capital invested by Chromex.

Profit differs from cash flow to the extent that depreciation has been charged in the accounts. The sum received from the sale of assets merely reduces the size of the capital investment.

This gives the following figures for the payback calculation (assuming that no further re-investment in plant is required):

Investment Cost = £150 million – £10 million (TN 1) = £140 million

If the labour cost savings are ignored,

Annual Cash flows from Bexell's operations
post take over   = £10 million + £0·5 million

                                                = £10·5 million

Payback period (in years)   = 140/10·5

                                                = 13·33 years or 13 years 4 months

This is a conservative estimate in that it ignores the possible cash flow effects of the anticipated operating savings from reduced labour costs. If the savings are assumed to have a cash flow value of £700,000, this gives an adjusted figure for cash flow as follows:

Annual cash flow   = £10·5 million + £0·7 million

                   = £11·2 million

Payback period is therefore equal to:

140/11·2   = 12·5 years or 12 years and 6 months

The inclusion of the labour cost savings therefore reduces the payback period by 10 months.

(b)   Additional information required would include:

Specification of a time scale for the appraisal.

Forecast cash flow details, year by year, for period specified in the time scale.

An estimate of the cost of capital for Bexell and the combined group.

A forecast of the realisable value of the investment at the end of the time period.

Details of corporation tax rates, capital allowances and tax relief on debt finance.

Forecast inflation rates, to facilitate calculation of an adjusted NPV.

Did you answer the question?

For five marks, it is likely that you need at least five pieces of additional information!

(c)   The government might seek to intervene in the take-over bid because of fears that the market share of the combined group would constitute a monopoly, which would not be in the interests of UK consumers. The case might thus be referred to the Monopolies and Mergers Commission for further investigation. The Commission investigates all such take-overs in relation to their anticipated effect on the 'public interest'. For example, the commission may take the view that the take-over reduces the level of choice available to buyers of bicycles in the UK to an unacceptable level. In such instances it has the power to request changes in the terms of a deal, in order to protect the public interest. Historical evidence suggests that when the Monopolies and Mergers Commission become involved in reviewing a bid or merger proposal (for example the recent talks between British Airways and American Airlines), it is frequently the case that the bid is delayed, sometimes for several years.

The UK government may also intervene, because it is required to do so in order to enforce EU regulations on fair competition. The European Union sets its own rules for maintenance of free competition, and the control of monopoly power, which are then enforceable throughout the whole of the Union.

(d) A great number of ratios might be suitable for this purpose, depending on the specific type of financial performance which is being compared. Amongst those suitable for such a purpose are:

Return on equity

Asset turnover (by classes of asset type)

Gross/net profit margins

Stock days

Debtor days

Interest cover

Dividend cover

Financial gearing

Operating gearing

P/E ratio

Did you answer the question?

Only four ratios were required - the examiner has included more for your information.

The ratios selected can be justified on the grounds that they measure the key determinants of financial performance, namely:

(1) The company's profit performance (gross and net profit margins) and the returns it offers its investors (ROE & P/E ratio).

(2) Liquidity, which will affect its ability to continue trading: stock/debtor days and dividend and interest cover.

(3) Capital structure and level of business risk : financial and operating gearing.

A comparison, which is to be used to assess the relative performance of a particular company, should be based on data from companies in the same sector, because other businesses in other sectors may have different production systems, operating technology and sources of finance. As a result, the average rates of return, the scale of operations, and the risks of a business will vary from sector to sector. For example, a retail bank may face very high fixed costs, as it has a large branch network to support. In contrast, a franchised restaurant chain will have very low fixed costs, because fixed assets are owned by the franchisees and not the main company. In such cases, judgement on the relative levels of operating gearing in the two businesses would be impossible, because of the variation in the cost structures. Similarly, the risks of operating a shoe factory are fundamentally different from those of a chemical plant, and so the financial ratios generated by each operation will differ widely.

At the same time it is useful to compare ratios with firms of differing sizes (in the one sector) because market dynamics and profitability may well be linked to the scale of a company's operations. For example, in some product markets larger companies may report higher net profit margins as a result of being able to exploit scale economies in production or distribution, or the benefits of vertical integration. By contrast, in other markets, specialisation and niche marketing may increase margins. Comparing ratios amongst companies of differing sizes facilitates some analysis of the factors, which can add to profit.

Tutorial note

1   The £10m reduction in initial investment represents the resale value of the land and buildings (£(15 - 5)m).

---

76   (Answer 3 of examination)

Examiner's comments and marking guide

Question 3: The economic environment forms a large proportion of Section 6 of the syllabus, and so this question should not have been totally unexpected. Answers to parts (a) – (c) were adequate. Section (d) caused great difficulties.

The causes of inflation, covered in Section (a) brought mixed answers. The best clearly saw that demand, cost push and money supply were all relevant. Marks were awarded where these causes were implied, even if they were not explicitly identified.

Answers to (b) were either 100% correct or totally wrong. Calculations on indices forms part of the syllabus for paper 3, and so should be familiar to all candidates at this level.

Part (c) generated a lot of repetition, mainly about rising costs. Candidates need to stop and think, before they write, about the variety of effects created by economic phenomena. Interestingly, the best answers came from overseas candidates who clearly worked in an inflationary environment.

Answers to Part (d) were very disappointing. Most candidates made suggestions about what the company might do in the future, instead of writing about how well they had managed inflation in the past. The other common error was to fail to notice the impact of volume changes on costs. This type of report is something which may well be required of candidates in their place of work, and it is expected that they should be able to critically break down costs into the different components, and analyse trends.

			Marks
(a)	One mark for each theory	3	
	'Floating' mark for quality of comment	1	4
(b)	Calculation of inflation rate and comment on figures,		
	2 marks for each one		4
(c)	Comment on overall effects re performance	2	
	One mark per relevant comment on more specific issues	Max. 4	6
(d)	Report: comment	4	
	cost change calculations	2	6
		Total Marks	20

Step by step answer plan

Step 1   Read the question again and make sure that you focus on precisely what is required. It examines the area of inflation, by general discussion, computations and with specific reference to the impacts on a small manufacturing company. Don't be put off - the examiner's answer is much longer than would be possible in the time

Step 2   (a) A good answer here will be a clear and concise explanation of the economic theories that purport to explain why inflation arises. If your economic knowledge is a bit weak, don't be tempted to waffle - write down what you do know as concisely as possible and move on.

Step 3   (b) The calculations should be straightforward, leaving time for a reasonable amount of comment, although not as much as included in the model answer. Start your discussion with a brief summary of the story told by the numbers, making comparisons both between the two types of index and from year to year. Think about the trends they are showing, and how they might be interlinked.

Step 4   (c) Throughout your studies, you will have come across separate requirements to discuss how inflation affects pricing, investment decisions, cash flow forecasts, discount/interest rates etc. Now you are asked to bring these together in one discussion. The requirement is to "describe, in general terms" - rather than going into detail on one or two of these aspects, a better answer will discuss as many effects as possible very briefly.

Step 5
(d) Don't forget report format here. In order to comment on management of inflation, you need to do some basic analysis on the figures given to try to isolate inflation effects from others, and to split costs up as much as possible. You will use the fact of a constant selling price to determine volume growth, which will clearly be contributing to cost and revenue increases in its own right. You can then use the information in note (2) to split the costs. Only once you have done this basic analysis will you be able to make meaningful comments.

Step 6
Now review your answer and ensure that it does precisely answer the question as set.

The examiner's answer

(a) The causes of inflation can be summarised under three broad headings: cost-push, demand-pull and monetarist theories.

Cost-push inflation arises when autonomous increases in production and operating costs lead businesses to raise their selling prices in an attempt to maintain profitability. One example of a cost increase which might generate such inflation is a rise in wage demands due to workers expecting annual increases in pay. The demand for higher wages, and the resulting cost increase for companies, is not caused by a shortage of workers, but simply by their expectation of increases and the resulting demand for a pay rise. When companies pass on the extra cost via price rises, retail inflation can result.

Changes in exchange rates can also lead to autonomous cost increases, and subsequent price inflation. If, for example, sterling weakens relative to other currencies, companies which import components will experience a rise in the sterling price of those components, and they may decide to pass the cost increase on to their own customers.

A rise in the rate of indirect taxation e.g. Value Added Tax is a third possible cause of cost-push inflation.

The second major cause of inflation is demand pressures leading to price increases. When aggregate demand exceeds aggregate supply, and the economy is operating at full capacity, demand is 'rationed' via price increases. In other words, inflation becomes the means whereby demand and supply are brought back into equilibrium.

Monetarist theory explains inflation in terms of changes in the money supply, and takes the view that money is only held for transactionary purposes. The Quantity Theory of Money states that:

$MV = PT$

Where,

M = Stock of Money

V = Velocity of Circulation

P = Price level

T = Total transactions in the economy

The monetarists suggest that V is stable, and the economy will generally be close to full employment, so that T is not variable. This means that any change in the stock of money (M) will lead directly to an increase in the price level (P). In other words, inflation is a consequence of changes in the money supply.

(b)

	1995/6	1996/7	
RPI	2·5%	3·3%	
WPI	1·8%	2·0%	(TN 1)

The figures show that the rate of retail price inflation has exceeded that of wholesale price inflation over the two-year period, and that the gap between the two rates is widening. The reason for the change is likely to be the move out of recession and the substantial increase in consumer spending, particularly during 1997. Wholesale prices are clearly just one of the factors determining retail prices, and even when wholesale prices are stable, there may still be retail price inflation.

Wholesale inflation rates have remained relatively low, for a number of possible reasons. Many economies have been suffering from economic recession during the early 1990s. In a recession, retailing companies tend to run down their stock levels, which lowers demand from wholesalers. They in turn become reluctant to increase prices for fear of losing what few sales opportunities remain. At the same time, more and more companies are looking overseas for new markets, but such companies are then sensitive to changes in exchange rates. When a currency becomes relatively strong, it becomes increasingly difficult to sell abroad, as price competitiveness is eroded. As the world develops, new countries begin manufacturing and wholesaling basic consumer goods, and the competition for a share of that market increases. In the face of such competition, and faced with the risk of exchange rate fluctuations, many wholesale companies have been reluctant to increase prices. Price competitiveness is seen as a means of preserving market share.

Despite the low rate of wholesale inflation, retail inflation has been rising. One of the reasons why this is the case is because changes in interest rates can have a significant effect on the RPI. This is one of the reasons why economists view interest rates and inflation as interdependent.

In the UK, the RPI index includes an allowance for housing costs, and these are strongly affected by the rates charged for borrowing, which are directly linked to base rates. During 1997 interest rates rose a number of times, and this had the effect, together with the mini consumer 'boom' of raising retail inflation rates. At the same time, a rise in interest rates will cause company borrowing costs to increase, and if companies wish to maintain their profit margins, they will need to pass on such increases to customers via price rises. Interest rates can therefore indirectly affect the price of all the goods which form the RPI.

(c) Inflation can affect a number of different areas of business including pricing decisions, investment decisions, wage settlements, cash flow and working capital management. High rates of inflation can also mean that the traditional measures of company performance need to be adjusted to take account of price changes. The rate of inflation will affect both the prices that a company has to pay for its labour and materials etc and the prices that it is able to charge its own customers. Consequently, inflation can influence the profit performance of a company.

Did you answer the question?

Note how the examiner has shown, right up front, that inflation has a variety of effects on companies - it is a very wide brief and encompasses far more than just rising prices.

Where inflation rates are very high, such as in Mexico or Turkey, businesses selling into such markets may find that they need very frequent price reviews. Monthly reviews are not uncommon, and weekly reviews not unknown. Inflation erodes the real return being earned on any sale, and so regular price increases are necessary to try and maintain real earnings. In contrast, when inflation rates are very low, a business make take care when contemplating price increases for fear of losing market share to competitors who hold prices stable.

Investment decisions are sensitive to the rate of inflation because interest rates and inflation rates are inter-related. Evidence suggests that business investment is lower in times of inflation, partly because of uncertainty regarding the real returns that can be expected from an investment. At the same time, companies may be tempted into investing in short term rather than longer-term projects, because they offer a faster and more predictable payback. This has the effect of distorting the pattern of industrial investment. It is also the case that specific classes of business assets are more likely to retain their real value during inflationary times, and investment patterns are thus adjusted in favour of the purchase of such assets. One such example is the UK property boom of the 1980s when rising commercial property prices attracted many investors at the expense of manufacturing industry, which offered comparatively poor real returns.

Wage settlements are clearly sensitive to the rate of inflation because workers do not wish to see their spending power eroded. It is therefore likely that when inflation rates are high, companies will be faced with higher wage demands, and a need to maintain profitability in the face of such rising costs. At the same time, because inflation erodes the relative value of currencies, the cost of imported components is likely to be increasing. Conversely, however, inflation can make a company's overseas sales much easier, as products become more price competitive due to the exchange rate movements. Thus inflation may be bad for importers but good for exporters.

Cash flow is sensitive to the rate of inflation because if costs are rising, and prices have not been increased, cash flow may come under severe strain. The strain may be exacerbated if higher selling prices lead to a drop in demand, as people forego new spending, in response to reductions in the levels of real income. Working capital management becomes even more important. Investment in stocks and debtors becomes increasingly expensive, and so tight control becomes important. At the same time care must be taken not to under invest in stock only to find that replenishment is more expensive as a consequence of the inflation. Precautionary stock holdings may well increase. Cash holdings should be kept to a minimum during inflationary times, because spending power is being eroded.

Measurements of profitability and returns to investors need to be changed under inflationary conditions, as historic cost accounts may give a misleading picture of company performance. Alternative approaches that have been suggested in the past include the use of either Current Purchasing Power, or Current Cost Accounting. Neither method is currently in widespread use in the UK, but this situation may well change if inflation rates return to the high levels they reached in the 1970s. In essence it is necessary to make sure that a company's financial performance is being measured in *real* as opposed to *monetary* terms.

(d) Report:

To: Board of Directors, Pellas Ltd   June 1998

Prepared by: A. N. Accountant

Subject: Management of Sales and Costs 1996/1997

Dear Sirs,

Over the period 1995–1997 Pellas Ltd has been faced with the difficulty of maintaining profits in an environment of rising costs, but low levels of demand. I believe that the company has responded well to this challenge, and that both sales and cost management have been very good over the period in question.

The decision to hold selling prices fixed was done in order to maintain sales levels in a weak market. In fact, sales volumes have shown a healthy rate of growth, increasing by 20% between 1995 and 1996, and 8% between 1996 and 1997. This would suggest that demand is price sensitive, and the competitive pricing of Pellas' products has allowed us to increase sales and, possibly also, market share.

At the same time, the company was faced with the problem of maintaining margins, given that the main component supplier has insisted on significant annual price increases. Pellas has succeeded in compensating for the higher component costs by tight management and reduction of the other costs of sales. This is demonstrated in the figures shown below.

Component cost $\quad\quad$ = 80% of cost of sales

$\quad\quad\quad\quad\quad\quad\quad\quad$ = £0·520 million in 1995

In 1996, given a 20% increase in volume, plus a 10% price rise, component costs can be estimated as:

$\quad\quad\quad\quad\quad\quad$ = £0·520 × 1·2 × 1·1 million

$\quad\quad\quad\quad\quad\quad$ = £0·686 million

For 1997, the component cost, adjusted for the sales volume and price rises is:

$\quad\quad\quad\quad\quad\quad$ = £0·686 × 1·08 × 1·1

$\quad\quad\quad\quad\quad\quad$ = £0·815 million

This gives a year by year breakdown of cost figures as follows:

	1995	1996	1997
		£ million	
Components	0.520	0.686	0.815
Other cost of sales	0.130	0.144	0.152
Cost of Sales	0.650	0.830	0.967

It can be seen that the rate of increase in the non-component element of the cost of sales is much slower than the rate of volume growth in the business. Whilst sales rose by 20% in 1996, the other costs increased by just over 10·75%. The comparable figures for 1997 were 8% and 4% respectively. This indicates greater efficiency, and a high level of internal cost control.

The reported profits (as per the accounts) show a fall in operating profit of just below 3% between 1996 and 1997. Clearly, any fall in profits is undesirable, but it is difficult to see how performance could have been bettered. If Pellas had chosen to increase prices in line with the RPI, as demonstrated above, profits could have been maintained and indeed increased. The calculations assume, however, that the market is insensitive to price changes, and this is unlikely to be the case in practice. Higher prices could serve to reduce demand to unprofitable levels, particularly if non-manufacturing expenses are high. No information is given on non-manufacturing costs, but it is reasonable to assume that Pellas has some scope to reduce these, and in so doing retain a fixed level of reported pre-tax profit.

Did you answer the question?

Note you are being asked to comment upon the success or otherwise of past inflation management, not advise about future strategy

---

Tutorial note

1 $\quad$ These rates are derived by looking at the increase in the relevant index from one year to the next. For example:

RPI 1995/6: $\dfrac{154.4}{150.7}$ =1.0246, showing an increase of approximately 2.46%, rounded to 2.5%

WPI 1996/7: $\dfrac{137.5}{134.8}$ =1.0200, showing an increase of approximately 2.0%

77   (Answer 4 of examination)

Examiner's comments and marking guide

Question 4: This question was designed to test the candidates' ability to (a) describe the role of the management accountant, (b) contrast profit-seeking and non-profit-seeking organisations and (c) discuss the role of the management accountant in providing appropriate information in a non-profit-seeking organisation.

Candidates had only modest success with this question. Part (a) was reasonably well done though some failed to elaborate their answers sufficiently for full marks, relying on brief reference to "gatekeeper" or "information manager". In (b) candidates often failed to achieve higher marks because they had a narrow perception of a non-profit seeking organisation (e.g., charity or club). Reference was often made to the service nature and the need for subjective performance evaluation which earned marks, but at times little more was developed from this. A common mistake in this part was to discuss the role of the management accountant rather than the features of the organisation, which was a failure to read the question. As a result candidates failed to pick up more marks here, though parts (b) and (c) were marked with some flexibility. In part (c) candidates did not earn as many marks as possible because they failed to incorporate in their answers the full range of techniques and approaches which may be available to the management accountant in the setting envisaged. In other words they failed to be able to apply appropriate management accounting principles to the environment they had previously described.

		Marks
(a)	Each role fully developed (2 each)	6
(b)	Each feature contrasted (2 each)	6
(c)	Reference to appropriate issues: VFM, 3E's, Cost/Benefit, ZBB, Performance Measures, etc. (2 each)	8
	Total Marks	20

Step by step answer plan

Step 1   Read the question again and make sure that you focus on precisely what is required. You are being asked to compare management accounting within profit-seeking and non-profit-seeking organisations. Take care not to overlap your answers, particularly between parts (b) and (c) - plan first.

Step 2   (a) (b) The marking guide indicates that at least three separate points were expected for each of these parts, attracting up to two marks each. Don't be put off by the length of the model answers. Thinking of the roles of the MA in (a) should be reasonably straightforward - focusing it around the functions of planning, control and decision making gives a good structure. Part (b) may need a little more thought - differences mainly stem from different objectives and different types of output. Don't forget that your answer can acknowledge that some of the roles in (a) will also apply here.

Step 3   (c) This is very much a follow on from (b), and you have to be careful to keep the two answers distinct to get maximum marks. You are being asked to discuss the procedures and techniques that the MA may use in a NPO environment, which are often very similar to those used in a profit-seeking organisation. The three E's are a good starting point for setting out the aims; the techniques themselves can again be structured under the planning, control and decision making headings.

Step 4   Now review your answer and ensure that it does precisely answer the question as set.

The examiner's answer

(a)   A major objective of a profit-seeking organisation is profit maximisation, this tends to influence the provision of management accounting information. The role of the management accountant (MA) involves the provision of information which directly or indirectly supports the achievement of this objective. Management accounting is a decision-making, planning and control facilitating activity. The management accounting system must provide information to enable managers to allocate scarce resources in the most efficient manner. Some writers subdivide the role of the MA into at least three distinct areas, stock valuation and product costing, decision making, planning and control.

Stock valuation and product costing involves the generation of a manufacturing cost of a product for the purposes of the preparation of periodic profit and loss accounts. This may be extended to the preparation of a full product cost as an input to the pricing deliberations of a management team. In a profit seeking service organisation there is no requirement to value stock but the average cost of a service may still be generated.

Accounting for decision-making involves the identification of costs and revenues associated with alternative courses of action so that their relative profitability may be ascertained. This may focus, for example, on the relevant costs and benefits concerned with a particular decision, the profit implications of a change in volume, or a trade-off between volumes and price.

Accounting for planning and control is concerned with the creation and use of systems in the organisation to establish responsibilities for particular outcomes and commit the resources to be devoted to achieve the outcomes especially profit. These are often contained within the organisation's budget, consisting of statements of organisational intent of both a financial and a non-financial nature.

An alternative perspective on the role of the MA that is often quoted is that of 'score-keeping, problem solving and attention directing'. These are not dissimilar to the areas mentioned above in that costing and the ascertainment of profit of a company, or department of it, is like keeping a score. Problems solving is the arrangement of information to enable managers to choose between alternative courses of action – i.e. decision making. Attention directing involves ensuring that activities are in line with management's intentions, or particularly, where this is not the case, to be alerted to cases which are at variance to plan – planning and control.

Whilst either of the above groups of activities describe the traditional role of the MA or management accounting department, this is not exhaustive. For example, with increasing competitive situations for many companies the MA should be concerned with looking outward rather than inward, that is, looking at competitors costs and the competitive position of his/her company. Likewise, rather than concern with merely short-term decision-making planning and control, a longer-term perspective may be appropriate involving, for example, lifecycle costing. These and other aspects can be grouped under a heading of strategic management accounting which, whilst not diminishing the importance of the traditional role is becoming an increasingly important part of the role of a management accountant.

(b) There are some general similarities between profit-seeking organisations (PSOs) and non-profit organisations (NPOs) but some important differences which will be outlined below.

By definition there are no profit objectives for NPOs; they do not exist to maximise, or optimise, profits over any period, unlike PSOs for whom periodic profit is an important statistic. The absence of a profit motive may imply the absence of a profit measure. A PSO can compare expenses and revenues to produce profit, a 'guide' to the success of the organisation. This same implication cannot be drawn from a comparison made for an NPO. It may only mean, in the latter case, that the NPO has spent an amount related to that which was allocated or funded. That is, some goods, or more likely services, have been provided for a predetermined cost. It says nothing about the adequacy of that provision or the efficiency with which it was provided. This will be expanded upon below.

That NPOs usually provide services rather than products adds further complexities. It is more difficult to measure in convenient quantitative and aggregate terms the amount of service provided and therefore make judgements about the adequacy of any costs involved. This is a complication when planning how much should be spent and in control when the adequacy of achievement, for a particular outlay, is assessed. It is exacerbated further by the difficulty of measuring the quality of the service provided.

In the non-profit environment there is a reduced role for market forces. A PSO is influenced and can take signals from the choice exercised by consumers. For NPOs no direct alternative may exist, or if it does comparison is confused by measurement and judgement issues caused by the not-for-profit and service dimensions mentioned above.

Did you answer the question?

In (a) you are asked to discuss the roles of a management accountant in a profit-seeking organisation. Note that the requirement in (b) is slightly different - being to discuss the *features* of a non-profit-seeking environment. Take care to give the examiner what he's asking for!

(c) The MA must endeavour to provide information which demonstrates the provision of value for money by the NPO. Value for money is a focus on, and regularly monitoring through performance indicators of, economy, efficiency and effectiveness. In a little more detail this implies:

- Economy in the acquisition of resources of the right quality and the right type for the right price.

- Efficiency in the use of resources i.e. the appropriate quantity of inputs are used to attain a given level of output.

- Effectiveness, the outputs achieved should be those that enable the organisation to achieve its pre-stated general objectives in all areas of delivering the service.

In the context of the earlier discussion the MA is required to provide information to assist in decision-making, planning and control. Decision-making involves selecting between competing alternatives. In this a statement of the costs of each alternative needs to be set out and these inputs must be compared with the benefits achieved or outputs. The latter are the more problematic and often involve a description and some approximate financial or non-financial measure of achievement. The outcomes for various competing alternatives can then be compared. This process, called cost-benefit analysis, is not easy because the features involved may not be easily aggregated or compared directly. It is also influenced by a high degree of subjective judgement and opinion, for example consider having to make a choice between spending for educational or medical purposes or judging the quality of service in different settings.

Planning and control involves the production of periodic budgets and the use of feedback to monitor actual attainment. In NPOs, budgets often identify a 'spending limit'. They are the decisions taken (as above) but codified in terms of organisation structure, responsibilities and timescale. The technique of zero based budgeting or a variation, priority based budgeting may be employed in order to help with the preparation of budgets and to systematise the choice between alternative spending categories or spending levels. Along with the authority to spend contained in the budget should be a statement of the expected outcomes to be achieved by the spending. This should be supplemented by regular reports of actual achievements against those required often using non-financial performance measures.

The MA should support management with a diverse range of statistics beyond the immediate objectives and achievements of the organisation. This will include information on other organisations and regions or other ways of achieving objectives. A maximum ingenuity is required to produce information in NPOs in order to overcome some of the difficulties and complexities involved. Some not-for-profit organisations are undertaking various forms of 'privatisation', creating 'artificial' markets or requiring compulsory competitive tendering in some areas of operation. These are further ways to attempt to obtain value for money in the non-profit environment. It is likely to increase the competitive element but it is unlikely to simplify the role of the MA in non-profit organisations.

---

78 (Answer 5 of examination)

Examiner's comments and marking guide

Question 5: This question required candidates to (a) explain some budget terminology, (b) determine the variable and fixed components of costs provided, (c) apply these to generate a budget profit statement and (d) determine and comment on the implications of a change in stock levels.

Overall performance, on what could be seen as a fundamental area of the syllabus for this paper, was only average. In (a) most had some idea of a rolling budget and its advantages but at times these were poorly expressed and some confused them with flexible budgets or Zero-based budgets. Part (b) proved problematic for some who failed to appreciate the need to identify the semi-variable nature of the costs contained in some of the data (even though cost behaviour was mentioned in line three of the question and referred to in the requirement). As a result, they failed to score marks. Some also failed to appreciate that selling overhead would be related to sales not production volume and therefore they did not score here. In (c) candidates had some success in formulating a budget profit statement. Credit was given here for the use of candidates' own figures from part (b) which is in line with general marking practices. Candidates failed to pick up marks if they failed to appreciate that the production level was not the same as the sales, as a stock reduction was implied, this had implications for the cost prediction and the need to adjust for stock value at the unit cost given. In (d) some candidates attempted to repeat a lengthy budget statement when a summary and discussion of changes was required. Candidates did not pick up all the marks available here if they left insufficient time, though selected reference to fixed overhead implication, bonus levels and motivation to maximise production was pleasing and did earn credit.

			Marks
(a)	Explanation	2	
	Benefit	2	4
(b)	Material	1	
	Labour	1	
	Factory overhead	1	
	Selling overhead	1	4
(c)	Production	1	
	Labour	1	
	Factory overhead	1	
	Selling overhead	1	
	Stock adjustment	1	
	Sales	1	6
(d)	Variable cost	1	
	Bonus	1	
	Stock change	1	
	Explanation and motivation	3	6
	Total Marks		20

Step by step answer plan

Step 1 Read the question again and make sure that you focus on precisely what is required. It looks at the role and preparation of rolling budgets. Budgeting is a highly examinable part of the syllabus, and you should be well prepared for such a question.

Step 2 (a) Even if you can't remember exactly what a rolling budget is, the question itself makes this fairly clear. Give a concise explanation of how such a budget is prepared, and then think about its advantages - again, even if you haven't specifically learnt these, you should be able to come up with some common sense ideas.

Step 3 (b) In the introduction to the data in the question, it refers to "the cost behaviour" of each cost item. This should alert you to the possibility that some will be fixed costs (which should be obvious), some will be purely variable (change proportionately with volume) and some will be semi-variable (change with volume, though not proportionately) - see TN1. You thus need to determine the fixed and variable elements of the costs from the Q1 to Q3 data, and apply these to Q4.

Step 4 (c) This budget is prepared for three different production levels, using the Q4 unit and fixed costs computed in (b). Note that as the stock adjustment (TN3) is at a standard cost, not necessarily matching that used in valuing Q4 production, you cannot simply use the sales volume to get cost of sales directly.

Step 5 (d) Given both the requirement to produce your answer in summary form only, and the number of marks you have for this and comment, you need to think before launching into long repetitious revised budgets. Basically, if you produce the extra 8,000 units (TN2) instead of using stock, the profit will be charged with the extra actual variable cost instead of the standard full factory cost for these units. The difference between these costs gives you most of the profit difference. You then need to recognise the impact of the bonus - which helps with the discussion part that follows.

Step 6 Now review your answer and ensure that it does precisely answer the question as set.

The examiner's answer

(a) Accounting budgets are typically prepared for the year ahead, each year being divided into months or quarters. A company can then monitor its progress as the year passes. A variation and extension of the annual budget is to regularly add a further quarter to a budget as the immediate quarter passes so that a full budget year is always in view. This approach is called a rolling or continuous budget. As Q1 progresses, Q2 is reviewed and revised in some detail, at the same time the budget for the other quarters are reviewed and updated.

Benefits of this approach are that management can always have in front of them plans for a full year. This will emphasise the longer term focus of the organisation. It also ensures that managers are constantly thinking about planning for the future and the validity of these plans. It keeps planning at the front of the manager's mind all of the year, not just at the annual budget round. As a result of this it is likely that the actual performance is being compared with a more realistic target than if the budget was prepared only once a year.

(b) The costs are variable, semi-variable or fixed. It is necessary to determine the cost behaviour from Q1–Q3, then adjust this for Q4. (TN 1)

	Q1 – Q3		Q4	
	Variable Costs £	**Fixed Costs £**	**Variable Costs £**	**Fixed Costs £**
Material	2·5	–	2·75	–
Labour	5·0	80,000	5·0	80,000
Factory Overhead	1·5	140,000	1·5	147,000
Admin Overhead	–	30,000	–	30,000
Selling Overhead	0·5	20,000	0·5	21,000

Note Sample calculations:

Material Q1 $\dfrac{£50,000}{20,000} = £2·5$

Labour Q3 – Q1 $\dfrac{£230,000 - £180,000}{30,000 - 20,000} = £5$

Fixed element £230,000 – (30,000 × £5) = £80,000

Factory Overhead

Q2 – Q1 $\dfrac{£200,000 - £170,000}{40,000 - 20,000} = £1·5$

Fixed element £200,000 – (40,000 × £1·5) = £140,000

Selling Overhead (based on Sales)

Q2 – Q1 $\dfrac{£37,000 - £29,000}{34,000 - 18,000} = £0·5$

Fixed element £37,000 – (34,000 × £0·5) = £20,000

Note Further calculations made with data from other quarters, would confirm the rates and costs computed above.

(c) Flexible Budget Profit Statements

	Low	Most Likely	High
	000s	000s	000s
Sales	38	44	50
Production (TN 2)	30	36	42
	£000	**£000**	**£000**
Material	82·5	99	115·5
Labour	230·0	260	295 (TN 3)
Factory Overhead	192·0	201	210
Admin. Overhead	30	30	30
Selling Overhead	40	43	46
Cost of Production	574·5	633	696·5
Add stock adjustment (TN 4)	104·0	104·0	104·0
Prodn. Cost of sales	678·5	737·0	800·5
Sales	684·0	792	900·0
Profit	5·5	55	99·5

(d) The change in profit will be caused by the change in costs as a result of greater production, rendering the stock adjustment undertaken for the quarter (based on absorption costing principles) unnecessary. Change in costs = 8,000 units × variable production cost £9·25.

Production (000's) units	38	44	50
	£000	£000	£000
Variable production costs	74	74	74
Additional bonus	–	10	20
Stock adjustment	104	104	104
Increase in profit	30	20	10

Under the assumption of a simple linear relationship of variable costs to volume the only extra costs for 8,000 units are the variable production costs which are £9·25 per unit. For any volume above 40,000 units there is also the bonus payment to incorporate (in the case of the high volume the incremental bonus payment). If the budgeted production volume is made equal to sales then the stock level at the start of quarter four will remain at the end. There is no need for a stock adjustment, or put another way, the adjustment made in part **(c)** can be added back. The above table shows the profit increase which will occur for the three volume levels.

Under the original volume prediction (and absorption costing principles) quarter four was being charged with fixed overhead contained in the opening stock value in addition to the fixed overhead of the period. Such overhead being transferred to that quarter from earlier accounting periods where production exceeded sales. With the revised stocking policy, the production for quarter four is equal to the sales of the quarter, and this fixed overhead is, in effect, being passed into the following year.

Did you answer the question?

This text is meeting the requirement to "comment on the reason for the profit change" - ie explain what you've just shown in numbers, in words.

Regarding managerial motivation and production levels, it is apparent that the reported profit levels, under absorption costing, respond to changes in the levels of production. We have seen that during a quarter, an increase in the production results in an increase in the reported profit. This presents the possibility of opportunistic behaviour by managers wishing to enhance the level of profit being reported in any one period. They may deliberately over-produce, compared to prevailing sales demand, this production would be held in stock to be sold later, and reported profits would increase. This action would occur if they were placed in a position of needing to achieve a target profit for their bonus or performance appraisal purposes. It may be storing up trouble for the future however, because future production may have to be cut back in order to allow stock levels to be reduced. It would really only be justified if, for example, future sales were expected to be so high that they could not be met by the existing production capacity.

Tutorial notes

1   To determine the behaviour of each cost, look at how they respond to changes in production volume. Looking at Q1 to Q2, for example, production doubles and so does direct materials (thus variable); production labour increases but doesn't double (thus semi variable) admin doesn't change (thus fixed).

2   As the company wishes to have closing stock at the end of the fourth quarter equal to the opening stock at the beginning of the first, then production must equal sales in total over the four quarters. Over the first three quarters, production has exceeded sales by (20+40+30) - (18+34+30) = 8,000 units; thus production must be 8,000 lower than sales in Q4.

3   42,000 × £5 + £80,000 + 2,000 × £2.5 (bonus) = £295,000

4   Cost of sales = production cost plus the decrease in stock at full factory cost (8,000 units (TN2) at £13 = £104,000)

79 (Answer 6 of examination)

Examiner's comments and marking guide

Question 6: This question involved (a) interpreting a joint product situation in a process costing environment, (b) sharing joint costs and (c) reference to an additional business opportunity.

This question was the least preferred in section C and the least well answered, though the scale of the numbers involved did not make it a complex problem. At times candidates tended to make it more complex by the use of unusual methods of sharing cost or wasting valuable time by making calculations for each cost element rather than combining some of them. The diagram for (a) was usually reasonable, earning some good early marks and mapping out the process. In (b) candidates failed to pick up more marks if they failed to split the common costs correctly, or inexplicably, failed to take any account at all of the common costs. There were varying interpretations of the net realisable value, often candidates made use of the gross sales value basis and partial credit was given here. Insufficient comment was given in the conclusion to this part and hence candidates failed to pick up marks as a result. In (c) full financial evaluations were rare and hence this resulted in marks not being gained. In particular candidates tended to use the full cost in simple comparison to the offer price with no qualifying comments, in spite of the presence of fixed costs and questions in other diets featuring this sort of marginal decision. Finally, it was pleasing to see some further points arise in the discussion part of (c), for example, discussing the availability of capacity and, on occasions, the potential available market for the other joint product.

Marks

(a) Diagram		2
(b) Joint costs	1	
Further processing	1	
Sales	1	3
NRV	2	
By product	1	
Profit	1	4
Comments		3
(c) Use of variable costs	1	
Common and finishing process costs	1	
By product	1	
Comment on shortfall	1	4
Clarifying comments		4
Total Marks		20

Step by step answer plan

Step 1 Read the question again and make sure that you focus on precisely what is required. This is a fairly standard joint products problem, involving allocation of fixed costs and decision making.

Step 2 (a) It is probably a good idea to do a *quick* sketch of the flow diagram to get the logic sorted, then produce the finished version with quantities etc on it.

Step 3 (b) These are two common methods of splitting fixed costs between joint products, and you should have a good idea of the best way to lay out your workings. Don't forget to comment.

Step 4 (c) When decision making comes into a joint products question, you must remember the golden rule - consider incremental costs versus incremental revenue, disregarding any unit costs you may already have calculated involving apportioned fixed costs. In this case, producing more of one product will inevitably mean the production of more of the other, with associated common costs. The decision will ultimately depend upon the possible uses of the excess "other" product.

Step 5 Now review your answer and ensure that it does precisely answer the question as set.

The examiner's answer

(a)

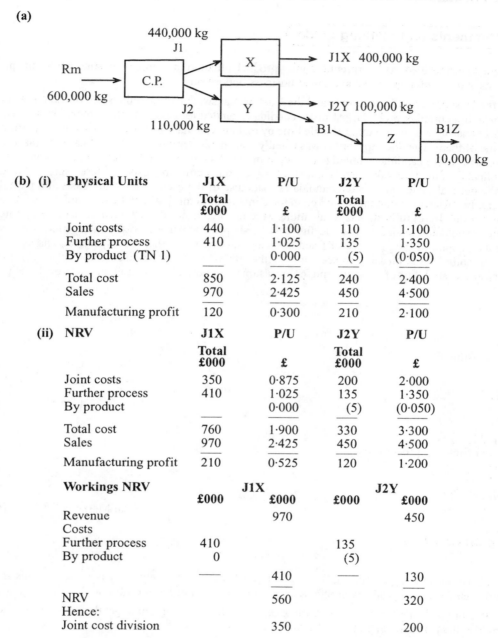

(b) (i)

Physical Units	J1X Total £000	P/U £	J2Y Total £000	P/U £
Joint costs	440	1·100	110	1·100
Further process	410	1·025	135	1·350
By product (TN 1)	___	0·000	(5)	(0·050)
Total cost	850	2·125	240	2·400
Sales	970	2·425	450	4·500
Manufacturing profit	120	0·300	210	2·100

(ii)

NRV	J1X Total £000	P/U £	J2Y Total £000	P/U £
Joint costs	350	0·875	200	2·000
Further process	410	1·025	135	1·350
By product	___	0·000	(5)	(0·050)
Total cost	760	1·900	330	3·300
Sales	970	2·425	450	4·500
Manufacturing profit	210	0·525	120	1·200

Workings NRV	£000	J1X £000	£000	J2Y £000
Revenue		970		450
Costs				
Further process	410		135	
By product	0		(5)	
	___	410	___	130
NRV		560		320
Hence:				
Joint cost division		350		200

N.B. The above tables enable the cost per unit and the monthly manufacturing profit to be extracted and are presented for the sake of clarity. A candidate would be able to produce the answers required in this question without reproducing all the detail in the tables.

There is no single correct way to divide the joint costs between the two products involved. The above are two possibilities. The physical units method is the most simple and results in the same unit joint cost of the two products. If management want to undertake this product costing for the purposes of stock valuation and stocks are not material in the context of overall volume then the physical unit method may be convenient and appropriate but it has little else to commend it.

The NRV method takes account of the respective market values in addition to the quantities produced. If management want to make some judgements about profitability of the products this method is to be preferred. However, they should be warned about drawing any conclusions about individual products. In joint product situations this is not possible. The emphasis must be on the whole process rather than individual products. With this method the individual products will be shown to be profitable if the whole process is profitable. It is preferable to produce cost and profit reports which show joint products with a similar level of profitability than for these to be distorted when products have very different market values and this is not taken into account.

(c) (i) Extra costs incurred for 10,000 kg of J2Y
(i.e. 10% of current volume of J2Y)

	£	£
Emphasis on variable costs only:		
10% of Common Facility costs		50,000
10% of finishing process (Y)		13,000
		———
Subtotal of costs		63,000
Sales revenue of J2Y		
10,000 × £4·00	40,000	
Contribution from sale of B1Z		
10% of current volume (1,500 – 700)	800	40,800
	———	———
Shortfall in revenue		22,200
		———

The price of £4·00 per kg is not sufficient to cover all of the costs of manufacturing the 10,000 of J2Y. On the face of it a price in excess of £6·22 would be more appropriate. It should be noted however that in undertaking this production of J2Y the company will also manufacture 40,000 kg of intermediate product J1 which can be developed into J1X. A decision rests on what can be done with this output. If J1X can be sold at a price which exceeds the shortfall in revenue and the variable further processing costs then this should be undertaken. The minimum revenue for the sales of the excess J1X to make the whole deal profitable is £22,200 plus £38,500 (10% of process X £385,000 variable further processing costs). This represents a minimum price of approximately £1·52 per kg.

(ii) There are a number of assumptions and further questions applicable to the above approach. It is stated that this business is extra to the present level of business, it needs to be confirmed that all present output is committed and cannot be used to meet this order. Following on from this it is uncertain that the company has the capacity to cope with this extra business, though it is only 10% of volume, not all businesses have the flexibility to cope with this sort of volume change, it depends on their existing capacity.

Given that some increase in production is likely if the approach is to be entertained then in the calculations above it is assumed that the extra costs will be variable costs only. This assumes that the unit variable costs have been identified with some accuracy and there are no incremental fixed costs incurred for this order. If there are any additional costs they need to be incorporated.

The attractiveness of the order may well depend on what can be done with the extra J1X that is produced, therefore its market potential and the price it can command may be a decisive factor in responding to this approach. This is presently unknown.

The prevailing market price of J2Y is £4·50, if this order is taken at £4·00, or close to it, the effect on the existing customers and the prices currently being achieved needs to be considered. If further discussion with this new customer takes place it may have to be made clear that business at this special price may not be possible in the future. Indeed, there is no indication of the chances that this approach may lead to further business, but this could be a factor which the company may wish to consider.

Tutorial note

1   The net gain from the by product is 10,000 × £1.50 (market price) - £10,000 (process Z cost) = £5,000. This will be deducted from the costs of process Y.

QUESTIONS TO DECEMBER 1998 EXAMINATION

Section A – This question is compulsory and MUST be answered

80   (Question 1 of examination)

You are an accountant with a practice, which includes a large proportion of individual clients, who often ask for information about traded investments. You have extracted the following data from a leading financial newspaper.

(i)

Stock	Price	P/E ratio	Dividend yield (% gross)
Buntam plc	160p	20	5
Zellus plc	270p	15	3·33

(ii) Earnings and dividend data for Crazy Games plc are given below:

	1993	1994	1995	1996	1997
EPS	5p	6p	7p	10p	12p
Div. per share (gross)	3p	3p	3·5p	5p	5·5p

The estimated before tax return on equity required by investors in Crazy Games plc is 20%.

(iii) The gross yield to redemption on gilts are as follows:

Treasury 8·5% 2000	7·00%
Exchequer 10·5% 2005	6·70%
Treasury 8% 2015	6·53%

Required:

Draft a report for circulation to your private clients which explains:

(a) the factors to be taken into account (including risks and returns) when considering the purchase of different types of traded investments.   **(6 marks)**

(b) the role of financial intermediaries, and their usefulness to the private investor.   **(8 marks)**

(c) the meaning and the relevance to the investor of each of the following:

  (i)   Gross dividend (pence per share)

  (ii) EPS

  (iii) Dividend cover

  Your answer should include calculation of, and comment upon, the gross dividends, EPS and dividend cover for Buntam plc and Zellus plc, based on the information given above.

                    (12 marks)

(d) how to estimate the market value of a share.
  Illustrate your answer by reference to the data in (ii) on Crazy Games plc, using the information to calculate the market value of 1,000 shares in the company.   **(5 marks)**

(e) the shape of the yield curve for gilts, based upon the information given in (iii) above, which you should use to construct the curve.   **(4 marks)**

(f) the meaning of the term 'gilts' and the relevance of yield curves to the private investor.

                    (5 marks)

                    (40 marks)

Section B – ONE question ONLY to be attempted

---

81   (Question 2 of examination)

(a) Explain the cash flow characteristics of a finance lease, and compare it with the use of a bank loan or cash held on short-term deposit. Your answer should include some comment on the significance of a company's anticipated tax position on lease versus buy decisions.   **(8 marks)**

(b) Prime Printing plc has the opportunity to replace one of its pieces of printing equipment. The new machine, costing £120,000, is expected to lead to operating savings of £50,000 per annum and have an economic life of five years. The company's after tax cost of capital for the investment is estimated at 15%, and operating cash flows are taxed at a rate of 30%, one year in arrears.

The company is trying to decide whether to fund the acquisition of the machine via a five-year bank loan, at an annual interest rate of 13%, with the principal repayable at the end of the five-year period. As an alternative, the machine could be acquired using a finance lease, at a cost of £28,000 p.a. for five years, payable in advance. The machine would have zero scrap value at the end of five years.

Note: Due to its current tax position, the company is unable to utilise any capital allowances on the purchase until year one.

Required:
Assuming that writing-down allowances of 25% p.a. are available on a reducing balance basis, recommend, with reasons, whether Prime Printing should replace the machine, and if so whether it should buy or lease.   **(12 marks)**
          (20 marks)

---

82   (Question 3 of examination)

PCB plc manufacture printed circuit boards for use in pocket calculators. Since 1995 business has been expanding very rapidly, and the company has now encountered a liquidity problem, as illustrated by the most recent balance sheets reproduced below:

PCB company balance sheets

	As at 30 November 1998 £	As at 30 November 1997 £
Fixed assets	308,000	264,000
Current assets		
Stock	220,000	95,000
Debtors	210,000	108,000
Cash	Nil	1,750
	430,000	204,750
Current liabilities		
Bank	158,000	41,250
Trade creditors	205,000	82,500
Net current assets	67,000	81,000
Capital and reserves		
Issued share capital	18,000	18,000
Reserves	357,000	327,000

Equity
Shareholders' funds   375,000   345,000

Other information

1. Sales for the year to 30 November 1997 were £1·7 million, yielding a gross profit of £330,000, and a net profit before tax of £82,000.

2. The corporation tax rate is 30%.

3. For the year ending 30 November 1997, dividends of £35,000 were paid out.

4. At the beginning of the year to 30 November 1998 the company bought some new manufacturing equipment and recruited six more sales staff.

5. Sales for the year to 30 November 1998 were £3 million, with a gross profit of £450,000, and net profit before tax of £60,000.

6. Dividends payable for the year to 30 November 1998 amount to £12,000.

Required:

(a) Illustrating your answer with figures taken from the question, explain why it is not unusual for manufacturing companies to face a cash shortage when sales are expanding very rapidly.

(4 marks)

(b) Explain why PCB plc has not increased its net profit, despite the large increase in sales between 1997 and 1998.

(4 marks)

(c) How has the mix of funding used by PCB changed between the two years, and what are the implications of such changes in terms of investor and creditor risks?

(6 marks)

(d) Suggest ways in which PCB might seek to resolve its current funding problems, and avoid the risks associated with over-trading.

(6 marks)

(20 marks)

Section C – TWO questions ONLY to be attempted

83 (Question 4 of examination)

The Zorro Company manufactures a line of four related products in a single factory which is currently operating below capacity. Annual sales and costs of the products are shown below:

	W £000	X £000	Y £000	Z £000	Total £000
Sales	2,000	2,500	1,000	500	6,000
Factory cost of sales:					
materials	300	400	200	40	940
labour	500	600	400	100	1,600
overhead	600	800	500	100	2,000
	1,400	1,800	1,100	240	4,540
Gross margin	600	700	(100)	260	1,460
Selling overhead	300	375	150	75	900
Operating profit/(loss)	300	325	(250)	185	560

The factory overheads costs allocated to products are based on predetermined overhead rates of which 40% is estimated to be variable at the current operating volume. Selling overheads are applied to products based on 15% of sales value, the variable component of this is approximately 5% of sales.

The loss being reported in the above table against product Y is indicative of recent results and has led the management to consider its withdrawal. It is estimated that if product Y were to be withdrawn a saving of fixed factory and selling costs of £100,000 would occur.

Required:
(a) On financial grounds should Y be withdrawn? Briefly explain and qualify your answer.

(7 marks)

(b) The chief executive has said that he believes in the long run a product that does not cover its costs should not be retained.

    (i)   Is it conceivable that in the long run it might be profitable to keep Y in the product line?

    (ii)   In what circumstances would it be appropriate to consider dropping product Y?

(6 marks)

(c) Following some further enquiries it is established that:

Product Z may in some cases be a substitute for Y. If Y were to be withdrawn, sales of Z would increase by £300,000.

Products W and Y are complementary. Twenty per cent of Y is sold in conjunction with W. These customers would not be able to substitute Z for Y and would be likely to move to other companies for their supplies if product Y is dropped. As a consequence sales of W would drop by 10% if Y were to be withdrawn completely. Product Y could however be retained as a service to these specific product W customers only, in which case the increased sales of Z, mentioned above, would still apply.

The saving of fixed costs achieved by the complete withdrawal of product Y would still be £100,000. If product Y was to be retained as a service to product W customers only the saving in fixed factory and selling costs would be £50,000.

Required:
In the light of this new information should product Y be continued, withdrawn completely, or continued as a service only to the specific customers for product W? Briefly explain your answer.   (7 marks)

(20 marks)

---

84   (Question 5 of examination)

A product manager has responsibility for a single product and is in the process of submitting data to be compiled into budgets for 1999. The manager has performance targets set in relation to sales volume, profitability levels and a target cash surplus from the product.

Shown below are the agreed budgeted sales for the product for December 1998 to May 1999.

	Dec	Jan	Feb	Mar	April	May
Units	14,000	16,000	22,000	17,000	20,000	24,000

The company policy is that, at each month end, the closing stock of finished goods should be 25% of the following month's forecast sales and the stock of raw material should be sufficient for 10% of the following month's production. Stock levels currently conform to this policy. One unit of raw material makes one unit of finished stock, there is no wastage.

Raw material purchases are paid for during the month following the month of purchase. All other expenses are paid for as incurred. All sales are made on credit and the company expects cash receipts for 50% of sales in the month of sale and 50% in the following month.

The company operates an absorption costing system which is computed on a monthly basis. That is, in addition to direct costs it recovers each month's fixed and variable manufacturing overhead expenses in product costs using the budgeted production and budgeted expenditure in the month to establish an absorption rate. This cost is used to place a value on the stock holding. Opening stock is valued at the unit cost which was established in the previous month. At 1 January 1999 finished stock should be assumed at £40 per unit. A flow of cost based on FIFO is assumed.

Sales are made at a price of £58 per unit.

Estimated costs to be used in the budget preparation for the product are:

Manufacturing costs:
material	£10·00 per unit produced
variable overhead and labour	£16·00 per unit produced
Fixed overhead costs	£210,000 per month
(including depreciation of £54,000 per month)	

Selling costs:
Variable	£7·00 per unit sold
Fixed	£164,000 per month

Required:

(a) Compute the monthly budgeted production and material purchases for January to March 1999.

(4 marks)

(b) Prepare a budgeted profit and loss account and a statement of cash receipts and payments for January 1999.

(7 marks)

(c) Explain briefly the implications of the company's treatment of fixed manufacturing overheads compared to a predetermined overhead rate prepared annually.

(4 marks)

(d) The preparation of budget data may be assisted by the use of a time series.

Explain what a time series is and the various components which comprise one.

(5 marks)

(20 marks)

---

85   (Question 6 of examination)

A major information source within many businesses is a system of standard costing and variance analysis.

Required:

(a) Describe briefly four purposes of a system of standard costing.

(4 marks)

(b) Explain three different levels of performance which may be incorporated into a system of standard costing and comment on how these may relate to the purposes set out in (a) above.

(6 marks)

(c) Comment on whether standard costing applies in both manufacturing and service businesses and how it may be affected by modern initiatives of continuous performance improvement and cost reduction.

(4 marks)

(d) A standard costing system enables variances for direct costs, variable and fixed overheads to be extracted. Identify and briefly discuss some of the complexities and practical problems in calculation which may limit the usefulness of those variances.

(6 marks)

(20 marks)

ANSWERS TO DECEMBER 1998 EXAMINATION

80   (Answer 1 of examination)

Report to Private Clients:
Subject: Traded Investments
Author: A.N. Accountant

(a)   The term 'traded investment' refers to the purchase of an investment asset, which is traded in the financial markets. Examples include government and company bonds, ordinary shares, preference shares, warrants, and options or futures contracts. The range of such investments is therefore wide, and it is important to recognise that each type of investment has unique characteristics in terms of its cost, rate of return and risk. All of these factors must be taken into account when selecting an investment.

The price of bonds and shares will vary, depending upon economic conditions and the financial performance of the individual companies. Interest rates directly affect the price of gilt-edged stock and corporate bonds, such that as interest rates rise, the price of bonds falls. This represents a capital risk to the investor, who cannot be certain of the price at which the bond can be sold. This uncertainty is counter-balanced by the fact that such investments offer a fixed rate of return. If an investor buys, for example, 10% Treasury Stock 2001, at a price of £105, he/she can be certain that the interest payable is £10 per bond, equal to a return of 10/105, or 9·5% gross. This interest is payable annually (usually in two instalments) until the date of maturity of the bond, when the bond is redeemed for the nominal value of £100. The return earned on bonds will generally, though not always, be higher than that available through interest bearing deposit accounts. Ordinary shares present a much riskier form of investment, particularly for private individuals, who may incur high charges for the purchase and sale of shares. The price of ordinary shares varies daily, depending on factors within the market in general, and also specific to the company. An investor may earn a return via dividends and/or capital gains. The amount of dividends receivable is dependent, amongst other things, upon the profits of the company, and hence is not predictable with certainty. Individual share prices are definitely not predictable with any level of certainty. Consequently, investment in ordinary shares is relatively risky, but may offer good returns, which historically have been shown on average to be higher than the returns on bonds.

The purchase of derivatives, such as futures or options, as a way of investing in traded securities, may be highly risky unless they are covered trades. The potentially very high returns from such investments reflects the associated high risk.

In conclusion, when comparing the different traded investments, it is essential that the composition of the investment portfolio matches both the liquidity and risk needs of each individual investor.

(b)   Financial intermediaries are important to the efficient functioning of the financial markets, as they act to bring the borrowers/companies and lenders/equity providers together. Financial intermediaries include pension funds, insurance companies, retail and merchant banks, and unit trust companies. In relation to private investors, their functions include:

(i)   the provision of investment advice and information.
Financial intermediaries provide investors with advice and information on the range of investment opportunities available, and the associated risks and returns. Access to such expert information and advice saves the private investor a great deal of time in searching for the investment most suited to his/her needs. Stockbrokers can act on client instructions to buy/sell stocks, but may also offer an advisory service which offers suggestions on investments to add to a porfolio. Many brokers also offer private investors hands-free investment management, whereby the investor leaves all the decisions on investment selection in the hands of the broker, in return for a management fee. The investor is protected from the risk of loss through negligence or mismanagement on the part of the intermediary, by the regulatory systems which govern the financial markets.

(ii)   reduction of risk via aggregation of funds
Intermediaries serve to reduce investment risks for individuals by creating an investment portfolio. Unit trusts are a good example of how the process works. An individual investor will usually lack

the funds to own an equity portfolio, but by investing money in a unit trust the trust can aggregate all the small individual investments and invest in a wide spread in stocks across the whole market. In this way, the returns to the individual investor are less volatile than if they invested in the equities directly on a small scale.

(iii) maturity transformation
It will often be the case that there is not a perfect match between the time period for which a company needs funds and the time period over which a private individual is willing to invest.

Financial intermediaries play a role here in performing the function of maturity transformation. For example, a building society will lend out money for periods of 20 or 30 years, but their investors will still wish to be able to withdraw cash that they have in deposit accounts at random intervals. By taking advantage of the constant turnover of cash between borrowers and lenders, the building society can lend long-term whilst holding short-term deposits. It is this process which is referred to as maturity transformation.

Financial intermediaries can therefore be seen to be extremely useful to the private investor, as they may provide useful advice and make it easier for the individual to take advantage of the returns that can be earned in the financial markets (via, for example, personal pension funds), whilst at the same time leaving investors with a wide range of opportunities because of maturity transformation, aggregation and reduced risk.

(c) (i) Gross dividend
At the end of the financial year, companies will announce the profits or losses that they have earned, and a figure for net profit after tax. A company can choose either to pay any profit out in dividends or to re-invest it in the business. Dividends are paid out per share, and so the more shares that you own in a business, the more dividend income that you will receive. Using the example of Buntam plc, the figures indicate a gross dividend yield of 5%. This means that the dividend paid equals 5% of the share price, or eight pence, in this case. The term gross means that this is the dividend paid before tax. The equivalent calculation for Zellus plc means that the dividend yield of 3·33% is equivalent to a gross dividend payment of nine pence. If an individual shareholder in Buntam plc pays tax at 20% on investment income then he will collect a net dividend of 6·40 pence per share. The company pays this basic rate of tax to the government as an advance payment of its corporation tax liability, when it pays out its dividends, and so investors receive the dividend after deduction of the basic tax payable.

The gross dividend figure is of relevance to an investor as it facilitates direct comparison of the dividend figure and dividend yield paid out by different companies, as well as comparison with interest yields on fixed return investments.

The tax liability is determined by the individual circumstances of each investor, and so its inclusion would serve only to confuse any comparative analysis. The dividend figure is also relevant to an investment decision because it is a way of earning income from investments, as opposed to capital gains, which can only be realised when the investment is sold.

(ii) Earning per share
Earnings per share (EPS) is calculated as profit attributable to equity divided by the number of shares in issue and ranking for dividends. EPS thus represents what is available to be paid out as dividends.

Clearly, therefore, if the number of shares in issue remains fixed, the EPS will rise as the net profit attributable to equity increase.

The value of EPS can be calculated by dividing the share price by the P/E ratio. For Buntam this means EPS equals eight pence. In other words, the earnings per share is equal to the gross dividend payable. For Zellus, the EPS is equal to 18 pence (270/15), which compares with a gross dividend of nine pence. On first sight, therefore, it is tempting to view Zellus as a better investment because its EPS is higher. On the other hand, an investor has to pay 270 pence per share to get earning of 18 pence, compared with 160 pence to get earning of eight pence. The EPS figure is of limited value on its own; it needs to be judged in conjunction with the share price, and hence the P/E ratio.

(iii) Dividend cover
Dividend cover measures the relationship between earnings per share and net dividends per share. The higher the level of dividends (for any given level of EPS) the lower will be the level of profit

retained and re-invested within the business. This can have an effect on the balance of returns available to an equity investor.

The returns from investing in shares may take the form of either income i.e. dividends, which are paid twice yearly or capital gain/loss which is earned when the shares are sold. Some investors may prefer one type of return to the other, often for tax reasons.

Dividend cover is measured as follows: Earnings per share (net)/dividend per share (net).

Using the example of Zellus plc, the net EPS is 18 pence. The gross dividend is nine pence, and so if tax is payable at 20%, then the net dividend equals 7·2 pence. Using the formula, dividend cover equals 18/7·2, which gives a dividend cover of 2·5.

In other words, Zellus' earnings are sufficient for the company to be able to pay out dividends at a rate 2·5 times their current level. By comparison, Buntam has an EPS of eight pence and a net dividend per share of 6·4 pence, giving a dividend cover of just 1·25.

Investors need to understand the relationship between dividend cover and investment returns. As a general rule, the greater the level of retention (and dividend cover), the greater the likelihood that a share will yield capital gain rather than income. From the examples given above, it would thus appear for Buntam plc (paying out almost all their earnings as dividends), there is limited scope for capital growth in the share price. By contrast, Zellus has a relatively high dividend cover, and so the reinvestment of profits should generate capital gains.

As with all investor ratios, dividend cover has to be interpreted with caution, and alongside a number of other measures.

(d) The dividend growth model suggests a method whereby share values can be estimated from information on the required return on equity and the expected dividend payable. The theory suggests that the value of a share is equivalent to the discounted value of the future dividend stream, where the discount rate is determined by the return required by the investor.

For example, if I decide that an investment is very risky, the result may be that I require a return of 20%, and the dividend flows will be discounted at this rate. In this way, the price that an investor places on a share is a reflection of his perceived risk re that investment together with his dividend expectations.

Using Crazy Games plc as an example, the formula for share valuation under the dividend growth model is as follows:

$$\text{Market value of share} = \frac{D_1}{R - G}$$

Where D_1 = Next year's dividend
R = Investor's required return on the equity
G = Growth rate of the dividends

From the figures given relating to Crazy Games plc,
$G = 16·36\%$
i.e. $\sqrt[4]{5·5/3} - 1$

$R = 20\%$
$D_1 = 5·5 \,(1·1636) = 6·40$ pence

$$\text{Market value} = \frac{6·40}{0·2 - 0·1636}$$
$$= 175·8 \text{ pence}$$

This means that to buy 1,000 shares in Crazy Games would cost £1,758.

It is important to note that the model bases share prices on dividend growth rates even though, as in this case, there is often a significant difference between the rate of growth of dividends and that of earnings.

(e) Based on the data given in the question, the yield curve has the following shape.

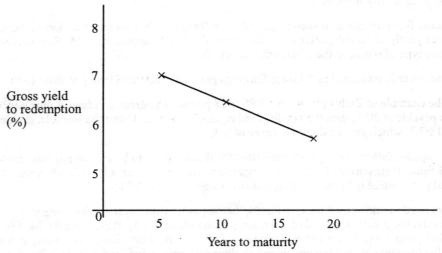

The yield curve clearly shows that as the years to maturity increase, the yield earned on the gilt investment falls.

The shape of the curve drawn above is contrary to that which would be expected from liquidity preference theory. Theory suggests that investors require *increasing* levels of compensation as the time to maturity lengthens – the curve drawn above shows the exact opposite. The reason for the difference between the theoretical and the observed shape of the curve is market expectations. The market believes that over the long term interest rates will fall, and the effect of market expectations is currently greater than the effects of liquidity preference.

The slope of the yield curve shows not only how much an investor can expect as investment returns, but also the cost of debt finance to the government.

(f) The term gilts refers to government issued bonds, which are 'gilt' edged because of the associated risk of default is negligible.

For the private investor, gilts are an attractive form of investment because they offer fixed rates of return, they may be index-linked, and the investment risks are low. Gilts have a nominal value of £100 but they may trade at prices above or below that value depending on the current level of interest rates. If the current interest rate exceeds the coupon rate payable on the gilt, then it will sell for a price below its nominal value, and vice versa.

Yield curves are relevant to the private investor because they give an indication of interest rate expectations and trends. A downward sloping yield curve, such as that shown above, indicates a long-term downward trend in interest rates. For a gilt investor, this means that he can expect gilt prices to rise over the same time period.

Tutorial notes

1. Students should be aware that Advance Corporation Tax (ACT) has been abolished with effect from April 1999. This has a number of implications for this question and answer:

    • Dividends and dividend yields are now shown in financial newspapers at net amounts rather than gross.
    • The payment of ACT described in part (c)(i) of the answer is no longer necessary after April 1999.

2. FRS 14 has now replaced SSAP 3 as the accounting standard dealing with earnings per share. FRS 14 defines basic EPS as the net profit or loss for the period attributable to ordinary shareholders, divided by the weighted average number of ordinary shares outstanding during the period. Shares no longer have to be ranking for dividend to be included in the EPS calculation (as was the case under SSAP 3).

81   (Answer 2 of examination)

(a)   A finance lease is usually arranged via a finance house, with the intention of providing a business with the funding to acquire an asset. The time scale of a finance lease is set such that at the end of the initial leasing period, the lessor has more than recovered the cost of the asset. At such a time, the lessee is given the option to continue leasing the asset at a nominal rental, or sell the item on behalf of the lessor, and retain the bulk of the proceeds.

The cash flow pattern of a finance lease is such that cash flow is evenly spaced throughout the leasing period, and the company acquiring an asset is not therefore required to pay out a large sum of cash in one go in order to obtain the use of that asset. The interest rate charged for the finance is usually fixed for the duration of the lease, and the predictability of the outgoing cash flow in such circumstances can be very useful in helping smaller companies to plan their finances. One possible area of uncertainty in relation to fact that under such an agreement the lessee is responsible for maintenance costs of the equipment/ machinery. Such costs may not be readily predictable, and be related to level of usage.

A cash flow advantage may arise because of the tax treatment of finance leases. Some businesses may be earning insufficient profits to allow them to take advantage of all the capital allowances that may be available to them if they choose to purchase machinery and equipment outright. Where a finance lease is used, no capital allowances may be claimed, but instead the company may claim tax relief against the full leasing cost. The lower annual cost may mean that the company is able to maximise its use of tax relief, and so reduce the effective cost of the leased equipment.

An alternative source of medium-term finance is a bank loan. In terms of cash flow, the loan agreement will define the level of regular repayments, which will be a mix of capital repayment plus an interest component. The loan may be subject to either a fixed or a variable rate of interest. In the latter case, the repayments may change over the life of the loan, if interest rates alter. Under such circumstances the cash flow pattern is clearly less certain than under a finance lease based on a fixed finance charge.

The company can claim capital allowances on the purchase, and so obtain tax relief to reduce its mainstream corporation tax liability. As indicated above, such tax relief is only of value if the company has profits against which the relief can be offset. This means that the tax paying position of a company plays a critical role in determining the comparative advantage of leasing versus borrowing to pay for a business asset.

A third source of finance to pay for acquisition of a business asset is the use of existing cash holdings/ funds on deposit. Where funds are withdrawn from deposit, there will be a cash-flow impact in terms of the loss of regular interest receivable. Furthermore, the conversion of the current asset of cash into a fixed asset (piece of equipment) alters the structure of the company's balance sheet. The outflow of a single large cash payment will reduce the liquidity of the business (at least temporarily). If cash-flows from operations are adequate to meet regular cash outgoings, this will not matter. If, however, there is a potential cash shortfall, this is not a sensible source of funding for asset purchases. As with loan finance, the purchase of the asset for cash means that capital allowances can be claimed, and the same considerations on the usefulness of those allowances need to be taken into account.

(b)   *Workings:*

(i)   Capital Allowances

		Allowances
Year 1	25% × 120,000	30,000
Year 2	75% × 30,000	22,500
Year 3	75% × 22,500	16,875
Year 4	75% × 16,875	12,656
		82,031

Year 5	Balancing allowance	
	(120,000 – 82,031)	37,969

(ii) *Taxable profits and tax liability*

£'000

Year	Cash savings	Capital allowance	Taxable profits	Tax at 30%
1	50	30	20	6
2	50	22·5	27·5	8·25
3	50	16·875	33·125	9·94
4	50	12·656	37·34	11·20
5	50	37·969	12·03	3·61

(iii) *Tax savings on capital allowances*

Year	Capital allowance	Tax relief at 30%
1	30,000	
2	22,500	9,000
3	16,875	6,750
4	12,656	5,063
5	37,969	3,797
6		11,390

Acquisition decision

Year	Equipment	Cash savings	Tax	Net cash flow	Discount factor at 15%	Present value
0	(120)			(120)	1·00	(120)
1		50		50	0·87	43·5
2		50	(6)	44	0·756	33·26
3		50	(8·25)	41·75	0·658	27·47
4		50	(9·94)	40·06	0·572	22·91
5		50	(11·2)	38·8	0·497	19·28
6			(3·61)	(3·61)	0·432	(1·56)
					NPV	24·86

The NPV is positive and so the company should acquire the machine.

Present value of purchase

Discounting cash-flows at the after tax cost of borrowing i.e. 13% × 0·7 = 9·1% (say 9%).

Note: This is approximate, as tax relief is lagged by one year.

Year	Item	Cash flow	Discount factor at 9%	Present value
0	Purchase cost	(120,000)	1·00	(120,000)
2	Tax savings from allowances	9,000	0·842	7,578
3		6,750	0·772	5,211
4		5,063	0·708	3,585
5		3,797	0·650	2,468
6		11,390	0·596	6,788
			Net PV of cost	(94,370)

Present value of leasing

Year	Lease payment	Tax savings	Discount at 9%	Present value
0 – 4	(28,000)		4·239	(118,692)
1 – 5		8,400	3·89	32,676
			Net PV leasing	(86,016)

This means that it is cheaper to lease the machine than to purchase it via the bank loan.

Tutorial note: There are a number of different ways of calculating the comparative cost of the lease versus purchase, but all methods yield the same result. Candidates will not be disadvantaged by the use of a specific method of approach.

82	(Answer 3 of examination)

(a) Manufacturing companies usually sell their products on credit. This means that increasing sales leads to a need for greater working capital in order to finance the higher levels of debtors, stock, and staff employed in sales.

PCB have seen their sales increase by 76% over 12 months, and the effect of this has been a need to increase their fixed asset base, as well as invest in more current assets. Between 1997 and 1998, the company has increased its fixed asset investments by £44,000 and its current assets by £225,250. The asset increase may well be more than is required to service the higher sales levels. These investments appear to have been paid for by a massive increase in both trade creditors and short-term bank borrowing. Bank borrowing has increased almost four-fold, whilst trade creditors have increased by almost 150%. This means that the company has run out of cash to pay for creditors, and is seeking to resolve the crisis by higher short-term borrowings.

The cash crisis faced by PCB is not unusual, as banks may often increase overdraft limits when companies have a full order book. It is also true that as the earnings from the increased sales feed through into the profit and loss account, the cash crisis should be eased.

(b) Extra sales do not always yield significantly higher profits and extra cash-flow in the short-term, because of the extra investment needed to facilitate the sales increase. The figures show that PCB has been forced to meet higher costs and perhaps sell at reduced prices in order to realise the extra sales, and profits (gross and net) have been hit. The gross profit margin has reduced from 19·4% to 15%. At the same time, the depreciation charge will rise because of new equipment having been purchased, and the wages bill will also be higher because of the new staff. The company will have to meet increased interest payments on its very large overdraft/short-term borrowings. As a result, and as the figures show, the company's net profits have actually fallen between 1997 and 1998, despite the higher sales. The net margin has fallen from 4·8% to just 2%; it could be difficult for the company to survive in the longer term when it earns such slim margins.

(c) As already indicated in (a) the company has become increasingly dependent on short-term borrowing from trade creditors and the bank in order to continue trading. Trade credit is a useful source of funding as it frequently does not incur an interest charge. The company may, however, risk forfeiting the goodwill of its suppliers if it takes excessively long periods of time to pay its debts. The ratio of bank loans: equity capital equals 1:8·4 approximately in 1997. By 1998 this ratio had fallen to 1:2·4. The company's balance of funding is moving away from the use of equity as the prime source, to increased dependence on short-term debt.

It is not wise for a company to fund large-scale long-term increases in its trading volume out of short-term funding. The company needs to match long-term investments with long-term finance. Furthermore, as net profit falls, the equity investor will see a drop in the return to equity, accompanied by an increase in equity risk. The higher risk comes from the fall in profit after interest, and the possibility that the lines of short-term credit may dry up for PCB, and they may be forced to cease trading.

Creditor risk is clearly increased, as the company is now committed to a level of short-term borrowing (£363,000) which exceeds its fixed asset base (£308,000). Creditors have no means of obtaining security against any loans (except against debtors). It seems very unlikely that any further credit would be made available to PCB.

(d) PCB needs to re-organise the funding of its business in a way which reduces its exposure to short-term debt. This could be done either by converting the short-term bank loan into a long-term debenture/loan or by increasing the equity investment in the business.

Conversion of the loan would not alter the overall level of financial gearing within the business, and so there would remain some high risks for both equity investors and creditors. Increasing the equity investment is the better alternative. The issued share capital is low, given the current level of sales. If current shareholders were to invest another £50,000, and the bulk of the short-term bank borrowings were re-arranged as a long-term loan, the balance sheet would look much healthier.

At the same time, PCB could look carefully at its current levels of working capital, and aim to reduce the level of stock and debtors as a means of releasing capital. In 1997 debtor and stock levels stood at 6·4% and 5·6% of sales value respectively. If the 1997 levels were maintained, the company's investment in these two current assets in 1998 could be reduced from £430,000 to £360,000, a saving of £70,000. The cash freed up by tighter working capital controls may then provide sufficient capital to pay for further sales expansion in the future without the need to look for additional outside funding.

The risk of over-trading arises when a company has insufficient working capital to service the volume of business. PCB would appear to have exhausted its sources of working capital, and any further increases in sales would therefore place the company under a great cash strain. By re-organising its financing, and increasing the long-term equity investment, PCB could regain access to additional short-term borrowing, and so avoid the risk of over-trading.

83   (Answer 4 of examination)

(a)   Workings

	W £000	X £000	Y £000	Z £000	Total £000
Sales	2,000	2,500	1,000	500	6,000
Variable costs:					
materials	300	400	200	40	940
labour	500	600	400	100	1,600
factory overhead	240	320	200	40	800
selling overhead	100	125	50	25	300
Total variable costs	1,140	1,445	850	205	3,640
Contribution	860	1,055	150	295	2,360
CS ratio	43%	42%	15%	59%	39%
Less fixed costs:					
manufacturing					1,200
selling					600
Net profit					560

The table given in the question includes an arbitrary allocation of fixed costs to product Y. This form of presentation is not always the most helpful in reaching product discontinuation decisions. From the workings above it can be seen that Y makes a contribution of £150,000 and this exceeds the £100,000 fixed costs which would be saved if Y were to be withdrawn. In the short-term if Y is discontinued all of the remaining fixed costs will still be incurred. Profit would fall by £50,000 to £510,000 if Zorro were to discontinue Y at this time. It is apparent however that Y, in financial terms, is the poorest performing product in the line and it should therefore receive some detailed consideration.

The above explanation assumes that variable costs can be accurately identified by the percentages given in the question. Labour costs are assumed to be variable, in other words there is some casual labour which can be reduced with immediate effect and there are no other costs, for example redundancy costs, related to the withdrawal of Y. The discussion regarding Y also assumes that the current situation will continue, that is, there is no scope for price rises in the future or for costs to be significantly reduced through efficiency or cost changes.

(b)   **(i)**   The decision related to product Y turns on the incremental expenditure and incremental costs involved in producing and selling the product over the relevant time period. In the present position of spare capacity and the fact that Y is making a contribution, in the short-term, it should remain in the product line.

If the amount of the fixed costs which may be saved by withdrawing Y are low and there are no other lump sum savings of expenditures by withdrawing Y then it could be retained over the longer term on the basis that it is contributing to profit. Additionally, if its abandonment would cause the reduction in the sales of other products in the line, then these implications should also be taken into account. However, to proceed too far with this argument could be dangerous and the company could find it is using this reasoning to retain a wide range of low volume/low contribution products. These would add to the complexity and hence the costs of manufacture, but very little to the overall profit. It would be wise therefore for the company to regularly examine the low volume/low contribution products in its range. This may be what the chief executive has in mind. The ability of a product to cover its costs, including its somewhat arbitrarily allocated costs may be a useful general indicator to its viability.

(ii) If the company were able to develop another product, offering a better contribution, with similar characteristics which would utilise the same plant as Y, then Y should naturally be re-evaluated. If sales of the existing products expand sufficiently to require the capacity currently devoted to Y, then Y would be a candidate for withdrawal. Alternatively, if the company was faced with significant capital expenditure to maintain its production capacity then consideration could be given to withdrawing Y rather than incurring that expenditure. This would depend on the capacity involved, amount of the investment and the extent to which withdrawal of Y would affect sales of other products in the line.

(c) If Y were to be continued the financial result would be the same as that shown in (a) above. This could be summarised in terms of the respective contributions of the products and the total fixed costs as:

Product		£000
W		860
X		1,055
Y		150
Z		295
Total contribution		2,360
Fixed costs		1,800
Net profit		560

If Y were to be withdrawn completely the implications would be £300,000 extra sales of Z and a reduction in the sales of W by 10%. Additionally, £100,000 fixed costs would be saved, thus:

Product		£000
W	Less 10% of the contribution	774
X	Unchanged	1,055
Y	Withdrawn	
Z	Additional £300,000 × 59%	472
Total contribution		2,301
Fixed costs	Less £100,000	1,700
Net profit		601

If Y were to be retained to service only the customers for product W, this would imply 20% of the present sales of Y would be achieved (i.e. 80% reduction). The extra £300,000 sales of Z would still apply and there would be no reduction in the sales of W because these customers would be satisfied. The fixed costs saved would be only £50,000 in this case as some manufacturing capacity of Y is retained, hence:

Product		£000
W	As original	860
X	Unchanged	1,055
Y	Only 20% sold	30
Z	Additional £300,000 × 59%	472
Total contribution		2,417
Fixed costs	Less £50,000	1,750
Net profit		667

On financial grounds it would appear that the best option for Zorro is to retain manufacture and sale of product Y for the customers of product W only. There is the implication that Y has a trend of poor profit performance in the recent past and no indication that this will change. The opportunity cost of dropping Y completely, given the consequent loss of sales of W, is high and this is the main reason for keeping it in the portfolio. It is still reasonable for the company to look to develop a product with a better level of profit than Y and one which has the characteristics suitable for product W customers. This would improve their profit position even further.

84   (Answer 5 of examination)

(a) Production Budget.

	Dec	Jan	Feb	Mar	Apr
Sales	14,000	16,000	22,000	17,000	20,000
Closing stock	4,000	5,500	4,250	5,000	6,000
	18,000	21,500	26,250	22,000	26,000
Opening stock	3,500	4,000	5,500	4,250	5,000
Production	14,500	17,500	20,750	17,750	21,000

Purchases Budget

	Dec	Jan	Feb	Mar
Production	14,500	17,500	20,750	17,750
Closing stock	1,750	2,075	1,775	2,100
	16,250	19,575	22,525	19,850
Opening stock	1,450	1,750	2,075	1,775
Purchases	14,800	17,825	20,450	18,075

Note. Columns for January to March only are required in an answer to (a) though candidates will find that they will need some data from December for the cash budget, as well as the production for April for the purchases budget.

(b) Working: Product unit manufacturing cost for January

	£
Material	10
Variable overhead and labour	16
Fixed overhead	12
	38

NB. The fixed overhead rate for January is calculated using the budgeted monthly overhead and production thus; £210,000/17,500

Budgeted profit and loss account January 1999

		£000	£000
Sales	16,000 × £58		928
Raw material usage	17,500 × £10	175	
Variable overhead and lab.	17,500 × £16	280	
Fixed overhead	17,500 × £12	210	
Manufacturing cost	17,500 × £38	665	

Closing stock	$5,500 \times £38$	209	
	$12,000 \times £38$	456	
Opening stock	$4,000 \times £40$	160	
			616
Gross Profit			312

Selling costs

variable	$16,000 \times £7$	112	
fixed		164	
			276
Net Profit			36

Cash budget for January 1999

		£000	£000
Receipts			
sales	$7,000 \times £58$		406
	$8,000 \times £58$		464
			870

Payments:		
Material	148	
Variable overhead & labour	280	
Fixed overhead $(210,000 - 54,000)$	156	
Variable selling	112	
Fixed selling	164	
		860
Cash surplus		10

(c) Under a system of absorption costing an overhead rate is used to apply overheads to each unit produced. At present the company applies each month's overhead to products based upon the budgeted production levels and the budgeted expenditure in each month which are used to establish a separate predetermined rate for each month. As a result unit overhead costs fluctuate if production levels fluctuate because the fixed overheads are spread over fluctuating volumes.

It can be disconcerting and misleading for production and sales staff to be dealing with product costs which fluctuate on a monthly basis. This is especially so when the fluctuation has not been caused by changes in production efficiency and it bears no relation to changes in the general market price.

One way to overcome this is to compute an overhead rate which is based on a longer time period, for example quarterly, or a predetermined annual rate as mentioned in the question. This enables large fluctuations in, and extreme values of, product costs to be avoided. This would mean that management would be able to monitor the business volume and overhead costs on which the calculations were based to ensure that over the longer-term the average product costs which were predicted were in fact achieved.

(d) A time series is the name given to a set of observations taken at equal intervals of time in order to obtain an overall picture of what is taking place. For example, monthly sales covering a period of, say, five years. A time series consists of various components, such as trend, cyclical, seasonal and residual components.

To develop this explanation a little further, the trend component is the way in which the series appears to be moving over a long interval, after other fluctuations have been smoothed out. The cyclical component is the wave-like appearance which occurs in the series when taken over a fairly long period, a number of years. Generally it is caused by the booms and slumps in an industry or trade cycle.

A seasonal component is the regular rise and fall of values over specified intervals of time, within say one year. Though the term seasonal is used it does not have to align with seasons, but any regular variations over short time periods. Residual components are any other variations which cannot be ascribed to any of those mentioned above, essentially random factors and due to unpredictable causes.

85   (Answer 6 of examination)

(a)   A standard costing system can support a wide range of management requirements. For example:

It can help in the development of budgets; standards are in effect the building blocks of periodic budgets.

If handled correctly by management the existence of an appropriately set standard can act as a target and hence become a source of employee motivation

To the extent that standards are measures of expected performance by departments or individuals, standard costs are the basis for measuring performance

Following on from the above, the variances that are derived from standard costs act as a control device by highlighting those activities which are different from plans. This signals to decision makers the need for action to take advantage of any circumstances which have produced favourable variances or minimise the repercussions of any adverse variances.

Standard costs are predicted future costs which can be used to support decision making, for example in making pricing decisions.

In manufacturing companies a key requirement of costing is the valuation of stock. Standard costs simplify the process of tracing costs to products for stock valuation.

NB. The question asks for *four* of the above.

(b)   Three different levels of performance are:

Basic standards – such standards are left unchanged for a long period, perhaps from the inception of the product or service concerned. They may be useful in demonstrating a progression of improved performance over a period of time, but do not represent current targets. Therefore, they do not motivate, they do not result in representative unit costs and are inappropriate as predicted costs for decisions.

Ideal standards – these represent perfect performance and the most efficient operating conditions reflecting the lowest possible costs. They are a useful objective to which the firm can aspire over the long term but firms will rarely achieve this level of performance consistently. As a result adverse variances will almost always be reported, this will inevitably have an adverse effect on employee attitude and motivation. They represent budget figures which are too tight and inappropriate from which to set prices or to use directly as performance measures in most circumstances.

Currently attainable standards – these standards represent costs which should be attained under current efficient operating conditions. They are a reasonable target and represent a likely level of future costs if operations are managed efficiently. They are a level of performance which does not demotivate staff. They are therefore the figures which can be used to manage the current operations of a business unit. They are figures which can support planning and decision-making and as current cost levels they are appropriate for stock valuation. It should be expected that most companies will run their systems based on these standards. The first two levels mentioned above may, on the other hand, be useful for strategic purposes, demonstrating on an adhoc basis, how far the company has come or how far it has to go.

(c)   Standard costing is most suited to organisations whose activities consist of a series of common or repetitive operations. Typically, mass production manufacturing operations are indicative of its area of application. It is also possible to envisage operations within the service sector to which standard cost may apply, though this may not be costed with the same degree of accuracy of standards which apply in manufacturing. For example, hotels and restaurants often use standard recipes for food preparation, dealing with conference attendance can be like a mass production environment. Similarly, banks will have common processes for dealing with customer transactions, processing cheques etc. It is possible therefore that the principles of standard costing may be extended to service industries.

In modern manufacturing and service businesses, continuous improvement and cost reduction are topical. In order to remain competitive it is essential that businesses address the cost levels of their various operations. To do this they have to deal with the costing of operations. But the drive to 'cost down' may mean in some cases that standards do not apply for long before a redesign or improvement renders them out of date. In such a setting an alternative to the use of standard costs is to compare actual costs with those of the previous operating period. We have seen in (a) above that a standard costing system has a variety of purposes. It is for management to judge their various reasons for employing standard costing, and consequently whether their aims of continuous improvement and cost reduction renders the system redundant.

(d) Standard costing variances are a convenient way of summarising the results of an operating period by focusing on the financial impact of deviations from a budgeted result. The variances, which can be identified as to cause and responsibility, are in total the absolute difference that actual results bear to an original plan. The exercise of variance analysis is not without difficulty however, and the following is a critique of the technique, bringing out some of the practical problems.

For direct costs the traditionally adopted formula creates an analysis of price and usage variances. However, this division is only by the convention of the variance formula and the existence of joint variances influenced by a combination of price and usage could also be compiled in certain circumstances, say when remuneration is based on the results of the reported variance. The complexity of the variance calculation can at times however, be taken too far, for example the extraction of mix, yield and price variances say in relation to materials costs can be questionable. Most of these variances can be inter-related. It is dangerous to interpret individual variances in isolation, interdependency should be recognised.

Concerning variable and fixed overheads, the level of costs are controllable against a budget and this is often a fixed budget. When activity levels change it is important to remember that the variable costs need to be flexed to allow for this. This raises the problem of which costs to flex and what measure of activity (i.e. number of units, hours of work etc.) to use as the basis of flexing. There is unlikely to be exact correlation between the measure of activity chosen (say labour hours) and the cost change, therefore care should be exercised in the interpretation of these variances. A comparison of the actual and standard activity levels facilitates the extraction of an efficiency variance in relation to variable overheads. Whether the results of such analysis reflect a more or less efficient use of variable overhead resources has been questioned.

Perhaps the variance which attracts most criticism is the fixed overhead volume variance. This variance represents the fixed overhead cost or benefit of working at a volume level below or above that which was budgeted. Though it is important to reconcile budget and actual volumes, the value applied to the volume variance does not report a meaningful cost in all circumstances. For example, as costs are fixed, by definition, extra volume, if available, is 'free' up to a certain limit. In other circumstances if time is scarce then the cost of any time wasted, for example, may be far higher than the fixed overhead rate. It has been pointed out that the calculation of an overhead recovery rate per unit or per hour applied to fixed overheads may be unhelpful because it is in effect treating fixed overheads as if they were variable costs.

N.B. In the latter stages of this question, especially parts (c) and (d), there is scope for slightly different content or views to be expressed than those in the outline answer. Credit will be given for points other than those stated above.

Certificate Examination – Paper 8
Managerial Finance   **Marking Scheme**

Section A

                                                                 Marks

1	**(a)**	Definition of traded investment	1
		Different types of investments	1
		Comparison of risk, rate of return and use of derivatives to reduce risks	4
			6
	(b)	Examples of financial intermediaries	1
		Provision of advice	2
		Maturity transformation	2
		Risk reduction	2
		Impact on private investor (general)	1
			8
	(c)	4 marks for each part. Maximum of 2 per section if the answer omits to use examples based on the data in the question	
			12
	(d)	Formula	1
		Growth rate	2
		Value per share	1
		Value of 1,000 shares	1
			5
	(e)	Construction of curve	2
		Comments	2
			4
	(f)	Explanation of gilts	2
		Relevance of yield curves to investors	3
			5
			Total marks 40

Section B

2	**(a)**	Explanation of finance lease	2
		Pros and cons of bank loan and cash (2 marks each)	4
		Relevance of tax position	2
			8
	(b)	Writing-down allowances	2
		Taxable profit and tax liability	2
		Acquisition decision	2
		Discount factor for purchase	1
		Tax savings on capital allowances	1
		Present value of purchase	2
		Present value of leasing	2
			12
			Total marks 20
3	**(a)**	Credit sales and working capital implications	3
		(one mark each for mention of stock, debtors and bank borrowings)	
		Fixed asset purchases	1
			4
	(b)	Higher depreciation charge	1
		Lower selling prices	1
		Increased interest payable	1
		Sales staff costs	1
			4

Marks

(c) Rise in short-term borrowing   2
     Changed bank loans: equity ratio   1
     Threat of lost access to short-term credit   2
     Borrowing: fixed asset ratio   1
                                                                                                    6

(d) 2 marks each for detailed comment on each of:
     Reduction in short-term borrowings
     Increased equity investment
     Reduction in working capital requirements
     Maximum of 1 mark for each if answers do not include illustrative figures
                                                                                                    6
                                                                                Total marks 20

Section C

4 (a) Contribution margin all products   2
        Profit implications   2
        Explanation and qualification   3
                                                                                                    7

(b) Each point 1 mark,
     Development of point 1 mark   6

(c) Clarify implications of continuation   1
     Re abandonment of Y   3
     Re partial abandonment of Y   3
                                                                                                    7
                                                                                Total marks 20

5 (a) Production budget   2
        Purchase budget   2
                                                                                                    4

(b) Unit cost   1
     Profit and loss   3
     Cash budget   3
                                                                                                    7

(c) Each point 1, development of point 1   4

(d) Explanation each term 1   5
                                                                                Total marks 20

6 (a) Each purpose briefly described 1   4

(b) Each level explained 1   3
     Each comment 1   3
                                                                                                    6

(c) Comment re manufacturing and service   2
     Comment re cont. improvement and cost redn.   2
                                                                                                    4

(d) Each developed point 2   6
                                                                                Total marks 20

Present value table

Present value of £1 ie, $\dfrac{1}{(1+r)^n}$ or $(1+r)^{-n}$

where   r   =   discount rate

         n   =   number of periods until payment

Discount rates (r)

Periods (n)	1%	2%	3%	4%	5%	6%	7%	8%	9%	10%	
1	0.990	0.980	0.971	0.962	0.952	0.943	0.935	0.926	0.917	0.909	1
2	0.980	0.961	0.943	0.925	0.907	0.890	0.873	0.857	0.842	0.826	2
3	0.971	0.942	0.915	0.889	0.864	0.840	0.816	0.794	0.772	0.751	3
4	0.961	0.924	0.888	0.855	0.823	0.792	0.763	0.735	0.708	0.683	4
5	0.951	0.906	0.863	0.822	0.784	0.747	0.713	0.681	0.650	0.621	5
6	0.942	0.888	0.837	0.790	0.746	0.705	0.666	0.630	0.596	0.564	6
7	0.933	0.871	0.813	0.760	0.711	0.665	0.623	0.583	0.547	0.513	7
8	0.923	0.853	0.789	0.731	0.677	0.627	0.582	0.540	0.502	0.467	8
9	0.914	0.837	0.766	0.703	0.645	0.592	0.544	0.500	0.460	0.424	9
10	0.905	0.820	0.744	0.676	0.614	0.558	0.508	0.463	0.422	0.386	10
11	0.896	0.804	0.722	0.650	0.585	0.527	0.475	0.429	0.388	0.350	11
12	0.887	0.788	0.701	0.625	0.557	0.497	0.444	0.397	0.356	0.319	12
13	0.879	0.773	0.681	0.601	0.530	0.469	0.415	0.368	0.326	0.290	13
14	0.870	0.758	0.661	0.577	0.505	0.442	0.388	0.340	0.299	0.263	14
15	0.861	0.743	0.642	0.555	0.481	0.417	0.362	0.315	0.275	0.239	15

	11%	12%	13%	14%	15%	16%	17%	18%	19%	20%	
1	0.901	0.893	0.885	0.877	0.870	0.862	0.855	0.847	0.840	0.833	1
2	0.812	0.797	0.783	0.769	0.756	0.743	0.731	0.718	0.706	0.694	2
3	0.731	0.712	0.693	0.675	0.658	0.641	0.624	0.609	0.593	0.579	3
4	0.659	0.636	0.613	0.592	0.572	0.552	0.534	0.516	0.499	0.482	4
5	0.593	0.567	0.543	0.519	0.497	0.476	0.456	0.437	0.419	0.402	5
6	0.535	0.507	0.480	0.456	0.432	0.410	0.390	0.370	0.352	0.335	6
7	0.482	0.452	0.425	0.400	0.376	0.354	0.333	0.314	0.296	0.279	7
8	0.434	0.404	0.376	0.351	0.327	0.305	0.285	0.266	0.249	0.233	8
9	0.391	0.361	0.333	0.308	0.284	0.263	0.243	0.225	0.209	0.194	9
10	0.352	0.322	0.295	0.270	0.247	0.227	0.208	0.191	0.176	0.162	10
11	0.317	0.287	0.261	0.237	0.215	0.195	0.178	0.162	0.148	0.135	11
12	0.286	0.257	0.231	0.208	0.187	0.168	0.152	0.137	0.124	0.112	12
13	0.258	0.229	0.204	0.182	0.163	0.145	0.130	0.116	0.104	0.093	13
14	0.232	0.205	0.181	0.160	0.141	0.125	0.111	0.099	0.088	0.078	14
15	0.209	0.183	0.160	0.140	0.123	0.108	0.095	0.084	0.074	0.065	15

Annuity Table

Present value of an annuity of 1 ie, $\dfrac{1-(1+r)^{-n}}{r}$

where   r   =   discount rate

      n   =   number of periods

Discount rates (r)

Periods (n)	1%	2%	3%	4%	5%	6%	7%	8%	9%	10%	
1	0.990	0.980	0.971	0.962	0.952	0.943	0.935	0.926	0.917	0.909	1
2	1.970	1.942	1.913	1.886	1.859	1.833	1.808	1.783	1.759	1.736	2
3	2.941	2.884	2.829	2.775	2.723	2.673	2.624	2.577	2.531	2.487	3
4	3.902	3.808	3.717	3.630	3.546	3.465	3.387	3.312	3.240	3.170	4
5	4.853	4.713	4.580	4.452	4.329	4.212	4.100	3.993	3.890	3.791	5
6	5.795	5.601	5.417	5.242	5.076	4.917	4.767	4.623	4.486	4.355	6
7	6.728	6.472	6.230	6.002	5.786	5.582	5.389	5.206	5.033	4.868	7
8	7.652	7.325	7.020	6.733	6.463	6.210	5.971	5.747	5.535	5.335	8
9	8.566	8.162	7.786	7.435	7.108	6.802	6.515	6.247	5.995	5.759	9
10	9.471	8.983	8.530	8.111	7.722	7.360	7.024	6.710	6.418	6.145	10
11	10.37	9.787	9.253	8.760	8.306	7.887	7.499	7.139	6.805	6.495	11
12	11.26	10.58	9.954	9.385	8.863	8.384	7.943	7.536	7.161	6.814	12
13	12.13	11.35	10.63	9.986	9.394	8.853	8.358	7.904	7.487	7.103	13
14	13.00	12.11	11.30	10.56	9.899	9.295	8.745	8.244	7.786	7.367	14
15	13.87	12.85	11.94	11.12	10.38	9.712	9.108	8.559	8.061	7.606	15

	11%	12%	13%	14%	15%	16%	17%	18%	19%	20%	
1	0.901	0.893	0.885	0.877	0.870	0.862	0.855	0.847	0.840	0.833	1
2	1.713	1.690	1.668	1.647	1.626	1.605	1.585	1.566	1.547	1.528	2
3	2.444	2.402	2.361	2.322	2.283	2.246	2.210	2.174	2.140	2.106	3
4	3.102	3.037	2.974	2.914	2.855	2.798	2.743	2.690	2.639	2.589	4
5	3.696	3.605	3.517	3.433	3.352	3.274	3.199	3.127	3.058	2.991	5
6	4.231	4.111	3.998	3.889	3.784	3.685	3.589	3.498	3.410	3.326	6
7	4.712	4.564	4.423	4.288	4.160	4.039	3.922	3.812	3.706	3.605	7
8	5.146	4.968	4.799	4.639	4.487	4.344	4.207	4.078	3.954	3.837	8
9	5.537	5.328	5.132	4.946	4.772	4.607	4.451	4.303	4.163	4.031	9
10	5.889	5.650	5.426	5.216	5.019	4.833	4.659	4.494	4.339	4.192	10
11	6.207	5.938	5.687	5.453	5.234	5.029	4.836	4.656	4.486	4.327	11
12	6.492	6.194	5.918	5.660	5.421	5.197	4.988	4.793	4.611	4.439	12
13	6.750	6.424	6.122	5.842	5.583	5.342	5.118	4.910	4.715	4.533	13
14	6.982	6.628	6.302	6.002	5.724	5.468	5.229	5.008	4.802	4.611	14
15	7.191	6.811	6.462	6.142	5.847	5.575	5.324	5.092	4.876	4.675	15

ACCA
AT FOULKS LYNCH

HOTLINES
Telephone: 0181 844 0667
Enquiries: 0181 831 9990
Fax: 0181 831 9991

AT FOULKS LYNCH LTD
Number 4, The Griffin Centre
Staines Road, Feltham
Middlesex TW14 0HS

Examination Date:
☐ June 99
☐ December 99

	Publications			Distance Learning	Open Learning
	Textbooks	**Revision Series**	**Lynchpins**	**Include helpline & marking**	

Module A – Foundation Stage

	Textbooks	Revision Series	Lynchpins	Distance Learning	Open Learning
1 Accounting Framework	£17.95 [UK] [IAS]	£10.95 [UK] [IAS]	£5.95 ☐	£85 ☐	£89 ☐
2 Legal Framework	£17.95 ☐	£10.95 ☐	£5.95 ☐	£85 ☐	£89 ☐
Module B					
3 Management Information	£17.95 ☐	£10.95 ☐	£5.95 ☐	£85 ☐	£89 ☐
4 Organisational Framework	£17.95 ☐	£10.95 ☐	£5.95 ☐	£85 ☐	£89 ☐
Module C – Certificate Stage					
5 Information Analysis	£17.95 ☐	£10.95 ☐	£5.95 ☐	£85 ☐	£89 ☐
6 Audit Framework	£17.95 [UK] [IAS]	£10.95 [UK] [IAS]	£5.95 ☐	£85 ☐	£89 ☐
Module D					
7 Tax Framework FA98	£17.95 ☐	£10.95 ☐	£5.95 ☐	£85 ☐	£89 ☐
8 Managerial Finance	£17.95 ☐	£10.95 ☐	£5.95 ☐	£85 ☐	£89 ☐
Module E – Professional Stage					
9 ICDM	£18.95 ☐	£10.95 ☐	£5.95 ☐	£85 ☐	£89 ☐
10 Accounting & Audit Practice	£22.95 [UK] [IAS]	£10.95 [UK] [IAS]	£5.95 ☐	£85 ☐	£89 ☐
11 Tax Planning FA98	£18.95 ☐	£10.95 ☐	£5.95 ☐	£85 ☐	£89 ☐
Module F					
12 Management & Strategy	£18.95 ☐	£10.95 ☐	£5.95 ☐	£85 ☐	£89 ☐
13 Financial Rep Environment	£20.95 [IAS]	£10.95 [IAS]	£5.95 ☐	£85 ☐	£89 ☐
14 Financial Strategy	£19.95 ☐	£10.95 ☐	£5.95 ☐	£85 ☐	£89 ☐

P & P + Delivery	Textbooks	Revision Series	Lynchpins	Distance	Open
UK Mainland	£2.00/book	£1.00/book	£1.00/book	£5.00/subject	£5.00/subject
NI, ROI & EU Countries	£5.00/book	£3.00/book	£3.00/book	£15.00/subject	£15.00/subject
Rest of world standard air service	£10.00/book	£8.00/book	£8.00/book	£25.00/subject	£25.00/subject
Rest of world courier service†	£22.00/book	£20.00/book	£14.00/book	£47.00/subject	£47.00/subject

SINGLE ITEM SUPPLEMENT: If you only order 1 item, INCREASE postage costs by £2.50 for UK, NI & EU Countries or by £10.00 for Rest of World Services

TOTAL	Sub Total £				
	Post & Packing £				
	Total £				

†*Telephone number essential for this service*   *Payments in Sterling in London* | Order Total £ | |

DELIVERY DETAILS

☐ Mr ☐ Miss ☐ Mrs ☐ Ms   Other _____

Initials _____ Surname _____

Address _____

_____

_____

Postcode _____

Telephone _____   Deliver to home ☐

Company name _____

Address _____

_____

Postcode _____

Telephone _____   Fax _____

Monthly report to go to employer ☐   Deliver to work ☐

PAYMENT

1 I enclose Cheque/PO/Bankers Draft for £_____
Please make cheques payable to AT Foulks Lynch Ltd.

2 Charge Mastercard/Visa/Switch A/C No:

Valid from: ☐☐☐☐   Expiry Date: ☐☐☐☐
Issue No: (Switch only) ☐☐

Signature _____   Date _____

DECLARATION

I agree to pay as indicated on this form and understand that AT Foulks Lynch Terms and Conditions apply (available on request). I understand that AT Foulks Lynch Ltd are not liable for non-delivery if the rest of world standard air service is used.

Signature _____   Date _____

Please Allow:	UK mainland	- 5-10 w/days
	NI, ROI & EU Countries	- 1-3 weeks
	Rest of world standard air service	- 6 weeks
	Rest of world courier service	- 10 w/days

Notes: All delivery times subject to stock availability. Signature required on receipt (except rest of world standard air service). Please give both addresses for Distance Learning students where possible.

Form effective at Jan 99   *All details correct at time of printing.*   *Source: ACRSF9*